Developing Managerial Competence

Developing Managerial Competence offers a comprehensive analysis of modern management development, emphasizing the benefits of linking management development with organizational strategy and the value added by adopting the occupational standards for managers developed by the Management Charter Initiative. In addition to developing a conceptual framework for evaluating the business benefits of management development, detailed case studies of sixteen organizations, in a range of sectors, illustrate how such evaluation works in practice.

Subjects covered include: Management development; Methodologies for measuring performance outcomes; Organizational strategy and management development; Human resource development strategy; Individual performance; Organizational performance; Business performance; Case studies.

The book is innovative in five respects: it demonstrates, after analysing the theoretical and methodological issues, how the impact of management development can be measured; it links management development with corporate strategy, in line with *Investors in People*; it entails a competence-based approach, and offers the first comprehensive assessment of the impact of using the Management Standards; it is endorsed by the Management Charter Initiative, with a Foreword by Professor Tom Cannon, Chief Executive of MCI; and it offers practical illustrations through in-depth case studies which show attainable benefits in a wide range of contemporary organizations.

As the first coherent analysis of competence-based management development, this book combines a clear methodological approach with strong empirical evidence of the effects of management development on performance at the levels of the individual, teams and the organization as a whole.

Jonathan Winterton is Professor of Employment and Human Resource Development and Director of the Employment Research Institute at Napier University, Edinburgh. His previous publications include *Managing Human Resources* (Routledge, 1994, with Chris Molander), and *Public Enterprise in Transition* (Routledge, 1993, with Andrew Pendleton). **Ruth Winterton** is a Lecturer in the Department of Psychology and Sociology at the same institution. Her previous publications include *The Business Benefits of Competence-Based Management Development* (HMSO, 1996, with Jonathan Winterton) and *Coal, Crisis and Conflict* (Manchester University Press, 1989, with Jonathan Winterton).

Developing Managerial Competence

Jonathan Winterton and Ruth Winterton

London and New York

First published 1999
by Routledge
11 New Fetter Lane, London EC4P 4EE

Simultaneously published in the USA and Canada
by Routledge
29 West 35th Street, New York, NY 10001

Typeset in Baskerville by Routledge
Printed and bound in Great Britain by
Creative Print and Design (Wales), Ebbw Vale

British Library Cataloguing in Publication Data
A catalogue record for this book is available from the British Library

Library of Congress Cataloging in Publication Data
Winterton, Jonathan
Developing managerial competence/
Jonathan Winterton and Ruth Winterton.
p. cm.
Includes bibliographical references and index.
1. Management–Study and teaching–Great Britain. 2. Executives–
Training of–Great Britain. 3. Executive ability–Standards–Great
Britain. 4. Competence based education–Great Britain.
I. Winterton, Ruth. II. Title.
HD30.42.G7W56 1999
658′.0071′041–dc21   98–30932

ISBN 0–415–18345–6 (hbk)
ISBN 0–415–18346–4 (pbk)

Contents

Figures

Tables

Foreword

Management competence is without doubt a key factor in developing strategies to further an organization's mission, in achieving an organization's objectives and in improving performance, whether this means competitiveness in global markets or delivering a better public service. Developing that competence among managers whose daily routines are frequently fragmented and reactive has become a quest of Herculean proportions for companies and business schools alike in the increasingly unpredictable and often precarious environment of the modern organization.

This book makes a major contribution to understanding how management development can support organizational strategy and how the benefits of development and training can be assessed at the levels of individual managers, teams and the organization as a whole. With the growing number of organizations and individual managers using the occupational standards developed by the *Management Charter Initiative* and increasing commitment to *Investors in People*, this book meets the needs of business schools, management consultants and human resource professionals for a resource which draws together essential information, argument and analysis concerning modern theory and practice of management development. Offering a systematic analysis of the value of a competence-based approach to management development, the findings are of immediate relevance to practitioners considering whether to adopt the Management Standards in their HRD systems and processes.

The study is grounded in a comprehensive review of the relevance to management development of theories of learning, individual, team and business performance, organizational strategies and HRD systems and processes. Using a conceptual framework derived from approaches to learning organizations and an innovative methodological approach, robust empirical evidence of the problems as well as best practice in relation to management development is analysed in sixteen organizations. Through these detailed case studies, undertaken as part of a study for the Department for Education and Employment, the Wintertons explore how the needs of organizations and individual managers are reconciled and how learning and development can support the achievement of business objectives.

The evidence shows convincingly how improvements in the performance of individual managers, teams and the organization overall can be identified and attributed to management development. Individual and business performance measures are found to be most reliable for monitoring the impact of management development, and are correlated with the more opaque measures of organizational performance. The strength of the link between individual performance and business performance provides a powerful argument for investing in management development. The conclusion that the most significant improvements in performance were attributed to management development where this is strongly linked with organizational strategy reinforces the importance of *Investors in People*, the national standard for investment in development. Similarly, their finding that performance is improved most where organizations adopt the Management Standards as a framework for development within HRD systems and processes demonstrates the additional value of the Management Charter Initiative.

In providing insights into how conflicting needs of the individual and the organization can be reconciled, this book will improve our understanding of the relationships between management development, managerial competence and business performance.

Professor Tom Cannon
Chief Executive, MCI

Acknowledgements

This book began with research undertaken on behalf of the Department for Education and Employment and we should like to acknowledge the role of the Steering Group (Peter Weller, Stephen Leman, Paul Kingslan and Ian Battersby, from the Department, and Bryan Fowler from MCI) for their guidance and direction of the competence-based management development project. We are grateful to the Department for funding the original research and for permission to publish in this form.

The research would have been impossible without the collaboration of a number of individuals, especially Judy Staton and Jackie Sturton who undertook some of the case studies and Lindsay Mitchell of PRiME Research and Development, who organized the evaluation of the case studies. Their tenacity and good humour with what became known among us as 'the project from hell' owing to its methodological complexity, ensured the timely completion of the fieldwork.

Equally, the research could not have happened without the chief executives in the sixteen cases studied who were not afraid to have a team of consultants crawl all over their organizations and ask awkward questions. Although they cannot be named for reasons of confidentiality, we are grateful to them, and to the managers at all levels of the organizations involved who gave their time as respondents and facilitated access to key individuals and documentary evidence.

Finally, other individuals have provided support and encouragement at key points since the original study was completed. Stuart Hay at Routledge kept us on schedule despite other work demands. When the book took precedence over other activities, colleagues at Napier University showed genuine understanding of the conflicting demands. Jenny Finder, Librarian at Bradford Management Centre, helped resolve obscure references at the eleventh hour. Carolyn Beattie from the Employment Research Institute sat at the word processor after hours to complete revisions to the case studies. We hope all involved will think it was worthwhile.

Abbreviations

APEL	Accreditation of Prior Experiential Learning
APL	Accreditation of Prior Learning
APP	Assessment of Professional Performance (government agency)
BDG	business development group
BMG	business management group
BP	business performance
BPR	business process re-engineering
BTEC	Business and Technician Education Council
BU	Business Unit
CBI	Confederation of British Industry
CBMD	competence-based management development
C&G	City and Guilds of London Institute
CMS	Certificate in Management Studies
CPS	Crown Prosecution Service
DEP	Developing Effective Performance
DfEE	Department for Education and Employment
DMS	Diploma in Management Studies
DQI	departmental quality index
DTA	Development and Training Agency
DTI	Department of Trade and Industry
ED	Employment Department (now DfEE)
EEF	Engineering Employers' Federation
EITB	Engineering Industry Training Board
EnTra	Engineering Training Authority
EPS	earnings per share
FTE	full-time equivalent
GP	general practitioner
HR	human resources
HRD	human resource development
HRM	human resource management
HSSM	Health and Social Services Management
IES	Institute for Employment Studies (formerly IMS)
IiP	Investors in People

ILB	Industry Lead Body
IMS	Institute for Manpower Studies (now IES)
IoM	Institute of Management
IP	individual performance
IPD	Institute of Personnel and Development (formerly IPM)
IPM	Institute of Personnel Management (now IPD)
IPR	Individual Performance Review
ISM	Institute of Supervisory Management
IT	information technology
ITB	Industry Training Board
ITO	Industry Training Organization
LCD	Lord Chancellor's Department
LEC	Local Enterprise Company
MBA	Master of Business Administration
MCC	Magistrates' Courts Committee
MCI	Management Charter Initiative
MCF	Management Competency Framework (charity organization)
MD	management development
MDA	Management Development Audit
MESOL	Management Education Scheme by Open Learning
META	Marine and Engineering Training Association
MHS	Management Health Services
MICS	Management Information and Control System
MIS	management information system
MSC	Manpower Services Commission
NACETT	National Advisory Council for Education and Training Targets
NCVQ	National Council for Vocational Qualifications (now QCA)
NFMED	National Foundation for Management Education and Development
NHS	National Health Service
NISW	National Institute for Social Work
NTA	National Training Award
NTO	National Training Organization
NVQ	National Vocational Qualification
OD	organizational development
OP	organizational performance
ORPI	outcome-related performance indicators
OS	organizational strategy
OSR	Objective Setting and Review
OTJ	on-the-job (training)
PC	personal computer
PDP	personal development plan
PEST	'political, economic, social, technical' (analysis)
PRP	performance-related pay

QA	quality assurance
QCA	Qualifications and Curriculum Authority (formerly NCVQ)
RHA	Regional Health Authority
ROCE	return on capital employed
RTDO	Regional Training and Development Officer
RTU	Regional Training Unit (Magistrates' Courts)
SCAA	Schools Curriculum and Assessment Authority
ScotVEC	Scottish Vocational Education Council (now SQA)
SM	standard minutes
SME	small or medium-sized enterprise
SMT	self-managed team
SQA	Scottish Qualifications Authority
SVQ	Scottish Vocational Qualification
SWOT	'strengths, weaknesses, opportunities, threats' (analysis)
T&D	training and development
TDLB	Training and Development Lead Body
TEC	Training and Enterprise Council
TNA	training needs analysis
TQM	total quality management
TUC	Trades Union Congress
VET	Vocational Education and Training
VFD	verified free distribution (newspapers)
VQSS	Vocational Qualifications Support Service (government agency)
WTC	Workplace Training Committee
YTS	Youth Training Scheme

1 Introduction

This book represents a response to that perennial question of management development: what impact does it have on performance? Senior strategic managers want to know whether developing their management team will add value to the organization and, if so, whether one approach is better than another. Individual managers want to know whether the time they invest in development will pay off in terms of improving their own performance and, as a result, their careers.

The book also reflects the context in which the research has been undertaken. Changes in the vocational training system in the UK, especially the adoption of a competence-based approach and the creation of employer-led bodies to establish occupational standards, have affected management development along with other training and development, but what the effects have been is far from obvious. The recognition in White Papers from the European Commission (1994) that skills must be raised at all levels if European enterprises are to compete in global markets, has been reiterated in successive Competitiveness White Papers in the UK (DTI 1994; 1995). The need to build a 'Learning Society' (EC 1996) taken up with the movement for Lifelong Learning (Fryer 1997) has reinforced the argument that 'investment in human capital will be the foundation of success in the twenty-first century' (DfEE 1998).

These are times of change, fitting for the dawn of a new millennium, where learning and development appear to be at the top of the agenda and are assumed to be the key to future organizational success. It is difficult not to become enthused by the momentum of developments in this new era, and the new priority placed upon developing human potential should be wholeheartedly welcomed. However, important questions remain concerning who pays, what they get for their money and whether it lives up to the promises and expectations. This contribution to the debate offers a perspective on what can be done to improve the impact of training and development and provides an analysis of some of the benefits in terms of improvements in performance.

This chapter is organized into three sections dealing with:

1   the changing context of training and development;
2   background to the empirical study;

3   structure and overview of the book.

In the first section, the implications of changes in vocational training policy and organizational contexts for the development of managerial expertise are considered. Why is the workforce in the UK poorly trained in comparison to their major competitors? Can MD initiatives raise the level of qualifications of the managerial workforce? What new demands are being placed on managers and on MD by the profound organizational changes taking place?

The second section outlines the background to the empirical study which originated with a decision by the Employment Department to evaluate the benefits to organizations of adopting the Management Standards. A study group was established to consider existing evidence and to recommend an appropriate methodology for empirical investigation. This section provides a summary of the deliberations of the study group and elaborates the hypotheses established for testing.

The third section provides an overview of the remainder of the book, explaining the logic of the structure and the purposes of each chapter. The aim is to guide the reader to the most relevant sections for their needs and to identify how the chapters are related. Two themes in particular recur throughout the book: the relationship between the individual and the organization; and the impact on performance of training and development for managers. Other broader themes developed concern HRD strategies centred on skill and autonomy; the relationships between the processes underlying individual, group and organizational learning; and a framework for developing a learning organization.

The changing context of training and development

By 1980 there was abundant evidence that the UK workforce was inadequately trained in comparison with their major industrial competitors and that the level of training and development was insufficient to meet the skills needs of the 1990s. The UK economy was characterized by a 'low skills equilibrium' (Finegold and Soskice 1988), and the impact of skill deficiencies on productivity, and hence competitiveness, was widely recognized. As a result, during the 1980s the government radically overhauled the system of vocational education and training (VET) in the UK. First, employers were given a leading role in determining local training priorities and in establishing sector-level training arrangements. Second, a competence-based approach to VET was adopted in order to establish a nation-wide unified system of vocational qualifications. After describing these changes in the framework for vocational education and training, this section reviews the main policy debates concerning management education and training, and outlines the changing organizational context in which management development is taking place.

The framework for vocational education and training

The Employment Department White Paper, *Employment for the 1990s* (1989), proposed new arrangements to overcome the UK skills deficit, which entailed devolving responsibility for achieving an increase in the volume of vocational training and development to the local level, a strategy 'to return the training problem to businesses' (Ashton *et al.* 1989: 150). Employer-led Training and Enterprise Councils (TECs) in England and Wales, and Local Enterprise Companies (LECs) in Scotland were created to give employers a major role in ensuring that training provision matches local labour market needs. Sector training bodies were also transformed into employer-led bodies with responsibility for determining training arrangements and establishing occupational standards. Recognizing the need to develop a national strategy for VET (IPM 1992) and to monitor its progress, National Targets for Education and Training were established from 1991 and since 1993 have been monitored by the National Advisory Council for Education and Training Targets (NACETT 1996).

Statutory Industry Training Boards (ITBs) had been established under the *Industrial Training Act 1964* as tripartite sector bodies to promote training through raising funds from a statutory levy on employers and disbursing grants to meet the costs of those employers training employees in accordance with the overall policies and directives of the ITB. The involvement of the social partners was seen as necessary to establish an 'industry view' which would transcend the sectional interests of employers and trade unions (Rainbird 1990). Under the *Employment and Training Act 1973*, levy exemptions were allowed to companies that could demonstrate the quality of their own training programmes. From 1979, the approach altered under the Conservatives, with statutory, tripartite arrangements giving way to voluntary, employer-led Industry Training Organizations (ITOs) (Hyman 1992; Senker 1992). Following a review of their operation, the *Employment and Training Act 1981* abolished seventeen of the twenty-four ITBs, and notice was given in 1990 that another five were to be abolished. There are now over 120 ITOs in existence and two ITBs (Construction and Engineering Construction).

The Manpower Services Commission (MSC), established in 1973 to create a coherent national policy for VET, published *The New Training Initiative* in 1981, putting the case for 'new standards' to define what people at work should be able to do. A year later, Hayes (1982) emphasized the importance of occupational competence in place of the traditional time-serving approach to VET. In 1986, a *Review of Vocational Qualifications* for the MSC and the Department of Education and Science recommended that new vocational qualifications should be centred on occupational competence, defined as 'the ability to perform satisfactorily in an occupation or range of occupational tasks'. The review led to the development of a unified system of National Vocational Qualifications (NVQs) based on occupational standards developed by employer-led Industry Lead Bodies (ILBs), which may be the same organization as the ITO for that sector or a separate entity. The functions of ITOs and ILBs are being combined in new National

Training Organizations (NTOs). Social partner involvement is crucial in the establishment of occupational standards, and even in the employer-led ITOs, trade union representatives play a major part in this process (Winterton and Winterton 1993b; 1994).

The removal of statutory union involvement in training at sector level focused union attention on the workplace level and the TUC proposed the formation of Workplace Training Committees (WTCs) with a statutory responsibility to develop a Training Plan for the enterprise (TUC 1989: 11). In the absence of statutory rights, union negotiators were to put training on the bargaining agenda and to develop a joint approach with employers (TUC 1990; 1996b). The TUC response to the National Commission on Education reiterated the unions' view that statutory underpinning of the training system was needed to give individuals a right to training (TUC 1992: 31). Despite the marginalization of the institutions of collective bargaining since the early 1980s, the unions are keen to establish new collaborative arrangements to promote lifetime learning (TUC, 1993; 1994a; 1995a; 1995b). Future social partner involvement in validation and recognition of vocational qualifications is likely to focus on the workplace and to involve some forum like the WTC proposed by the TUC (Winterton and Winterton 1998).

The National Council for Vocational Qualifications (NCVQ) was established to oversee and monitor the NVQ process, accrediting the qualifications based on standards developed by ILBs. The qualifications are certificated by Awarding Bodies such as the City and Guilds of London Institute, the Royal Society of Arts and the Business and Technician Education Council, which had been the traditional qualifying bodies for vocational training before the introduction of NVQs. In Scotland, the Scottish Vocational Education Council (ScotVEC) was established to accredit the equivalent Scottish Vocational Qualifications (SVQs). In 1996 NCVQ merged with the Schools Curriculum and Assessment Authority (SCAA) to form the Qualifications and Curriculum Authority (QCA), while in Scotland, ScotVEC was re-named the Scottish Qualifications Authority (SQA).

An NVQ (which should be taken to imply SVQ also, henceforth) comprises units of competence, each of which can be separately achieved and certificated, and the emphasis is on the assessment of competence, not the route through which competence is achieved. The units of competence are broken down into elements of competence, each of which is related to performance criteria and range statements. The occupational standards are therefore specified as elements of competence, range statements and performance criteria. The NVQ framework covers five levels, from the basic competences required to undertake elementary, routine and predictable work activities (level 1), through intermediate skills and competences required for supervisory and craft work (level 3), to competences involving the application of complex principles in unpredictable contexts, and associated with responsibility for substantial resources (level 5).

The assessment of NVQs is competence-based, involving judgement of how an individual performs in a work context against the criteria established in the standards, irrespective of whether the learning takes place via open or flexible learning, through off-the-job training or on the job. Workplace assessors are trained to the standards laid down by the Training and Development Lead Body, and the quality of their assessment is overlooked by internal and external verifiers (Fletcher 1991; Holyfield and Moloney 1996). Crediting competence, including validation of experiential learning and the recognition of tacit skills (Manwaring and Wood 1984), is an important part of shifting the emphasis away from traditional learning and has the potential of offering qualifications and opening up access to further training for groups of individuals who have been disadvantaged in traditional education, or made redundant through restructuring, but have developed competence through experience.

Acceptance of NVQs has been far from universal, as evidenced by the slow rate of take-up and extensive criticism of the approach (Toye and Vigor 1994). NCVQ and the TECs have, therefore, introduced various marketing initiatives to raise awareness, and have established quality control procedures to build commitment, with the objective of increasing the take-up of NVQs (Winterton and Winterton 1995). Some observers have criticized the competence-based approach for neglecting underpinning theory and knowledge.

Others have argued that crediting *existing* competences does not provide developmental opportunities for gaining new competences, a source of criticism from both employers and individuals in relation to the Accreditation of Prior Experiential Learning (APEL). While raising the level of qualification does not necessarily raise the skills and competences of individuals, the value of APEL as a means of recognizing and validating tacit knowledge should not be underestimated (Winterton and Winterton 1998). With the emphasis on the competence to perform defined tasks, more importance is attached to establishing the infrastructure necessary to facilitate access to assessment services (Crowley-Bainton and Wolf 1994).

Policy debates concerning management education and training

There is a broad consensus that the inadequacy of training and development in the UK equally applies to managers. Hussey (1988: 65) claimed that the estimate that 'most managers receive no training at all is by no means restricted to managers in the smaller companies'. The CBI (1989) noted that while 24 per cent of top UK managers are graduates, in France and Germany the percentage is more than twice that, and in Japan and the USA, 85 per cent of top managers have degree-level qualifications. In 1985, a staggering 54 per cent of management board members in the top 100 German companies were qualified to doctorate level (Randlesome 1990: 48).

In 1987 two reports were produced as part of a review of management education and training, prompted by the recognition that the UK lagged behind other industrialized nations in terms of its formal management education, and the belief that developing managers would improve the competitive advantage of UK industries. The first report, *The Making of Managers*, by Handy *et al.* (1987), presented recommendations in the form of a 10-point agenda, which included the following:

*   encouraging leading corporations to set a standard of five days off-the-job training per year per executive;
*   furthering good practices in MD by encouraging larger corporations to act as trainers and consultants to suppliers.

Among the recommendations of the second report, *The Making of British Managers*, by Constable and McCormick (1987), were two of particular relevance to the present study:

*   MD should be seen as a career-long process involving in-company training and external education;
*   MD should be an integral part of strategic plans and, where appropriate, developmental activities should be associated with the development of strategic changes.

In 1992, the Institute of Management began a review of management education, training and development, and established two working parties investigating management development, chaired by Professor Tom Cannon and Dr F. Taylor, respectively. Their findings were published as *Management Development to the Millennium* (IoM 1994). Professor Cannon was subsequently appointed chief executive of the Management Charter Initiative (MCI). The remit of the Cannon Working Party was to explore the extent to which the medium-term goals established in the earlier Handy and Constable reports had been attained, and to make policy recommendations in the light of changes since 1987. The Taylor Working Party was established to recommend policies for the period 1994–2000, taking into account the key issues expected to affect organizations in that period in the view of practising managers.

Noting the renewed interest by the Department of Trade and Industry (DTI) in the contribution which management education can make to raising the competitiveness of British industry, the Cannon Report (1994) sought to establish the extent of MD activity in the UK. Constable and McCormick (1987) had estimated that there were 2.5–3 million managers in the UK, excluding those in very small enterprises (< 20 employees) and the self-employed. The Cannon Report (1994) calculated that the number had shrunk to 2–2.25 million due to the recession of the 1990s. With the addition of an estimated 2.9 million self-employed and 1.6 million managers of very small firms, the total managerial labour pool is between 6.5 and 6.75 million. Since 'the majority of managers who can affect the performance of their organizations up to and beyond the millennium are already in post' (Cannon 1994: 21), their development is critical for raising the competitiveness of British industry.

Like the Handy and Constable reports, the Cannon Report noted the difficulty of obtaining an accurate estimate of the volume of MD in enterprises. The

Constable Report found over half of UK companies made no provision for training managers, a problem which was especially pronounced in companies with 20–99 employees. Although no estimate was made of MD in firms of < 20 employees, the situation can be assumed to be even more serious given their lesser resources and even more acute job demands. According to MCI (1992), the situation improved slightly from 1987, with 80 per cent of larger organizations (> 500 employees) reporting that they had a formal management training programme, but still only 50 per cent of all organizations and half that proportion of smaller firms (< 100 employees) having similar arrangements.

The Taylor Report (1994) noted several ambiguities in the views of senior managers interviewed in the study undertaken for the Working Party by Ashridge Management Research Group. Managers expected in the remainder of the 1990s to consolidate the evolving practices they had already begun to implement, a philosophical approach which the authors felt inappropriate for millennium thinking:

> In the chaotic and ambiguous world painted for us by the opinion formers, a search for clarity, certainty and solutions may be misguided. The challenge for organizations will lie in having to manage issues that are divergent, incongruent, and on occasions inherently contradictory at one and the same time.
>
> (ibid.: 3)

The changing organizational context

The Ashridge survey confirmed the extent of organizational changes underway, and established that UK managers thought the biggest challenges for the year 2001 to be contracting out, de-layering and empowerment. Other key issues of concern were persistent high levels of structural unemployment, increasing competitive pressures from low-wage economies, rapid technological change and standards in education which are inappropriate to the needs of employers (Taylor 1994: 26).

Given the expectation of continued organizational development, the Taylor Report (1994: 5) emphasized the need for organizations to create 'an environment where employees can develop and flourish and where change can be seen as a positive experience'. Respondents in the survey anticipated key challenges which would present new demands on MD, including the following:

- contracting out, both in the sense of outsourcing and the adoption of flexible firm strategies, leading to new measures of outcomes and frameworks for managing new working arrangements (ibid.: 44);
- empowerment, in terms of increased delegation of responsibility throughout the workforce, and 'drawing on the brainpower of all employees' (ibid: 34), requiring management to earn authority and to demonstrate ability (bid: 45);

- de-layering will increase the need for generalist managers to be 'aware of the totality of operations conducted by the organization' (ibid: 39) and necessitate team working and multiskilling of managers paralleling that of other empowered employees (ibid:36).

As a consequence of these challenges and changes, managers will be operating in organizations which are *constantly evolving*, so will have to be more flexible and undertake 'continuous learning rather than periodic training' (ibid: 37).

The comments of the Taylor Working Party are consistent with the approach developed in 1984 by the Institute of Personnel Management (now the Institute of Personnel and Development), which published a Code of Practice on continuous development, designed to promote continuous self-development and to integrate learning with work in order to improve operational performance (IPM 1984). The Code recommended that the operational plans designed to implement corporate strategy should identify learning needs and opportunities, leading to the development of a learning plan. Managers' job descriptions should outline their responsibilities for appraising, counselling and developing subordinates as well as the responsibility for their own continuous development. Appraisals should review improved performance goals and identify learning needs, while special reviews of the learning system should be regularly undertaken by 'diagonal slice' working parties.

Background to the study

It was in this context of renewed concern over developing the UK managerial workforce that the Employment Department needed to appraise the use of the Management Standards developed by MCI (see Chapter 5). To this end, a study group was established to identify what types of evidence could be considered to explore links between the use of competence-based standards and improvements in business performance, and to recommend the most appropriate methodology to investigate those links empirically. The study group comprised Stephen Leman (Employment Department), Lindsay Mitchell (PRiME Research and Development), Stuart Sanderson (Bradford Management Centre), Brian Sturgess (Putnam Hayes and Bartlett) and Jonathan Winterton, each of whom had distinct methodological expertise of relevance to the project. Members of the group held discussions with Paul Kingslan (Employment Department) and representatives of MCI and proceeded to assess the relevant literature, to develop a theoretical framework and to design a methodology for future empirical work. The existing evidence and the performance measures considered are reviewed below before outlining the hypotheses developed for testing.

Existing evidence

The study group found that the existing evidence of the benefits of using the Standards was largely anecdotal, comprising reported perceptions based on respondents' implicit criteria rather than systematic evaluation by an impartial observer using explicit criteria. Nevertheless, the literature provided a means of identifying hypothetical benefits which could be explored through more rigorous empirical study and analysis. Inevitably, the case studies produced by MCI of organizations adopting the Standards emphasized the Crediting Competence approach being marketed by MCI, rather than a wider consideration of the impact of competence-based management development (CBMD) in general. Also, the MCI case studies reported benefits without indicating whether these were outcomes perceived by an independent researcher or by individuals inside the organization. Studies attributed outcomes such as 'financial and other benefits' to MD without citing evidence, and most appeared to have been based on a single interview with a training manager. Most of the outcomes described in the MCI literature at that time related to broad improvements, like embedding quality in the company's systems and procedures, rather than quantifiable financial benefits. Several cases cited intermediate-level process-related outcomes: for example, customizing the Management Standards, becoming a Crediting Competence Centre, or achieving *Investors in People* status (see Chapter 4).

The MCI case studies were designed to illustrate the adoption of the Management Standards and persuade companies of the benefits of that approach, rather than to make an objective assessment of outcomes. Nevertheless, the MCI literature provided a useful starting point in providing a list of ascribed benefits which could be considered as criteria for evaluation purposes. The list (Leman *et al.* 1994: 12–13) included the following:

- raising the standards of management performance;
- managing change more effectively;
- improving staff morale, motivation and retention;
- gaining external recognition (e.g. *Investors in People*);
- promoting empowerment;
- identifying training needs and becoming self-reliant in training.

Coopers and Lybrand (1992) published case studies of MD in small and medium-sized companies (SMEs), and although this was not competence-based, the outcomes reported were comparable with those cited in the MCI cases, and included:

- generating commitment;
- improving the focus of the business;
- providing a broader strategic view of issues;
- improving team working and developing an integrated management approach;
- improving the customer focus;
- increasing turnover and gross margins.

A study of Management NVQs included in a report published by IMS (Callendar *et al.* 1993) identified other anticipated benefits of adopting the Management Standards. One enterprise viewed the Standards as a tool for organizational development, enabling a transformation towards a flatter, team-based structure. In another context, management similarly emphasized improving the quality of debate and understanding about the processes involved in changing the company's style. In a third case, the motivation of managers was expected to improve as a result of having their existing competences formally recognized through Accreditation of Prior Learning (APL).

A study (Corlett 1992) of the views of managers who participated in the piloting of APL assessment against the MCI Standards provided another list of anticipated benefits to individuals and their organizations, which included the following:

* increased motivation to take part in developmental activities;
* increased confidence and greater involvement in decisions;
* being better organized;
* improved clarity and focus of organizational objectives;
* achievement of *Investors in People* status;
* greater consistency of product quality.

These findings were echoed by a later study (Cheetham 1994) involving candidates for NVQs based on the Standards. Candidates reported improvements in management performance, and knowledge of both techniques and theory, particularly when an external agency was involved in providing developmental support.

These earlier studies provided no indication of appropriate methodologies to isolate the business benefits from the use of the Management Standards, and in all cases fell short of robust evidence attributable without ambiguity. Nevertheless, the list of potential benefits to individuals and organizations represented a starting point in considering the types of performance measures which might be addressed in further research. From this initial list, the study group considered potential measures of performance at different levels, as outlined below.

Measures of performance

The study group (Leman *et al.* 1994: 2–3) recognized the considerable difficulties in assessing the outcomes of management training and development because the causal chain between MD and performance involves three ascending levels:

* first-level outcomes involving improvements in the personal effectiveness of managers, such as focus on organizational objectives or greater motivation;
* second-level outcomes involving improvements in the functioning of the organization, such as better customer relations or improved team work;

- third-level outcomes reflecting improved business performance, such as increased market share or higher profit margins.

It was recognized that different performance measures and even different analytical techniques are appropriate at each level. Nevertheless, the three levels were thought to be inter-related in that, for improvements at a higher level to be attributable to the use of the Management Standards, it is necessary for benefits to be attributable to the Standards at the level(s) below. Thus a causal link needs to be demonstrated between the Standards and improvements in individual performance, and then with organizational effectiveness before a link can be demonstrated between the Standards and business outcomes.

The Standards developed for managers by MCI are particularly identifiable with individual performance since, like all occupational standards, they were created through a process of functional analysis whereby a functional map is produced describing what is expected of people working in that occupational domain. A functional map provides a classification of what people are expected to achieve in employment, rather than describing jobs, grades or educational and training requirements. Occupational standards are based on a broad strategic view of competence based on whole work roles, rather than on a narrow mechanistic view of the performance of routine, repetitive tasks and procedures. For example, four aspects of occupational competence are identified in the Job Competence Model: task or technical skills; contingency management; task management and role environment (Mansfield and Mathews 1985). A functional map should therefore offer an holistic specification of work roles bound together by a common key purpose clearly linked to the strategic aims of the sector.

Irrespective of the use of the Standards, the study group concluded that it should be relatively unproblematic to investigate improvements in individual performance of the sort claimed in earlier studies. The possible benefits ranged from perceived improvements in personal effectiveness and motivation to the acquisition of specific managerial skills leading to demonstrable improvements in performance. Less measurable outcomes like individuals taking responsibility for their own development, and managers adopting a more strategic approach to identifying training and development needs were also considered to be significant.

At the second level, organizational performance is often assessed in terms of economic measures such as profitability, earnings per share and market share, and in terms of other appropriate performance indicators in not-for-profit organizations. However, organizational effectiveness can be examined at a lower level of aggregation than such strategic and holistic measures by considering functions within the organization. In considering the influence of MD on organizational effectiveness, for example, the speed of the decision-making process or the effectiveness of team work might be assessed. Other aspects of organizational effectiveness might relate to the responsiveness of the organization to new ideas, as measured by the speed of adoption of innovative techniques and technologies, and the ease with which organizational change is accomplished or different cultures accommodated. The extent to which there is a 'learning culture' might be measured in terms of the extent to which individual learning and development is encouraged and how far vacancies are filled through internal promotion as opposed to externally.

At the level of business performance, financial measures such as pre-tax profit rates are complicated by the effects of a firm's capital structure on performance, so operating performance ratios are more useful, although these are not without pitfalls (Holes and Sugden 1991). Three corporate ratios are commonly used to measure business performance: trading profit/turnover; trading profit/capital employed; and turnover/capital employed. Increasingly, non-financial measures of business performance are also employed (see Chapter 8).

Hypotheses for evaluation

The study group concluded that to assess the effect of CBMD on performance, the three levels of performance first needed to be considered independently through appropriate measures. The central research question was therefore translated into three initial hypotheses appropriate to each of the levels of results discussed above:

1   CBMD will improve individual performance (IP);
2   CBMD will improve organizational performance (OP);
3   CBMD will improve business performance (BP).

The study group placed considerable influence on establishing links between the different levels of performance. The key relationship is between the organizational strategies in response to a changing external environment and how the necessary organizational development is supported by activities to develop the new managerial competences. The organization's environment defines the critical success factors and the impact of MD can be assessed in terms of its contribution to reskilling the organization's managers in order that they can implement the strategic objectives developed in pursuit of those critical factors.

The relationship between organizational strategy and performance is shown in Figure 1.1. The critical success factors, defined by the organization's environment, influence the objectives which are translated into strategy. The HRD processes within an organization are the mechanisms through which CBMD translates into performance, at the level of individuals, the organization and in 'bottom line' terms, which is evaluated against the organization's objectives. A conditional hypothesis was therefore constructed as follows:

4   CBMD is more likely to improve IP, OP and BP if linked to organizational strategy.

The study group also recognized that the central research question presented

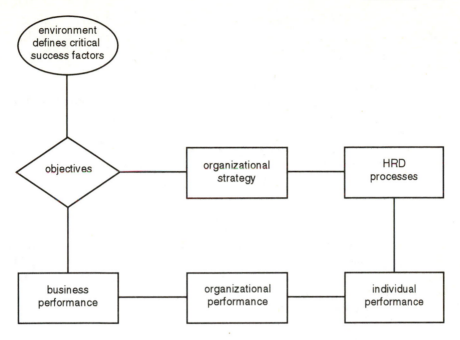

Figure 1.1 Relationship between organizational strategy and performance
Source: Leman *et al.* (1994)

the greatest methodological difficulty: identifying the extent to which performance improvements followed from the adoption of the Management
Standards. Improvements in performance might be attributed to MD and MD
linked with organizational strategy, without the Standards being necessarily
embedded in HRD systems and processes. Occupational standards represent
benchmarks against which individual performance can be assessed at a particular point in time, but to evaluate improvements in performance against the
standards requires some monitoring of individual achievement over time. Thus
an organization can adopt the Management Standards as a tool to assess the
performance of individual managers by incorporating the Standards in HRD
systems and processes. The rationale for this approach was described in the
report of the study group (Leman *et al.* 1994: 18).

Since occupational standards are designed by the appropriate lead body, they
reflect the organizational culture and values of the sector or occupation, identifying both the desired outcomes and the processes by which these may be
attained. By adopting a common, coherent set of standards, the same performance indicators, describing what individuals and teams are required to achieve,
can be used in all HRD systems and processes, facilitating the closer integration
of separate HRD activities. The Standards are influenced by the organization's
goals and provide integrated instruments to improve the effectiveness of the
HRD systems and processes, but decisions must still be made concerning the
ways in which the HRD activities will be used to achieve strategic objectives.

Finally, the Standards themselves can be used in the accreditation and qualification of managerial competence, and can support the achievement of other forms of external recognition, at the level of individuals (NVQs/SVQs) and organizations (*Investors in People* and quality standards such as ISO9000). The relationship between organizational goals and the Standards, the intervening role of HRD activities and the mediating influence of external systems is shown in Figure 1.2. A second conditional hypothesis was therefore constructed thus:

5   CBMD is more likely to improve IP, OP and BP if HRD systems and processes are based on a common, coherent set of competence statements (e.g. the Management Standards).

These hypotheses are explored in subsequent chapters, starting with the two conditional hypotheses, then moving on to performance at the three levels. Beforehand, the concept of MD is explored with a review of the literature concerning management training and development, while the methodological approach adopted in the study is elaborated in further detail. The logic and structure of the remainder of the book are outlined in the following section, which provides an overview of the purpose of each chapter.

Structure and overview of the book

The previous sections of this chapter have established the context of training and development in the UK and the background to the study of competence-based management development. This section provides a brief overview of the logic and structure of the remainder of the book.

Chapter 2 offers an overview of current debates in relation to the nature of MD, what it is seeking to develop and how its effectiveness can be assessed. The concept of MD is explored by asking why managers need developing, what it entails and how it can be most effective. Management skills, competences and competencies are compared, with an important distinction made between occupational competence and individual competency. This chapter also considers how MD can be evaluated in terms of its impact upon performance.

Chapter 3 explores the methodological issues involved in measuring the impact of MD, and in particular CBMD, on performance. After reviewing the nature of a case study approach, the development of the case study protocol and research design is explained. The chapter explains how the fieldwork was carried out, achieving access to the organizations, operationalizing case study protocol and collecting the evidence through interviews and written evidence. The chapter also explains how evaluation of the case reports by independent experts was used to test the five hypotheses outlined in the previous section.

Chapter 4 examines MD from an organizational perspective and explores the link between MD and organizational strategy (OS). Organizations need to develop core competences as a route to competitive advantage; translating the business plan into strategy and operationalizing it depends crucially upon

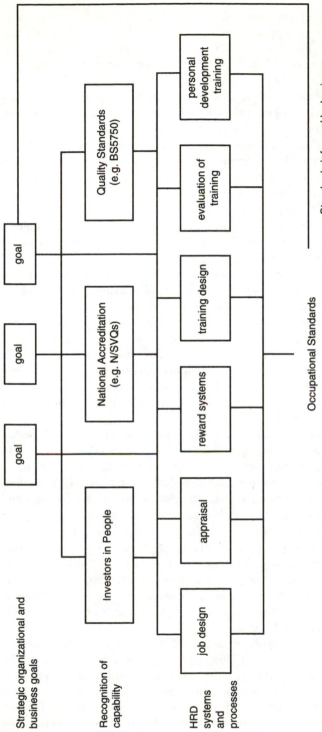

Figure 1.2 Relationship between occupational standards and strategic goals
Source: Leman *et al.* (1994)

developing managerial competence. This chapter also considers how development can be designed to support strategy and how integrating the two ensures both the effectiveness of MD and of OS, hence the significance of the *Investors in People* initiative. The empirical findings from the case studies are discussed in relation to linking MD and OS.

Chapter 5 is concerned with the adoption of competence standards by organizations and the relationship with CBMD. Combining the developmental aspects of HRM with a pluralist philosophy to establish a high-trust relationship with all employees is shown to be conducive to establishing such a culture. Forms of work organization must be consistent with the culture, and the combination of responsible autonomy and multiskilling is proposed as a new form of 'anthropocentric' work organization. The value of adopting a competence-based approach is considered along with the use of the Management Standards developed by MCI to provide a framework and structure for MD. The empirical findings from the case studies are discussed in relation to the adoption of the MCI Standards in HRD systems and processes.

Chapter 6 explores MD from the perspective of the individual manager and considers improvements in individual performance (IP) identified in the organizations studied. Mechanisms for identifying training and development needs of individual managers reveal tensions between development, assessment and rewards, but form an essential part of the performance management and assessment processes. Processes of individual learning and different types of occupational learning are discussed in relation to the learning cycle and the relationship between cognitive and affective learning. The empirical findings from the case studies are discussed in relation to demonstrated improvements in IP which were attributed to MD.

Chapter 7 addresses the role of MD in improving organizational performance (OP), exploring the meaning of organizational efficiency in terms of the effectiveness of departments and work groups. The effectiveness of teams depends upon both the competences and personalities of team members along with a wide range of organizational characteristics. Means of developing teams and team working, and ways of measuring team performance are considered. Team learning is distinguished from individual learning and factors identified which are conducive to learning and development *of* teams, as well as *in* teams. Action learning is shown to facilitate learning at the team level, while the concept of organizational learning is viewed as a bridge between individual learning and the development of a learning organization. The empirical findings from the case studies are discussed in relation to demonstrated improvements in OP which were attributed to MD.

Chapter 8 is concerned with the relationship between MD and business performance (BP), exploring how improvements in individual and team performance are translated into corporate success. Corporate success is considered in terms of both financial and non-financial measures and shown to depend upon the organization achieving certain critical success factors, which in turn, depends upon the organization's capacity to maintain and develop core competences.

The scope for learning between teams and at the level of the organization as a whole is addressed as a means of linking MD with improvements in BP. The utility of the concept of a learning organization as a framework for developing core competence is discussed and a model for building a learning organization is proposed. The empirical findings from the case studies are discussed in relation to demonstrated improvements in BP which were attributed to MD.

Chapter 9 draws together the empirical analysis developed in Chapters 4–8 by comparing the cases studied in terms of the performance improvements at the different levels. The importance of linking MD with OS and the value of basing HRD systems and processes on the Management Standards are assessed statistically. The conclusions, which have considerable significance for recent policy relating to MD, can be summarized as follows:

- there is a strong link between MD and both IP and BP which shows that developing human potential contributes to business success;
- the *Investors in People* approach, through which development is intergrated with business strategy increases the performance improvements from MD;
- the adoption of the Management Standards in HRD systems and processes provides coherence and further increases the performance improvements from MD.

2   Management development

The purpose of this chapter is to provide an overview of current debates in relation to the nature of management development (MD), what it is seeking to develop and how its effectiveness can be assessed.

The chapter is organized into three sections:

1   conceptualizing management development;
2   management skills, competences and competencies;
3   evaluating the impact of management development.

The first section explores the concept of MD, asking why managers need developing, what it entails and how it can be most effective. Are the objectives of MD concerned with developing individuals, organizations or both? Is MD more effective with a pedagogic or auto-didactic learning approach? What conditions are likely to make MD most effective in achieving its objectives?

In the second section, management skills, competences and competencies are discussed. Can management be defined as an occupational group or are management activities too diverse? What key skills and knowledge must managers possess and how can competence be demonstrated? How does occupational competence differ from individual competency?

In the third section, the principles and practices of evaluating MD in terms of its impact upon performance are considered. What is the value of evaluation frameworks for assessing the impact of training and development initiatives? What difficulties are encountered with evaluating MD in practice? How can evaluation be re-focused so that the effectiveness of MD is assessed in terms of its lasting impact on performance? The chapter concludes with a brief overview of the salient points by way of summary and conclusion.

Conceptualizing management development

To explain the concept of MD, this section contrasts ends, means and results, first establishing the purpose of MD, then outlining what it entails, and finally considering how it can be made more effective.

Why develop managers?

Motives vary according to context, but Molander (1986: 21) offers the general reason for management development as 'the identification and release of individual potential' through matching the growth needs of the individual manager with the needs of the organization. Career development is perceived as an objective goal for the individual which is analytically distinct from organization development (Schein 1978) but which can be moulded in such a way as to be consistent with corporate needs (Beer *et al.* 1984: 86). Managers involved in MD must see some value in the process for themselves; the business has its own strategic objectives which require the development of managers, but these need to mesh with the objectives of the individual (Abrams 1981). Wallace (1991: 206) believes that this can be achieved by requiring managers involved in MD to prepare a profile of their own strengths and weaknesses, review this profile in the context of any MD they are undertaking and at the end of a specific programme reassess what they need for future development (Hague 1973). Managerial learning and development are relevant in two senses: managers exert control over the learning of others (Hendry *et al.* 1995: 160) but also pursue learning for their own 'free agent careers', rather than the employing organization's purpose (Kanter 1989).

Reconciling parallel, and perhaps conflicting, individual and organizational objectives is a recurrent theme in the literature (Storey 1989b; 1990) which is also reflected in the analysis of this book. While MD is crucially concerned with improving performance, Lees (1992: 104) notes other rationales which are important in 'making managers feel whole'. Although skills and competences are transferable, there are certain areas of learning that may be firm specific and which will contribute largely to the strategic interests of the firm. This can cause conflict between individual aspirations for learning and skill development and the developmental needs of the company, which may restrict new learning that is deemed inappropriate to company strategic objectives (Hendry *et al.* 1995: 139). Hussey (1996) notes that the most common approach to MD involves developing the individual manager, and this is limited by their superior's ability to assess what development each individual requires to facilitate the achievement of the company's strategic objectives, especially when such objectives are not widely known.

Watkins (1989: 427) describes the purpose of human resource development (HRD) in general as fostering 'a long-term, work-related learning capacity at the individual, group and organizational levels' through 'training, career development and organizational development.' Pedler *et al.* (1989a: 92) similarly emphasize the role of both individual and organizational development in raising generic problem-solving capacity to facilitate the creation of a 'learning company'. While such an approach may be criticized for attributing human characteristics to institutions, it nevertheless embodies the notion of synergy between individual and organization, whereby the learning company 'facilitates the learning of all of its members and continuously transforms itself in order to meet its strategic goals'.

The concept of the learning organization is valuable because it explicitly links learning with the workplace context in which it occurs. Moreover, writers on learning organizations frequently integrate individual and organizational development. Argyris and Schön (1978: 29) emphasize the importance of developing managers through error detection and correction, whereby 'double-loop learning' challenges prevalent assumptions within an organization and transforms the way individuals relate within an organization from unilateral control to mutual collaborative learning. De Geus (1988: 70) defines institutional learning as 'the process whereby management teams change their shared mental models of their company, their markets and their competitors'. Senge (1990a) focuses on metanoic learning, representing a major change in managers' thinking, as the key to developing a learning organization. 'Organizations learn only through individuals who learn. Individual learning does not guarantee organizational learning. But without it no organizational learning occurs.' (Senge 1990b: 139).

Watkins and Marsick (1992) build on these learning organization concepts and focus on learning at the individual, team and organizational levels in order to raise the organization's capacity to change. As Tate (1995a; 1995b) argues, management development is concerned not only with developing individual managers, but also with developing *corporate competence*, the management of the organization as a whole. The foundation of an organization's capabilities is the competences of its individual members (Stinchcombe 1990: 63), whose routinized skills must be constantly built upon and modified to produce improved organizational performance and competitive advantage (Cohen 1996: 189).

Recent attention has been drawn to the identification of core skills, competences and competencies (Prahalad and Hamel 1990; Hamel 1994) and ways of developing these to support corporate renewal (Doz 1997) and competitive advantage (Barney 1995). Herriot and Pemberton (1995) similarly emphasize the role of innovation and learning in developing managerial and corporate competence for competitive advantage. De Geus (1988) even goes so far as to claim that the only source of competitive advantage for the organization of the future is its managers' ability to learn faster and continually to revise their mental models of the world.

What is management development?

MD has been defined as 'any attempt to improve managerial effectiveness through a planned and deliberate learning process' (Training Services Agency 1977: 1). Mumford (1994: 3) modifies that definition 'to include *informal* and *accidental* processes, as well as those defined as planned and deliberate'. Similarly, while MD, and HRD in general, should emphasize strategic goals, especially in the preparation and follow-up stages, Watkins and Marsick (1992) argue that it should also include informal and incidental learning alongside formal development. Burgoyne and Stewart (1976) acknowledged that managers learn from a variety of sources, especially experientially, but argued that planned education and training still play an important part. Mumford (1993a) similarly emphasizes the need to combine formal and informal opportunities for development. The Taylor Report (1994: 84) noted a widening in the concept of MD, which now 'embraces a wide range of developmental activities...such as job rotation, project work, [and] self-managed learning'.

Peel (1984) distinguished management education from management training in terms of the duration of the provision: long courses represented education, short courses were viewed as training. The value of making a distinction between the two is debatable, but it would seem equally valid to characterize education as broad and of general applicability, whereas training is narrower and with a specific application. Thus a manager might be educated in the principles of financial accounting, but trained to maintain accounts. Management development includes both education and training, but also embraces 'reading, job rotation, projects and other ways of trying to bring in the dimension of learning by experience in a managed way' (Hussey 1988: 58).

Molander (1986: 6) classified MD activities in terms of the level at which they are focused and the style in which initiatives are introduced. The focus may be on the individual, the group or the organization, while the style may be prescriptive or consultative. At the individual level, the prescriptive approach includes management courses and qualifications, while the consultative approach includes coaching, needs analysis and career planning. At the group level, Molander identifies project-based learning as a prescriptive approach and action learning as a consultative approach. Finally, at the organization level, organizational development may be prescriptive, while organizational analysis and feedback are consultative. While a prescriptive approach based on the required qualifications for a post is suitable in some contexts, if the principal objectives are concerned with change, then a consultative approach with the active involvement of the individual manager is likely to be more appropriate.

Snape *et al.* (1994: 73) distinguish pedagogical (trainer-led) and androgogical (self-directed or auto-didactic) training and development activities, and this classification of delivery methods is more meaningful in learning terms than Molander's dichotomy of prescriptive/consultative styles. In contrast with traditional structured learning, self-organized learning focuses on enabling the learner to diagnose personal needs and to manage their learning (Harri-Augstein and Webb 1995). In the learning company people are encouraged to manage their own learning and career development in this way: 'learning starts from the job itself which is designed to be developmental' (Pedler *et al.* 1997: 164). Small groups, such as project teams, task forces, quality circles and productivity improvement teams facilitate self-development as an integral part of action learning development where an individual with a problem to address is supported by a small group of colleagues.

Marchington and Wilkinson (1996: 194) combine the learning dimension with a focus dimension, distinguishing between individual and group learning to create four categories of training and development methods. If development at the organizational level is added, six categories are distinguished which then makes explicit the need to consider individual and group development as part of a broader strategy to develop organizational capacity, at the same time illustrating the range of, and relationship between, different approaches to developmental activity. Table 2.1 shows the different categories and examples of each.

Taking an holistic view of the complete MD cycle, a particular developmental activity merely represents the programme delivery stage. Wallace (1991: 15) identifies three phases: preparation, in which problems are identified and aims established; execution, comprising needs analysis, programme design and delivery; and follow-up, including 'diplomatic advertising and internal marketing'. By focusing on the complete MD cycle, the diagnosis and analysis of problems may lead to non-training solutions, such as new systems or procedures, as well as to training and development solutions. The contribution which MD can make should not be overlooked, but neither should it be viewed as a panacea for all an organization's problems.

What makes management development effective?

Many authorities emphasize the importance of individual ownership in making MD effective. Thus for Molander (1986: 98), in addition to a climate of mutual respect between the individual and their senior manager, the learner should set the goals for MD, be involved in its planning, be a resource in the implementation and undertake the evaluation. A self-development action learning approach, requiring the learner to take responsibility for what they want or need to learn, is advocated by Pedler *et al.* (1997: 172), who argue that it should form an integral part of any well-designed development programme today. It is especially the case in small firms that individuals have to grasp the limited learning opportunities available to them and Hendry *et al.* (1995: 157–9) suggest that there are three ways of achieving this objective. First, they need to take the 'initiative', push themselves forward and demand the training and development they need. Second, they can take advantage of 'interpersonal learning' from others on-the-job. Third, individuals can learn in teams, which can be an important vehicle for occupational development.

Developing competence may meet individual needs, but Nordhaug (1993: 43) notes that 'the utilization of competence depends on the employee's motivation to work, defined as a drive toward attaining the best possible job performance'.

Table 2.1 Approaches to management training and development

learning/focus	individual	group	organization
pedagogical	instruction	lecture	organizational development
auto-didactic	self-managed learning	team building	learning organization

Applying cognitive motivation theory to individuals demonstrates that work motivation is influenced by rewards, whether 'extrinsic', like pay and promotion, or 'intrinsic', such as empowerment to allow individuals more control of their working lives. For highly educated personnel, intrinsic rewards, which are a direct function of personal and professional development, are assuming an ever increasing importance, especially since this group of employees have often already attained high pay and status . However, 'extrinsic' rewards do influence the 'utilization' of competence: 'If employees feel that they are not sufficiently valued in terms of salary and status, the incentive to utilize their knowledge and skill will diminish.' (ibid.: 44). The learner-centred approach, where the individual manager takes responsibility for their own development, increases the motivation to learn, but does it make for more effective MD in terms of the needs of the business? When considering the effectiveness of MD, it is important that evaluation takes place at both the individual learning level and at the organizational level in terms of the extent to which the development leads to performance improvement in line with organizational strategy.

In addition to individual ownership and commitment, the existence of a supportive environment is thought to be a key factor in making MD effective. Waterman (1994: 17), for example, argues that it is the organizational arrangements of top companies that gives them the leading edge over other organizations: 'They are better organized to meet the needs of their *people*, so that they attract better people than their competitors do and their people are more greatly motivated to do a superior job, whatever it is they do.' Management is no longer telling people what they must do but rather 'understanding what motivates people and aligning culture, systems, structure, people, and leadership attention toward things that are inherently motivating'. In an action learning or learning company context, learning is central to the organization with all kinds of opportunities being available to employees, such as job shadowing, task forces, action learning groups, quality circles, self-learning materials, resource centres, courses, seminars and workshops (Pedler 1996; Pedler *et al.* 1997). A genuinely supportive environment involves serious commitment from senior management which goes beyond the organizational rhetoric of terms like 'employee involvement', 'empowerment', and total quality management (TQM). These notions have been systematically undermined by the prevalent 'hierarchical financial culture' and Taylorist attitudes which militate against generating a more collaborative, high-trust relationship with employees (Jones 1996: 121).

An assumption consistent with the action learning, learning company and learning organization approaches is that it is more effective to take the work group or the organization as the target for change when seeking to develop the individual manager (Varney 1976). This perhaps explains the finding of Wallace (1991) that the most cost-effective approaches to MD were associated with 'business change' and had a 'dual focus', addressing both the individual manager and the organization. Similarly, Watkins and Marsick (1992) note that changing workplace demands challenge HRD specialists to alter their focus from training individuals to facilitating learning by individuals, teams and organizations.

Organizations still need leaders, but rather than the traditional managers of the past, these are likely to be individuals who coach, train and support others in the company (Molander and Walton 1984; Mumford 1993b) as well as enabling the development of innovative business strategies. It is not always easy to achieve this level of self-direction, however, because managers cling to their role as controllers rather than facilitators: 'their need for control is just as high as it is in the rest of the population, probably higher' (Waterman 1994: 44).

Management skills, competences and competencies

Early management theorists like Fayol (1949) and Barnard (1938) criticized the lack of management education, the absence of management theory and the inadequate understanding of management practice. As with Taylor's (1911) approach, management was portrayed in terms of rational, systematic, scientific processes like planning, coordination and control. The recognition of a gap between the rhetoric of academic management thought and the reality of management practice is relatively recent (Ashton *et al.* 1975; Mumford 1988a). When Mintzberg (1989) described what managers actually do, the role was seen to be far removed from rational actions in a predictive environment.

Others, equally, have emphasized the complexities and contradictions of managerial work, and the enormous variations in the tasks, roles and contexts of management which make generalization of the management role so elusive (Hales 1986: Hirsh and Bevan 1988; Whitely 1989; Knights 1992). Graves (1976) suggested that development is more likely to be successful than training because of the differences between what managers do and what they *say* they do.

Defining skills and competences

Clearly, it is necessary to identify the skills and competences which are required of managers before effective MD can be designed (Margerison 1985; Hornby 1991; Johnston and Sampson 1993). Despite the vast range and variety of activities in which managers are involved and the fragmented nature of a 'typical' manager's day, it is possible to identify managerial roles and the skills associated with these. Mintzberg (1980), for example, includes such roles as leadership, handling resources and negotiation in his definition of management activities. Since few individuals can aspire to peak performance in all of these diverse roles, Belbin (1981) argued that managerial teams comprising individuals with complementary strengths should be constructed.

For MD to facilitate improved performance in particular roles, it is necessary to identify the factors contributing to the execution of a particular role, which first requires a distinction to be drawn between skill, knowledge and understanding. Skill was defined by Hans Renold in 1928 as 'any combination, useful to industry, of mental and physical qualities which require considerable training to acquire' (More 1980: 15). Proctor and Dutta (1995: 30), who provide an authoritative text on skill and performance, note that 'a defining property of skill is that it develops over time, with practice'. Like Renold, Proctor and Dutta include perceptual and problem-solving skills as well as motor skills. Thus skill encompasses both manual facilities, including dexterity, and conceptual ones, including relevant knowledge and understanding. Knowledge includes underpinning theory and concepts relevant to an area of activity, as well as tacit knowledge gained as a result of the experience of performing tasks. Knowledge may therefore be gained through formal or informal learning, or, typically, through both routes. Understanding refers to more holistic knowledge of processes and contexts, and may be distinguished as know-why, as opposed know-how (skill and competence) or know-that (knowledge). Collin (1997: 297) cites Gardner's association of know-how with tacit knowledge and know-that with propositional knowledge.

The competence-based approach adopted in the UK since 1986 is concerned with the practical demonstration of skills, knowledge and understanding in a work setting, and therefore relates to job performance: 'the ability to put skills and knowledge into action' (Day 1988). Since the assessment of competence is undertaken in the work context, and the standards adopted are those expected in employment, the issue of transfer of training to the workplace becomes unproblematic (L. Miller 1991). Hirsh and Strebler (1994: 83) identify three 'recurring features' in the notion of competences:

- a competence is seen in the context of a particular job or job role and the organization in which that job exists;
- competences are positively associated with superior performance;
- competences can be described in terms of specific behaviours which can be observed in the job.

There is nevertheless considerable confusion and debate concerning the concept 'competence', which may relate to personal models, outcome models or education and training models, as well as to the standards approach in which benchmarking criteria are used. The definition of occupational competence provided by the Manpower Services Commission (MSC) (1986) and adopted by *Investors in People* (1995: 41) was 'the ability to perform activities in the jobs within an occupation, to the standards expected in employment'. However, the definition also included 'mastery of skills and understanding' and 'aspects of personal effectiveness'. As Mansfield and Mitchell (1996: 46) note, this definition 'appears to include a mix of models: work expectations, input measures (knowledge and skills) and psychological attributes'. Nevertheless, the MSC definition of competence was subsequently adopted as the official Employment Department approach in defining occupational standards as 'a description of something which a person who works in a given occupational area should be able to do…[and] able to demonstrate' (Training Agency 1988: 5; 1989; Employment Department and NCVQ 1991).

In everyday language, if an individual is 'competent', they can perform the task or job in question, but are not necessarily demonstrating any particular *skill* in executing that role. As Tate (1995b: 82) notes, 'the word "competent" suffers from the connotation of bare sufficiency or adequacy, as opposed to expertise'. Moreover, the UK notion of threshold competence may be contrasted with the US approach where competence is against the yardstick of the best performers. The term 'incompetent' is usually applied to a person who is inept at the tasks they perform, and likely to remain so, whereas 'not yet competent' implies that the individual is expected to attain competence as a result of further development and training. Burgoyne (1988a) questions the use of generic managerial competences in MD, as well as the dichotomous nature of competence in the NVQ approach: competent/not competent. It is perhaps more realistic to imagine a continuum of *degrees* of competence, with a threshold of competence where the individual meets the defined standards, but has scope for developing further skills, knowledge and understanding. Such an approach is more consistent with an organization's 'continuous improvement' strategies and the notion of individual career progression through MD.

Another source of confusion in discussions of skills and competences is whether these relate to the job or the job holder. As Figure 2.1 shows, competence represents the link between the demands of the job and the attributes of the manager, whose performance is assessed against the standards defined.

Beyond competence

The attraction of a generic core of management competences is self-evident when it comes to designing training, development and assessment. Equally, such an approach is essential to ensure transferable skills and portable qualifications. Some commentators, however, believe that for the environment in which managers now operate, the 'nanosecond nineties' as Peters (1992) puts it, organizations need more than managerial competence. Noting the radical changes in the UK financial sector, for example, Higgs (1988) argued that in addition to traditional technical competence, managers in that sector needed attributes like flexibility, tolerance of ambiguity and ability to learn. Brown (1994) similarly argues that without prerequisite 'managerial capacities', like judgement and intuition, any demonstration of competence is meaningless.

In contrast to the job-related concept of *competence* (and *competences*), Boyatzis (1982) defines managerial *competency* (and *competencies*) in terms of the attributes of an individual which are 'causally related to effective or superior performance in a job'. Burgoyne (1988a) similarly distinguishes 'being competent' (meeting the job demands) from 'having competencies' (possessing the necessary attributes to perform competently).

Unfortunately, competence and competency are frequently confused or conflated. Pedler *et al.* (1997: 141), for example, refer to 'competencies that are needed in certain jobs' and the 'skills, competences and capabilities that will be required in the company', without articulating the distinction between the two terms. Snyder and Ebeling (1992) refer to competence in the sense used in this book, but use 'competencies' in the plural. Some authors consistently use

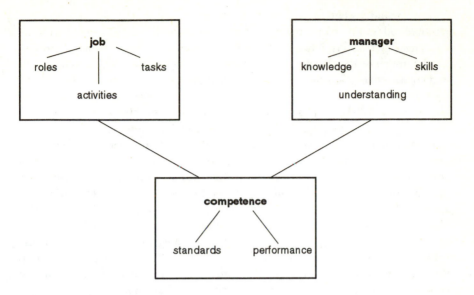

Figure 2.1 Competence in context
Source: Winterton (1994)

'competency' when meaning competence (Boam and Sparrow 1992; Mitrani *et al.* 1992; B. Smith 1993; Hendry *et al.* 1995) or treat the two as synonymous (McBeath 1990; R.B. Brown 1993; 1994; Doyle 1997). Dale and Iles (1992) distinguish occupational skills from psycho-social characteristics, but use competence and competency to describe both in discussing their role in assessing managerial skills.

Spencer (1995: 144) offers a typical North American definition of competency as a 'relatively enduring characteristic of a person causally related to effective or superior performance in a job', but also refers to this as competence (Spencer and Spencer 1993). Similarly, the Hay/McBer definition of competency as 'a characteristic of an individual that has been shown to drive superior job performance' includes both visible 'competencies' of 'knowledge and skills' and 'underlying elements of competencies', like 'traits and motives' (Hartle 1995: 107). Elkin's (1990) association of competences with micro-level job performance and competencies with higher management attributes is unconvincing.

Boak (1991) argues that 'competency' in the American sense complements 'competence' as used in the UK occupational standards. Woodruffe (1991) offers the clearest statement, contrasting areas of competence, defined as aspects of the job which an individual can perform, with competency, referring to a person's behaviour underpinning competent performance. Woodruffe's definition is endorsed by Tate (1995b: 86) who warns against confusing 'input competencies with output competences'.

There is a broad consensus between the policy reviews on management education and recent management literature that whatever competences are required today, tomorrow's managers will need more than these to cope with the challenges and uncertainties of the future. The management attributes emphasized in much of this debate invariably include competencies as well as new skills and competences. Constable (1988) identified personal qualities such as decisiveness, intiative, tenacity and creativity as essentials for the competent manager. For Morgan (1988), getting the balance right between chaos and order, and managing in a more egalitarian environment are among the important attributes. Kanter (1989) similarly mentions the ability to operate without hierarchy across traditional functional boundaries. In defining 'managerial competencies for the future', Cockerill (1989) combines output competences, like effective presentation skills, with input competencies such as self-confidence. Likewise for Burgoyne (1989a; 1989b) tomorrow's managers need higher-order abilities such as 'learning to learn', forecasting and analysis, as well as personal competencies, including diligence, tenacity and integrity. The common theme with such lists of 'meta-competences' (R.B. Brown 1993) are that they relate to the cognitive aspects of management concerned with reflection and ability to cope with uncertainty (Burgoyne and Stewart 1976; Kolb *et al.* 1986).

Evaluating the impact of management development

It is a popular assumption that HRD in general and MD in particular provide a route to improving performance and maintaining competitive advantage, yet robust empirical evidence to support the hypothesis is rare and the methodological tools with which it can be tested are relatively under-developed. To assess the effectiveness of MD, according to Mumford (1994: 4), it is necessary to have a definition of effective management behaviour, a developmental process which emphasizes activities in which managers are required to be effective, and the identification of learning processes which are effective for the individual or group concerned. The emphasis of MD should therefore be on what a manager can achieve: 'in terms of the results actually secured...not by the knowledge someone possesses' (ibid.: 7). Evaluating MD should involve a number of different levels, but in practice it is usually far less comprehensive. The theory and practice of evaluation are contrasted below.

Levels of evaluation

Kirkpatrick (1983) distinguished four different levels at which the effectiveness of MD may be assessed:

1   reaction level provides information on what participants thought of a training programme;
2   learning level evaluates the effectiveness of training in providing participants with the ability to show the attainment of principles, facts, techniques and skills presented in the training programme;

3   behavioural level is concerned with how well training skills or behaviours have been transferred to the job and involves collecting information from participants, superiors and subordinates;
4   results level measures the results of training through assessing organizational improvement, in terms of company's return on investment, cost savings, quality changes and improvements in work output.

Alternative approaches to evaluation, such as the Bell system (Jackson and Kulp 1979) and Parker's (1973) framework, have much in common with Kirkpatrick's, which has become the most widely adopted.

Evaluation at the reaction level is really no more than a customer satisfaction index – in the worst case the 'happy sheets' completed by participants at the end of a course. Such measures of 'reaction outcomes' (Bell) or 'participant satisfaction' (Parker) may yield valuable information to training providers and help future training and development, but both providers and participants have a vested interest in exaggerating the success of developmental activities. Customer evaluation therefore provides little information about the effectiveness of training and development programmes.

Evaluation at the learning level, which entails a performance-based check on individuals before and after a training course or developmental activity, is more relevant in evaluating the effect of MD on individual performance. The purpose is to measure 'capability outcomes' (Bell) including 'knowledge' acquired (Parker), to assess improvement in the individual's potential. It is important that the evaluation system collects base-line data before training begins and this forces an identification of what the objectives of training are in terms of training outcomes or results. Such evaluation can be part of the regular performance review, where subordinate and superior examine the extent to which a training event or other experience has provided the desired development of competence (Margerison 1993).

Evaluation at the behavioural level is concerned with whether individuals are applying what was learned (including both observable and non-observable results). Such 'application outcomes' (Bell), reflected in 'job performance' (Parker) are relevant both to individual and organizational performance (Margerison 1991). One mechanism is for managers to keep a 'time manager' log of activities to monitor the effectiveness of their personal development in terms of more strategic behaviour (A. Smith 1993).

Tracking the effect of training in results or operational terms is concerned with 'worth outcomes' in the Bell terminology, which emphasizes the value added by training and development. In the Parker framework, however, 'group performance' is the highest evaluation level, which reflects the difficulty of identifying the impact of development on business performance. In such a cost–benefit analysis there are problems in identifying what costs of training are to be included, and in assessing the benefits, there is great diversity in what are the most appropriate measures:

For a sales training programme, you may calculate the change in sales volume, the size of average sale, or the number of new accounts; for a management development programme those indicators would be meaningless. In that case, you might need to determine the benefits by calculating the change in productivity, the decrease in production costs, or the increase in output.

(Robinson and Robinson 1989: 256)

In order to evaluate training and development, it is necessary to identify (a) specific operational indicators related to the training effort, which are (b) amenable to monitoring. In addition to quantifiable benefits, there are unquantifiable results from improved competence; such effects are long-term and difficult to disaggregate. This is especially the case with development, which invariably has a longer time-scale than training (Endres and Kleiner 1990). Establishing clear aims that can be monitored as results is therefore the key to successful follow-up. By juxtaposing an evaluation framework with the stages of the MD cycle, Wallace (1991: 60) produces a 'value chain for management development'. In cost-effective MD, evaluation at the start of the cycle begins with pressures for change in terms of business results, moves to learning and reaction levels in the middle of the cycle, and then returns to the application and results level at the end of the cycle.

Evaluation in practice

The four levels of evaluation may be seen as complementary, each offering insights into a different aspect of the effectiveness of the adoption of a development or training initiative. In addition to their structural characteristics, Phillips (1990) notes that the four levels of evaluation differ in three important respects:

- the value of information increases with the level of evaluation, from reaction to results;
- the difficulty of assessment also increases from reaction through to results;
- the frequency of use decreases from reaction to results evaluation, showing an inverse relationship to the degree of difficulty.

Noting the lack of information which could be used by senior management to assess what was being achieved by MD in an organization, Ashton and Easterby-Smith (1979) proposed an audit of existing development in order to operationalize a systems approach to MD. The Management Development Audit (MDA) approach (Easterby-Smith *et al.* 1980: 6) contrasts three distinct views of MD:

- a formal view of what is supposed to happen;
- managers' perceptions of what is actually happening;
- what managers would like to see happen in MD.

The MDA is based upon the perceptions of the individuals concerning MD *inputs*, rather than an evaluation of the MD *outputs*. The MDA therefore constitutes little more than a reaction level evaluation and does not offer a prescription for demonstrating the effectiveness of MD in terms of performance.

Clement (1981) found evaluation of training was inadequate in the USA: where any evaluation was undertaken, this was usually at the level of trainee reaction, and rarely considered improvements in individual or business performance. Clement also noted that few studies had attempted to compare the relative effectiveness of two or more techniques to achieve the same objective, nor had they explored the influence of individual differences to the outcome of training. Similarly, in the UK, there is evidence that evaluation of training is rare and usually limited to a reaction level questionnaire following a course. Coopers and Lybrand (1985: 10) found few companies evaluated the cost-effectiveness of their management training, a situation confirmed by Hussey (1988: 68), who noted that most companies could not indicate the criteria by which the success of a training programme was measured.

Hussey (1988: 68–9) offers five reasons why little evaluation is undertaken:

1   There is little top management pressure for this.
2   Money spent on evaluation cannot be spent on training.
3   Training is based on individual, not corporate, needs, and it is difficult to measure all aspects of individual performance compared with corporate performance.
4   The objectives of many internal training initiatives are unclear.
5   Widespread ignorance of evaluation.

Peel (1984: 35) explained the paucity of evaluation in terms of the difficulty of attributing causality: 'at best, management development and training must always be an act of faith'. Not only is it difficult to identify operational results that are amenable to improvement through training and development, causality is difficult to establish because:

> no single factor, including training, could by itself have brought about the change that has taken place. The change has occurred because all factors have worked together, producing a synergistic effect, to improve performance. Attempting to say how much of the change can be strictly attributed to any one factor is an exercise in futility.
>
> (Robinson and Robinson 1989: 275)

In addition, there are often 'political' considerations which deter proper evaluation, of the sort recommended by Rae (1997) for training, from taking place. Those responsible for the evaluation may have a vested interest in demonstrating the effectiveness of MD opportunities for which they are responsible or to which they have committed time or money (Fox 1989; Currie 1994; Easterby-Smith

1994). These factors may explain the lack of obvious value from team survival exercises reported by Newstrom (1985).

Any major MD programme inevitably makes demands on limited company resources and organizations seek to maximize the return on this investment. The effectiveness of MD can prove difficult to measure in the short term, as MD outcomes are not always obvious in limited time periods, but Wallace (1991: 235) argues that 'short-term effectiveness is more important for us than long-term effectiveness, because short-term effectiveness helps us make timely decisions'. While conceding that long-term effectiveness is important to the organization, it is difficult to estimate or measure because of extraneous organizational and environmental factors, so Wallace recommends that an investment framework should concentrate on short-term effectiveness.

Where evaluation gets beyond the reaction level at all, organizations are likely to adopt such a pragmatic approach and focus on short-term effects, but it is possible to conceive of a more strategic approach taking into account longer-term effectiveness. For example, Pedler (1996: 77–8) acknowledges the difficulties in evaluating action learning outcomes, but notes that the more specific the success criteria, the easier it is to assess the value added by the programme. It is important to clarify whether evaluation is being undertaken for developmental purposes (to improve action and learning) or for judgemental reasons (to assess the impact or contribution). It is also necessary to undertake evaluation at different levels (individual, group and organization) as well as at different points in time to assess the true value of a particular contribution. Obviously, other factors may produce a cost reduction or greater efficiency or productivity: 'Often the best we can do here is to get people's opinions on the likely causes of such changes' (ibid.: 80).

To increase the effectiveness of evaluation requires senior management to re-focus training on to areas of strategic importance and to 'insist on evidence that training is economically effective' (Hussey 1988: 174). The Cannon Report (1994: 49) similarly recommended that MD should be re-focused to emphasize 'its impact on corporate performance and improved competitiveness'. The national occupational standards should help in this respect because they describe work role expectations and there is therefore a direct link with business performance. At the same time, the need to demonstrate value added from investment in human capital, just as with investment in plant and machinery, highlights the need to develop effective measures of performance at all levels in order to assess the impact of MD.

Summary and conclusions

In this chapter we aimed to do three things. The first was to explore the concept of MD, analysing its objectives and nature, while considering the conditions under which it can be made most effective. Second, this chapter has been concerned with identifying management skills, competences and competencies, relating these to the development of the Management Standards by MCI. The final objective was to consider how the effects of MD can be evaluated in terms of improvements in the performance of managers and organizations.

In exploring the concept of MD, tension between the twin objectives of developing individuals and raising core competence within an organization was identified. In order to achieve the best fit between the two objectives, the approach to MD needs to involve auto-didactic learning at the individual, group and organizational levels. Individual ownership coupled with a supportive environment, such as action learning or a learning organization, appears to be most conducive to effective MD.

Any discussion of skill is invariably complex and controversial, especially when addressing managerial work with its diversity and ambiguity. This chapter has aimed to clarify the discussion by defining skills and competences, and distinguishing them from competencies. The changing context in which managers must operate demands new competences and competencies, which are related to the results which managers can achieve, rather than simply with their possession of knowledge. The Management Standards are shown to provide a comprehensive framework of key management roles and elements of managerial competence, and the adoption of these Standards in human resource development structures and processes is encouraged by the *IiP* initiative.

Various frameworks for assessing the effectiveness of MD have been considered and these have in common a hierarchy of evaluation from the reaction level, through learning and behavioural levels, to the results level. In practice, the effectiveness of MD is seldom adequately evaluated beyond the short-term and reaction level rather than the longer-term and results level. The paucity of evaluation is explained by difficulties of measuring performance and attributing causality. However, if the objectives of MD are sufficiently tied to organizational goals and anticipated results are specified unambiguously, it is possible for the evaluation of MD to be re-focused to emphasize its impact on corporate performance and competitiveness. The Management Standards have the potential to provide the necessary link between developing competence and improving business performance since they describe work role expectations.

3   Methodological approach

The previous chapter showed that MD is rarely evaluated adequately beyond the reaction and learning levels so that it is difficult to identify the impact of MD in terms of organizational and business results. This is surprising given the extensive and established literature supporting the crucial role of HRD in improving organizational performance and sustaining competitive advantage (Arthur 1994; Carter and Lumsden 1988; Coopers and Lybrand 1992; Cutcher-Gershenfeld 1991; Downham *et al.* 1992; Huselid 1995; King 1993; MacDuffie 1995). Despite such claims, there is a paucity of robust evidence capable of building a 'cumulative body of knowledge' (Becker and Gerhart 1996: 790).

In the absence of a common, coherent conceptual framework, there is little scope for comparison between the different studies until theory has been advanced by developing 'specific, testable propositions' and elaborating 'more complete structural models' (Becker and Gerhart 1996: 791, 793). Given the 'causal ambiguity' concerning the mechanisms by which HR practices translate into improved business performance (Barney 1991), more rigorous methods of analysis are also required. While some observers believe such analysis should ideally assess 'the *magnitude* of the effect of HR on organizational performance' (Becker and Gerhart 1996: 791), others have noted that increased productivity from investment in human resources 'depends upon the contribution of employees to a firm' and the extent to which its competitiveness is a function of employee competences (Youndt *et al.* 1996: 839).

There is, in short, a need to develop a conceptual foundation, and a more robust methodological approach towards empirical testing of the theories in order to assemble an adequate body of knowledge. This lack of an adequate methodological framework of analysis was recognized when the Employment Department established a study group to prepare for evaluating the impact of the Management Standards on performance (see Chapter 1).

The purpose of this chapter is to explore the methodological issues involved in measuring the impact of MD, and in particular CBMD, on performance. There were valuable lessons in the operationalization of the methodology proposed for the study undertaken on behalf of the Employment Department.

The chapter is organized into three sections:

1　case study evaluation methodology;
2　research design;
3　case study fieldwork.

The first section is concerned with the case study approach to assessing the business benefits of MD. The implications of the case study method are reviewed and the principal stages in case study design and analysis are explained. The initial case study protocol developed by the study group is then outlined. The second section elaborates the research design and relates this to the hypotheses constructed. After tracing the progress of achieving access to the organizations included in the study, the modifications made to the initial design are explained.

The third section, concerned with the fieldwork, describes how the initial case study protocol was operationalized, piloted and refined. The modified protocol, entailing a series of interview schedules, a list of written evidence to be collected and a template for case reports, is described. The evaluation of the case reports by independent experts is explained in relation to testing the five hypotheses. Finally, a brief summary of the chapter is provided by way of conclusion.

Case study evaluation methodology

The choice of an appropriate methodology to test hypotheses depends upon the research question(s) being formulated, the degree of control over behavioural events and the extent to which the focus is on contemporary issues. The proposed research was to be exploratory, in that it would investigate the concept of CBMD in actual work settings and attempt to move from an abstract theoretical concept to an operational model. The study would be illustrative in that it would give examples from those considered to be lead sites in different industrial sectors. Moreover, the study would be explanatory, analysing the processes by which MD translates into bottom-line results. The study group considered a variety of methodological approaches and recommended that case studies would be appropriate for investigating the five hypotheses constructed. The implications of a case study approach are outlined below, before the initial case study protocol is described.

Case study method

The case study offers a distinct advantage in examining 'a contemporary set of events, over which the investigator has little or no control' (Yin 1984: 20). While case studies may be exploratory, descriptive or explanatory, all conform to Yin's (1981) definition of the case study as an empirical inquiry that: investigates a contemporary phenomenon within its real-life context; when the boundaries between phenomenon and context are not clearly evident; and in which multiple sources of evidence are used.

Three problems are commonly raised in connection with a case study approach:

- bias and lack of rigour;
- difficulty of generalization;
- cumbersome to research, report and read.

None of these problems is entirely justified, nor are the problems sufficiently serious to warrant rejection of the case study approach where it is an appropriate methodology. All researchers must guard against bias and there are no grounds for assuming the problem to be any greater with the case study approach than with experimental, statistical or historical methodologies. Given appropriate research design, a series of case studies may be generalized to theoretical propositions, not to a universal population as is the goal with analytical generalization of theory or statistical generalization from a sample. While some case studies are cumbersome, lengthy narrative and time-consuming participant observation are not essential for effective case study research. In recommending a case study approach, the ED study group recognized that observation would play a very minor role in data collection and agreed that the case study reports should be kept concise and focused on the issues relating to the hypotheses outlined in Chapter 1.

Rigorous research design is as important to case study as to any methodology. In formulating the research design, five areas were addressed, following Yin (1984: 29–35):

- the research question to be explored: how does CBMD or the adoption of the Management Standards developed by MCI, improve performance?;
- propositions or hypotheses: such as the hypotheses that CBMD will improve both individual and organizational effectiveness;
- unit of analysis: the primary unit of analysis is the organization, but within this sub-units such as functional areas and individuals may be defined;
- logic linking data to propositions: evidence of improved performance following the adoption of the Management Standards;
- criteria for interpreting a study's findings: it was necessary to establish criteria to assess what would constitute a significant improvement in performance.

It was recognized that the research design for the case studies must embody the theoretical and conceptual underpinnings of what was being studied. As the elements of the design were developed, so the theory was more clearly articulated. Only when the theory has been developed is it possible to make analytical generalization, which should be distinguished from the statistical generalization of a survey method:

cases are not 'sampling units' and should not be chosen for this reason. Rather, individual case studies are to be selected as a laboratory investigator selects the topic of a new experiment. Multiple cases...should be considered like multiple experiments (or multiple surveys). Under these circumstances, the method of generalization is 'analytical generalization', in which a previously developed theory is used as a template with which to compare the empirical results of the case study. If two or more cases are shown to support the same theory, replication may be claimed. The empirical results may be considered yet more potent if two or more cases support the same theory but do not support an equally plausible, *rival* theory.

(Yin 1984: 38)

A range of case study research designs are possible and it is useful to distinguish between single-case and multiple-case designs. The single-case study may be adopted when it is the critical case for testing (or falsifying) a well-formulated theory; when it is an extreme or unique case, offering an opportunity to illustrate an unusual situation; or when it is revelatory, providing an opportunity to explore something which is normally invisible. Multiple case studies offer the advantages associated with replication when cases are selected to offer either literal or theoretical replication, the theoretical framework establishing the conditions under which a phenomenon should be, and should not be, found. A multiple case study approach was identified as most appropriate for this research and Figure 3.1 illustrates the replication approach to multiple case studies.

As Figure 3.1 shows, after the initial theory development stage, the cases for study are selected and the hypotheses operationalized by defining appropriate measures and identifying methods of data collection. Each case is a self-contained study, and the investigation seeks convergent evidence in order to reach conclusions for one case which will define the information which needs to be replicated in another case. Each case report should reach conclusions concerning the propositions to be tested, while the cross-case report should seek to explain convergence and divergence between cases in terms of the *a priori* predictions made as part of the replication logic at the design stage.

The number of cases to include in a multi-case design depends upon whether literal or theoretical replication is involved, the degree of confidence required in the results, and the resources available. For literal replication, the number of cases can range from two to six or more, the number increasing with the degree of certainty required and decreasing with the extent of difference between rival theories. For theoretical replication, the number of cases also depends upon the complexity of external factors anticipated to influence case study results. Thus if different industrial sectors, company sizes and market structures are expected to create different contexts which would influence the effects of CBMD within organizations, the number of cases would need to be sufficient to capture some of the anticipated variation. If the external environment is not expected to create much variation in the phenomenon being studied, a smaller number of theoretical replications will suffice.

It is also useful to distinguish between holistic and embedded case studies, whether single-case or multiple-case design. In the holistic study, the concern is with the global nature of the phenomenon, as is appropriate where the theory is of a holistic nature and no logical sub-units can be identified. Where a case

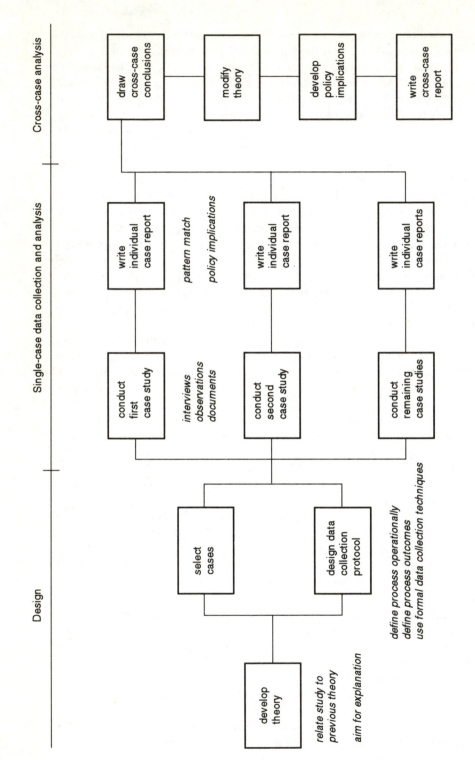

Figure 3.1 Case study evaluation methodology
Source: Yin (1984)

study involves more than one unit of analysis, the study is an embedded one. An embedded design offers the advantage of focusing a case study inquiry and uncovering clear measures and data. Where an embedded design is used in a multiple-case study, it may entail a survey conducted at each case study site. In such circumstances, results are not pooled across centres (as would be the case in a survey design) but the survey data for each case will be part of findings for that case and can only be used within that context. An embedded design was agreed as the most appropriate for this research since each case would involve a consideration of different functional areas and different levels of analysis.

Case study protocol

Having established the case study design, the case study protocol was developed, comprising all the research instruments to be used, along with the procedures and rules to be followed in administering the instruments. It was essential to have a thoroughly developed case study protocol, first, because a multi-case design was being employed, and second, because a team of researchers were involved in order to ensure the reliability of the research. In accordance with the approach developed by Yin (1984: 70), the protocol contained the following:

- overview of the case study project (project objectives and auspices, case study issues, and relevant readings about the topic being investigated);
- field procedures (credentials and access to the case study 'sites', general sources of information and procedural reminders);
- case study questions (the specific questions that the case study investigator must keep in mind in collecting data, 'table shells' for specific arrays of data, and the potential sources of information for answering each question); and
- guide for the case study report (outline, format for the narrative, and specification of any bibliographical information and other documentation).

In developing the protocol, the theoretical framework was reviewed and the nature of the evidence to be sought was identified in preparation for data collection. The objective was to create a 'recipe' to be followed exactly in each case, irrespective of the researchers involved. At this stage it was thought essential to clarify the hypotheses being investigated and to establish:

- why the study was being undertaken;
- what specific hypotheses were to be tested;
- what would constitute supportive or contradictory evidence;
- what sources of evidence could be used.

Data collection could not begin until the theoretical framework had been elaborated and the research protocol developed, including designing the research instruments and refining the measures to be employed. It was anticipated that data collection would involve a combination of three sources. First, documentary sources, including letters, agendas, reports of meetings and administrative documents were to be consulted, including portfolios held by individuals. While care is always needed in the interpretation of documentary evidence, it was recognized to be free from influence by interaction with the researcher in the way that is possible with other sources. Second, interviews were expected to be the primary data gathering technique for the case studies, and it was agreed that questions should not be completely open-ended, but a mixture of focused (where the interviewer has an agenda but allows respondents to elaborate in their own way) and more structured questions (where a consistent set of questions are asked of a number of respondents in an identical fashion). Semi-structured interviews have the advantage of allowing the protocol to be followed more closely in each case and facilitate more systematic cross-case analysis. Structured interviews also enable links to be established between case studies and survey material, the survey providing a large volume of low-level data establishing the generality of a phenomenon, and the case studies identifying circumstances affecting the phenomenon and the processes by which the effects occur. In this research, however, a survey was deemed inappropriate. The third source was from observation, taken to include all information gathered on-site about a particular case other than from interviews and documentary evidence. Formal observation was expected to include making notes of meetings, identifying and measuring the incidence of particular forms of behaviour in a work setting, or monitoring other activities. Informal observation was also expected to provide valuable insights into the context of a particular case or respondent. The reliability of observation is significantly increased by the use of more than one observer but logistics dictated that each case would involve only one researcher, so less importance was attached to this source of information.

It was agreed that the following three principles of data collection would be applied with all sources of evidence. First, multiple sources of evidence would be employed in each case study to increase the reliability of data collection through offering scope for triangulation, or the corroboration of an event by independent sources. Construct validity is more easily assured when there are multiple measures of the same phenomenon. Second, a case study database would be created so that the evidence on which conclusions are reached could be examined independently of the report containing those conclusions. For each case, the database would contain case study notes, documentary evidence, accounts of observations and a narrative, where the investigator would present answers to the questions developed in the protocol as a first attempt to integrate the available evidence and offer an interpretation for that particular case.

Third, a chain of evidence would be maintained to demonstrate how the evidence links the initial questions to the ultimate conclusions. Specific documents and interviews would need to be cited, and the database would indicate that the information was collected in accordance with the protocol, which should demonstrate the link to the initial questions.

After the collection of data for each case study an individual report was to be written, considering the evidence in accordance with the analytical strategy outlined in the protocol. It was suspected that some evidence might be amenable to statistical testing, but for the most part we recognized that case study evidence requires the deployment of other analytical techniques. In studying the effects of CBMD, it would be necessary for cases to demonstrate an improvement in individual performance, for example, after and as a result of, introducing CBMD within an organization.

A pattern-matching logic is often employed in case study analysis (Eisenhardt 1989). For example, the three initial hypotheses relate to three sets of outcomes representing different dependent variables, each of which can be assessed with different measures and instruments. The study is therefore based on non-equivalent dependent variables, about which an overall pattern of outcomes has been hypothesized. If the results in a case are as predicted, then robust conclusions can be drawn about the impact of CBMD. The cross-case conclusions would be written once all the individual case study reports were complete, and used to modify the theory and develop policy implications before completing the cross-case report.

The ED study group developed an initial case study data collection protocol, beginning with criteria for evaluating the satisfaction of the two conditional hypotheses, since these were important in selecting appropriate cases in accordance with the research design. For each enterprise it was necessary to identify where and how MD fitted with the organizational strategy by tracing the links through the organization and unpacking the 'article of faith' approach to MD. It was necessary to establish the extent to which HRD systems and processes were based on the occupational standards and how far appraisal, for example, was used as a tool to support MD.

In terms of individual performance, measurement mechanisms mentioned in the protocol included appraisal reports, peer and self-assessment and NVQ portfolios. Despite different institutional norms and practices, and potential problems of access, it was thought that the individual level was most easily assessed against the occupational standards because it is closest to the initiative and improvements were probably also most easily attributable to MD.

At the organizational level, it was concluded that measures of efficiency would need to be developed within each case using the perceptions of key actors as well as functional measures. Many such measures would inevitably be organization-specific, and unsuitable for quantitative cross-case comparison, but analogous measures could form a basis for cross-case analysis. Interview schedules would need to be constructed to establish whether MD had facilitated the attainment of group objectives, and to what extent the adoption of the Standards affected team development and the operation of organizational systems and processes.

The study group recognized that while it is easiest to standardize business performance indicators, these are most remote from the original MD initiatives and more susceptible to influence by a wide range of factors. The difficulty of identifying matched pairs of organizations eliminated a statistical or econometric approach, but it was thought possible to identify improvements over a time period consistent with MD activities becoming embedded in the organization and to seek senior management views on causality. The risk of subjectivity in this approach is less serious than the false precision of using quantitative measures which are subject to extraneous influences since senior managers ought to be able to offer well-informed opinion. Guest and Peccei (1994: 224), for example, argue that the effectiveness of HRM is best analysed by asking key individuals for their assessments rather than focusing on quantitative measures.

The initial protocol drafted by the study group showed how the different sources of evidence are inter-related as well as their role in testing the hypotheses (Leman *et al.* 1994: 58–60). This formed the basis of the list of written evidence summarized in the DfEE Report (Winterton and Winterton 1996: 73).

Research design

The study group offered a tentative case study design, based on an embedded, multiple-case study approach. The three initial hypotheses (for short-hand referred to as IP, OP and BP) defined sub-units of analysis which would be possible within each case. Five cases were recommended for the purposes of literal replication, and to provide adequate theoretical replication, it was recommended that five further cases should be identified for each conditional hypothesis, and five for the two in combination. Thus the case study design would comprise twenty organizations applying CBMD where five are in each of the four cells represented in Figure 3.2.

Accessing suitable cases for study

Identifying suitable cases was seen to be a critical aspect of the research, and the criteria for attributing cases to particular cells made it necessary to elicit information from potential case organizations before any fieldwork took place. To do this, contact names in organizations were first approached with a letter of introduction from the ED (DfEE) project manager, followed by a letter from the researchers, who then followed this up with a brief telephone interview. From the telephone contact, the objective was first to establish whether the organization would, in principle, collaborate, and then obtain the information from which to allocate each organization, tentatively, to an appropriate cell.

Contenders for study were identified from discussions with MCI, the ED (DfEE) steering group, and from previous research. The primary factors for selection of cases were to be the criteria outlined in Leman *et al.* (1994: 53), in order to provide adequate replication to test the two conditional hypotheses (concerning the relationship between CBMD, organizational strategy and HRD). The organizations were to be drawn from a range of different economic sectors and to include public and not-for profit organizations, as well as commercial and industrial enterprises. In addition, the Steering Group asked that one-third of the organizations studies should be SMEs (fewer than 200 employees), even if this necessitated some compromise of other sample requirements.

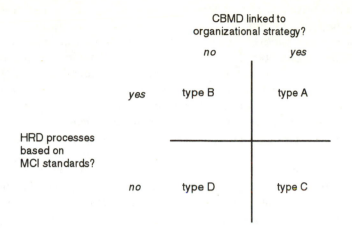

Figure 3.2 Organizational types for case study

A list of twenty-five organizations known to have adopted the Management Standards was supplied by MCI. An initial contact letter was sent from the ED (DfEE), which was followed up by a letter from the researchers and then with successive telephone calls. A second tranche of eighteen organizations, known to practise CBMD but not thought to be users of the occupational standards, was identified by the researchers and contacted in the same way. Difficulties in achieving access, particularly to SMEs, made it necessary to explore further routes, and an approach was made to twenty TECs for assistance in identifying suitable organizations for study.

In each organization approached, the project objectives, the data collection protocol, and the benefits of involvement were explained to the contact person. Cases were selected from those organizations agreeing to participate with the aim of satisfying the process criteria and obtaining an equal number of cases of each type (A–D).

Negotiating access to cases took considerably longer than had been antici-pated. In one case, for example, over forty telephone calls, in addition to letters and faxes, were made before a decision was reached, and in most cases, gaining access entailed protracted negotiations involving senior management. In over half of the cases contacted, there were additional complications involving the absence of the contact person in the organization (reasons included holidays, sickness, maternity, marriage and redundancy). On average, the elapsed time from first contact to a firm decision was about six weeks, and the process took twelve weeks in the most difficult case.

From the first tranche of twenty-five organizations supplied by MCI, eleven initially agreed to collaborate and the remainder declined. Out of the second tranche of eighteen organizations known to the researchers, nine initially agreed to be involved and the remainder declined. However, two of the first tranche and three of the second tranche later withdrew from the study owing to time pressures or failure to gain the support of senior management. The approach to twenty TECs achieved a positive response from seven of them, who supplied a total of eighty-three organizations, mostly via an associated Business Link. All eighty-three organizations were approached by letter and followed up by telephone, but only two agreed to participate in the study. With seventeen organizations involved, the project manager agreed that further resources should not be committed to seeking collaboration from other organizations.

All cases entailed extensive discussions because the case protocol required access to senior executives and an opportunity to examine written materials, so inevitably senior staff were involved in the decision to cooperate. There was a high rate of attrition of the organizations approached, which was directly proportional to the 'distance' of the target organization from the researchers and consultants involved. The highest success rate was with organizations where contacts had been personally recommended by MCI (36 per cent) or were known to the researchers from earlier work (33 per cent). The overall response rate from organizations approached from the TECs was exceedingly low (2 per cent).

Difficulties encountered

The attempt to access organizations through the TECs met with limited success for a variety of reasons. The TECs were contacted directly without an introductory approach from DfEE, and the project offered no immediate returns for cooperation, hence very few TECs agreed to assist the research. Even where TECs collaborated, the information supplied by them, or an associated Business Link, often proved unreliable; they had been asked to provide contacts in SMEs undertaking a significant amount of CBMD. Some of the organizations identified were very large, including one major multinational, so these were not approached.

Of the eighty-three organizations which were approached, a significant proportion (about 30 per cent) were no longer in business, or the details provided were inaccurate, so mail was returned. A similar proportion reported that they had not initiated any MD in the organization. Eliminating these organizations from the eighty-three approached left thirty-four eligible cases, so the response rate for this third tranche may be viewed more accurately as 6 per cent. Three factors possibly contributed to the greater attrition rate of this third group: the absence of a formal approach to the organizations from DfEE; the absence of personal contacts known to the MCI or the researchers; and the predominance of SMEs, where managers might be expected to have less scope to accommodate the demands of the project.

In all three tranches, organizations declined to cooperate for similar reasons, which are summarized below in order of importance:

- the organization was undergoing a period of rapid or major change, restructuring or 'downsizing';
- HR specialists saw the evaluation as potentially sensitive, fearing that the research might fail to identify sufficient business benefits to warrant further resources for MD;
- the organization had only recently adopted the MCI Standards and these were insufficiently embedded to warrant study;
- there was a reluctance to commit the time of key individuals;
- the organization was already 'over-studied' because of the success of its training and development arrangements, and could not accommodate more researchers.

The first of the seventeen organizations which agreed to collaborate was subsequently eliminated from the study because the case study protocol could not be adequately applied. It proved impossible to conduct face-to-face interviews, and the schedules were completed instead as questionnaires by a small number of managers in the organization. The difficulty was a result of the size of the organization (forty employees) and some of the 'managers' involved had no line responsibility for other employees. The exercise was useful in helping further to refine the piloted interview schedules, but the outcome was not comparable with the other cases.

When the remaining sixteen cases were tentatively allocated to the four categories on the basis of preliminary discussions with the contact in each organization, the cases appeared to be weighted in favour of Standards users, and especially in favour of those claiming that MD was closely linked with organizational strategy. The tentative classification of achieved cases by type is shown in Figure 3.3.

There were early indications that the double dichotomy which was used as a basis for categorizing cases as A, B, C, D was an over-simplification and would prove less useful than intended. Each dimension is better seen as a spectrum, with cases located somewhere along each continuum. The differences between A and B or C and D were difficult to establish, since most respondents believed that their CBMD was linked to organizational strategy; several respondents suggested that otherwise there would be no point in having any development. Clearly, CBMD may be integrated with organizational strategy in some respects and not in others, and the difficulty in establishing to what extent it is integrated with organizational strategy is reflected in the different perspectives of individuals in the same organization.

It was feared that these problems with the A/C versus B/D divide would impose limitations on the extent to which the first conditional hypothesis (concerning the impact of linking CBMD with organizational strategy) could be tested. The differences between A/B and C/D appeared less problematic, and cases were provisionally labelled as users and non-users (of the occupational standards developed by MCI). However, the case studies demonstrated that some organizations which were ostensibly users of the Standards had not, in fact, adopted them comprehensively (see Expert evaluation on p. 47).

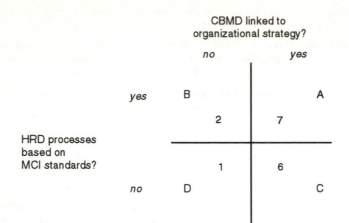

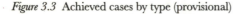

Figure 3.3 Achieved cases by type (provisional)

The case study fieldwork

While access to organizations was being arranged, the protocol from the study group report (Leman *et al.* 1994) was operationalized, piloted and refined. The fieldwork was then undertaken in the organizations that had agreed to collaborate and case reports were written in accordance with an agreed schedule. The case reports were validated with the organizations and, after re-drafting, evaluated by independent experts.

Operationalizing and piloting the protocol

The protocol from the study group was initially operationalized into three interview schedules, for senior strategic managers, line managers, and members of functional teams, and a list of corroborative written evidence. The protocol was submitted to the Steering Group for approval and amended following discussion with members of the project team and piloting with individual managers not involved in any of the cases studied. As a result of the discussions and piloting, the questions were improved and the schedules more tightly focused, and separate interview schedules were produced for the following respondents:

- chief executive or managing director
- senior financial manager
- senior human resources manager
- line managers
- team members.

The final versions of the five interview schedules were included as Appendices to the DfEE report (Winterton and Winterton 1996: 75–101).

Even when collaboration was agreed and cleared with senior management, there were invariably problems in arranging interviews. The case study protocol required interviews with specified senior strategic managers; these individuals often had few spaces available in their schedules, and there was little latitude for substitution. Moreover, it also proved very difficult to obtain written evidence (since this involves a substantial amount of work for the contact in the collaborating organization), and to coordinate interview times with several individuals, so each case required more site visits than anticipated (up to twelve separate visits).

In each case, face-to-face interviews were conducted with the three senior strategic managers, and on average four line managers and four team members, using the interview schedules. Multiple sources of evidence were collected in every case to increase the reliability of data through triangulation. The interview schedules were designed to allow for corroboration. Thus the different schedules all had interlocking questions so that the views of senior strategic managers, for example, were contrasted with those of line managers. Individuals were encouraged to elaborate at length in interviews and to provide additional information in support of their claims.

An extensive range of written evidence was collected or examined on site to cross-check the oral evidence from the interviews, to demonstrate claimed improvements in performance, and to illustrate the nature of HRD systems and processes. Thus, managers' job specifications gave an indication of the extent to which responsibility for MD was a feature of all managers' roles. Similarly, as evidence of improvements in BP, company accounts were examined, and to demonstrate improvements in OP, minutes of team meetings, for example, were consulted. Table 3.1 provides a summary of the written evidence collected or consulted.

Wherever possible, corroboration was attempted through documentary sources and from individuals at different levels in the organization. The average interview lasted about 90 minutes, and some individuals freely gave further time by gathering substantial amounts of information with the research team. For each organization studied, a dossier was compiled of written evidence and a case report was written in accordance with the protocol. The case reports provided background details of the organization, written to preserve anonymity, details of the organizational strategy, the HRD systems and processes, including roles and responsibilities for management development, and the evidence from the interviews and written materials of the improvements in IP, OP and BP which were attributed to MD by respondents. The case reports were validated with the organization and revised before being evaluated by independent experts and used in the cross-case analysis.

Expert evaluation

In order to test the conditional hypotheses adequately, each dimension was treated as a continuum, and independent experts were asked to evaluate the

Table 3.1 Sources of evidence in relation to hypotheses

Hypothesis	Evidence sought	Written material	Expected source
OS	CBMD key strand in organizational strategy	Mission or vision statement	Chief Exec/HHR
OS	CBMD linked to departmental strategy	Departmental strategy statements	Section
OS	CBMD feature of all managers' roles	Managers' job specifications	HHR/Section
HRD	HRD based on management standards	HRD systems and processes	HHR
HRD	Appraisal/assessment developmental	Appraisal reports	HHR/Section
HRD	Responsibility for development	Documents relating to HRD	HHR/Section
IP	Improvements in IP	Individual managers' portfolios	Section
IP	Ongoing improvements in performance	Current documentary evidence	Section
OP	Improvements in team performance	Records of team meetings and achievements	Section/Team
OP	Improvements in use of teams	Minutes or other guidance on team roles	HHR/Section
OP	Quality improvements	+ standards of output: accidents/failures/complaints	Section/Team
BP	Improvements in production rates	Trends of production statistics	Section/Team
BP	Market share increased	Trends of sales/market statistics	Chief Exec/Section
BP	Improved company accounts	Turnover, profit, share price, etc.	Chief Exec/Finance

degree to which MD was linked with organizational strategy, and the extent to which each organization had adopted the Management Standards in HRD systems and processes. This evaluation was coordinated by an expert on the Management Standards who had participated in the original study group but had not been involved in the case studies. While familiar with the protocol, the experts would not be biased by knowledge of particular cases (which were kept anonymous).

The independent experts evaluated the validated case reports and written evidence against the criteria elaborated in the protocol developed by the study group. The cases were re-classified on the basis of this evaluation, producing the achieved cases shown in Figure 3.4. In this final classification, only four cases were defined as type A, while five were viewed as type D, and the remainder type C. Type B, in which HRD systems were based on the Management Standards but MD was not linked to organizational strategy, proved to be an empty cell, which confirms empirically, for the cases studied, what might be assumed *a priori*: an organization is unlikely to adopt the Management Standards and fail to link MD to organizational strategy.

The sector, size and final classifications of the sixteen cases which were involved in the study are shown in Table 3.2. More detailed information is provided in the case studies section of the book, subject to preserving the anonymity of the organizations. In terms of sectors involved, the cases were drawn from: primary (2); manufacturing (5); private services (3); public services (3); and the health service (3). In terms of the size distribution (by number of employees), the cases were drawn from: < 201 (4); 201–499 (3); 500–1,999 (3); 2,000–3,999 (3); and > 3,999 (3).

When the cases had been evaluated, they were ranked on continua in terms of the two defining characteristics relevant to the conditional hypotheses: the degree to which MD was linked to organizational strategy and the extent to

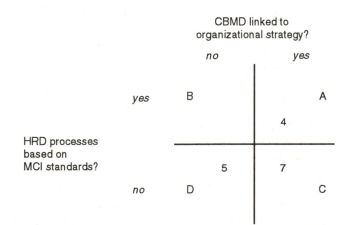

Figure 3.4 Achieved cases by type (reclassified)

Table 3.2 Characteristics of collaborating cases

case	sector	size	category
01	mining	200	D
02	galvanizing	103	A
03	retail	410	A
04	oil	4,000	C
05	engineering	3,500	C
06	civil service	68,000	C
07	insurance	260	A
08	charity	2,300	D
09	law courts	560	A
10	newspapers	3,200	C
11	NHS Trust	1,400	C
12	aeroplane components	274	C
13	NHS Trust	7,000	D
14	clothing	170	D
15	footwear	167	C
16	NHS Trust	1,400	D

which the Management Standards had been adopted in HRD systems and processes. In addition, the cases were ranked according to the extent of improvements in IP, OP and BP attributable to MD, taking into account the robustness of the evidence, against the criteria outlined in the report of the study group. The rankings were again undertaken by independent experts.

The rank order of the cases according to the three performance measures and the two defining characteristics was used to structure the cross-case analysis which is contained in Chapters 4–8. The rankings made it possible to test for any correlation between the defining characteristics and performance improvements measured at the three levels, as well as correlation and concordance between the three performance measures. In addition to the case study evidence, therefore, the hypotheses were examined using robust non-parametric techniques. The results of the statistical tests are reported in Chapter 9.

Summary and conclusions

This chapter has outlined the methodological issues involved in measuring the impact of MD on performance. Following the recommendations of the study group established by the Employment Department in 1994, the five hypotheses outlined in Chapter 1 were to be tested using an embedded, multiple-case study approach. The case study protocol proposed by the study group was operational-ized in the form of interview schedules and details of written evidence to be collected. Once the research instruments were piloted and refined, they were used to examine the benefits of CBMD in selected organizations. The research design which envisaged case studies of twenty organizations was modified when it was recognized that one of the four categories of cases would be unlikely to exist. Serious difficulties were encountered in obtaining access to suitable organizations for study: out of 128 organizations approached, access was gained to seventeen after protracted negotiations, and one of these proved unsuitable. Fieldwork was successfully conducted in sixteen of the collaborating organizations, involving interviews with managers at various levels and the collection of written evidence. Resource limitations precluded studying more cases in the time available. Case reports were written in accordance with the protocol, validated with the organizations, revised and kept anonymous. These validated case reports were then evaluated by independent experts familiar with the Management Standards to re-classify the organizations, and the organizations were ranked in relation to the criteria being investigated. The ranking of each criterion was used to structure the cross-case analysis and to subject the hypotheses to statistical tests.

The following chapters present the results of the study in relation to the conditional hypotheses concerning the link between MD and organizational strategy and the use of the Management Standards in HRD systems and processes, and in relation to the three levels of performance improvements, IP, OP and BP. The evidence in each chapter is contextualized by an introduction which discusses the role of MD and appropriate learning processes at the different levels of analysis.

4 Organizational strategy and management development

This chapter examines MD from an organizational perspective and explores the link between MD and organizational strategy (OS). The need to reconcile the different needs of the organization and the individual manager was outlined in Chapter 2 and this chapter takes the argument forward by exploring how the strategies formulated by senior management influence the competences needed within the organization. The concerns include how the 'needs' of an organization are expressed in terms of MD, the relationship between MD and OS and empirical evidence of that relationship in the organizations studied.

The chapter is therefore organized into three sections:

1 organizational strategy;
2 development to support strategy;
3 linking development to strategy in practice.

In the first section, different approaches to strategy are outlined and linked to the need for organizations to develop core competences as a route to competitive advantage. Corporate planning is discussed as the key leadership role of senior strategic managers. How the business plan is translated into OS and operationalized by management is shown to depend crucially upon developing managerial competence.

In the second section, the perspective is altered by considering how development can be designed to support strategy. Integrating development with strategy is shown to be important in ensuring the effectiveness of MD, yet much MD is undertaken in isolation from OS. Ways of linking MD more effectively with OS are explored and the *Investors in People* initiative is examined as a framework for linking human resource development (HRD) to OS.

The third section presents the empirical findings from the case studies of sixteen organizations. The evidence is presented first from those organizations where a robust link was identified between MD and OS, then from the organizations found to have a more moderate link between MD and OS. The roles and responsibilities for MD are shown to be a major determinant of linking MD most effectively with OS; in the best cases responsibility for MD was devolved to individuals and their line managers, typically through partnership arrangements involving personal development plans. Finally, the problems of linking MD with OS are considered. The chapter concludes with a brief summary identifying the salient points of the discussion.

Organizational strategy

In order to link MD with OS, it is important to articulate the approach to strategy that is adopted since this has implications for the emphasis placed on development. Equally, it is necessary to progress corporate strategy beyond a mission statement, to operationalize the corporate plan developed by senior strategic managers and to translate strategy into action. Each of these issues is considered in turn in this section.

Approaches to strategy

Whittington (1993: 11–41) distinguishes four major theoretical approaches to strategy: classical; processual; evolutionary; and systemic. The classical approach emphasizes the pursuit of profit maximization through rational planning, coupled with a separation of conception from execution. The approach is typified by the orthodox corporate strategy tradition (Ansoff 1965) and the more recent theories of strategic competitive advantage (Porter 1985). Recognizing the limitations of attempting long-term rational planning, the processual approach emphasises the need for political compromise and *ad hoc* responses in formulating strategy. The processualists favour an incremental process of adapting to changes in the external environment (Mintzberg 1987), which leads to an 'emergent' strategy (Mintzberg and Waters 1985) rather than a rational plan. The evolutionary approach places less reliance on top managers and rational planning, attributing profit maximization to the operation of free market forces. In place of strategy, attention is focused on efficiency and survival through cost minimization: 'economy is the best strategy' (Williamson 1991: 87). For the systemic approach, different contexts influence the underpinning rationale of a strategy, so strategy can only be understood in a specific sociological context. Systemic strategy is therefore embedded in local culture and thus sensitive to diversity within increasingly globalized markets (Granovetter 1985).

Whittington (1993: 40) views the four approaches as divergent and associates each with one of the four last decades of the twentieth century: the classic approach with the 1960s, the processual with the 1970s, the evolutionary with the 1980s and the systemic with the 1990s. This periodization reflects the changing contexts as well as changing fashions in strategy; as markets have become globalized and the competitive environment more complex and uncertain, so strategists have been forced to adopt a more flexible and contingent approach.

While the approaches are analytically distinct, in practice those responsible for strategy, who are unlikely to articulate their activities in theoretical terms, may behave in ways which reflect elements of several of these approaches simultaneously. Thus, senior managers may combine a classic profit maximization strategy with its emphasis on internal plans, with an evolutionary survival strategy focused on external markets, and in doing so be forced to take a processual view of internal political constraints as well as a systemic view of the cultural dimension of global markets.

To a large extent, the value of drawing the analytical distinction is in making explicit the theories which delimit both the conceptualization of context and the possibilities for action. Making individual theoretical approaches to strategy explicit is also important for facilitating the transfer between individual learning and organizational learning (Senge 1990a; Kim 1993) since this depends upon the development of shared mental models (see Chapter 7). Corporate learning takes place through the progessive incorporation of tacit knowledge (Spender 1996) into shared mental models and the adoption by the organization of individual routines which improve existing practices to develop core capabilities (see Chapter 8).

Such resource-based perspectives of business success fit readily with a processual approach to strategy (Collis 1991). The key to competitive advantage lies in the capacity within the organization for developing and maintaining core competences (Grant 1991; Barney 1991). Strategies which recognize core competence as a key organizational resource that can be exploited to gain competitive advantage are prevalent in the recent literature (Prahalad and Hamel 1990; Mitrani *et al.* 1992; Tobin 1993; Barney 1995; Thurbin 1995; Hussey 1988; 1996; Campbell and Sommers Luchs 1997). However, the importance of core competence for competitive advantage was recognized even in the era of classical strategy as 'distinctive competence' (Andrews 1965) and 'firm capabilities' (Ansoff 1965). Clearly, therefore, the development of core competence, including managerial competence, is a crucial part of OS irrespective of the particular approach to strategy adopted.

Corporate planning and leadership

Corporate planning emerged as a result of the problems created by using financial criteria alone as the rationale for future planning. The starting point of corporate strategy usually constitutes some description of the vision for the future of the organization, frequently articulated as a general mission statement. These are then elaborated in a business plan, defining key organizational goals and providing a broad indication of how these will be pursued. Corporate planning represents the foundation of any organization, defining what products and services will be offered in which markets to ensure the achievement of the business plan, whether this relates to maximizing shareholder return, long-term survival, a combination of business objectives, or the optimization of a public service.

Most managers are involved in the planning process to a degree, but the key part of corporate planning involves senior strategic managers formulating long-term strategic plans at board level. Senior strategic managers need strategic awareness beyond the broad mission, including an analysis of the market, competitors and customers and an understanding of how organizational capacity can meet customer needs. Bal (1995: 23) identifies three areas of strategic awareness which senior managers need when developing the corporate plan. First, they must be able to define 'what the business stands for', which entails identifying a range of organizational values indicating to shareholders, customers and managers the purpose of the business. Second, they need to understand how to create competitive advantage from delivering maximum value to shareholders and customers through providing a commodity or service in a unique manner. Third, they need to be aware of the organization's core skills as a basis for business development, continuous improvement and innovation.

In developing strategies to support the business plan, senior management need to provide leadership, which should not be seen as some mystic personality trait of a charismatic individual (although such individuals featured in two of the cases on which this study is based). Wickens (1995: 92) argues that leadership is not simply embodied in the leaders of an organization because the ability to transform an organization and lead it to success is achieved by working through others who are themselves leaders in their own areas of work. For Wickens (ibid.: 95–102) successful leaders possess 'personal attributes, strategic perspective and communication and achievement'. In relation to the 'strategic perspective' leadership involves 'aligning' the organization, ensuring that all its members accept that they are working towards a clearly defined set of goals firmly entrenched in a shared vision and strategy. This vision and strategy need to be a long-term plan not just a short-term response to problems in the organizational environment as they arise. In the 'ascendent' organization the leadership role involves challenging the status quo and being determined to succeed while taking into consideration all the other stakeholders in the business.

Bal (1995: 176) emphasizes the importance of leaders having clearly defined goals, knowing in which direction they wish the organization to develop and having the ability to implement a strategic plan to achieve this organizational vision. Organizations which are experiencing radical change need 'decisive' leaders who stimulate the energy and commitment necessary to implement change and respond to the needs of customers and the market environment in which they operate. The crucial theme can be summarized as a need for leaders who inspire, energize and polarize individuals and teams in line with an organizational vision, as a result of which shared mental models are created.

Strategy and managerial competence

Organizational strategy is concerned with operationalizing the corporate plan developed by senior strategic managers and with translating strategy into action. From the mission statement and business plan, a set of specific strategies is developed outlining what, where, when and how various actions will be performed. Far more effort is expended by senior managers implementing strategies than selecting them, as business success is a function of the former rather than the latter (Whittington 1993: 112).

In order to operationalize a particular organizational strategy it is necessary to win the support of various groups and individuals to support the achievement of specified goals. Managers throughout the organization need to understand the strategic business objectives and be able to integrate these into divisional or departmental targets. Strategic change requires organizations to create conditions conducive for managers at all levels to develop, adopting learning organization principles to overcome scepticism, inertia and sectional interests (see Chapter 8). Benchmarking techniques must be applied in order to match organizational performance and practice to that of other organizations in the pursuit of excellence. The strategy must be contextualized by carrying out PEST and SWOT analyses in order to capitalize on organizational strengths and tackle organizational weaknesses in relation to the external environment.

Senior management are focused on long-running core strategies and maintaining core competence, so continuity strategies are more evident in practice than the change strategies so popular in the business school literature (Mintzberg and Waters 1985). Nevertheless, the rapidity of technological developments and the dynamism of markets render traditional specific sources of competitive advantage liable to obsolescence and being superseded by innovation. As a result, sustainable competitive advantage derives more from the ability of individuals and organizations to adapt and learn faster than the competition (De Geus 1988: 74; Whittington 1993: 123). In order to promote this learning, development must therefore be designed to support the strategy.

Different approaches to strategy, however, lead to different emphases in the prescriptions for developing managerial competence. The classic approach involves exhortations for greater investment in MD through voluntary means, which Whittington (1993: 137) associates with the Handy Report and the background to MCI. From a processual perspective, instead of developing generic management skills, what is needed is detailed 'craft knowledge' of specific sectors. The evolutionists believe that market forces will eliminate inefficiencies through restructuring and that this pressure will act as an impulse on organizations to develop the competences needed for survival. From a systemic viewpoint, the specific cultural context of the UK demands state involvement to overcome short-termism and the barriers to investment in MD.

What is of merit in three of these approaches is not necessarily mutually exclusive; indeed, elements of the prescriptions are complementary. The voluntarist arrangements associated with the classic approach have limitations, but it was the employer-led arrangements that created the occupational standards on which the competence-based approach to VET was based (see Chapter 1). There can be little doubt that the competence movement has increased the relevance of training and development and brought vocational qualifications closer to employers' needs. The processual emphasis on knowledge of the specific sector is equally important but it is unclear why this needs to be an alternative to generic managerial competences; in our view, the two are complementary.

Consider the comparable argument that graduate engineers in the UK (and to an even greater extent in France) have little experience of practical production techniques compared with their German counterparts. The solution may be to incorporate *additional* craft skills into the chartered engineer learning route, but should this be at the expense of the theoretical underpinning of an engineering degree? The evolutionist approach adds little value since the market can be a disastrous mechanism of resource allocation in terms of long-term strategic interests, as demonstrated by the restructuring of the UK coal industry (Winterton and Winterton 1992).

Development to support strategy

Hussey concluded that most training and MD is wrongly focused:

> What is needed in most companies is a mental shift from the common idea that training should be for the improvement of the individual because this will benefit the firm, to the concept that training should be for the benefit of the firm and this will benefit the individual.
>
> (Hussey 1988: 69)

If management training is to contribute to the attainment of corporate objectives, and is to be used as a competitive weapon, Hussey (ibid.: 84–5) argues that the initiative must come from the chief executive and training needs must be assessed against corporate requirements. Moreover, formal training should relate to the corporate need first, with individual needs being 'incidental': 'this implies that the annual training assessment of individuals, or the results of the residential assessment centre, have to be related to an understanding of the company aims, strategy, the business environment, and the desired company culture' (ibid.: 190).

Clearly it is important to link MD with OS, but such a relationship often does not exist in organizations. This section therefore addresses the difficulties in integrating MD with OS and considers the role of the *Investors in People* Standard as a mechanism for creating that link.

Integrating development with strategy

Many authorities share Hussey's view that MD must be linked with OS. Burgoyne (1988b) put forward a model for integrating the development of the individual and the organization. Kilcourse (1988) showed how this strategy of developing the individual and the organization in parallel was successfully adopted in Leicestershire Co-operative Society. Wild (1993) describes a Corporate Strategy model, designed 'to integrate the MD activities of an organization with its strategy in order to provide a framework for the specification of priorities for MD for that organization', while enhancing the organization's 'capability and competitiveness'. Noting that firms have tended to conduct MD without any clear purpose, Michael (1993) argues that 'executive training must be linked to organizational strategy, so that executives can manage the substantial change that is required of them'. Robinson (1994: 368) similarly argues that organizational development (OD) and MD should be closely integrated, since OD is concerned with strategic level initiatives to improve OP, and uses the label 'learning organization' to capture this harmonization of MD with OD strategies (ibid.: 373).

The importance of linking MD with OS has been emphasized where it is used to support strategic change (Marsh 1986; Pate and Nielson 1987) and restructuring (Oram and Wellins 1995). Similarly, where strategic MD is seen as the key to competitive advantage (Schroder 1989; McClelland 1994).

Despite the substantial expenditure on MD each year in the UK, 'few companies have yet integrated it into their strategic planning process and it is poorly implemented' (P. Miller 1991). There is some evidence that the situation has improved. A survey by the Harbridge Consulting Group (1993) found that in the decade 1982–92, the proportion of UK business organizations in which MD was explicitly linked to corporate strategy increased from 33 per cent to 54 per cent. Nevertheless, the Taylor Report (1994: 47) noted the continued conflict between individualism and corporate goals. The inherent tension is between the need for organizations to encourage empowerment and individual responsiveness while simultaneously promoting corporate cohesion and team work. Managers will be required 'to take responsibility for their own part in corporate success'.

Moreover, while HRD involves both strategic and functional activities, the latter are often prevalent as a result of the marginalization of HRM and its dislocation from OS (Stewart and McGoldrick 1996: 10). Pont (1995: 27) similarly argues that the HR function has traditionally had relatively little impact in terms of OS because it is largely preoccupied with operational matters. Marchington and Wilkinson (1996: 374–5) note the difficulties in making clear links between HRM and business strategies and doubt the potential for HRM to have a structured role in strategic decision-making. If the personnel and development function is represented at board level there is more likelihood that HRD will form an intrinsic part of OS, yet only 30 per cent of companies employing over 1,000 workers have any HRM function represented at board level (Marchington and Wilkinson 1996: 375). There is a danger of HRD specialists having to take on the role of facilitating strategic decisions taken by senior management without consulting them.

Tyson (1995: 97–102) cites MD as one of three distinctive areas where personnel and development professionals can make a key contribution to OS (the other two are employee relations and organizational development). Temporal (1990) similarly identifies the role for HR professionals in ensuring that MD is linked to future business needs. Armstrong (1989: 195–7) argues that the greatest scope for HRM to have an impact on OS is through strategies which develop the culture and values of the business. However, MD can only form an effective part of OS if the strategy is adequately communicated to all managers and resources are available to fund the necessary training and development (Pont 1995: 13).

Hussey (1988: 88–9) suggests that training can be used as a tool for implementing corporate strategy in several ways:

* a very clear understanding can be gained, of both the broad strategy and what it means to the individual in his or her job;
* commitment can be built, as people discover the reason for the strategy and decide for themselves that there is sense behind it;
* the implication of implementation can be explored and converted into personal action plans;
* suitable training can be given so that the appropriate individuals are able to implement the strategy.

Hussey (1988: 91) provides examples of how MD workshops to develop individual managers differ from traditional training and offer greater potential for relating MD to business needs because of the following:

* They are concerned with 'live' company problems, identified by a survey and agreed with the chief executive, instead of lectures and simulated case studies.
* They seek to influence the perception and attitudes of managers and are action-orientated. Implementation of agreed solutions is reviewed during the workshops.
* The emphasis is on improving effectiveness of management teams, rather than individual managers. There is greater understanding of the jobs of other managers, and improvement in communications horizontally and vertically.
* They enable managers to determine priorities for achievement of their job objectives, and they help integrate the efforts of the management team to achieve the business plan targets.

The benefit of such an approach, it is claimed, is seen in the improved effectiveness of the management team in achieving the company's business objectives. Such an argument underlies the national standard for development, which is becoming the main initiative for linking HRD with OS.

Investors in People

The concept of investing in people is less widely accepted than the principle of investment in plant and machinery, although economists have occasionally addressed human capital as a resource like other 'factors of production' (Tsui *et al.* 1997). As Tobin (1993: 139–46) states, there are several difficulties in evaluating investments in people. The return on investment cannot be predicted because the duration of the benefit stream depends upon retention of human capital. Isolating the benefits of investment in training and development is notoriously difficult, as was demonstrated in Chapters 2 and 3. Also, it is unethical to attempt to quantify the value of human resources just as it is impossible to place a value on knowledge assets, which can be far more important to business success than physical resources. Notwithstanding these difficulties, the concept of investing in people, developing human resources, is generally viewed as a positive and progressive development (Critten 1993).

It is therefore particularly significant that the name *Investors in People* (*IiP*) was chosen for an initiative launched by the Employment Department in 1991 on the recommendation of the National Training Task Force, involving representatives of the CBI, TUC and IPD. The year before, the ED (1990) had published as best practice examples, details of businesses reporting improvements in 'performance through investing in people'.

These best practice cases exhibited four common characteristics:

- a public commitment from the organization to develop all employees to achieve business objectives;
- regular review of the training and development needs of all employees;
- action to train and develop individuals when recruited and throughout their employment;
- evaluation of the benefits of investment in training and development.

IiP is a national programme which is administered at a regional level by the TECs in England and Wales and the LECs in Scotland (IiP UK 1995). The TECs and LECs may provide support and advice for organizations striving to attain *IiP* status, usually via approved consultants, and are responsible for the assessment programme by which *IiP* recognition is granted to achieving organizations. Government aims for 50 per cent of UK organizations to be recognized as having attained, or be committed to attaining, the *IiP* national standard by 2000 were incorporated in the National Education and Training Targets (NETTs). Gilliland noted in 1996 that only 5 per cent of organizations had made progress towards *IiP*, a statistic repeated in the second edition (Gilliland 1997).

Although *IiP* focuses on the organization as the unit of analysis, the proportion of committed organizations is a misleading measure of the penetration of the Standard in terms of the proportion of people at work who are brought under its scope. The 1995 Competitiveness White Paper (DTI 1995: 82) reported 'over 15,200 organizations covering 19 per cent of the employed workforce are now committed to the *Investors* standard'. By 1 May 1995, 1,960 organizations had attained *IiP* recognition, and another 16,383 had made the commitment to becoming an *IiP*, representing 24 per cent of the workforce (Taylor and Thackwray 1995: 2). According to Investors in People UK, the latest position, (as at 31 May 1998) is that 10,249 organizations have attained *IiP* recognition, and a further 20,801 are committed to the process of attaining recognition. The organizations that have either gained or are working towards

IiP recognition now represents 32.8 per cent of the total number of employees in employment (excluding self-employed).

On the basis of the 1995 figure, the proportion of eligible employees was on target to exceed 50 per cent by 2000, assuming the base year of 1991 represented no attainment of the Standard, whereas extrapolating between the 1995 and 1998 figures, the proportion of employees is likely to be around 40 per cent in 2000. This may indicate that the take-up of *IiP* is slowing down, or that the assumption of a zero base year is unrealistic, given the existence of best practice cases which were used in defining the Standard. Most likely both issues are relevant, but it is difficult not to conclude that the achievement of the target will take longer than anticipated. Nevertheless, the achievement to date should be acknowledged: the involvement of organizations accounting for one-third of the employed workforce in seven years is significant and demonstrates the importance that companies have attached to the need to raise the level of workforce skill in the UK.

Using the Investors Standard

The *IiP* Standard incorporates a range of good practice in a structured framework to promote training and development in the interests of business objectives, linking business and human resource development. *IiP* involves developing individuals, teams and the organization as a whole, which translates into empowerment for individual employees and facilitates managing change to achieve strategic business goals. Taylor and Thackwray (1995 :19) believe that *IiP* has had a profound effect on organizations, encouraging managers to formulate clearly defined and measurable objectives for training and development, analysis of the competences available within the organization and the relationship between existing competences and those required to meet business objectives. The process of continually reviewing development and training plans in relation to strategic organizational development forms an integral part of the *IiP* process.

Gilliland (1997: 31–101) outlines how the principles can be achieved in practice. First, an employer needs to outline the organization's objectives, specifying the role of employees in achieving these targets and explaining how the development requirements of the business will be identified and met. All employees need to be aware of the future direction of the organization and what contribution they will be expected to make to its successful development. The business plan must earmark the resources necessary for training and development and a system for regularly reviewing individual development targets needs to be in place, and linked to NVQs/SVQs where appropriate. Employees should be involved in identifying these targets and matching them with their own development needs. The training and development process should be a continuous improvement of individual competences, which in turn needs to be evaluated against the utilization of these to achieve business goals. The evaluation of the effectiveness of training and development strategies should be undertaken at the highest level of management and the results used in establishing new training and development objectives.

Taylor and Thackwray (1995: 148) believe that the feedback from the assessment process is welcomed by organizations who regard it in the spirit of *Kaizen* (continuous improvement) and utilize the information in developing the organization's strategic action plan for the next three years. Recognition is valid for three years because of the time taken to demonstrate significant improvements from strategic planning. The *IiP* process has been associated with the creation of a learning organization (see Chapter 8) in both major commentaries on the Standard (Taylor and Thackwray 1995: 158; Gilliland 1997: 13). In an early evaluation of the benefits of *IiP* for employees, Rix *et al.* (1994: 14) found that most employees wanted 'more and better training and development, seeing both personal and organizational benefits in this', but a minority feared that multi-skilling would lead to redundancies. In most cases, where employers are working towards *IiP* recognition, employees recognize the advantages. The support for *IiP* from the trade unions is demonstrated by the TUC's *Bargaining for Skills* initiative (TUC 1995b), as a result of which some employers have been persuaded of the benefits of IiP recognition by their workforce representatives.

Linking development to strategy in practice

The extent to which MD was linked with OS was investigated in the sixteen organizations studied for the competence based management development project (Winterton and Winterton 1996). The sixteen cases were evaluated and ranked in these terms using the three key criteria identified in the report of the study group (Leman *et al.* 1994) as follows:

- CBMD is a key explicit strand in OS;
- a range of CBMD systems and processes are linked to OS;
- CBMD is not solely the responsibility of personnel or training departments but a key feature of all management roles.

Overall, the cases were ranked against these criteria along a continuum according to the extent to which MD was linked with OS and the robustness of evidence identified. The ranking was undertaken by independent consultants on the basis of the validated case reports and written evidence.

In the best cases, the links between MD and OS were pervasive. Written evidence and corroborated interviews showed how OS influences MD, and how MD supports OS to achieve commercial objectives. In two cases the Management Standards were seen to link MD most effectively with OS. Roles and responsibilities for MD were devolved to individuals and their line managers, with only limited HR intervention, thereby embedding MD within OS.

In cases where the link between MD and OS was more modest, evidence was provided of MD initiatives to support specific aspects of OS. Where extensive restructuring or business process re-engineering (BPR) was taking place, this provided opportunities for linking MD to OS and focused attention on the competences required to achieve the organizational transformation.

Towards the bottom of the ranking, there was little evidence of any systematic link with OS, and MD was geared to the needs of individuals rather than the organization. The examples of linkages between MD and OS draws upon the eleven best cases, while the problems of measurement and attribution also include details from the remaining five cases.

The evidence is presented under four headings:

1   major link between MD and OS;
2   moderate link between MD and OS;
3   roles and responsibilities for MD;
4   problems of linking MD with OS.

Major link between MD and OS

The five cases identified as having particularly strong links between MD and OS provided corroborated evidence of how OS influences MD, and how MD supports OS to achieve commercial objectives. Two cases cited the role of the MCI Standards in linking MD most effectively with OS.

In the galvanizing company, MD is influenced by OS in that it is designed to meet business needs, and through *IiP* the linkage has been strengthened so that the 'business plan drives personal development'. In the *IiP* submission, the company identified 'personal competence and technical capability, properly assessed and continuously enhanced' as the key to achieving its objective of progressively increasing market share (case 2). In the oil company, the consensus amongst senior staff was that the company's business strategy has a general influence upon its approach to MD. Several changes in OS, such as outsourcing, were viewed as having an impact on the company's MD activities, creating a need to develop the commercial awareness of managers over the next five years (case 4).

In the engineering company, one example of OS influencing MD related to the offshore safety case, which makes it essential to demonstrate competence to potential customers. The belief that MCI certification will give the Group a competitive edge underpins its policy of encouraging and enabling its subsidiary companies to offer their managers access to MCI (case 5). In one of the NHS Trusts, all managers noted very close links between OS and MD, and most felt the link could not be stronger. The Senior Managers' Development Programme is explicitly linked to the business objectives of the Trust. Interviews and written evidence confirmed that MD was aimed both at changing attitudes and approaches to meet the demands of the new business environment and that a range of organizational development and team development work is being planned and implemented to support the Trust's strategic priorities over the next few years (case 11).

In the newspaper organization, MD is cited as an area for further action in the Business Plan, with key tasks focused on appraisals, in-house programmes and conferences and seminars. The extent to which OS influences MD was a matter of some debate among senior strategic managers interviewed, but most line managers were unequivocal that OS influences MD, and gave a wide range of concrete examples. Team members referred to Training Plans tailored to individual needs and supporting OS. A team working course was singled out as particularly effective in showing the virtue of 'trying things out and taking risks' (case 10).

The adoption of MCI Standards provided a mechanism for linking MD with OS in two organizations. In the engineering company, increased investment in systematic MD via the route of MCI certification was attributed by senior managers to market changes. Customers are now outsourcing responsibility for managing the whole project or task to the company, so the management capabilities of staff need to be developed. MCI qualifications provide a mechanism both for improving management skills and for creating career pathways to retain managers (case 5). In the oil company, OS has moved the organization towards management by process rather than 'by silo', so change management and the ability to work in teams are priorities for MD. These trends and developments supported broad-based MD such as the company's two MCI-based programmes which are specifically intended to facilitate flexible use of staff in line with the company's needs (case 4).

In another two cases, NVQ certification plays a similar role in linking MD with OS. HRD documentation in one NHS Trust puts the business strategy firmly in the centre of the model for MD, and the specific strategic objectives include ensuring that all staff have an up-to-date personal development plan (PDP) which contributes to strategic objectives, and access to appropriate training and development, including where appropriate NVQs (case 11). Similarly, in the galvanizing company, line managers described the link between OS and MD in terms of the arrangements for developing staff through NVQs at levels 3 to 5. Team members at supervisory level quoted the achievement of NVQ 3 in supervisory management using portfolio evidence in preparation for a shift manager role (case 2).

Moderate link between MD and OS

In a further six cases there was also evidence of links between MD and OS, which were elaborated in terms of the MD to equip individuals with the competences required by the OS. In two cases, extensive BPR was shown to have both necessitated and facilitated MD linked to OS.

In the Magistrates' Courts, the Action Plan of one MCC shows how strategic objectives, linked to senior management indicators, have been mapped onto senior management performance standards. The basic framework for the development of managers was established in 1990 by the Training Policy Committee of the Lord Chancellor's Department. MD is linked into NVQ standards, competence must be demonstrated against the needs of the organization, and everyone is to have a PDP related to the Business Plan. There was universal support for MD initiatives among the team members interviewed, especially for the way that 'MCI Standards have been adopted and given a qualifications structure to MD' (case 9). Similarly, all senior and line managers in the retail company studied were unanimous in their opinion that OS influenced their MD. A rapidly expanding organization must have a MD programme which is closely linked with the planned expansion. Since OS is limited by the competences of staff, the identification of both strengths and weaknesses of employees has enabled a development strategy to emerge which complements the strategic goals of the organization (case 3).

In the government agency, the business plan for one district focused on service delivery and MD had been used to raise business awareness following the introduction of market testing and outsourcing. The agency's OS required managers to provide the same service with fewer staff, so they have to acquire motivational skills and the ability to 'get people to work smarter, not necessarily harder'. The link between business needs and strategy is competence, and managers following the NVQ route are supposed to have a PDP which links the individual's needs with those of the organization (case 6). In the footwear company, OS and MD were also very closely linked, and because of a culture change in the organization 'management must develop the skills necessary to manage this change' (case 15).

In two organizations, there was evidence that BPR, leading to flatter structures, had created a need for MD to equip front-line managers with the competences to accept more responsibility and autonomy. The BPR strategy applied in the insurance company restructured operations around multi-disciplinary customer-service teams, in place of specialist departments involved in sequential processing. All senior strategic managers and most line managers agreed that OS 'fundamentally' influences MD, and that departmental strategies also influence MD. Each autonomous Business Unit (BU) created in this new flatter structure is headed by a general manager, and the BUs develop annual business plans, identifying appropriate training plans to support these. All managers have a list of competences against which they are appraised, and competences have been established to support organizational objectives (case 7).

Similarly, in the aeroplane components company, the functional structure was altered through BPR and re-organized into Business Development Groups (BDGs), so business strategies influence MD 'indirectly', since the strategies developed by BDGs create MD needs. MD is intimately related to OS according to the chief executive, and most line managers noted that departmental strategies influenced MD: the strategy 'cascades down to MD requirements'. As a result of 'giving ownership for business to the BDGs and cells', it became necessary 'to train team people with appropriate leadership skills'. Line managers identified clear links between OS and MD and stressed how 'major changes in business development led to MD', and the BPR strategy played a significant role because 'moving ownership into appropriate areas creates a need for independent MD in those areas' (case 12).

Roles and responsibilities for MD

In the organizations where MD was linked most effectively with OS, responsibility for MD was devolved to individuals and their line managers. Partnership arrangements, which typically centred on a PDP established through appraisal, involved individuals taking responsibility for self-improvement and line managers facilitating developmental opportunities, with guidance from HR staff.

In the galvanizing company, MD strategy was developed from above and responsibility devolved to line managers and individuals. Line managers are responsible for 'developing team members', while individuals are responsible for 'developing their own competences' (case 2). In the oil company, responsibility for MD rests primarily with the individual and their supervisor. Personnel planners are involved in organizing job experience and career moves, which are the most important form of MD within the company (case 4). In the engineering company, responsibility for MD is again shared between the manager and their line manager. The individual is expected to contribute to identifying training needs, while line managers undertake appraisals and, where their staff are undertaking MCI qualifications, may take on the role of mentor (case 5).

In one of the NHS Trusts, individuals have a key part to play in their own development as managers and this is embedded within the Trust's objective setting and review process. Line managers are also involved in coaching, mentoring and appraising their staff on an ongoing basis. The central Training and Development Agency has a strategic role of identifying organizational needs and designing, developing and providing interventions to meet both organizational and individual needs (case 11). Management in the retail organization believed that individuals had a responsibility for their own development, while the HR role in MD is an enabling one (case 3).

In the newspaper organization, responsibility for MD is largely devolved to the individual and their line manager. Individuals are responsible for identifying training and development needs, while their managers are charged with identifying people to develop and facilitating MD in line with OS. The HR function manages the HRD process, but this represents only 10 per cent of the activity. All managers are expected to promote their own MD via career development reviews (case 10). Similarly, in the Magistrates' Courts the individual and their line manager are expected to work together to assess current competence and to complete a PDP. The line managers' role was mainly seen as providing 'encouragement and support', but since the MD often involves the use of 'internal expertise', line managers and senior managers may have considerable involvement in MD delivery. Line managers accepted their role, as 'team leader rather than boss', in developing staff in line with the OS (case 9).

In the government agency all players involved in the MD process have specific responsibilities. The individual has to take the initiative and play a proactive role, using the PDP as the mechanism, which is linked to business unit objectives. The HR role is strategic, ensuring that all agency staff are given the opportunity to develop. Line management are the catalyst, ensuring that MD occurs by encouraging staff to adopt a PDP (case 6).

In the insurance company, responsibility for MD is also shared between the individual, the HR function and line managers. Individuals are responsible for self-improvement, while line managers are the primary facilitators of MD. The HR role is a minor one of providing a training needs analysis (TNA) service and maintaining a global overview of the availability of opportunities for MD (case 7).

The responsibilities for MD in the aeroplane components company amount to a 'partnership' between the individual, who needs to have 'interest in self-development and career advancement', and their line manager, who should 'generate a supportive environment and a culture where individuals can express aspirations'. All managers are expected to contribute to the development of their staff, while the HR role is a minor one, a 'business responsibility' to establish the means of finding what MD is needed and to establish the necessary structure (case 12).

Problems of linking MD with OS

Linking MD to OS was not unproblematic even for the five exemplary cases, although the difficulties were more pronounced in organizations lower down the hierarchy. The major problem was in translating the needs of the organization into developmental needs of individuals, especially given the decentralization of responsibilities for MD. Much MD remains focused on the needs of individuals rather than the needs of organizations.

In one company, senior management recognized that 'the join between MD and OS was not seamless' and thought that MD lagged somewhat behind professional technical development. If MD were to be linked closely to business strategy, this 'would require each of us to analyse what are the real requirements that I need to bring to this particular job to maximise bottom line results'. It would also be necessary to examine what constituted a good management team rather than trying to develop similar qualities or competences in all managers (case 4). In another company, decentralization makes it difficult to achieve a closer link between MD and OS because each company has its own approach to implementing MCI (case 5).

Most line managers in the newspaper organization thought that MD could be more effectively linked with departmental strategies. Among team members, the perception of MD was largely that it was related to their individual needs, with the needs and opportunities for MD being largely identified by their line managers (case 10). Similarly, in the Magistrates' Courts, some senior strategic managers believed MD could be linked more closely with OS, and with departmental strategy (case 9). In the government agency, most development initiatives have been at staff level, rather than at managerial grade, where MD appears limited to those managers pursuing NVQs. Moreover, a training manager expressed the view that MD is actually being 'held up, because of a lack of a clear strategy at lower level' (case 6).

The chief executive in the aeroplane components company thought that MD could be linked more closely with OS, but the company 'is not ready for this yet, because the development of OS via the Task Force is ongoing'. The Training and Development Manager acknowledged that 'not all training is strategic, but the purpose is to make all training focused on strategic vision'. Line managers thought that MD could be linked more effectively with departmental strategy. Two managers believed departmental strategies were 'starting to influence' MD more, although another noted that 'business pressures impose limitations' (case 12).

The factory manager in the footwear company also felt that MD could be linked more closely with organizational strategy: the development of people needed to be more systematic and the operating unit strategy needed to be more closely linked to people. He opposed MD for development's sake; MD should be sharply focused and generate business advantage as well as advantage to the individual (case 15).

In the mining company, line managers were generally doubtful about the extent to which OS influences MD, but the managing director explained that they are using *IiP* as a 'tool' to link MD more closely with OS (case 1). Some of the more junior managers in the charity similarly thought the links between corporate and divisional strategies and MD were less clear, partly because they felt there is no comprehensive strategy for MD nor pathways for progression, and because their management role and responsibilities were not clearly defined (case 8). In one NHS Trust, objectives currently tend to be short term and unconnected to overall organizational objectives (case 13).

Summary and conclusions

This chapter set out to consider the relationship between MD and OS. In doing so, it was necessary to investigate different approaches to OS, to discuss ways of integrating development with strategy and to analyse the experience of linking development to strategy in practice.

The chapter started from the premise that analytical distinctions between the different theoretical approaches to strategy needed to be considered as part of the process of developing shared mental models. The need to develop core competence in line with OS was shown to be relevant whatever approach to strategy is adopted. To progress corporate strategy beyond a mission statement, it was concluded that leaders must inspire, energize and polarize individuals and teams in line with the organizational vision. In operationalizing the corporate plan developed by senior strategic managers and translating strategy into action, the different approaches to strategy were shown to offer complementary prescriptions which can be optimally combined.

This chapter was also concerned with how development can be designed to support strategy. Despite the consensus that MD should be linked with OS, and evidence that the proportion of UK business organizations in which MD is explicitly linked to corporate strategy is increasing, much MD is undertaken in isolation from OS because HRM and HRD are overlooked at the strategic level.

Investors in People, the national standard for training and development, was shown to be steadily increasing, providing a proven structure for linking HRD with OS.

Finally, this chapter reviewed the evidence from the sixteen organizations studied in relation to linking MD and OS in practice. In the organizations where MD was most closely linked with OS, the link was demonstrated in a variety of ways, those most often mentioned including the following:

- management development is an intrinsic part of the business plan;
- MD initiatives respond to changes in the organization's environment;
- MD supports strategic priorities;
- strategic objectives are mapped onto performance standards;
- business objectives are linked to OS through defined competences;
- personal development plans relate to business plans;
- major changes provide both the opportunity and necessity of linking MD to OS;
- Standards and NVQs/SVQs provide a structure for the link.

In the organizations where management development was linked most effectively with organizational strategy, responsibility for management development was devolved, typically entailing the following:

- management development is a partnership between individuals and their line managers;
- personal development plans are agreed in appraisal;
- individuals accept responsibility for self-improvement;
- line managers facilitate management development and provide coaching, mentoring and support;
- the HR function is limited to strategic issues, policy and advice.

There were problems in linking management development to organizational strategy, especially in the organizations in which the links were unclear. The main difficulties identified were:

- no systematic analysis of the competences individuals need to develop to improve business performance;
- the apparent paradox of devolving responsibility for management development and linking it to organizational strategy;
- management development lags where organizational strategy is especially dynamic;
- immediate priorities for management development take precedence over longer-term strategic management development;
- much management development is focused on the needs of the individual, not the organization.

5 Human resource development strategies

This chapter is concerned with the adoption of competence standards (including the Management Standards developed by MCI) by organizations and the relationship between CBMD and the use of Standards. The importance of providing a framework and structure for MD was identified in Chapter 2 and this chapter explores the value of adopting a competence-based approach in human resource development (HRD) systems and processes. The concerns include different approaches to HRD, the relationship between MD and the Management Standards and empirical evidence of the use of the Management Standards in the organizations studied.

The chapter is therefore organized into three sections:

1   human resource development;
2   competence-based management development;
3   competence-based management development in practice.

In the first section, different approaches to HRM strategy are outlined and linked to the need for organizations to establish a collaborative employee relations culture in order to promote learning. Combining the developmental aspects of HRM with a pluralist philosophy to establish a high-trust relationship with all employees is shown to be conducive to establishing such a culture. Forms of work organization must be consistent with the culture, and the combination of responsible autonomy and multiskilling is proposed as a a new form of 'anthropocentric' work organization. This approach can be seen as contributing to the need expressed by Handy *et al.* (1988) for a UK (or European) model for MD in place of imported Japanese or American approaches.

The second section is concerned with the adoption of a competence-based approach to HRD in general and MD in particular. The Management Standards developed by MCI are outlined and the main critiques of the competence-based approach to MD are considered. The value of adopting a competence framework in HRD systems and processes is discussed, followed by the experience of organizations using a competence-based approach to MD.

The third section presents the empirical findings from case studies of sixteen organizations concerning the adoption of the MCI Standards in HRD systems and processes. The evidence is considered first from those organizations which had comprehensively adopted the Management Standards, then from the organizations which had partially adopted the Standards, before summarizing the benefits and limitations of using the Standards. The chapter concludes with a brief summary identifying the salient points of the discussion.

Human resource development

The Taylor Report (1994: 49) noted managers will increasingly be concerned with managing people, the manager will become a coach and responsibility for MD will rest with the individual. Nevertheless, organizations need to create a framework to support this development, which demands that HR needs are defined strategically, especially as the HRD function becomes increasingly absorbed into general line management activities. The role remaining for HR specialists will be as managers of the skills transition, acting as enablers rather than providers, and extracting added value from the HR function (ibid.: 82). This change in role, purpose and function of HRM creates an apparent paradox that while people are becoming seen as the most important assets of an organization, the HR department is assuming a lower profile (ibid.: 84).

It is important in addressing these issues that HRD is considered in the context of wider HRM strategy. Equally, organizations need to establish a high-trust, 'integrative' culture with all employees by combining a pluralist approach with collaborative employee relations. An 'anthropocentric' form of work organization is consistent with such a culture, and is built on multiskilled autonomous teams. Each of these elements is considered in turn in this section.

Approaches to HRM

The emergence of HRM, in place of personnel management, along with the associated rise of HRD in place of training and development, prompted debate as to whether this marked more than a semantic trend (Armstrong 1987; Torrington 1988; Guest 1989a; Legge 1989; Sisson 1994). What became clear over the past two decades as HRM displaced personnel in managerial vocabulary, is that HRM involves a range of approaches. Two main variants were distinguished as 'hard' HRM, with an emphasis on the strategic business of deployment of labour, and 'soft' HRM, with an emphasis on human relations, motivation and leadership (Storey 1989a: 8).

Sisson (1994: 9) claimed that the HRM paradigm is inherently ambiguous because of a 'major discrepancy between the rhetoric of HRM and reality of practice', with the rhetoric reflecting the people-centred 'soft' version, while in reality the cost reduction approach of the 'hard' version was actually being adopted. The ambiguity rests upon a combination of hard and soft HRM, but Chapter 4, which emphasized the strategic role of HRD, suggests that the dichotomy is a false one. There is no inherent ambiguity in integrating HRM strategy with the corporate plan and emphasizing employee development.

Rather than contradictions between the strategic and developmental aspects of HRM, the ambiguities reflect inconsistencies between the espoused models of HRM and the practice of organizations. HRM has been associated with a new recognition by senior managers of 'the people factor' as critical to competitiveness (Storey 1989a: 2), but the corporate chorus line of 'people are our greatest asset' has a very hollow ring when accompanied by the adoption of the 'flexible firm' strategies described by Atkinson (1984). Often there are inconsistencies between strategies designed to develop individuals and teams which coincide with other initiatives that erode terms and conditions, and effective development in line with OS cannot be expected when the culture gives a contradictory message. When British Coal brought in consultants in an effort to reduce operational delays in the Selby mine complex, the initiative failed because of the low trust culture created by strategies designed to undermine the union (Winterton and Winterton 1993a).

Many managements took the opportunity in the political and economic climate of the 1980s to individualize reward systems and decollectivize labour relations. As a result there was concern within the trade union movement over HRM because of practices such as individualized performance-related pay and flexible working practices (TUC 1994b). This resurgence of unitary values during the 1980s led Guest (1989b: 47) to conclude that HRM is incompatible with pluralist industrial relations, and to suggest that 'management is not practising effective HRM…[where] the door is left open for the unions to play a role'. Yet if HRM is inevitably unitary and individualist, then managements which adopt HRM practices run the risk of creating a pattern of workplace relations which is inherently conflictual. A paternalist culture depends upon employees failing to organize and challenge management over differences which inevitably arise in the employment relationship. Managers adhering to unitary values deny the existence of such everyday disputes, and remain ill-prepared for any challenge from below.

The traditional approach to employee relations was pragmatic and reactive, rather than strategic and proactive. While HRM appeared to involve a more strategic approach to employment, these strategies largely neglected the collective dimensions of employee relations. The emergence of HRM marked a move away from the presumed norm of 'bargained constitutionalism', with its adversarial industrial relations and a cost minimization approach to labour, to a developmental approach which either entailed unitarist human relations or a co-operative, consultative style (Purcell and Ahlstrand 1993; Storey and Sisson 1993).

An integrative approach

There can be little doubt that the 1980s witnessed a fundamental transformation of labour relations in the UK, presenting the trade unions with their greatest challenges since before the Second World War. The coverage of union representation and collective agreements contracted, but shop-floor trade unionism appeared to hold up in the private sector, at least in major manufacturing plants (Millward and Stevens 1986). Workplace union organization and collective bargaining remained reasonably intact and most employers refrained from any systematic attack on the unions (Edwards 1985; Kelly 1987). Nevertheless, there were some notorious examples of 'union busting' (Claydon 1989), especially in the provincial newspaper sector (Smith and Morton 1990), and the incidence of derecognition intensified between 1988 and 1994 (Gall and McKay 1994). Signs of the erosion of collective bargaining increased towards the end of the 1980s, when a significant contraction in the coverage of collective agreements, a narrowing in the scope of bargaining and a decline in the depth of union involvement was reported (W. Brown 1993). The most dramatic examples of institutional deconstruction were in the public sector, where unions were marginalized and in some cases completely excluded (Smith and Morton 1993; Winterton and Winterton 1993a). Despite notable conflicts and a dramatic restructuring of labour relations, there was still some continuity with the past (Pendleton and Winterton 1993).

While in some cases HRM conformed with the unitary, anti-union stereotype, other anti-union initiatives during the 1980s were unrelated to the adoption of HRM techniques, suggesting that the determining influence was the permissive environment which altered the balance of power in management's favour. A unitary perspective is not an essential part of HRM, and the developmental aspects under the HRD umbrella are quite consistent with recent ambitions of the trade unions to promote learning opportunities in the workplace (TUC 1995c; 1996a). The developmental aspects of HRM can be combined with a pluralist perspective and the maintenance of traditional representative arrangements to build collaborative employee relations (Molander and Winterton 1994).

The competing trajectories of the HRM movement can be summarized in terms of the management philosophies which underpin them and the employee relations culture. In practice, each dimension represents a continuum but for simplicity, we posit two alternative management philosophies, unitary and pluralist, and two styles of employee relations, adversarial and collaborative. The resultant options are as shown in Figure 5.1.

Employee relations during the 1960s and 1970s was founded upon pluralist values and adversarial relations, the 'bargained constitutionalism' referred to earlier. This has been labelled 'traditional' since it represented a policy norm, although in practice paternalist and anti-union managements continued to exist; even in celebrated cases of reform, managers did not necessarily embrace pluralist philosophies (Ahlstrand 1990). Those approaches to HRM that are founded on a unitary philosophy are associated with two alternative trajectories away from this assumed norm of pluralist, adversarial.

One approach involved a crude reassertion of managerial prerogative, the 'macho-management' approach, while the other was based on a 'paternalist' human relations approach. Whereas macho management was concerned with managers regaining control at the point of production, the paternalist approach

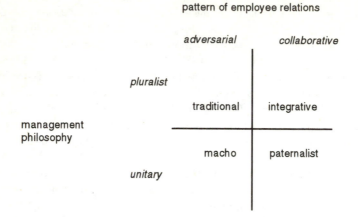

Figure 5.1 Competing trajectories of HRM

involved the workforce within clearly prescribed limits, often through TQM initiatives.

The third trajectory, an employee-centred approach which builds a collaborative relationship on an existing pluralist institutional framework, is termed 'integrative' because it forms a point of departure from traditional 'zero-sum' bargaining. By combining the developmental aspects of HRM with a pluralist philosophy, a high-trust relationship can be established with all employees. Such an approach is complemented by a new form of work organization, based upon responsible autonomy and enhanced skills, which we describe as 'anthropocentric'.

Anthropocentric work organization

Different form of work organization can be distinguished in terms of the strategies adopted in relation to skill and employee discretion or management control. Again, in practice, each dimension is really a continuum, but for simplicity we propose two extremes in terms of skill: multiskilled (broad and deep skills base) and Taylorist (narrow, shallow skills), and a similar dichotomy for discretion: monitored (close surveillance by supervisors or via computer) and autonomous (where workgroups are responsible for their own internal management and discipline). The four combinations are shown in Figure 5.2.

In manufacturing industries, at least, the prevailing mode of production remains Taylorist in nature: individuals perform a narrow range of tasks requiring only shallow skills. Moreover, their work is closely monitored and individuals have little task discretion. Such separation of conception and execution, where managers are supposed to do the thinking and operatives carry out their instructions, is the very antithesis of developing human resources. Organizations that retain Taylorist work organization are not conducive to developing human

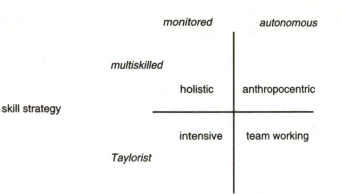

Figure 5.2 Options for work organization

potential, no matter how often senior management proclaim their commitment to do so. Since the purpose of Taylorist job design is to intensify the rate of production, such work organization is characterized as 'intensive'.

The limitations of Taylorist work organization have gradually come to be appreciated in the UK (Kelleher 1996), although somewhat belatedly in comparison with Japan (see Konsuke Matsushita quoted in Molander and Winterton 1994: 147). Management recognition, though popularized in the cliché that 'with every pair of hands a brain comes free' (Cannell 1993: 64), has rarely been translated into attempts to get individuals to *use* their brains. The problems associated with Taylorist work organization led some companies to redesign work in ways that demanded broader and deeper skills. In the chemicals sector, for example, process operatives and maintenance craft workers increasingly need to have diagnostic and analytical skills to troubleshoot and keep the plant running. To do this they need a conceptual understanding of the process which goes beyond a daily operational working knowledge, and a broader range of skills and competences (Winterton and Winterton 1998). This approach is described as 'holistic', in contrast to the fragmented skills and knowledge associated with Taylorist work.

Another solution has been to devolve a degree of decision-making and control to work groups. In the clothing sector, for example, while tasks remain fragmented, a proportion of production is now undertaken by teams that are assigned a bank of stand-up sewing machines to cover the full range of operations. Team members need a broader range of skills but also have more control over their pace of work and are empowered to take operational decisions. This 'team working' approach is generally preferred by operators, even though their work rate is invariably higher than in the traditional bundle system of garment production (Barlow and Winterton 1996).

The most comprehensive initiatives involving autonomous work groups and self-directed teams are found in Scandinavia. When the Volvo motor vehicle plant at Kalmar was in operation, for example, the adoption of autonomous team working resulted in significant improvements in quality and efficiency, and workers overwhelmingly preferred this work organization to the traditional assembly line (Aguren *et al.* 1984). In the UK, empowerment has usually involved less extensive employee participation measures (Marchington *et al.* 1992), although there is renewed interest in the effect of employee involvement on performance in the USA (Cotton 1993). Relatively few companies have introduced both substantial multiskilling and work group autonomy but one such workplace, identified in the FORCE project on trade union involvement in vocational training (Winterton and Winterton 1994), was re-visited as part of the competence-based management development study (case 12). Fully multiskilled production teams have responsibility for certifying that their work is to the standards required by the relevant aviation authorities (Winterton and Winterton 1997: 161–2). Such a combination of multiskilling and autonomy is described as 'anthropocentric' since work organization is centred on human capacity for self-expression.

The design of jobs to promote skill and autonomy is essential for the development of a high-trust relationship and a motivated workforce. The importance of the integrative approach to HRM is that it recognizes the possibility of interests which are divergent from those of the organization, whether at the level of individuals or groups, and irrespective of institutional arrangements for the representation of collective interests. Once the plurality of interests is recognized, systems and procedures can be developed to accommodate differences and establish a collaborative culture complemented by anthropocentric work organization. Parallel arguments can be applied to managers, whose development must also include gaining the competences required for managing autonomous, multiskilled teams.

Competence-based management development

Following the adoption of a competence-based approach to vocational training in the UK and the development of the Management Standards by MCI, there has been controversy over the value of CBMD but relatively little analysis of the experience of its adoption within organizations. This section discusses the origins and nature of the Management Standards, addresses the main critiques and considers the value of incorporating the Standards in HRD systems and processes.

The Management Standards

The Handy Report (Handy *et al.* 1987) recommended that a group of top companies form a Charter Group and establish a Charter of good practice for MD (Constable 1991). Among the standards proposed for the Charter were:

- a corporate development plan;
- a minimum of five days off-the-job development per year for every manager;
- a personal development plan for every manager;
- reimbursement of tuition fees for education.

From these origins, the Management Charter Initiative (MCI) was established in 1988 as the operating arm of the National Forum for Management Education and Development and by the end of 1991 had the support of over 800 companies. The MCI was recognized as the lead body for management and developed a generic set of occupational standards relating to areas of activity in which managers need to be competent (L. Miller 1991). Standards were developed for supervisory management (level 3), first line management (level 4) and middle management (level 5). The 'Winning' Report identified the importance of innovation, leadership and empowerment, and the Management Standards incorporate many of these elements. The M3 standards for senior managers, first drafted by MCI in February 1995, focus on strategic issues, and similarly include such elements as leadership. The final version of the M3 standards is expected to be available for use before the end of 1998. In July 1998 MCI officially became a National Training Organization, with the mission 'to shape and promote management development, particularly competence-based management development for the benefit of organisations and individuals'.

As with other occupational standards, functional analysis was used to produce a framework of management competences, from which the occupational standards for managers were developed. The Management Standards were mapped to NVQ criteria to fit the new framework of vocational qualifications and equate to the following levels:

- M1S Supervisory Management = NVQ level 3;
- M1 First Line Management = NVQ level 4;
- M2 Middle Management = NVQ level 5;
- M3 Senior Management.

Like all occupational standards, the Management Standards identified key roles, and in the case of the M1 standards, for example, there were four key management roles:

- to manage operations;
- to manage finance;
- to manage people;
- to manage information.

Each key role was broken down into a number of *units of competence*; the 'manage people' role, for example, comprised four units:

- to contribute to the recruitment and selection of personnel;
- to develop teams, individuals and self to enhance performance;
- to plan, allocate and evaluate work carried out by teams, individuals and self;
- to create, maintain and enhance effective working relationships

Each unit was in turn further sub-divided into *elements of competence*; the second of the above units, for example, was broken down into three elements:

- to develop and improve teams through planning and activities;
- to identify, review and improve development activities for individuals;
- to develop oneself with the job role.

For each element of competence, performance criteria were defined which form the basis of assessment and range indicators were provided for guidance. In the case of the first element above, examples of performance criteria were:

- the strengths and weaknesses of the team are identified against current and anticipated work requirements;
- any unproductive friction between team members is minimized;
- development activities optimize the use of available resources.

Examples of range indicators relevant to these performance criteria are:

- development objectives and activities cover all areas in which the teams are expected to produce results and meet quality standards;
- development activities include specifically designed work activities, formal training and informal training.

The Management Standards were reviewed in 1996 and as a result revised Standards were published in 1997 (Boutall 1997). First, there have been significant linguistic changes in the new Standards, which were re-written in a more appropriate and accessible language free from jargon.

Second, there are now *two* sets of Standards: the Vocational Qualifications Version relates to individuals as before, while the Business User Version relates to organizations. The two versions constitute an integrated whole in order to promote complementarity between individual and organizational needs for development. A system of core units and options has also been introduced in order to make the Standards more flexible and easier to apply in different organizational contexts.

Third, in place of the four key roles, there are now seven:

- to manage activities;
- to manage resources;
- to manage people;

- to manage information;
- to manage energy;
- to manage quality;
- to manage projects.

The empirical study reported here was based on the original version of the Standards and the revisions represent improvements in terms of the difficulties encountered in the cases studied and some of the criticisms outlined below. Therefore, the changes do not invalidate the performance outcomes identified from the original Standards, which probably understate the benefits of adopting the revised Standards. It is reasonable to assume that a study based on the 1997 Standards would not result in any less significant performance outcomes.

Critiques of competence-based management development

There has been considerable criticism of competence-based management development, some of which is concerned with aspects of the process which are common to the competence-based approach to vocational education and training in general, and some of which relate specifically to the management function.

In the first category, criticism has been made of the process of functional analysis by which key roles and competences are defined. Stewart and Hamblin (1992a) argued that functional analysis is less effective as an analytical tool for MD than established methods such as task and job analysis. They are not alone in challenging the value of functional analysis for management tasks:

> the disaggregative approach of functional analysis has had no empirical verification. For this, the MCI would have to show that managers who are judged to be competent on each element are also judged to be competent overall, using independent criteria.
>
> (Holmes and Joyce 1993: 43)

The assessment associated with the competence-based approach and the use of the Management Standards for qualifications have also been criticized for being bureaucratic (Canning 1990; Currie and Darby 1995). For small employers in particular, the framework was seen as too complex and the language too rigid (Hirsh and Strebler 1994: 91). The dichotomy of 'competent' or 'not yet competent' is seen as too simplistic in failing to differentiate levels of competence and therefore not taking into account continuous improvement (Stewart and Hamblin 1992b), while the developmental steps in the MCI approach have been viewed as too hierarchical, neglecting the possibility of strategic thinking at lower levels (Wille 1990). Moreover, in an empirical study of the introduction of level 3 and 4 Management NVQs using APL, Currie and Darby (1995) criticized the scheme for not being developmental. These issues are common to the NVQ/SVQ approach in general and we found them to act as serious barriers to take-up by individuals at all levels (Winterton and Winterton 1995). Nevertheless, problems in the operation of vocational qualifications should suggest a need to streamline the system, not abandonment of the competence-based approach.

Criticisms relating specifically to using a competence-based approach for managers have tended to argue that the special nature of managerial tasks makes it impossible to capture and define the required competences or competencies (Wille 1989). The Training Commission (1988) reiterated the MSC definition of competence in relation to management development, but some observers claim that management skills and competences are too complex and varied to define (Hirsh 1989; Canning 1990) and that it is futile to attempt to capture them in a mechanistic, reductionsit fashion (Collin 1989). Others believe that the use of generic competences leads to a neglect of qualitative aspects of management (Jacobs 1989) or that inter-personal skills, for example, cannot be measured or assessed (Hay 1990; Donnelly 1991). Hirsh and Strebler (1994: 92) are uncertain whether and how personal competencies can be incorporated into such a task-based structure. Thorpe and Holman (1997) conclude that 'the methodology of MCI has caused it to overlook or inadequately address factors thought to be important in managing which are difficult to describe or reduce to behavioural terminology'.

The essence of these objections is that managers are like alchemists and magicians, whose mysterious arts defy description and analysis. Complexities and ambiguities in the management role are well known, but there is a serious risk of mystification and obfuscation in claiming such a special status for management skills. The Management Standards, like other occupational standards, are grounded in concrete functional analysis of managerial activities in a variety of contexts (Mansfield and Mitchell 1996), and while this inevitably results in abstraction, the Standards offer a valuable framework for MD.

A related criticism was that the competence-based approach puts too much emphasis on the individual and neglects the importance of organizational development in making MD effective (Burgoyne 1988b) and the differences in organizational contexts (Kilcourse 1994). Equally, it has been argued that generic lists of managerial competences cannot be applied to diverse organizations (Burgoyne 1989b; Collin 1989; Canning 1990). Yet managers as an occupational group are employed in a wide range of organizations and their mobility between enterprises demonstrates the validity of common transferable managerial competences.

Otter (1994) claimed that the competence-based approach presents problems for MD since NVQs are construed in terms of competence within a specific occupational context, whereas managerial competences are generic rather than occupationally specific. There is a danger of confusing sector with occupation; managers as an occupational group, like electricians, are found in a range of sectors and it is the occupation, rather than the sector which is the focus of competence.

Some of the criticisms of CBMD and the Management Standards have been addressed in the revised Standards, and some criticisms are exaggerated. The difficulties that remain are endemic to the competence-based approach in general, the use of APL and the degree of bureaucracy. While the system may be improved, some of the difficulties may simply be the price to pay for relevance in vocational education and training.

Adopting the Standards in HRD systems and processes

The Management Standards offer a comprehensive framework of management competences. Noting their value for strategic coherence, Iles (1993: 79) demonstrated how competence-based personnel strategies can assist in the internal integration of the HR system, providing consistency and coherence in all HR activities. As was anticipated in Chapter 1, the Standards can be used to structure MD activities by providing a means for basing HRD systems and processes on a common, coherent integrated set of competence statements. This in turn should facilitate the development of management competences which support OS and lead to improvements in IP, OP and BP. To the extent that the Standards are being adopted, therefore, organizations should be developing more robust HRD frameworks linking MD with OS.

The Harbridge Consulting Group (1993) found that by 1992, 10 per cent of organizations had adopted 'competency-based assessment'. A survey undertaken by MCI in the same year estimated that 11 per cent of organizations were using the Management Standards (King 1993). Among organizations having a formal system for MD, 20 per cent were already MCI users and a further 18 per cent were planning to apply the Standards in the near future. Among the 20 per cent of organizations using the MCI Standards, almost half had contextualized them within the organization (MCI 1993). The 1997 Survey (MCI 1997) found 30 per cent of organizations were aware of the Management Standards and 15 per cent were using them. By the third quarter of 1997 the cumulative number of Management NVQ registrations (levels 3–5) was in excess of 100,000.

In the management context, competence has been defined as 'the ability to perform effectively functions associated with management in a work-related situation', yet the Cannon Report found 'few employers have any real understanding of the meaning of competence in this context' (Cannon 1994: 35–6). Burgoyne (1988a) noted 'the impact of MCI has been minimal so far', but as a result of working towards *IiP* status (see Chapter 4), increasing numbers of organizations will be adopting MCI standards and linking MD with OS in the future, especially following the introduction of the Business User Version of the Standards.

The MCI approach appears to have had less impact on academic provision (Cannon 1994: 48, 51). The main academic concern is that a competence-based approach may lead to a neglect of underpinning knowledge and theory, the same criticisms which have been raised by some employers about NVQs in general (Toye and Vigor 1994; Winterton and Winterton 1995). In the light of this, the Cannon Report (1994: 50) recommended a programme of research 'to bring out the distinct, specific and complementary roles of competence, knowledge, understanding and skill-based management education and training'.

Hirsh and Strebler (1994: 91) noted that many employers had already developed their own competence frameworks or adopted other generic models instead of the MCI Standards. Iles (1993: 68) distinguished the generic (MCI) competence models from organization-specific competence models, but regarded both as having considerable potential. Mathewman (1995) claimed that organizations prefer to use behavioural competencies rather than the competences embodied in the Management Standards, as was the case with Natwest Bank (Cockerill 1989).

The Safeways supermarket chain developed competence-based HRD systems and processes before the MCI Standards. A strategy was developed in the 1980s 'to ensure that employees and prospective employees are matched against specific competence-based specifications for each job' (Stringfellow 1994: 293). The twelve 'management dimensions' identified were later termed 'competences'. They are as follows:

- problem analysis;
- problem solving;
- planning and organization;
- delegation;
- management control;
- leadership;
- human relations skills;
- personal effectiveness;
- verbal communication;
- oral communication;
- stress tolerance.

Once the competence-based approach was established, it was adopted throughout the company in selection, training and appraisal. In the selection interview, for example, questions were introduced which were designed to identify the candidates' 'competence traits and behavioural indicators' for comparison against the 'established competence profile bands' (Stringfellow 1994: 296). The competence-based training programme involves in-store assessment by trained observers as well as written and oral assessment. The appraisal review 'focuses on the behaviours under the various job competences, and matches them against stated performance criteria' (ibid.: 297). Significantly, operating results are considered separately from the appraisal, thereby emphasizing the developmental purpose of the review. Once the national Management Standards were published by MCI, the Safeway competences were linked to these and the company was involved in piloting the M1 standards. As a result of the experience in these trials, the training programme was modified because the old scheme was too work-related and the generic management competences involved were insufficient.

Competence-based management development in practice

The extent to which HRD systems and processes were based upon the Management Standards was investigated in the sixteen organizations studied for the competence-based management development project (Winterton and Winterton 1996). The sixteen cases were evaluated and ranked according to three key criteria identified in the report of the study group (Leman *et al.* 1994) as follows:

- all HRD systems and processes are based on the occupational standards (and for management these are the MCI Standards);
- assessment and appraisal systems are designed to inform development rather than punish the incompetent;
- every manager in the organization views MD as their own responsibility for their own development and for those with whom they work.

Overall, the cases were ranked against these criteria along a continuum according to the extent to which the Management Standards were adopted in HRD systems and processes and the robustness of evidence identified. The ranking was undertaken by independent consultants on the basis of the validated case reports and written evidence.

In four organizations, the Management Standards were comprehensively adopted in HRD systems and processes. Written evidence and corroborated interviews demonstrated the ways in which the Standards were used and the benefits of building MD initiatives around the MCI Framework. In three cases, the Management Standards had been partially adopted, and were used to a limited extent in some HRD systems and processes. The remaining nine organizations had either not attempted to adopt the Management Standards or had only made limited progress in this direction, so that they are regarded as non-users.

The evidence is presented under four headings:

1   comprehensive adoption of the Management Standards;
2   partial adoption of the Management Standards;
3   benefits of adopting the Management Standards;
4   limitations of using the Management Standards.

Comprehensive adoption of the Management Standards

In the four organizations where the Management Standards had been adopted comprehensively in HRD systems and process, a competence-based approach had been adopted for all or most MD activities. The Management Standards were central to appraisal, and training and development, but used less extensively in job descriptions, recruitment and selection, and remuneration.

The most comprehensive adoption of the Management Standards was found in the galvanizing company, where MD was described as 'entirely competence based', with additional 'academic top-up' where necessary. The Standards were adopted in 1989, since when they have been used in all HRD systems and processes except recruitment and remuneration. Line managers explained that there is a 'continuous process' of informal appraisal by the senior manager, who has a very close understanding of every manager's activities. At shift manager level, the process involves regular discussion with senior management throughout the day, while supervisors see the appraisal as 'an opportunity to identify further training needs'. The Standards are viewed as the 'very foundation' of training and development, and targets for personal development are 'related to the MCI Standards' (case 2).

The majority of HRD systems and MD in the retail company are also now competence based; all training programmes have been reviewed and focus on key tasks in line with MCI standards and the company became an Accredited Competence Centre approximately two years ago. Appraisal systems are now designed to support the achievement of the MCI standards. The Performance Appraisal system is being reviewed and a new set of appraisal criteria are being developed which are directly linked with the Management Standards. A personal action plan will be a direct outcome of the new appraisal system and areas for development will be identified, with details of how, by whom and when this will be carried out (case 3).

In the Magistrates' Courts the approach to MD was described as '100 per cent competence based'. Most HRD systems and processes are based on the MCI Standards, which were adopted in 1991. Among line managers, current job descriptions were seen as inadequate: 'a list of tasks, not linked to competences' and 'based on an historical view of what the job involves'; although it was recognized that in the future, 'they will be linked to competences' and 'the MCI Standards will be used'. Some job descriptions have been 'refined in terms of MD', so that as well as the competences of the job, there may be an expectation that the individual 'will develop to BTEC level 5'. Some courts are using the Standards in recruitment and selection, but the practice is not yet widespread. No formal appraisal systems are yet in place in the Magistrates' Courts, although 'continuous monitoring against targets is in progress', and it is intended to build appraisal around the Standards. Team members anticipated that, once operational, the appraisals would provide an opportunity 'to identify problems and to seek improvement'. The Management Standards form the fundamental framework for MD and training. Staff are given performance indicators for their region and asked to compare performance and explain variations, using the Lord Chancellor's Department guidelines on interpretation. Moreover, PDPs are 'work-related and linked to the achievement of standards' (case 9).

In the insurance company, almost all HRD systems and processes are based on the Management Standards, which were adopted 18–24 months before the research. The organization's Management/Supervisory Competency Standards and Staff Competency Standards represent contextualized and modified forms of the Management Standards. The competences outlined in job profiles in the insurance company reflect 'what the job entails', 'the steps involved in the work process', and were defined in relation to the Management Standards. Recruitment, selection and appraisal systems are based on the Management Standards, and the individual and their manager agree the job profiles as part of the appraisal process. Personal development objectives incorporate the Standards, and a Training Development form is completed 'to identify the expectations and purpose' of any training or development activity, and 'checked afterwards against outcomes'. The remuneration system involves salary bands with grading based on the job role, and a performance-related aspect determines where an individual incumbent is placed within their band (case 7).

Partial adoption of the Management Standards

Three organizations had partially adopted the Management Standards in some of their HRD systems and process. These organizations had largely adopted a competence-based approach and the Management Standards were used to some degree in appraisal, training and development.

For many of the oil company's managers MCI supplements their technical standards because there is a large technical or safety component to their work (for example, managing major emergencies) to which MCI is not thought to be relevant and for which they continue to be assessed against company standards. Job descriptions are worded in terms of accountability rather than competences, which would make it difficult to incorporate the MCI Standards. Recruitment and selection processes, broadly speaking, are not based on MCI or other competences. For a number of years the company has operated a highly structured system of staff appraisal or performance review which is common to the Group as a whole. Competence in the appraisee's present job is assessed using the Group's framework which is mandatory for all the companies in the Group. The competences listed are very general, e.g. managing resources, planning and organizing work. For the purposes of appraisal, MCI competences are not explicitly linked to particular work roles (case 4).

In the engineering company, the majority of MD is competence-based in the sense that MCI is the basis of most management training, but some subsidiaries continue to second staff to MBA programmes. Job descriptions are linked to duties and responsibilities, as defined by management systems, and are kept as flexible as possible. 'Person' specifications prescribe minimum qualifications and level of experience rather than being based on competences. Personal development objectives and targets are set and progress against these is reviewed through an annual review and appraisal system. The criteria or categories specified on appraisal forms currently in use are not explicitly linked to MCI competences, but the form has recently been revised in line with the MCI Standards. Most of the supervisors working off-shore on one project and the majority of the supervisors in one on-shore company are undertaking level 3, and two or three managers per company are undertaking MCI at level 4 with similar numbers projected for level 5 (case 5).

The MCI standards were considered by the charity but were not found to meet the organization's needs, so a Management Competency Framework (MCF), based on the MCI standards, was developed internally and adapted to reflect working practices within the voluntary sector. The appraisal system is designed to support achievement of the MCF, and the framework is referred to in the appraisal documentation. Of the external courses used by the organization, the Certificate of Management Studies (CMS) is based on the underpinning knowledge requirements of the MCI standards. Other external courses do not claim to be based on the MCI Standards, but these programmes are only being followed by five or six managers (case 8).

Benefits of using the Management Standards

In all the cases where the Management Standards were used, respondents cited extensive benefits, irrespective of the extent of adoption. The MCI approach provides a coherent framework for HRD systems and processes, criteria for more systematic appraisal of competence and developmental needs, and a structure for training, development and qualifications.

In the galvanizing company, the Management Standards have been adopted to provide a coherent structure for training, MD and personal development. Key management were developed using the M2 (NVQ 5) Standards. Line managers and supervisors are trained to generic standards experientially within the business. The production manager had attained NVQ 5 through MD and was devising with other managers an NVQ 3 programme and assembling the supporting documentation, while the organization was developing an NVQ 2 in galvanizing with the Engineering Training Authority (EnTra) (case 2).

The Management Standards have been used similarly to structure training and development in the Magistrates' Courts. A guide to the Management Standards was produced by MCI and the Magistrates' Courts Service in October 1992, which outlines the framework of MD in the Magistrates' Courts, based on the Standards. The Senior Management Development Initiative, a development and accreditation process central to MD in the Service, was introduced in 1994 (Magistrates' Courts Service 1994) (case 9).

The benefits of linking appraisal to MCI were acknowledged in the engineering company, since this will enable gaps in competence to be identified and training needs framed in these terms. Some objectives identified during appraisal are clearly relevant to competence in terms of the Standards. For many of those interviewed, MD appeared to be synonymous with management training and, indeed, with MCI. Prior to the introduction of MCI, there was apparently little systematic management training or development (case 5).

In the review of the performance appraisal system, management in the retail company identified the benefits of using the Management Standards to establish new performance appraisal criteria (case 3). The performance review being developed around the Standards in the Magistrates' Courts will similarly assist in 'identifying training and development needs', through comparing 'job profiles and Personal Development Plans' (case 9).

In line with the oil company's decision in 1993 to use the MCI Standards as an 'off the shelf' solution for its structured management training programmes, the Standards were introduced that same year as a tool for assessing competence, both managerial and personal, within its appraisal system. According to the company's personnel director, the MCI standards were intended to be used not as a tool to measure everyone's performance in detail but to help managers think about where competence improvement could lead to business benefits and to identify more specific competence development targets (case 4).

Because the Management Standards provide criteria for HR planning and career succession in the retail organization, line managers identified the reward for achieving competence in terms of promotion opportunities, as well as the personal satisfaction of obtaining an NVQ, and in the smooth running of the department for which they are responsible (case 3).

Limitations of using the Management Standards

In those organizations which had adopted the Management Standards, particularly where they were only partially used, there were limitations to the implementation of the MCI approach. The limitations were manifest in the extent of adoption throughout an organization and in the range of HRD systems and processes involved.

Some difficulties related to the adoption of the MCI approach appear to be the result of the time it takes for the use of the Management Standards to percolate through an organization. In the retail company, for example, where HRD systems and processes had been comprehensively restructured around the Standards, line managers were nevertheless unable to identify what the competences outlined in their job description were based upon. Team members commented that they had no job descriptions, and were not convinced that the competences required for particular functions had really been identified (case 3).

Similarly in the charity, where the Management Competences Framework (MCF) incorporates elements of the Standards, the use of the Framework was limited and not disseminated widely. The central personnel team believed that the Management Standards were used in recruitment and selection procedures, but usage seems to be limited to the central team, rather than widespread throughout the organization. Other interviewees made no mention of the Framework and a number of respondents commented that the organization has no agreed definition of what is expected of managers. Managers thought that personal development objectives are not expressed in terms of the MCI Standards or the organization's MCF, although the appraisal policy states that they should be (case 8).

Even in the cases where the Management Standards had been comprehensively adopted in HRD systems and processes, their use was more limited in systems of recruitment and selection, which are inevitably geared towards application forms, references and interviews, for evidence of candidates' qualifications and experience. Qualifications will increasingly be competence based with further take up of NVQs/SVQs, but even where job profiles use the framework of the Management Standards, none of the organizations had developed mechanisms for assessing an individual's competence against the Standards at the selection stage. In the galvanizing company, where the MCI approach has been most comprehensively adopted, the Management standards are not used in recruitment because supervisors and managers are developed internally 'from within' the existing workforce (case 2). The use of the Standards for job descriptions has not been considered in the engineering company, and the feasibility of using them as a basis for assessment at the selection stage was questioned. The company therefore does not use the MCI standards in recruitment and selection, except in the sense that possession of an MCI qualification would be relevant (case 5).

Organizations which had adopted the Standards generally used them in appraisal, but in some cases, additional criteria were used. In the retail company, for example, personal development objectives are not fully defined in terms of the Standards (case 3). Similarly, in the oil company, there is a large technical or safety component to the work of managers and the Management Standards are not thought to be as relevant as company standards (case 4).

The Management Standards were not used in reward and remuneration systems, other than in relation to payment for attaining a qualification, and there was little enthusiasm for linking pay to the achievement of competence. In the retail company, a small one-off payment is made to those managers attaining NVQ 3 or 4, but senior management believe the individual reward for attaining competence is in obtaining a nationally recognized qualification and having the opportunity for self-development with company support (case 3). Similarly, in the galvanizing company, the reward system is not built around the Standards because 'competence is the standard for the job', although there is additional remuneration for production workers who achieve NVQ 2 (case 2).

Summary and conclusions

This chapter set out to explore the adoption of a common, coherent set of competence statements (including the Management Standards) in HRD systems and processes and the relationship between CBMD and the use of Standards. To do this, it was necessary to investigate different approaches to HRM, to discuss the nature of competence-based HRD and to analyse the experience of adopting CBMD in practice.

The chapter started by outlining the different theoretical approaches to HRM and emphasized the diversity and ambiguity of HRM strategies. The case was made for establishing a culture of collaborative employee relations by combining the developmental aspects of HRM with a pluralist philosophy to establish a high-trust relationship with all employees. To complement this approach, a new form of 'anthropocentric' work organization, based upon responsible autonomy and enhanced skills, was proposed.

This chapter was also concerned with the value of a competence-based approach to management development. The origins, nature and revisions of the Management Standards developed by MCI were outlined before considering critiques of the use of the Standards for MD. Finally, evidence was reviewed from the sixteen organizations studied in relation to CBMD and the use of the MCI Standards. In the organizations where the Management Standards have been extensively adopted, the HRD systems and processes had the following characteristics:

- virtually all management development was competence based;
- job profiles or job descriptions related to the competences outlined in the Management Standards;
- appraisal systems were designed to support the attainment of the Management Standards;
- training and development is structured around the MCI competence framework.

Where the Management Standards had been adopted, the following benefits were identified:

- there is a coherent structure for training, management development and personal development;
- gaps in competence are more readily identified through appraisal;
- training and development needs are specified more precisely in relation to the competences required for individuals to meet the needs of the organization;
- there are clear criteria for human resource planning and career succession;
- management development is linked to a qualifications framework.

There are limitations to the adoption of the Management Standards both in the extent to which they have percolated through an organization and in the range of HRD systems and processes involved. The main limitations identified were as follows:

- familiarity with the Management Standards is less extensive outside the HR specialists;
- the Standards are not extensively used in recruitment and selection, other than in relation to job profiles;
- additional criteria are sometimes used alongside the Standards, especially in relation to specific technical competences;
- reward and remuneration systems are rarely linked to the achievement of competences defined in the Management Standards.

6 Individual performance

The purpose of this chapter is to explore MD from the perspective of the individual manager and to analyse the improvements in individual performance identified in the organizations studied. MD is concerned both with the renewal of individuals and with the continued improvement of their performance. It was argued in the 1995 Competitiveness White Paper (DTI 1995: 116–18) that 'management performance can be improved...by spreading best practice...developing standards and qualifications for management...with linked development and training opportunities'.

The MD cycle described by Wallace (1991: 15) and outlined in Chapter 2, is viewed from an organizational perspective. From the perspective of an individual manager, there is a parallel cycle entailing the identification of individual needs, the learning experiences through which competence is developed and the outcomes in terms of improvements in individual performance.

This chapter is therefore organized into three sections:

1   identification of training needs;
2   learning to develop competence;
3   individual performance outcomes.

In the first section the main mechanisms for identifying the training and development needs of individual managers are considered. Tensions are shown to exist between development, assessment and rewards, which are highlighted in the common failings of performance management systems. Assessment centres are shown to offer an alternative approach which recognizes individual development in line with organizational needs. Finally, it is argued that tools for analysing individual training and development needs represent a common and essential part of the performance management and assessment processes.

In the second section the processes of individual learning are considered in order to identify factors conducive to learning and development. Different types of occupational learning are discussed, and the learning processes emphasized in different approaches are then related to a hierarchy of stages of learning. The limitations of a sequential view of learning are demonstrated in the learning cycle and the relationship between cognitive and affective learning. Senior managers are shown to have an important role in promoting an environment supportive of learning and development, and their own development needs are identified.

The third section presents findings from case studies of sixteen organizations. The use of the Management Standards is shown to be associated with the seven cases where the greatest improvements in IP were demonstrated and attributed to MD. The chapter concludes with a brief summary identifying the salient points of the discussion.

Identification of training needs

In keeping with the philosophy of taking responsibility for their own MD, individual managers should be involved in identifying their training and development needs. Equally, for MD to support organizational strategy and to link with performance improvements, the individual's senior manager should have a role in identifying developmental needs and opportunities. It is logical, therefore, for an organization's performance management system to include mechanisms for identifying the training and development needs of individual managers. Evaluating competence can involve specialist tools, so assessment centres have been used increasingly in recent years. Whatever combination of mechanisms is involved, some form of training needs analysis must also be employed. These three aspects of identifying training and development needs are considered in turn below.

Performance management systems

Hartle (1995: 12) describes performance management as 'a process for establishing a shared understanding about what is to be achieved, and how it is to be achieved, and an approach to managing people which increase the probability of achieving job-related success'. The performance management process should reflect both organizational and individual objectives since the performance of the organization rests on the achievements of the individuals who work within it. To be effective, performance management must be designed to deal with the development needs of individual employees on both a long-term and short-term basis and be capable of exploring in specific detail how individual performance can be improved. However, as Marchington and Wilkinson (1996: 156) note, 'despite the rhetoric, much of the practice in British industry and commerce is based upon *ad hoc*, unplanned and poorly conceived ideas about how to improve employee performance'.

An IPM survey in 1992 found that performance appraisal was the commonest performance management system, and that employers with formal performance management schemes were more likely to have implemented other schemes such as total quality management (TQM) and performance-related pay (PRP). An annual appraisal interview of subordinates by their boss is the most common means of identifying individual training needs in major UK companies, but there is often dissatisfaction with the appraisal process as a result of trying to deal with too many issues (Hussey 1996: 126). It is difficult to deal with pay and promotion in the same context as development, but the performance management process is often expected to do this. Performance appraisals are heavily criticized where pay is linked to the outcome of the appraisal, which militates against the parties involved being open and honest. Individual managers are reluctant to discuss performance weaknesses if this may affect the salary increases they will receive.

The lack of consistency frequently found in appraisals can be attributed to the degree of commitment individuals bring to the process as well as their understanding of which particular aspects of an individual need to be developed. Also, because appraisal often takes place as an annual event, it tends to become a bureaucratic organizational process, rather than one which occurs throughout the year, as and when required by individuals and their managers. An appraisal which is meant to achieve development and career progression needs to be a more flexible and continuous process involving both appraiser and appraisee as partners who can make an equally important contribution to the outcome of the performance appraisal. Moorby (1996: 196) argues that performance appraisal has the potential to be 'a privileged occasion to obtain feedback' and an 'ideal platform for discussing and agreeing developmental opportunities'. The appraisal system itself should be reviewed on a regular basis and must be sensitive to the comments and suggestions for change of those involved.

Overall performance management systems can improve organizational performance without including PRP, and PRP is found to be more effective when part of a performance management system. Surveys conducted by the Hay Group identified recurrent problems with performance management and PRP. Frequently, objectives are inappropriate to individual aspirations, employees are unhappy with their ratings and top management feel that they do not need to be involved in the process. The performance appraisal is often inadequate, with individuals being unaware of what actually constitutes good performance, and there is a widespread lack of understanding of the purpose of performance management and its potential benefits to the individual and the organization. Where PRP is used, employees are often unclear of the relationship between achieving objectives and subsequent pay enhancement. Hartle (1995: 27) suggests that one reason for these problems is that 'many organizations have underestimated the level of managerial skills needed to provide support to the effective management of performance'.

The process known as 360° feedback can be utilized as a part of performance management to improve individual performance and to assess an organization's skills, strengths and deficiencies. Information is gathered from a wide range of individuals and organizations with which an individual interacts in a variety of capacities, as well as from the managers themselves. A profile of the individual manager's performance is built up from this information in order to identify areas for development which can then be addressed through a personal development plan and the utilization of relevant management training programmes. Hussey (1996: 138) believes that the use of this process is limited as it is not 'possible to design valid feedback tools to assess functional and professional skills'.

Faced with such evidence of widespread dissatisfaction with traditional systems, Hartle (1995: 57–61) proposed that an organization's performance management process should entail the following:

- an integrated management process, involving an ongoing process throughout the year which can be reviewed and changed and which is geared to measurable and achievable performance outcomes;
- an holistic approach, ensuring that performance management is an integral part of an organization's business strategy and relates to other key business initiatives like TQM or employee development;
- total performance management, using a competence-based approach, ensuring that people are aware of the standards required to perform their job satisfactorily and the best means of achieving these standards through examples of best practice;
- a fit with work cultures, recognizing that the performance management process differs with the culture of the organization;
- self-managed individuals and teams, encompassing de-layering to empower individual employees and to encourage individuals and teams to assume greater ownership of the performance management process;
- effective links with rewards, ensuring that individual performance promoted by the performance management process is recognized and results in a well-motivated workforce;
- a motivating work climate in which managers adopt a supportive management style, allowing individuals scope to develop their performance to the best of their ability.

Assessment centres

Assessment centres are most widely used by large companies, normally for recruiting new staff and for assessing the suitability of existing staff for promotion. An individual's competencies and competences are measured against those required for a particular function and their strengths and weaknesses are identified (Woodruffe 1990). A development programme can then be devised which is tailored to the individual and the requirements of a particular job. Assessment centres offer the benefit of 'objective observations of the strengths and weaknesses of the participating individuals and it is possible to focus the process so that the assessments are business driven' (Hussey 1996: 139). In the UK, development has received less attention than assessment, and the two have only recently been linked (Bolton and Moreira 1995: 10). The use of assessment centres has stimulated development which takes into account an individual's strengths and weaknesses. In a situation where opportunities for promotion are limited, individuals must be encouraged to think in terms of development without obvious promotion (Bols *et al.* 1995: 101–2).

Assessment centres can involve external or internal assessors and may be time-consuming and expensive, so it is important to decide whether the benefits of intensive off-the-job assessment outweigh the costs (Wallace 1991: 206). The use of audio-visual material as a pre-selection tool can go some way towards reducing the cost of the exercise, but simulation is not always an accurate substitute for a real situation. Computers can be used to track individual responsiveness, but this is limited to certain role plays and produces quantitative rather than qualitative data. Also group rather than individual role plays can be used, but this can mask individual ability as the behaviour of each group may not be consistent (Bols *et al.* 1995: 103–4).

There is a trend to rename assessment centres development centres in line with the philosophy that their activities are wider than selection (Lee and Beard 1994). Assessors and participants meet after the assessment and discuss the event and a proposed plan of action for development, initiating this process as soon as possible after the assessment is complete. One disadvantage of this is that 'there may be confusion about whether it is intended to be a development programme or an assessment of future capabilities and the need for development' (Bols *et al.* 1995: 108–9).

Self-assessment and development are a relatively new approach in assessment centres, whereby individuals devise their own development plans with expert assistance, which involves the participating managers being trained as assessors and feedback counsellors. Although the process takes longer, it is anticipated that costs will be offset by reducing the number of assessors and senior management involved in the process. Confidentiality is assured because the individual owns the results and can decide whether or not to share them with superiors (Bols *et al.* 1995: 110–11).

Training needs analysis

Training needs analysis (TNA) represents the first stage of all forms of HRD, including MD, and involves identifying the competence requirements of individuals in relation to the organization's strategy (Hall 1984; Bartram and Gibson 1997). Hussey (1996: 127) estimates that approximately 60 per cent of organizations carry out training needs assessments, which normally involve managers and sometimes their superiors. It is a common failing of TNA that insufficient attention is paid to how training and development will fit with organizational culture and strategy (Fairbairns 1991). While MD needs to reflect organizational needs and fit with company culture, the mechanisms for identifying the development needs of individuals should also be seen as an inherent part of the career management process.

The objective is therefore to identify MD which best meets the needs of the organization and the needs of individual managers. Responsibility for development rests primarily with the individual, but individual and organizational training and development objectives can conflict. Development for the individual could be undertaken as a means of becoming a more attractive commodity in the labour market rather than aiming to meet the learning needs of an organization which are determined by company objectives (Moorby 1996: 193). Individual and organizational needs can be most effectively reconciled when MD (and HRD in general) is explicitly linked with organizational strategy (see Chapter 4).

The TNA process entails two complementary activities, focusing on the job (and by implication the organization) and the individual, respectively. The job role must be defined accurately and the required competences identified. Highly structured job descriptions have been associated with demarcation and inflexibility in the past and run the risk of allowing job roles to ossify. Job profiles entailing an analysis of key tasks and broader responsibilities can more adequately reflect an emergent organizational strategy. An accurate job profile facilitates an analysis of required competences against the MCI Standards (Fowler 1991). Hussey (1996: 127) recommends holding a workshop for senior managers to consider the strategic changes facing the organization and to identify what is needed to implement the organizational strategy.

The individual manager's existing competences are analysed from personnel records and reports from performance appraisal and assessment centres. Ideally, the development needs of managers should be assessed by combining feedback from these sources with observation, reflection, counselling and personal action planning. The personal profile based on this information will reveal areas where competence needs to be developed to improve performance in the current or anticipated job role. The individual can then agree with their senior manager a Personal Development Plan (PDP) designed to fill the competence gap identified. As with the required competences of the job, the acquired competences of the individual manager can be analysed against the Management Standards.

By comparing the skills required to ensure that company objectives are achieved with an audit of existing skills, the organization's competence gaps are identified. The TNA process may also reveal a lack of competence in areas that were not necessarily recognized as important in an assessment of organizational needs. A management development audit should identify initiatives to fill skill and competence gaps, although in practice the degree of success is limited by the quality of the organization's personnel records. Training and development needs must be categorized and a list of MD priorities drawn up in order to fill the competence gaps identified. Hussey (1996: 140) suggests that they could be categorized as gaps which 'have a fairly immediate business imperative', gaps 'which are indirectly business driven, which have less direct benefit, and perhaps longer term orientation' and gaps which 'relate to individual desires' and which do not benefit the company directly.

Wallace (1991: 211) argues that good MD depends upon 'identifying business change opportunities, matching managers to these opportunities, supporting managers while they tackle the opportunities, and helping them reflect on what they learned'. Creating a network of managers keen to improve performance through business change facilitates MD in line with the business needs of the organization. Harris (1989) cites best practice examples where training and development are devolved to line management, who have a 'charter' to improve their subordinates' competences and where training programmes are evaluated against measurable productivity improvements and reductions in employee turnover.

Learning to develop competence

Stewart and McGoldrick (1996: 1) define HRD, which includes MD, in terms of planned interventions intended to have an impact on individual and organizational learning. Mabey and Iles (1994: 1) note how 'the development process has overtaken the training event at individual, group and organization level'. Individual learning is intended to contribute to personal development and to the extent that the organizational and individual needs are congruent, should also lead to performance improvement (Dale 1993). By definition, employee development represents the 'provision of learning experiences in the workplace in order that performance can be improved' (Harrison 1992: 4), but it should be noted that learning does not necessarily lead to improvement in performance (Stammers and Patrick 1975: 23).

Individual learning and maturation together contribute to development, defined by Collin (1997: 285) as 'the process of becoming increasingly complex, more elaborate and differentiated'. The processes and stages of individual learning must be understood in order to identify factors conducive to learning and development. After considering these, this section explores the role of senior managers in promoting an organizational environment that is free from barriers to learning and which will motivate managers, and other employees, to maximize their opportunities for development.

Individual learning processes

Learning is generally thought of as both a cognitive process involving the assimilation of knowledge and an affective process leading to changes in behaviour. The stages in learning identified by Fitts (1962) link the two processes: in the cognitive stage, the individual understands what is required and how to achieve it; the associative stage involves practice to attain correct behaviours; while in the autonomous stage external sources of information are unnecessary and the individual's capacity to perform secondary tasks increases. In Kolb's (1983) widely accepted model, experiential learning is seen as an integrated cognitive and affective process involving two dimensions: the concrete/abstract dimension (involvement/detachment) and the active/reflective dimension (actor/observer). The learning cycle moves from concrete experience, through reflective observation and abstract conceptualization to active experimentation (Kolb *et al.* 1984). Individuals have a preference for a particular phase of the cycle, and appropriate learning styles can be adopted to suit the individual (Honey and Mumford 1992).

The hierarchy of managers' learning proposed by Burgoyne and Hodgson (1983) parallels the stages identified by Fitts: at the first level, factual information is immediately relevant; while at the second level tacit knowledge is acquired which enables them to deal with events; and the third level involves conscious reflection on their conception. These three learning levels can be broadly associated with the three dimensions of what is learnt in an occupational setting: knowledge (know what), skills and competences (know how), and understanding (know why). The Dreyfus five-stage learning model (Dreyfus and Dreyfus 1984; Dreyfus *et al.* 1986) describes levels of skill acquisition from novice through advanced beginner to a level of basic competence, then further to proficiency and on to the highest level of expertise, where the individual demonstrates 'intuitive grasp' and 'vision'.

The hierarchical approach is echoed in the four types of occupational learning which Hendry *et al.* (1995: 141–9) contrast in a generalized occupational learning model:

- basic occupational learning entails training and development undertaken in the early stages of an individual's career and should provide them with basic job competence in the form of recognized, transferable skills;
- extended occupational learning entails learning skills beyond recognized job competence, whether through extended job duties or other developmental opportunities, and generally takes place during the first stage of career development, although it can continue as long as the opportunities exist;
- learning from the job context, which involves skill development beyond that required for a specific job, generally occurs during the middle or advanced stage of an individual's career through collaborating with others in the organization. At this point, 'tacit knowledge' and 'tacit skills' become significant in the operations of the firm and lead to the achievement of 'occupational mastery'.
- learning new occupational skills involves learning at the forefront of one's chosen occupation, ahead of the generally recognized skill base in the industry, and focuses on 'different' rather than 'better' skills.

Each of these types of learning can be associated with the learning processes emphasized in different approaches, and it is tempting to treat these as a hierarchy of stages of learning. Identifying different stages of learning provides a convenient framework for distinguishing learning for basic occupational competence from routes to learning higher skills and new competences. In doing so, however, it must not be assumed that the stages are necessarily sequential, since the learning cycle, with its continual interaction between cognitive and affective learning, inevitably reintroduces individuals at all stages of their career to different types of occupational learning.

Stages of learning

For basic occupational learning, Moorby's (1996) description of how individuals learn is important, since the learning process is unique to each person and is a function of a number of criteria, 'brain hemisphere preference, preferred learning styles, the circumstances in life the individual encounters, specific motivations to learn, individual capabilities and, of course, available opportunities. Wherever possible the effectiveness, speed and relevance of learning need to be enhanced' (ibid.: 187).

Self-organized learning, where individuals do not depend on others for direction but rather take responsibility for their own learning, is relevant for acquiring skills beyond basic job competence (Boydell and Pedler 1981). In achieving self-organized learning an individual needs to recognize their own needs and how to achieve them by 'initiating flexible learning strategies and recruiting appropriate resources for achieving the expressed purposes' (Harri-Augstein and Webb 1995: 10). The process is continuous, with individuals critically evaluating their achievements and implementing new and more effective cycles to meet their future needs. 'The self-organized learners need to recognize and challenge existing partially-developed skills, including learning to learn so that such skills are transformed to achieve greater competence' (ibid.: 11). Such on-the-job learning is viewed as inherently challenging, exciting and contributing to broader individual development (Pedler 1986; Pedler *et al.* 1986; 1990).

The concept of action learning, pioneered by Reg Revans (1971) at the National Coal Board after the Second World War as a process which aimed to utilize the knowledge and experience of fellow workers for problem solving (Moorby 1996: 201), is also relevant in extended occupational learning. The fundamental principle that 'there can be no learning without action and no action without learning' (Revans 1983: 16) demonstrates the importance of learning from extended job duties and from the wider job context. Building on this approach to action learning, Pedler *et al.* (1997: 170) argue that work should inherently be a developmental experience in itself. While often difficult to achieve in practice, development is more likely to occur where a greater range of learning opportunities is available. Learning on the job may be inappropriate if a change in career direction is required or if it is necessary for an individual to develop new skills or knowledge not directly related to their current job (ibid.: 174). Self-development can be stimulated by giving control and responsibility to each individual and by creating opportunities to review learning and development through appraisal.

The highest stage of learning from job content and beyond to acquire innovatory occupational skills is widely seen as the route to 'personal mastery'. Although personal mastery is 'grounded in competence and skills', according to Senge (1990b: 141), it goes beyond these to entail a level of proficiency which should be regarded as a process rather than something that an individual comes to possess. 'People with a high level of personal mastery live in a continual learning mode. They never "arrive"...They take more initiative. They have a broader and deeper sense of responsibility in their work. They learn faster' (ibid.: 142–3). Traditionally, individual development was seen as a means of making an organization more effective, but Senge argues that personal mastery is more than this and that the fullest development of the individual is of equal importance to business success. This approach is intended to generate a complete relationship between the individual and the organization where shared commitment exists in the truest sense of the word.

Personal mastery is a learning discipline which increases an individual's capabilities, as well as having the potential to improve the abilities of those with whom they interact; 'an organization develops along with its people'. Senge *et al.* (1994: 193) argue that 'no one can increase someone else's personal mastery. We can only set up conditions which encourage and support people who want to increase their own.' Establishing such conditions is worthwhile because learning does not last unless an individual is motivated to learn: 'without commitment the trainees stop using the new skills. Gradually, they systematically forget them, often beginning with the principles and theories which made the training seem so worthwhile in the first place.'

Motivation and barriers to learning

Mumford (1988b: 26) identified ten types of blocks to learning experienced by managers, ranging from motivational, cognitive and intellectual barriers of individuals, to situational, physical and environmental barriers of the organization. At the individual level it must be recognized that managers, like all employees, are motivated when they feel individually in control of their working lives and are empowered to make decisions to achieve work goals. Waterman (1994: 32) found that in the top-performing companies, 'people who believe they have a modicum of control over their lives are healthier, happier and more productive'. People need to feel that they are performing a useful and meaningful function by working, and valuing their own work can only have a positive effect on an individual's performance. Work needs to be challenging and development continuous so that individuals can constantly expand and learn. Also, individuals need recognition for their achievements at work, whether these are financial or this is acknowledged by other means (Waterman 1994: 18–21).

In terms of the learning environment, organizational forms conducive to learning need to be developed by focusing attention not only on individual learning (Binsted 1980) but also on facilitating organizational learning (see Chapter 7) and working towards developing a learning organization (see Chapter 8). Clearly, it is difficult to achieve personal mastery when, as Deming (1993) noted, instead of stimulating 'intrinsic motivation' many organizations seem determined to make this as difficult as possible for their employees to attain. Development opportunities have tended to focus on managers, but in a learning organization these opportunities are equalized by spreading resources amongst all employees (Pedler *et al.* 1997: 164). Personal Development Plans and career planning can help to equalize learning and development, provided learning opportunities are made available.

Some organizations have introduced 'learning contracts', written agreements between the learner, tutor and trainer, detailing a set of rules to which each party involved in the contract will adhere (Boak and Stephenson 1987; Boak and Joy 1990). Harri-Augstein and Webb (1995: 72) are concerned that such a contract is merely 'an organizational commitment involving the completion of certain tasks within an agreed schedule', whereas a 'Personal Learning Contract' comprises a contract that learners make with themselves, and is completely under the individual's control rather than externally organized with others. Individuals are initially supported by a learning coach but as they become more familiar with the whole process, they take full control of the conception and execution of their own PLCs. 'The PLC empowers the learner to think positively and constructively about his or her learning competence' (ibid.: 74).

Senior managers have a major role in removing barriers to learning for managers and all employees, especially given the increasing responsibility of managers for the career development of their subordinates. In order to create a supportive environment for development, senior managers themselves need to develop key competences, which are both functional and behavioural in nature. Alderson (1993) identified six behavioural characteristics of top management teams which contributed to the success of the enterprises studied:

- interpersonal relationships must be good within the top team;
- there must be a capacity for openness and a willingness to discuss any issues;
- members of the top team must have a high level of trust in one another;
- the top team must be approachable and able to accept feedback and criticism;
- the team must have sufficient discipline and cohesion to implement their decisions;
- they must have the capacity to discuss and understand both long-term and short-term issues, a competence which comes in part from a broad and deep understanding of the business.

Senior managers are often not given the same opportunities for development as those further down the management hierarchy (Mumford 1989), yet there is considerable evidence that the competence of the top team is a major source of competitive advantage (Schuler and Jackson 1987; Alderson 1993). These are the managers who are often most in need of 'learning how to learn' (Mole *et al.* 1993). Strategic company change may demand skills that no one has previously been required to possess (Hussey 1996: 120), yet Vicere *et al.* (1994) found the budget for executive development was not formalized in major corporations. Spencer (1995: 159) argues that in order to re-engineer an organization's HRM systems and processes 'top management will change from controllers to leaders', which requires three main competencies. First, senior managers must have 'anticipatory strategy', which is the ability to take a long-term view of the business and the environment in which it operates and to plan accordingly. Second, they must be able to exert 'change leadership' which motivates all parties who have a stake in the business to be committed to a company's strategic objectives and to provide the necessary resources in key areas to be able to facilitate change. Third, senior managers need to establish 'relationship management' which involves creating networks of influence with groups and individuals and organizations whose cooperation is vital for the success of the business, but with whom there is no authority relationship.

Senior management must be involved in assessing the performance of individual managers and identifying their developmental needs and opportunities, but the process is not without difficulties. Herriot *et al.* (1993) explored the differences in perceptions between individual managers and their bosses with respect to individual performance and careers. Individual managers tend to be more optimistic about their own promotion than their superiors are, and while both parties believe that they share the same perceptions, this is seldom the case in reality. According to Nordhaug (1993), competence development amongst employees is a direct function of the ability of managers to promote this throughout the workforce by stimulating development, providing the right opportunities for individuals and generating feedback on the newly acquired competences.

Individual performance outcomes

One of the issues examined in the sixteen organizations which were studied for the competence-based management development project (Winterton and Winterton 1996) was the extent to which MD had contributed to improvements in IP. The three key criteria used were identified in the report of the study group (Leman *et al.* 1994) as follows:

* improvements in IP have been tracked (against the Management Standards);
* individuals are clear of the work expectations demanded of them and how their role links to the overall purpose of the organization;
* individuals are offered a range of support to improve their performance.

Overall, the cases were ranked against these criteria along a continuum according to the extent of improvements in IP and the robustness of evidence attributing the improvements to MD. The ranking was undertaken by independent consultants on the basis of the validated case reports and written evidence (see Chapter 3).

In this section, the best cases are considered first, where the central importance of MD to major improvements in IP was demonstrated through written evidence and corroborated interviews, before considering cases where improvements in IP were more modest. The role of the Management Standards is then discussed since the greatest improvements in IP were associated with the use of the Standards. Finally, problems of measurement and attribution are examined, where there was ambiguity in relation to reported improvements in IP or where improvements had occurred but could not be attributed to MD activity. The evidence of improvements in IP draws upon the eleven best cases, while the problems of measurement and attribution also include details from the remaining five cases. In two organizations MD activities were recent and it was too early to assess their effect.

Major improvements in IP attributed to MD

In five cases, the central importance of MD to overall improvement in IP was demonstrated unequivocally through written evidence and corroborated interviews. Examples from these organizations are quoted below, with the most robust evidence considered first.

In the retail company, senior management had no doubt that MD had improved IP: the managing director believed 'there would be no development [of the company] without MD'. The senior HR manager explained that MD had given managers increased competence, confidence and awareness of responsibilities, and this had improved their overall performance. For line managers the benefits in their performance attributed to MD were numerous: 'it made me stand back and look at my performance more carefully to find out what I am doing right, what I am doing wrong and what I could be doing better'; 'the contribution has been awesome. I have been given a helping hand all the way'; 'I started as a YTS trainee and am now an area manager for the company. I could never have done this without MD'. All team members also felt that their performance had improved because of MD; they had been given more responsibility, taught how to manage themselves, and encouraged to take a wider view of issues (case 3).

The traditional 'authoritarian style' of management in the Magistrates' Courts has given way to 'the empowerment of middle management', and as a result, IP is 'measured by self-empowerment'. Senior strategic managers believed that MD had contributed to improved IP, for example in developing the 'consultative style' of managers and providing a 'better understanding of the needs of the organization'. Line managers cited a wide range of ways in which MD had contributed to improved IP: for example, it had 'boosted confidence' and made managers 'more aware of their potential'. Gaining qualification to NVQ level V had brought 'recognition of achievements', which made managers 'more motivated to continue to improve performance'. Improved IP had come from gaining a better 'appreciation of their role in the organization' and 'understanding the organization's objectives'. Further improvements in IP included 'more systematic interviewing for youth trainees and permanent staff' as a result of a course in interviewing techniques (case 9).

At one of the NHS Trusts interviewees reported improved IP as a result of MD, such as increased personal confidence and competence, and achieving outcomes more quickly with fewer mistakes. Managerial skills, such as negotiating, managing change and project management, had improved noticeably and were applied to situations which managers encounter as part of their normal work (case 11).

In the engineering company, improvements in IP were measured by the extent to which work targets are met. Along with a general increase in self-confidence as managers, respondents were able to cite examples of specific areas in which they had developed knowledge or skills, such as developing budgets and representing the company at meetings. Managers' attitudes had changed in relation to their own development, to the company and with respect to their own work roles (case 5).

In the galvanizing company, managers noted that MD had led to 'improved understanding' and had helped to develop a 'more methodical and structured approach' to work. For shift managers, MD had given 'increased awareness of their responsibilities' and helped to 'structure the way experience has developed the individual'. Most importantly, MD had 'improved the quality of documentation, in both production and training'. For example, shift managers had established a training programme for operatives and developed all the supporting documentation: 'the loss of apprenticeships had left little training of operatives; we have now developed a reputation as a company with good training, and our workers will accept responsibility' (case 2).

Moderate improvements in IP attributed to MD

In a further six cases, verified evidence was provided of specific or isolated improvements in IP arising out of MD activities.

In the oil company, the annual appraisal is intended to be supplemented by quarterly reviews at which progress is monitored and both work and development targets are adjusted as necessary. Manager and mentor respondents identified various areas of improvement: personal development, contributing to meetings/problem solving discussions and communication. Examples of improvements in IP included leading and formalizing meetings, managing time, and presentation skills (case 4).

In the newspaper organization, a chief executive explained that MD made a significant contribution to IP not only through developing existing staff, but also through the organization attracting 'good people because of its reputation for MD'. Senior strategic managers involved in HRD and line managers were convinced that MD had been 'a major source of improvements in IP' and gave examples of how MD initiatives had provided individuals with an underpinning of confidence which led to 'major improvement in their performance'. One employee, with no background in the newspaper industry, had been developed through three significant training events and had been appointed as 'distribution manager, replacing a manager with 13 years' experience' (case 10).

In the insurance company, managers were unanimous in attributing improvements in IP to MD activities. Examples of self-development were given and line managers cited their application of skills developed through 'coaching on disciplining staff', 'interviewing' and 'presentation skills'. The benefits of various courses were also identified, including 'telephone training, which improved phone technique substantially', and training in leadership, which helped managers to 'understand people' and 'to manage upwards'. Competence-based training for account managers was reported to have improved their performance, while 'team management' had improved as a result of situational learning (case 7).

In the aeroplane components company, line managers gave examples of how MD had improved IP for themselves and for members of their departments. Managers had changed their behaviour 'as a result of a Continuous Improvement Group which focused on HR issues', and this had raised the motivation of staff. An Engineering Manager had developed from a shop floor position, 'attaining NVQ 5 in Operations Management', without which he 'could not have done this job'. Cell leaders attributed specific improvements in IP to various MD initiatives, such as team working courses, which gave 'greater confidence and a better understanding of the work of other departments', experiential development, which improved 'planning of work flows', and Pareto courses, which helped 'to solve production problems' (case 12).

In the government agency, senior managers had been involved in a development programme based on the agency's 'core competencies' which involved them constructing a personal development plan (PDP). This process demonstrated the importance of PDPs for the organization and managers are now encouraged to develop a PDP. Line managers believed that MD had improved individual management performance, although to varying degrees. The majority of team members interviewed felt that MD had made a positive contribution to improved IP. Secondment, job shadowing, opportunities to work on detached duties, and training courses had enabled individual managers to develop in ways that they had never previously thought possible, with MD being geared to individual needs (case 6).

In the footwear company, the factory manager felt that MD had made a significant contribution towards improvements in IP. For example, one manager had been educated purely as an industrial engineer, so had to acquire competence in new areas and now performs well in a managerial capacity. Team members felt that MD had made a significant contribution to their managerial performance, developing coaching skills which improved team performance (case 15).

Use of the Management Standards

In the seven cases where the greatest improvements in IP were demonstrated, the improvements were associated with the use of the Management Standards. Examples from these organizations are quoted below.

In the retail company, the Management Standards are viewed as a mechanism for developing individuals in all aspects of their role and providing guidance by producing a yardstick for best practice. The introduction of the Standards encouraged the adoption of a system of upward assessment, which brought a whole new dimension into appraisal, and to the MD which resulted from this exercise. One manager commented, 'working to MCI competence Level 4 helped me in every aspect of management from handling employees to handling finance, it even helped me in my personal life and totally changed my outlook' (case 3). Similarly, in the Magistrates' Courts, the functional model and the personal competence model from the Management Standards are used in MD to trace personal development through a 'log book, counter-signed and corroborated by a third party, showing both functional and behavioural achievements'. Moreover, 'linking MD to Standards has given benchmarks and criteria for individuals to perform to, and has structured recruitment and selection' (case 9).

All the respondents in the engineering company believed that use of MCI had already had, or would have, a positive impact on performance: undertaking the programme had resulted in new ways of thinking about their work. The MCI approach encouraged staff to take personal responsibility for their own development, strengthened their commitment to the company, and increased people's confidence and willingness to put themselves forward for promotion. Findings from a recent study undertaken by the local university on the business benefits of the Certificate in Management (MCI level IV) were broadly in line with those identified above but also cited development of skills in stress management, communication, delegation, motivating and relating to staff, as well as in financial budgeting and control (case 5).

In the oil company, informal feedback on the competence improvement workshops, which are cross-referenced to the Management Standards, has been positive. Participants felt that they had significantly improved their skills across a wide range of the MCI standards with most improvement in the 'soft' or 'people management' areas and least in the management of finance (case 4). Of those managers involved in programmes using the MCI standards in one NHS Trust, some found these useful and made them more reflective about their jobs (case 11).

In the newspaper organization, the NVQ open learning exchanges have 'enabled managers to identify best practice', and as a result 'management skills have improved' (case 10). Portfolios of NVQs from levels 3 to 5 similarly show how the developmental needs of individuals have been identified by senior management in the galvanizing company. The claim that MD had improved operator training was supported by written evidence: since 1990, when the documentation was developed, detailed training records demonstrate what competences individuals have achieved and show how this has been supported by assessor training (case 2).

Problems of measurement and attribution

The problems of measurement of IP and attributing improvements to MD were greatest in those organizations providing the least robust evidence, but some difficulties were also noted in the best cases. For example, in the retail company team targets are established and it is difficult to separate individual targets (case

3). Similarly, in the engineering company, systematic evaluation of the impact of MD on individuals would require taking a base-line measurement, appraising individuals against the standards in order to identify outcomes that they could not yet meet, and then re-assessing against these same outcomes following a learning opportunity (case 5).

In some organizations, the extent of improvement in IP from MD was seen to vary significantly between individuals. The HR specialist in the footwear company noted that in some cases MD has made a noticeable difference to IP, whereas in others it has had no effect whatsoever (case 15). In the government agency , an area manager believed the contribution MD has made to IP varies considerably and is a direct function of 'what an individual manager wants for themself' (case 6). Similarly, in one NHS Trust, in some cases MD had significantly improved a manager's IP and yet for other managers MD had very little effect; managers who had been involved in a long-term development programme had benefited significantly more than those on shorter programmes (case 13).

Major ambiguities and difficulties of attribution were apparent in the weakest cases. In two NHS trusts, MD activities are currently being transformed, which makes it difficult to identify improvements in IP and to attribute them to MD. In one NHS Trust, the appraisal and development scheme is relatively new, so interviewees found it difficult to identify improvements in IP due to management training and development (case 16). In the other Trust, there was disagreement within the senior management HRM team concerning the contribution which MD had made towards improvements in IP (case 13). In the mining company, none of the senior management thought that improvements in IP to date could be attributed to MD activity, but they anticipated that the MD strategy would do this in the future (case 1).

Summary and conclusions

This chapter set out to consider MD from the perspective of the individual manager. In doing so, it was necessary to investigate how training and development needs are identified, the learning processes associated with developing competence and the outcomes of increased competence in terms of improvements in IP.

The starting point of the chapter was a consideration of mechanisms for identifying individual training and development needs. These mechanisms were examined within the context of performance management systems, which illuminate the inherent tensions between development, assessment and reward management. The use of assessment centres was related to the adoption of competence and competency in recruitment and development. Training needs analysis was shown to entail a procedure for identifying the gap between the competences required by the organization for a particular role and the competences acquired by the individual in that role.

This chapter was also concerned with how competence is developed through learning. The individual learning process was shown to involve a cycle of cognitive and affective learning, and to pass through levels of skill acquisition. The types of occupational learning distinguished were associated with stages of learning from self-organized learning to personal mastery. The stages are not necessarily sequential since individuals attaining mastery in one sphere could be faced with a need to acquire basic occupational competence in another. The barriers to effective management learning and development were seen to include factors affecting individual motivation and, crucially, organizational constraints. Personal Development Plans and Personal Learning Contracts were discussed as means of overcoming both types of barriers to learning. The involvement of senior managers is of pivotal importance in creating organizational forms conducive to learning and development; equally, it is important for those senior managers to have adequate training and development themselves for this role.

Finally, this chapter reviewed the evidence of improvements in IP arising out of MD in the sixteen organizations studied. In the organizations where there was most robust evidence of significant improvement in IP attributed to MD, the improvements most often mentioned included:

- personal confidence, awareness of potential and continuous improvement;
- general managerial skills and competences;
- understanding of organizational objectives and individual responsibilities;
- empowerment of middle management;
- individual career advancement;
- methodical approach to developing others;
- planning, time management and effectiveness in running meetings;
- project management, change management and problem-solving skills;
- communications and presentation skills;
- leadership and motivational skills.

In these cases where MD had made an unambiguous contribution to improvements in IP, this was frequently associated with the use of the Management Standards and the implementation of NVQs/SVQs which provided the following benefits:

- criteria for performance;
- benchmarking best practice;
- new ways of conceptualizing work tasks;
- individuals take responsibility for own development and can track this;
- increased commitment and motivation.

There were some difficulties of measurement of IP and of attributing improvements to MD, especially in those organizations which provided less robust evidence, the main problems being:

- separating individual and team performance measures;
- time and cost of systematic measurement and evaluation;

- outcomes of development vary between individuals;
- isolating effect of development when other major changes are taking place.

Having considered the individual level, the following chapter addresses the next level of analysis, where the focus is on the organization at the level of teams and departments.

7 Organizational performance

This chapter addresses the role of MD in improving organizational performance (OP). Allied to the concept of organizational development (OD), the focus is upon how MD can renew organizations and improve the performance of groups of individuals. The concerns include developing structures to promote organizational efficiency through developing effective team working, implementing systems to enhance learning in organizations and measuring improvements in performance at the level of teams and departments.

This chapter is therefore organized into three sections:

1   organizational efficiency;
2   learning in organizations;
3   organizational performance outcomes.

The first section explores the meaning of organizational efficiency in terms of the effectiveness of departments and work groups. The growth of team working in organizations requires more effort to be directed towards developing employees at all levels to perform in groups. The effectiveness of teams is widely held to depend upon both the competences and personalities of team members, but it is argued that team dynamics requires a consideration of more than the psychological characteristics of individuals since effective work groups are influenced by a wide range of organizational characteristics. The notion of phases of group behaviour and the concept of a team development cycle are helpful in considering means of developing teams and team working. The measurement of team performance has been neglected in comparison with the performance of individuals, but can involve both output criteria, such as efficiency or productivity, and process measures, such as group capacity for future performance.

In the second section, team learning is distinguished from individual learning and factors conducive to learning and development *of* teams, as well as *in* teams, are identified. Recognizing the importance of the work team in attempts to promote organizational efficiency, approaches such as action learning are shown to facilitate learning at the team level. The concept of organizational learning is examined as a bridge between individual learning and the development of a learning organization. Distinctions are drawn between single-loop and double-loop learning, lower and higher level learning, and tactical and strategic learning at the organizational level. Stages of organizational learning are discussed, whereby cognitive and behavioural learning lead to visible performance improvement for the organization. Interactions between conceptual and operational learning at the organizational level are shown to parallel the relationship between cognitive and affective learning at the individual level, while the learning function of active memory is important in the transfer from individual to organizational learning. Small enterprises are shown to present particular problems as well as offering different opportunities for organizational learning and development.

The third section presents our findings from case studies of sixteen organizations undertaken in researching the business benefits of competence-based management development. The evidence is presented first from those organizations where major improvements in OP were attributed to MD, then from the organizations where more moderate improvements were demonstrated. Innovations and improvements in team working were associated with significant improvements in OP that could be attributed to MD. Problems of measurement and attribution of improvements in OP are discussed. The chapter concludes with a brief summary identifying the salient points of the discussion and the main findings of the case studies.

Organizational efficiency

For MD to be translated into real business benefits, improvements in IP must be paralleled by improvements in OP, otherwise there is a risk of organizational dysfunction through individuals improving their performance in isolation. In distinguishing OP from business performance (see Chapter 8), an intermediate level of analysis is proposed between individuals and the organization as a whole, centred on the work group or team. This section considers the requisites for building effective teams, how teams, as opposed to simply the individuals they comprise, can be developed, and ways of measuring team performance.

Effective teams

Belbin's (1981) influential work on teams demonstrated that effective teams are not just a function of the skills and expertise of their members, but also of the personalities of the individuals involved. Teams need a balance of complementary competences and *competencies*, since teams formed solely on the basis of technical expertise or creativity are unlikely to comprise a sufficient range of the requisite individual skills, qualities and attributes. Belbin identified eight ideal-types of team members in terms of their psycho-social characteristics (using psychometric tests) and the roles they adopted within a team. The 'co-ordinator' establishes the goals of the group, while the 'shaper' clarifies and moves forward these objectives. The 'plant' contributes ideas and provides new recommendations to overcome problems, while the 'evaluator' challenges and tests the team's decisions. The 'implementer' puts the ideas and proposals into practice, while the 'team worker' maintains the internal cohesion of the group, ensuring that everyone works together. Finally, the 'resource investigator' explores opportunities on behalf of the team and the 'completer' ensures all aspects of the project are completed.

According to Belbin (1981: 90–2) there are critical factors which must be met in order for a team to succeed. The leader of the team must be patient, commanding respect and generating trust, while looking for and knowing how to use ability. The ideal team leader does not dominate proceedings but can draw discussion to a close in order to reach a critical decision, working with the most talented contributors to the group. The inclusion of one 'strong plant', a creative and clever member of the group, with ample opportunity to fulfil themselves in their team role is also a prerequisite for success. High team performance is associated with a wide spread of mental abilities rather than with teams that are intellectually more homogeneous. Similarly, a wide range of 'team role strengths' minimizes conflict within the team, as individuals will not be competing for the same roles. Team members of a winning team found team roles suited to their psychological traits and abilities, or developed more flexible arrangements where more than one person would be responsible for a specific critical function which could not be covered by one individual. Therefore, teams that are able to recognize and compensate for areas of weakness are more likely to succeed.

The 'classic mixed team', identified experimentally, was the team structure most likely to generate success, but this is not evident from winning teams in industry. Belbin (1981: 97–8) acknowledged that the 'classic mixed team' was not the only possibility for a winning team. Successful teams in industry were less likely to be mixed teams than teams of 'co-operative stable extroverts', containing team workers, resource investigators and company workers, and in these cases the introduction of a 'shaper' could improve team performance. Moreover, Belbin (ibid.: 83) found that 30 per cent of managers tested would not fit well into any team, since 'no appropriate team role' could be found for them, and suggested that although classic mixed teams exist in business, none had been identified as they are 'very difficult to detect' (ibid.: 104).

Despite its popularity and pervasiveness, therefore, there are clearly limitations to the practical application of Belbin's work. Herriot and Pemberton (1995) argue that the Myers-Briggs personality types offer a more useful framework for understanding how teams accomplish tasks than Belbin's team role model. It has also been noted that the classic mixed team is no guarantee of success since decision making in groups can be complicated by diversity (Maznevski 1994) and the team can be dominated by those with formal authority (Herriot and Pemberton 1995). The difficulties probably reflect a deterministic over-reliance on psychometric tests, irrespective of whether the Belbin or Myers-Briggs framework is adopted, to the detriment of social and organizational factors. Teams and team working are of crucial importance to OP, but team dynamics are not readily reducible to the psychological characteristics of team members. As Campion *et al.* (1993) have shown, effective work groups are influenced by a wide range of organizational characteristics, especially self-management and participation.

Team development

As Downham *et al.* (1992) noted, when individual executives are targeted for development, they benefit personally but the competence can be lost by the company if they leave. By focusing on teams, in addition to individual learning, there is an opportunity to 'develop collective knowledge that stays within the organization'. Therefore, the organization benefits much more when teams are the core learning targets.

Adair (1986) described four phases of group behaviour as forming, norming, storming and performing, which can be related to the team development cycle proposed by Bal (1995: 148–9). The start of the cycle, when the team is formed, is characterized by 'uncertainty' as team members begin to understand the task and identify the roles each will play in the team. At the 'clarification' stage of the cycle, team members question 'the validity of the task or the qualifications of individual members including the leader' and strive to steer the team in the most appropriate direction. When team members begin to recognize how individuals can work together to achieve team objectives, the 'agreement' stage has been reached. When objectives and the means of attaining them are clearly recognized, the team cycle is characterized as 'full-steam ahead'. Successful team effort can result in 'complacency' when a team loses its 'vitality', and Bal argues that this is the time for the team development cycle to begin again.

Team working has become a major focus of initiatives to raise OP, and self-managed teams (SMTs) have been associated with productivity improvements of up to 30 per cent (Hoerr 1989). The benefits claimed for SMTs include individuals assuming greater responsibility and developing more comprehensive skills, as well as 'a longer-term, more strategic perspective' (Mullen 1992). A key purpose of SMTs, and a major source of increased motivation and performance, is the self-actualization of individuals, so the manager, supervisor or team leader role moves away from supervision towards developing team members (Manz and Sims 1987; Bundy and Thurston 1990).

The introduction of SMTs inevitably offers opportunities for de-layering, with the removal of a tier of supervision, but this also demands that teams are developed to internalize supervisory roles (Simmons and Blitzmann 1986). While empowerment of SMTs has been widely associated with improved OP, implementation is difficult because 'the approach challenges our traditional ways of managing' (Salem *et al.* 1992). Mullen (1992) explored the implications of introducing SMTs in the MD curriculum to establish a common set of team work skills across the organization and provide a framework for structuring experiential activities.

Teams were often established for group problem-solving, but as organizations invested in team-building dynamics to improve their effectiveness, it became necessary for SMTs to adopt management tools. Team-based anticipatory learning, where SMTs develop the necessary skills for future activities, is seen as the key development issue for the next decade (Sashkin and Franklin 1993). Fulmer (1992) cites such authorities as Tom Peters and the *Harvard Business Review* in arguing the importance of team-based anticipatory learning for developing competitive advantage.

Feedback is another tool which has been widely used to develop effective teams. Lawrence and Wiswell (1993) reported positive effects of training in feedback skills which was designed to improve managers' interactions with their natural work groups. Hackman (1987) similarly stressed the importance of feedback in the design and operation of effective work teams. Thomas *et al.* (1992) described the use of upward feedback at PBX to enable managers to improve their people management skills and to build team work. Difficult areas of discussion were more easily raised through upward feedback, which came to represent 'an important symbol of change to the staff'. Feedback can illuminate performance gaps which can be corrected through developing new competences, but in well-established organizations negative feedback is slow to evolve, creating barriers to learning and the development of learning systems (DiBella *et al.* 1996: 44).

Bal (1995: 146) argues that effective team development is dependent upon establishing trust and collaboration, without which the environment is not conducive to an exchange of ideas and learning. Effective communication within and between teams is also vital for the success of team objectives in order to facilitate debate and feedback. Multiskilling enables team members to utilize a wider range of skills, enabling the team to solve problems without the need to bring in external expertise. Senior management sponsorship of the team ensures the most effective outcomes of team working. Teams also need to be allocated time to devote to projects and should be located on the same site because 'working in close proximity engenders a feeling of belonging' and encourages freer discussion and debate (ibid.: 147).

Team performance

Team working has provided the means of utilizing the skills and competences of a whole range of employees rather than being restricted to the limited capabilities of individuals, and the effective use of teams has a major impact on OP (Shea and Guzzo 1987). Performance management, however, has tended to remain focused on IP, which is of little use in understanding team performance (Baker and Salas 1992). Where team performance is measured, output criteria, such as effectiveness, efficiency, quality and productivity, are commonly used (Sink *et al.* 1984). Alternative process measures have been proposed which focus on group-produced outputs, the implications of group membership and group capacity for future performance (Guzzo and Dickson 1996). Russ-Eft *et al.* (1997: 137) reconcile the two approaches to present composite range of performance criteria and indicators for teams.

It is widely recognized that HRD plays a crucial role in improving OP, but the relationship between individual competence and OP is poorly understood. Given the case for reframing MD to focus on organizational renewal (Lippitt 1982; Doyle 1995), there is a need to develop greater understanding of how development operates at the intervening organizational levels. What limited research is available tends to focus on 'key or core organizational competences', at the level of the firm, so that individual and organizational competences are rarely linked (Nordhaug 1993: 80). Individual performance is commonly viewed as more important to the business than team performance, especially in sectors like computing, where 'the durability of vital competences is generally very short' and developing employee competences is a crucial determinant of OP (Nordhaug 1993: 92). As a consequence, attention is focused on core employees responsible for generating most revenue, neglecting the potential for performance improvements involving all employees through team working (Bal 1995: 145).

Team work is viewed as a critical factor in gaining competitive advantage because of its contribution to increasing responsiveness to changing markets and its potential to improve BP in a relatively easy and cost-effective way. The establishment of multiskilled SMTs with the authority and responsibility to introduce new processes to raise efficiency and increase value added, creates the conditions in which HRD becomes a continuous process. Effective performance is achieved through empowerment which allows the team a sufficient degree of self-sufficiency to make the decisions necessary to achieve team goals, and cooperation can be enhanced by focusing remuneration on team performance rather than rewarding individuals.

Since individuals and work teams embody the competence of the firm, there is a need to explore the link between individual and team competence in relation to the competence base of the organization (Nordhaug 1993: 244). Aoki (1986: 25) argues that 'team competence' can only be formed in the context of the organization and since it is related directly to a specific group of individuals, ceases to exist if the team is disbanded. For Bal (1995: 145), however, once a project team is disbanded and its members join other teams in the organization, this provides a mechanism for organizational learning, disseminating best practice and breaking down organizational barriers through cross-fertilization.

The success of a company is not necessarily a function of individual managers carrying out their responsibilities because there are often conflicts between the objectives of different departments. Organizational success depends upon developing a corporate way of thinking through adopting a team-role approach to management and avoiding functional dominance (Belbin 1981: 87). Team performance is a function of the performance of all its members and not of individuals, but if individuals within the team underperform in relation to their colleagues then the group will exert pressure to conform and contribute to collective output (Nordhaug 1993: 234). However, the informal group norms which regulate teams are not necessarily directed towards achieving high performance. Developing new competences and improving performance may be difficult where there is collective resistance to the acquisition of new competences, for example, where a team is suspicious of management motives for enskilling (ibid.: 204).

Learning in organizations

Given the central role of the work team in raising organizational efficiency, it is important to develop mechanisms to facilitate team learning beyond the level of individuals. This section therefore explores how learning takes place in teams and how team working may be promoted, how this relates to the concept of organizational learning and the special conditions which apply in small enterprises.

Learning in teams

Nordhaug (1993: 223, 248) argues that the 'joint capacity to learn in organizations' is the critical factor for the future survival of the firm, and 'learning in teams is likely to be the dominant type of competence generation' at all levels of the organization. Reducing learning barriers and identifying the factors that facilitate learning are therefore key to maintaining the foundation for efficient OP. Certainly there is abundant evidence that organizations are establishing teams to undertake 'learning' tasks, such as developing new products or re-engineering processes, recognizing that single individuals do not have the capacity or range of competences to take on such projects.

Despite the extensive literature on teams and group dynamics, relatively little is known about the collective learning process in teams, although much of what is known about adult learning processes appear to be relevant (Dechant *et al.* 1993). Starting from Kolb's perspective of learning as the transformation of experience into knowledge, and of knowledge as 'socially distributed and socially constructed', Brooks (1994) explored the process of team learning and identified the distribution of formal power within teams as a critical determinant of the production of knowledge by teams. DiBella *et al.* (1996: 44) stress the value of identifying performance gaps even when teams cannot identify exactly what knowledge or skill is missing, since 'awareness of ignorance can be a powerful motivator of learning initiative'.

Action learning programmes have been developed around MD involving groups to improve OP (Revans 1971). Henderson (1993: 22) argues that action learning provides an ideal mechanism for focusing development on organizational needs. Storey *et al.* (1997: 96) similarly note a revival of interest in 'competency-based action learning'. In an action learning programme established at GEC in the 1970s, it was found that 'it was possible to combine personal development with improvements in organizational effectiveness' (Casey and Pearce 1977: 121). Participants in the programme demonstrated 'increased ability and willingness to consider wider corporate issues'. Drew and Davidson (1993), who describe the use of management simulation for individual, group and organizational learning, note that 'organizational learning has become an important strategic concern'.

In 1986, the BAT Industries Group Management Centre attempted to integrate education and skill development for managers, with a view to improving IP in implementing OS. The pilot programme was successful, but it was evident that business objectives would have been better served if the managers had involved their whole teams in the programme. Teams were involved in future MD initiatives and Butler (1990: 37) found evidence that each of the teams that had participated 'subsequently implemented new strategies, the success of which has yet to be fully validated'. Wille (1990), researching best practice in MD with respect to the relationship between MD and business policy, similarly concluded that the most effective approaches were those which developed all employees and not just a management elite.

Nordhaug (1993: 128) identifies the neglect of competence transfer between teams and employees, recommending that teams document, in writing, their knowledge, skills and experiences so that these can be used by other individuals and teams. Some organizations require project teams to routinely produce this type of material to facilitate competence transfer. However, individual team members who are 'egocentric' rather than 'collective' in their attitudes will resist learning from other team members (Driskell and Salas 1992).

Organizational learning

In the pioneering work of Argyris and Schön (1978: 3), single-loop learning, which involves detecting and correcting errors, is distinguished from double-loop learning, which entails modifying norms, policies and objectives. Where organizational learning is most effective, it represents 'deutero-learning':

> members [of the organization] learn about previous contexts for learning. They reflect on and enquire into previous episodes of organizational learning, or failure to learn. They discover what they did that facilitated or inhibited learning, they invent new strategies for learning, they produce these strategies, and they evaluate and generalize what they have produced.
>
> (Argyris and Schön 1978: 4)

The distinction between single-loop and double-loop learning is paralleled in what Fiol and Lyles (1985) term lower and higher level learning, and Dodgson (1991) terms tactical and strategic learning. Low-level, tactical learning is concerned with adding to the organization's knowledge base, whereas high-level, strategic learning is concerned with developing organizational competence. In addition to adaptive learning to cope with external change Senge (1990a: 8) argues that organizations need to develop generative learning based on more holistic understanding of systems.

Employing the distinction introduced in relation to individual learning, between cognitive learning to understand and use new concepts, and behavioural (affective) learning related to the physical ability to act, Garvin (1993) identifies three stages in organizational learning. During the initial stage, cognitive learning leads to the alteration and improvement of thought patterns and knowledge base. These changes are translated into new work practices in the subsequent behavioural learning stage. During the third stage, the actions which followed cognitive and behavioural learning lead to visible performance improvement for the organization considered. Despite the intrinsic appeal of such a rational analysis of organizational learning, it fails to recognize the importance of interactions between cognitive and affective learning, and, crucially, does not articulate the mechanisms by which individual learning translates into organizational learning.

Kim's (1993) analysis also incorporates the learning function of active memory, of pivotal importance in the transfer from individual to organizational learning. Kim's terminology of 'conceptual' and 'operational' learning (instead of cognitive and affective learning) is perhaps more readily applicable to an organizational context. Conceptual learning occurs through assessment and design, while the ensuing implementation and observation correspond to operational learning. The conceptual–operational learning cycle describes the knowledge acquisition process. It is not built around linear cause and effect relationships, but on the interaction between the two types of learning. Indeed, in some cases, conceptual learning may lead to operational learning and in others the reverse may be true.

Both Senge (1990a) and Kim (1993) suggest that the transfer between individual learning and organizational learning is based on the development of shared mental models and is essentially incremental. Individual learning experiences and individual mental models progressively become explicit and lead to the formation of shared mental models, more commonly described as organizational culture (Schein 1985). Organizational learning is a complex process (Starkey 1996), representing more than the cumulative effect of individual learning experiences: 'organizations do not have brains, but they have cognitive systems and memories' (Hedberg 1981: 3). The existence of a common organizational culture, or shared mental models, facilitates the progessive adoption by the organization of individual routines that improve on existing practices. The incorporation of tacit knowledge (Spender 1996) and individual routines into organizational routines represents a concrete operationalization of the organization's memory and knowledge base. Andreu and Ciborra (1996: 112) similarly demonstrate how core capabilities are developed in organizations through a transformation which combines resources with organizational routines; 'the transformation is a path-dependent learning process'.

Waterman (1994: 15) concluded that a small number of American firms perform well because they 'learn from the best' and 'find role models to emulate' in the same way that people learn naturally, rather than through the more common 'trial and error learning' adopted by most companies.

Organizational learning in small firms

The small firm represents a particular environment for learning which provides individuals with opportunities to undertake a wider range of tasks than would normally be available, and which demands a correspondingly broader range of competences in order for individuals to perform effectively. Definitions of tasks and skills are often more flexible and change more often than in larger organizations. Standards and vocational qualifications have limited relevance in a context where day-to-day issues form the basis of learning and the specification of occupational skill is so dynamic. Experiential learning is therefore a key process in smaller firms, where the emphasis is on learning from the job context and acquiring new occupational skills, as opposed to providing basic occupational learning (Hendry *et al.* 1995: 153).

Against these advantages, small firms have limited resources for training, often no formal training budgets, and owners may feel that it is not worth training individuals as they are poached or leave (Hendry *et al.* 1995: 155). Where the company has only a limited scope of tasks and activities it is unlikely that staff will be trained beyond this level, and if the firm is growing quickly there is often no time available for training. The general trend in organizations towards de-layering, self-management and empowerment is not particularly relevant in SMEs, but similar results arise naturally because of the small number of managers they typically employ. Small firms are generally unable to provide the type of career structure which would naturally promote MD and managers need to move between firms to attain any significant degree of career progression and development (ibid.: 162–4). Managers in the fastest-growing smaller firms are more likely to have been previously employed in larger organizations, as these types of companies have growth aspirations and need supporting managerial expertise. However development did not occur through changing firms, but as a result of promotion, a new job providing the context for individual learning and development. The whole process is largely *ad hoc* and the only formal training and development arise from the need for 'remedial and keeping up to date in technical aspects, rather than as preparation for a new job or involving fundamental education' (ibid.: 165). The three exceptions to this were studying for professional qualifications, specific behavioural skills training (such as to improve team work) and coaching. The 'succession issue' is identified as a means of stimulating management development; although there are many entrepreneurs who find it hard to address this issue viewing the firm as an extension of themselves and their own particular skills which no one else would be able to replicate.

Organizational performance outcomes

The extent to which MD had contributed to improvements in OP was explored in the sixteen organizations studied for the competence-based management development project (Winterton and Winterton 1996). The sixteen cases were ranked according to the robustness of evidence that MD had contributed to improvements in OP using the three key criteria identified in the report of the study group (Leman *et al.* 1994):

- improvements in team performance have been tracked (and can be shown to relate to the Management Standards);
- improvements in the use of teams and their specialist roles can be demonstrated;
- lower rates of accidents, failures, returns, wastage, complaints, etc. can be demonstrated.

Overall, the cases were ranked against these criteria along a continuum according to the extent of improvements in OP and the robustness of evidence identified. The ranking was undertaken by independent consultants on the basis of the validated case reports and written evidence (see Chapter 3).

In this section, the best cases are considered first, where the critical importance of MD to major improvements in OP was demonstrated through written evidence and corroborated interviews. Cases are then discussed in which evidence was provided of specific moderate improvements in OP arising out of MD activities. In the best cases the central importance of MD to overall improvement in OP was corroborated by interviews and written evidence. In three of these organizations, improvements in OP were explicitly linked to the use of the Management Standards. The importance of team performance and team working is highlighted. More effective team performance, involving flexibility and team working were reported in most of the cases where improvements in OP were identified, while quality initiatives were emphasized in other cases. Difficulties in measuring OP were acknowledged even in the best cases, either because the measures were subject to external influences or because OP was difficult to isolate from IP and BP. The evidence of improvements in OP draws upon the eleven best cases, while the problems of measurement and attribution also include details from the remaining five cases.

The evidence is presented under four headings:

1 major improvements in OP attributed to MD;
2 moderate improvements in OP attributed to MD;
3 team performance and team working;
4 problems of measurement and attribution.

Major improvements in OP attributed to MD

The five cases which were ranked highest provided robust evidence of improvements in OP, which were attributed to MD and, in three cases, to the use of the Management Standards. Improvements in OP were measured in terms of productivity, efficiency and quality of service, and often centred on more effective team working.

In the engineering company, organizational and departmental productivity and effectiveness are measured by means of contractually specified milestones (deadlines for completion of stages of the project), productivity and other types of targets which are cascaded down to teams from project level. Examples of improved OP arising from MD included improved procedures for controlling and handling materials as well as the identification of potential areas for improvement in the future, e.g. in relation to information systems. Several respondents also suggested that a heightened awareness of the importance of maintaining and developing the customer base was resulting in improved relationships with customers (case 5).

In the Magistrates' Courts, objectives are set and agreed between the Management Board and the Magistrates' Courts Committee (MCC) and OP is measured in terms of achievements against these objectives. Targets are established in terms of 'volume of processing' and 'response rates', as well as customer service measures, which are monitored through the official management information system (MIS) statistics, considered in this report as measures of BP. The MIS statistics are used to judge the effectiveness of departments, as is inter-departmental feedback. As a result of MD activities, quality improvements were evident: 'improvements in dealing with customers and reduced queues' (case 9).

In the retail company, the senior financial manager felt that almost every aspect of team performance was measured against the designated budgets for each area, for example, sales and expenditure were all compared against budgets under various headings. MD was necessary in order to facilitate the introduction of a computerized stock system which has cut costs enormously. MD has provided managers with the necessary skills to operate and train staff to use the new system (case 3).

The HR specialists in the aeroplane components company distinguished the Business Development Groups (BDGs), in which OP is measured by 'sales', from manufacturing, in which OP is measured by 'standard hours as a percentage of actual hours' (a measure of output achieved per unit of labour input). Line managers outlined how OP is measured in each department against fixed objectives and targets outlined in the Departmental Plan, which reflects the impact of business objectives on the 'functional requirements of the department'. The HR Director related MD to OP because of the role which MD played in 'restructuring operations to reduce ineffective working and the focus on environmental issues' (case 12).

Improvements in OP were explicitly linked with the use of the Management Standards in three cases. Respondents from the engineering group independently cited improvements in internal communications as a result of participation in MCI. In one company, supervisors and charge-hands had begun collecting written evidence for portfolios and continued the practice because staff were then able to check whether actions agreed at meetings and quality circles had been carried out (case 5). In the Magistrates' Courts, it was noted that 'groups of people working on the Standards together raises awareness of the constraints and pressures on colleagues', which improves OP (case 9). Similarly, in the retail company, having followed the MCI development programme, managers are able to identify weak performance and keep a branch and its staff on track. The senior HR manager also mentioned debt control, service delivery and first time fix on repairs as elements of OP monitoring (case 3).

Moderate improvements in OP attributed to MD

In a further six cases, verified evidence was provided of specific or isolated improvements in OP arising out of MD activities. Examples from these organizations are quoted below, with the most robust evidence considered first.

In one of the NHS Trusts, team or departmental performance is measured against agreed objectives through the business planning system in areas such as service development, cost efficiency and overall budgetary performance. Various service improvements were reported, including reduced length of stay, increased number of finished customer episodes, a higher rate of bed occupancy and more effective, multi-disciplinary working. Services are now more targeted on patient needs and quicker discharges are possible because of better 'patient management' skills (case 11).

In the mining company, measures of OP depended on the section or department involved, and in the mine there are very clear production targets. Written evidence demonstrated the major improvements in OP which have occurred: the development rate has increased by 24 per cent, and tonnage has increased by 8 per cent on the previous year's monthly average. Senior managers noted that as a result of MD, people are thinking more, there is more strategic behaviour, better relationships and more transparency (case 1).

In the newspaper organization, OP involves both financial measures of departmental performance and 'key tasks', such as 'time targets' for editorial departments and 'effectiveness of delivery' for distribution, which define the success factors – 'what must be achieved'. Senior managers with responsibility for HRD believed that there were 'indications that MD has delivered benefits' in OP (case 10).

In three cases, quality and service improvements were highlighted. In the insurance company, for example, the Management Information and Control System (MICS) which recorded work performance against targets set for individuals and teams was being dismantled and replaced by Customer First. The new system focuses on the achievement of team targets agreed in the annual plan, in accordance with defined 'standards of service to achieve the mission', which are measured daily and monitored monthly. Team targets, 'derived from the business plan', are 'agreed annually and may be reviewed'. Senior managers noted that MD had led to improved OP because 'all managers have expanded their knowledge base and built effective teams'. Line managers similarly explained how team building courses had created 'identity and bonding' within departments. Departmental performance standards include quality measures, such as 'turnaround times' and 'telephone standards', which are combined into a Departmental Quality Index (DQI), reporting on business produced within standard and quality. The senior financial manager believed that MD had made a significant contribution to improving quality throughout the organization (case 7).

In the government agency, the major measurable aspect of OP is how well teams perform to nationally determined targets, measured by computer monitoring of budgets, delivery, quality and time. In one district, teams were meeting 31 out of 36 targets, which was a vast improvement on the previous year's performance when 23 out of 36 targets were achieved. Senior management attributed these improvements to MD, which developed and trained staff to provide a more efficient level of service. A Quality Framework was launched in May 1993 and has enabled all parts of the organization to monitor their progress towards improving quality, consolidated performance in new target areas and improved the accuracy of payments. A 'Mystery Shopper' has been introduced to monitor customer service standards against criteria such as how long it takes for the telephone to be answered and the quality of information provided (case 6).

In the galvanizing company, there are various departmental and team targets, such as materials consumption, which is important because zinc is an expensive metal. Senior managers believed that the organization operates more effectively because MD has brought a more structured organization of work, a greater understanding of responsibilities and a willingness to work flexibly. Maintaining quality standards is crucial to the success of the business, and MD has contributed to this (case 2).

Team performance and team working

More effective team performance, involving flexibility and team working, was reported in seven organizations where improvements in OP were identified. Improved team performance was noted by managers in the Magistrates' Courts, and attributed both to individual MD and to team development projects, which resulted in increased 'team awareness and effectiveness'. Team members explained how job rotation had resulted in 'better team working: individuals will automatically move to help where there is workload pressure' (case 9). Team members in the retail company also felt that MD had improved team performance: 'MD motivates people and makes them more aware of the direct importance of company profits to each individual and how they can work together as a team to improve them' (case 3).

In the aeroplane components company, managers identified improved team performance, such as more 'flexibility and commitment', as a result of MD introduced to support business process re-engineering (BPR). Half of the supervisors were returned to manufacturing activities, and the remainder were trained as cell leaders, in 'problem solving, setting objectives and meeting targets'. All tasks are now undertaken within multiskilled cells, and OP has improved in terms of quality, efficiency and effectiveness. Evidence of 'more effective team working' and of 'more cooperative relationships between teams' was attributed to 'team working courses for department heads and cell leaders' (case 12).

In the footwear company, team working is perceived as being the key to improving OP, making the company competitive and staying in business. MD has allowed the development of team working, and the two developments have fostered greater flexibility. Managers had no reservation in identifying the beneficial effects of shopfloor team working on productivity in the factory. MD enabled managers to develop the skills necessary to form and motivate the teams to pull together and vastly improve their performance and hence the performance of the factory (case 15).

As an example of improvements in team performance arising from MD in one of the NHS Trusts, some interviewees noted how several managers from the same department undertook development activities at the same time, and therefore were able to work better as a team as each became more aware of the others' roles. With the skills gained from their MD, the team was able to take forward and implement a new 'patient focused care' initiative (case 11).

In the mining company, two line managers cited improvements in OP as a result of MD designed to promote team working. For example, relations between the 'mining and engineering departments had improved because engineering staff were now involved in production target meetings'. Another manager anticipated significant improvements in team working following the development of shift bosses because 'the shift boss is the crucial linchpin and all communication should go through him without management circumventing this'. Team members cited 'better liaison between the engineering and mining departments', and 'more effective organization of manpower by shift bosses' as a result of MD initiatives (case 1).

Line managers in the newspaper company thought that improvements in OP as a result of MD initiatives were visible in the changes in team behaviour, including performance and the dynamics of work groups. Team members reported improvements in OP resulting from MD in most departments. In sales, training had 'enabled the team to perform better on features', although one team member believed it was difficult to identify improvements in OP in the sales environment. In distribution, after seventeen years of 'authoritarian management', the new manager introduced 'improved communication and team working', and the team demonstrated 'increased confidence and performance improvements within six weeks'. In the editorial department, 'weekly news meetings improved performance through better communication and getting the team to take responsibility for generating new ideas' (case 10).

Problems of measurement and attribution

Difficulties in measuring OP were acknowledged even in organizations where there was evidence of improvements, either because measures were subject to external influences or were difficult to separate from IP or BP. Problems of measurement and attribution were greatest in the cases where the evidence was least robust. In the weakest cases, the measurement of OP at all was inherently problematic, while the problem of separating OP from IP was emphasized in over half of the organizations studied. Either OP measures were seen to be indistinguishable from IP measures, or OP was viewed as a function of the manager's IP. In two cases where there was robust evidence of improvements in OP, the measures were nevertheless confounded by extraneous influences or were difficult to isolate from measures of BP.

Improvement in OP in the newspaper company were 'less dramatic' than improvements in IP 'because more effective team working is difficult to identify' (case 10). Similarly, in one of the NHS Trusts, measures for team or departmental performance are in some areas similar to those for the managers of those teams or departments. Interviewees found it difficult to identify improvements in performance across teams or departments as a result of MD (case 16). In another NHS Trust, there are no explicit standards of performance measurement, other than meeting deadlines and producing work of an acceptable standard, and a senior financial manager felt that this lack of standards made it difficult to achieve meaningful measurement of the performance of management teams (case 13).

In the government agency, team and individual targets are essentially the same, so team members felt that team performance targets didn't really exist; in their place was a set of IP measures amalgamated at district level (case 6). In the clothing company, team results are arrived at by individual effort and although team targets are the major performance measurement, managers need to be aware of an individual operative's contribution to those targets, 'in order to increase team performance it is necessary to look at individual performance' (case 14). In some instances, IP is measured rather than team performance in the oil company. At the organizational level the impact of participation in the MCI programme was more difficult to identify than the benefits accruing to individuals (case 4).

In the retail company, team or OP is viewed by senior management as a direct function of a manager's IP. If the individual manager develops, this has a knock-on effect on their team, 'the more competent the manager, the more competent the team; they set the standards for others and this is how we achieve quality of operations' in the company (case 3).

Similarly, for the majority of managers in the aeroplane components company, improvements in OP, such as 'reduced direct labour costs per hour', were attributed to the 'effectiveness of training cell leaders', and the 'improved motivation' in the Engineering Department was associated by a development engineer with the appointment of a new manager, and perhaps his MD (case 12). In such cases, the improvements in OP ought to have been captured by IP.

In two cases, measures of OP were confounded by extraneous influences or were difficult to isolate from measures of BP. While performance within the Magistrates' Courts is most closely measured, monitored and analysed at the level of OP, these measures are complicated by diverse national targets and the impact of others involved in the administration of justice; new Police Standards, for example, have slowed down the Magistrates' Courts performance (case 9). In the aeroplane components company, senior managers noted the difficulty in separating departmental measures of OP from the measures of BP and suggested that it is problematic to relate improvements in OP to MD. The Task Forces determined business strategy, which had led to MD, but the process was 'informal: MD arose out of the need to be competitive and from BPR and the associated changes' (case 12).

Summary and conclusions

The objective of this chapter was to investigate what contribution MD makes to improving team performance, which is viewed as a level of analysis linking the individual with the organization as a whole. To do this, it was necessary to investigate factors influencing organizational efficiency, the nature of learning in organizations and the outcomes of increased competence in terms of improvements in OP.

In considering organizational efficiency, attention has focused on building effective teams through combining individual competences and competencies, and creating a supportive organizational environment. Stages of group behaviour were discussed and related to the cyclical development of teams. The measurement of team performance was shown to have been neglected in comparison with individual measurement, and output measures were contrasted with process measures.

This chapter also addressed issues of developing team working and team competence as distinct from the competence of individual members. Approaches to team learning such as action learning were discussed. The concept of organizational learning was introduced, and stages parallel to those in individual learning process identified. Attention was focused on the crucial question of the transfer from individual to organizational learning. The special difficulties and opportunities for organizational learning in SMEs were also discussed.

Finally, this chapter reviewed the evidence of improvements in OP arising out of MD in the sixteen organizations studied. In the organizations where there was most robust evidence of significant improvement in OP attributed to MD, the improvements most often mentioned included the following:

- quality of service;
- cost reductions and efficiency gains;
- focus on customer needs;
- reduced queues;
- better procedures and monitoring of actions;
- more effective debt control;
- better telephone standards and improved customer relations;
- more strategic behaviour.

Where significant improvements in organizational performance were attributed to management development initiatives designed to promote team working, the following benefits were identified:

- flexibility;
- awareness of team responsibilities and more effective working as a team;
- increased commitment and motivation;
- improved inter-personal and inter-departmental relations;
- better communications.

There were major difficulties of measurement of organizational performance and of attributing improvements to management development, especially in the organizations which provided less robust evidence. The main difficulties identified were:

- the same measures were used for organizational performance and individual performance;
- organizational performance was seen as a function of manager's performance;
- organizational performance was affected by extraneous factors;
- organizational performance was difficult to separate from business performance.

8 Business performance

This chapter is concerned with the relationship between MD and business performance (BP). The focus is on how improvements in individual and team performance are translated into corporate success. The concerns include how business success is related to core competences, ways of creating the conditions for a learning organization and measuring improvements in BP at the organizational level.

The chapter is organized into three sections:

1   defining corporate success;
2   corporate learning;
3   business performance outcomes.

The first section considers corporate success in terms of both financial and non-financial measures of BP. However defined, business success depends upon the organization achieving certain critical success factors. The attainment of these factors, in turn, depends upon the organization's capacity to maintain and develop core competences, those activities and collective skills which give the organization its competitive advantage. Through developing core competence to attain critical success factors, MD can contribute to identifiable improvements in BP.

The second section considers the scope for learning between teams and at the level of the organization as a whole, focusing on how MD can be linked with improvements in BP. The nature of 'corporate learning' is explored in terms of how cognitive systems and organizational cultures adapt or adopt routines and shared mental models to improve on existing practices. The utility of the concept of a learning organization as a framework for developing core competence is discussed and a model for building a learning organization is proposed.

The third section presents our findings from case studies of sixteen organizations undertaken in researching the business benefits of competence-based management development. The evidence is presented first from those organizations where major improvements in BP were attributed to MD, then from the organizations where more moderate improvements were demonstrated. The ways in which MD had led to specific improvements in BP are outlined and problems of measurement and attribution of improvements in BP are discussed.

The chapter concludes with a brief summary identifying the salient points of the discussion and the main findings of the case studies.

Defining corporate success

What constitutes corporate success is neither self-evident nor unambiguous. In for-profit organizations, it might be assumed that profitability is the main measure, but for some organizations operating in a hostile environment, survival itself may constitute success. Where it is appropriate to consider success in financial terms, there is a range of possible measures. In the long run, even in financial terms, growth and increased market share may be more important than profitability as measures of the future capacity for producing profit. In not-for-profit organizations, non-financial measures of BP have been developed and many organizations have adopted these in the pursuit of competitive advantage. The environment in which an organization operates defines the critical success factors which must be attained in order to survive in terms of BP. The business plan and organizational strategy are therefore designed to support the attainment of these critical factors (see Chapter 4). The organization's core competences must be developed and maintained against these critical success factors in order to be successful. In this section, measures of BP, critical success factors and core competences are therefore considered in turn.

Measuring business performance

Measuring and evaluating BP is a recurrent theme in the management literature. Much of the work in the for-profit sector is concerned with financial measures of performance such as profitability, earnings per share (EPS) and market share, although a better indication of BP in terms of financial performance is provided by operating performance ratios. The most widely used is *trading profit/turnover*, which is susceptible to influence by exchange rates and short-run fluctuations in demand and can be misleading when an organization accepts low margins in order to raise market share. A second performance ratio commonly employed is *trading profit/capital employed*, or the return on capital employed, which varies with factor intensity and accounting policies on the valuation of capital assets. A third ratio is *turnover/capital employed*, which can give a misleading impression where a firm is either failing to invest or investing heavily. Although these three ratios are inter-related, they provide a better overview of business performance when considered together, rather than in isolation.

Depending upon the nature of a company, there is a wide range of other criteria of business performance which may be used. For example, a crude measure of a firm's profitability in relation to its size is provided by *profit/employee*, although *profits/wages* is better because it is less susceptible to distortion by differences in labour costs. Where *value added/employee* is used, this focuses attention on how the firm's activities contribute to wealth creation, although *value added/wages* similarly takes into account variations in labour costs.

The ratio of *stock/turnover* measures the number of times stock is turned over in sales during a particular trading period, and shows whether a business is expanding or contracting in relation to past business performance. Financial ratios are inevitably sector-specific, reflecting operating constraints and the market conditions in which firms compete.

Financial performance indicators form the key performance measures common to organizations and systems for tracking financial performance are embedded in organizational structure, although they are not necessarily comparable because of different accounting methods. The measurement of other indicators like quality, customer satisfaction and market share is less embedded in organizations and data are gathered on a more sporadic basis. Resources need to be invested to develop systems for monitoring other performance measures and if such information is widely disseminated, the possibilities for increasing management autonomy are increased, as managers have adequate information available to make key developmental decisions for themselves and the organization.

There has been a shift in emphasis from largely financial to a more broadbased set of performance indicators, which develop with the organization and the changing environment in which it operates. Information technology facilitates monitoring a wider range of performance measures, so organizations need to determine the key categories of performance and establish adequate measurement systems. Individual organizations pursuing different strategies may require different performance measures, but a few critical measures appear common to all companies.

Eccles (1991) argued that managers were increasingly recognizing that performance measurement should no longer be based solely on the measurement of financial statistics and that other criteria were equally important. Although other aspects of performance such as quality and market share are traced by management in many organizations, these had not, until relatively recently, been given equal emphasis with financial performance measures. The search for a longerterm strategy for business success has led managers to identify what constitutes the most important measures of BP for their organization. Performance measures related to quality became prevalent during the 1980s as the TQM movement promoted the view that quality could give businesses a leading edge in highly competitive markets. Concern for customer satisfaction in the 1990s evolved from the quality movement of the 1980s and benchmarking best practice is the natural progression, measuring performance against competitors (Dence 1995).

Critical success factors

Fonda (1989: 50) defined critical success factors as those things which absolutely must be achieved for an organization to survive, grow and be profitable: 'The organizational capability to achieve these "critical success factors" is a result of the management capability of the firm'. Hence MD contributes to improved BP by developing managerial competences and thereby raising the organization's capability to achieve the objectives necessary to satisfy the critical success factors.

Kay (1993) argues that the key measure of corporate success is value added, defining this as the difference between the value of an organization's outputs and the costs of its inputs. While corporate success is normally judged in terms of returns to investors, market performance may be an inadequate indicator of corporate effectiveness, which is better judged by comparing the performance of different companies in the same markets. Although the profitability of an organization or its size or its share of the market are all important aspects of its success, it is value added which produces shareholder dividends, generates higher financial returns and provides the financial basis for the future development of the organization.

Although factors may be defined as critical to performance and hence to competitive advantage, these differ between industries and enterprises (Goold *et al.* 1995). Business plans should address the critical success factors and these need not be reiterated in developing corporate strategy, but it is necessary to explore the extent to which they have altered as a result of changes in the external environment.

In order for an organization to attain the critical success factors and gain competitive advantage, its managers need to learn from best practice in other organizations. Appropriate performance measures, such as comparative cost and quality performance, must be identified to benchmark. Benchmarking may involve comparing an organization's performance with similar organizations or divisions of the same corporation, or with leading edge organizations in *different* sectors that have comparable business processes (Zairi 1996). Benchmarking forms an important part of a BP improvement strategy, since it identifies those aspects of processes which give competitive advantage enabling the performance gap between the organization and best practice organizations to be assessed. Benchmarking can be a positive source for change, but cannot predict the future performance of comparable organizations and must therefore be continually revised.

The public sector, health service and local government have shown considerable interest in benchmarking and Dence (1995) notes that the performance indicators introduced in these sectors focus on providing better customer service and value for money. Smith (1993) explores the effectiveness of outcome-related performance indicators (ORPI) in the public sector. There are particular problems when applying these to public rather than the private sector. There is little agreement regarding what the output objectives of public sector organizations should be, how to measure these outputs and what the results of any systematic analysis actually mean. Nevertheless, initiatives like the Citizen's Charter which advocates the wider dissemination of public sector performance data cannot be ignored. The aim is to produce a more efficient and effective manager, but there is a risk of management disaffection over a system being imposed on them. When individual rewards are linked to ORPI schemes, managers may be tempted to focus on the narrow objectives addressed by the ORPI system to the exclusion of other more strategic organizational objectives.

Not-for-profit organizations can be assessed by means of performance indicators. These approaches are essentially strategic in that they assess the performance of the whole organization. A way of avoiding the distinction between for-profit and not-for-profit is to break down the corporate or holistic into a more functionally oriented view and examine the effects of various functions within the total organization. The adoption of a 'balanced scoreboard' approach to benchmarking similarly offers a more reliable assessment of BP by introducing a wider range of performance measures (Kaplan and Norton 1993). In this approach, an organization is benchmarked against four sets of performance measures: having a customer perspective; process capability; focus on innovation; and value added for shareholders.

Core competences

Hussey (1996: 115), referring to Tovey (1992), argues that core competences are synonymous with and have replaced the concept of critical success factors. In our understanding, however, critical success factors define the organization's operational parameters for success in a particular environment, whereas core competences define the activities for which the organization has a special aptitude. To assess the impact of MD on BP, it is necessary to analyse the organization's environment and identify the critical success factors against which it has to develop competences to be successful. Therefore, MD can be seen as a strategic tool which organizations can use as a source of strategic advantage. The result of this approach is that, to be effective, MD needs to be driven by strategic issues instead of the fragmented approach of the past where individuals were sent on primarily knowledge-based programmes.

According to Hamel (1994), for a competence to be considered as core to an organization it must deliver competitive advantage and it must be recognized by customers as being key to the business in terms of its 'contribution to customer perceived value'. Therefore, while core competences do not refer to the competences of individuals, but of the organization as a whole (Hussey 1996: 38), they may represent a group of skills (of individuals and teams) and technologies which together form a critical focus for strategic success, including the ability to manage organizational assets in a unique manner. Organizational strategy (see Chapter 4) should be based on core competences and HRD strategies (see Chapter 5) should develop capabilities and skills as the company's strategic demand for core competences as these evolve with the changing external environment.

Egan's (1993) model for managing business and organizational processes identifies 'master tasks' which are broken down into sub-tasks focusing on the policies, systems and processes serving the needs of the organization rather than the individual manager. These master tasks include creating an organizational structure dedicated to the optimum flow of information and work, developing competent leaders to promote organizational innovation and to facilitate the

work of others, and establishing HRD systems and processes to raise commitment and performance. Such master tasks should not be confused with core
competences, but should be seen as creating the conditions to optimize the maintenance of the organization's core competences through developing individuals
and teams.

Tate (1995a: 140) argues that improvements in BP can only be brought about
by building 'collective management competence', but top managers may be less
enthusiastic about the development of a strong organization which reduces the
power of a small number of individuals. For Tate (ibid.: 6), dealing with
managers as individuals is an inadequate strategy for business development since
management and organization development should be integrated in order to
address organizational problems and generate business success.

Corporate learning

The need to develop mechanisms to facilitate team learning beyond the level of
individuals was emphasized in Chapter 7, and this chapter is concerned with the
scope for learning between teams and at the level of the organization as a whole.
This section therefore explores how MD can be linked with improvements in BP
and the nature of 'corporate learning'. Corporate learning represents more than
an aggregation of all the individual and team learning in an organization and is
concerned with how cognitive systems and organizational cultures adapt or
adopt routines and shared mental models, improving on existing practices to
develop core capabilities. The first challenge is in establishing a tangible link
between MD and BP, since the two can appear remote and dislocated. After
considering the link between MD and BP, this section explores the utility of the
learning organization as a conceptual framework then proposes a model for
building learning organizations.

Linking MD and BP

While the measurement of BP may involve fewer dimensions than the measurement of IP, improvements in corporate performance, which is affected by a
whole complex of internal and external factors, as well as wholly extraneous
influences, are more difficult to attribute directly to MD or training initiatives.

A Coopers and Lybrand study (1985: 9) found that the link between training
and competitive success was not acknowledged in most companies. Training
managers and senior executives alike did not view training and development as
'the cutting edge of competitiveness' of their organization. As a consequence,
training managers and HRD departments tend to have a relatively low status
within firms, they are rarely expected to be proactive in suggesting training activities, and in several companies they were not thought capable of determining the
most cost-effective responses to business needs. In the firms surveyed by Coopers
and Lybrand, training was rarely discussed at board level, with the occasional
exception of MD, while Hussey's (1988: 59) research suggested that these excep-

tions were 'more illusory than real'. The Coopers and Lybrand study also found that few companies perceived any link between training and profitability, except in so far as training was viewed as a cost which would reduce profits. Berry (1990) similarly argues that despite significant expenditure, few MD programmes really affect an organization's ability to compete.

By contrast, a later Coopers and Lybrand study (1992) provided case studies of MD in SMEs, which demonstrated a variety of benefits including increased turnover and gross margins, a more customer-oriented approach and improved ability to respond to change. Similarly, a survey of MD activity in 510 organizations undertaken by MCI found that 62 per cent of organizations reported 'improved efficiency, productivity and quality as the main benefits gained from expenditure on developing managers, whilst other gains include better qualified and motivated staff (27 per cent) and improved company profits, at 12 per cent' (King 1993: 38). Two cases studied by Downham *et al.* (1992) also demonstrate how development activities designed and executed by a company's HRD staff can contribute directly to competitive advantage.

The case of Hewlett Packard is an interesting example of how improved BP can result from MD initiatives (Carter and Lumsden 1988). In 1984, there was a major slow-down in key markets and a need to invest in new product development, while costs were rising and margins under pressure from increasing global competition. In 1986, the company experienced a 10 per cent drop in market share for PCs and pre-tax profits were almost halved. The management response in Europe centred on three corporate objectives: increased productivity; faster market response; greater customer orientation. To address these objectives, a MD programme was initiated because 'although the challenges to managers were clear, their competence and ability to respond to them needed to be considered'. The company's performance improved significantly in market penetration, cost reduction and increased competitiveness: 'managers attribute many of the substantial gains in the company's business…to the programme, both in terms of building competence and in providing a vehicle to understand what is needed and to encourage risk taking' (ibid.).

Many organizations would treat MD as an investment and, as with other investments in plant and equipment, it would be expected that benefits would be realized over a long period, often with a significant gestation or commissioning period. The impact of MD should therefore be assessed over a sufficient time period in order to allow BP improvements to be identified.

Learning organizations

The learning organization concept has its roots in several originally distinct traditions. Early writers on cybernetics (Beer 1959), organizational learning (Argyris 1962), systems theory (Miller and Rice 1967) and systems dynamics (Forrester 1961), have clearly influenced the modern ideas of the learning organization. Argyris and Schön (1996: 181) suggest that socio-technical systems, as espoused by Emery and Trist (1960), also contributed to the notion of a learning organization with 'the idea of collective participation by teams of individuals, especially workers, in developing new patterns of work, career paths, and arrangements for combining family and work lives'.

The increasing interest in learning organizations from the 1980s is evident from publications in the organization theory (Argyris 1982; Argyris and Schön 1978; 1996; Levitt and March 1988) and management literature (Garratt 1987; De Geus 1988; Moingeon and Edmondson 1996). In the UK, learning organization principles were advanced most by the Learning Company project in Sheffield (Pedler *et al.* 1988; 1989a; 1989b; 1997), while at the European level, the EUROTECNET Technical Assistance Office promoted learning organization principles in its vision for HRD on behalf of the Task Force on Human Resources, Education, Training and Youth (Nyhan 1991; Stahl *et al.* 1993).

Dodgson (1993: 376) believes that the recent resurgence of interest in learning organization principles is attributable to the conjuncture of three factors. First, there is a general recognition that large organizations must become more adaptable and responsive to change, as evidenced in recent management writing (Kanter 1989; Wickens 1995; Morgan 1997). Second, technological developments behind process and product transformations (Piore and Sabel 1984; Kern and Schumann 1987; Womack *et al.* 1990) are having a profound impact on organizations, demanding faster learning (Hayes *et al.* 1988) to facilitate accelerated restructuring (Winterton and Taplin 1997). Third, the concept of learning has 'broad analytical value' as a dynamic, 'integrative concept that can unify various levels of analysis: individual, group, corporate, which is particularly helpful in reviewing the cooperative and community nature of organizations' (Dodgson 1993: 376). Senge's (1990a; 1990b) seminal work undoubtedly both reflected and stimulated this renewed interest in the learning organization, and has become as influential as the work of Argyris and Schön.

Despite the popularity of the concept of the learning organization, Raper *et al.* (1997: 9) believe that there is no agreed definition which can be attached to the concept of the learning organization, claiming that discussions have been 'essentially aspirational and prescriptive'. Mabey (1994: 3) similarly regards Senge's view as essentially an optimistic one in assuming that 'individual employees will subscribe to a given organizational vision' and neglecting the 'incipient plurality of mass organizations'. Other critics have noted the paucity of concrete examples of learning organizations, but Dale (1993: 219) believes that attempts to identify best practice examples of learning organizations which could be replicated missed the point of the concept. While the learning organization may be an ideal to be approached and never completely attained, it is nevertheless possible from the now extensive literature to identify key principles which are recurrently associated with the concept and to point to some examples of organizations working towards the ideal.

Senge (1990a; 1990b) relates learning organization concepts to the adoption of systems thinking, team learning, shared vision, personal mastery and the use of mental models. Alexander (1987) identifies the contribution of MD to developing shared values. For Morgan (1997) the key to the learning organization is the power of metaphor in understanding processes inside organizations. Megginson and Pedler (1992) similarly emphasize the importance of vision and metaphor in their concept of the Learning Company. Pedler *et al.* (1989a) define a learning organization as one which 'facilitates the learning of all its members and continuously transforms itself'.

Building a learning organization

Several useful models and frameworks for building a learning organization have been proposed (Brooks 1992; Braham 1995; Pearn *et al.* 1995; Marsick and Watkins 1996). To build the conditions for a learning organization, learning must take place in a number of domains, representing different levels and different purposes, as shown in Figure 8.1. The starting point is learning at the individual level to meet the immediate business needs for basic occupational competence, represented by the bottom left building block in the figure. Building from this point, individual learning must be advanced to meet the organization's future needs which are known, through what Hendry *et al.* (1995: 143–5) term extended occupational learning and learning from job context, to achieve extended occupational competence. Further learning of new occupational skills (ibid.: 149) beyond the foreseeable needs of the organization leads the individual to what Senge (1990b: 142–3) describes as 'personal mastery', and represents progression towards the organization's future needs which are *unknown*.

Once individuals have achieved basic occupational competence, team learning can be developed to meet the immediate needs of the organization, drawing on the synergies of individual learning and focusing on developing the team competences discussed in Chapter 7. The attainment of team competence to meet immediate needs and extended occupational competence of individual team members in line with future predicted needs provides the foundations for developing team competences to meet the organization's predictable future needs. Action learning can provide a route to operationalize collective learning through the creation of new team routines in the same way that individual learning can precipitate organizational action (March and Olsen 1975). Team learning can progress to address areas that may constitute future unknown needs once individual team members are working towards personal mastery.

Finally, at the level of the organization as a whole, learning can be promoted between teams to meet immediate needs, provided the necessary foundations at team and individual level have been accomplished. It is futile to attempt to introduce a framework for a learning organization without establishing the foundations at the level of individuals and teams. Once these building blocks are in place and shared mental models emerge, the organizational culture is sufficiently altered to permit learning to be transferred upwards and outwards, while development increasingly focuses on the organization's future known needs. The diagonal line in Figure 8.1 shows the broad trajectory proposed to build a learning organization by progressively addressing the learning domains associated with higher levels and further needs of the organization.

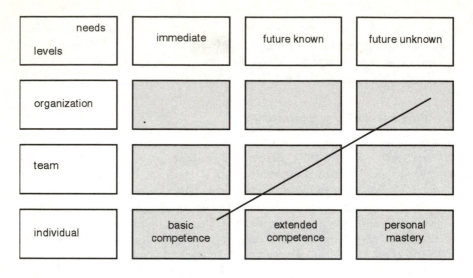

Figure 8.1 Learning domains in the learning organization

An organization may be expected to pass through several stages of development in pursuit of these ideals of a learning organization, establishing new
practices along the way. Jones and Hendry (1992) identify five stages in the development of a learning organization: a foundation phase where the emphasis is on
helping people learn how to learn; a formation phase where individuals initiate
their own development; a continuation phase where individuals take responsibility for deciding their own learning activities; a transformational phase where
at both the individual and organizational levels the required skills and actions are
reassessed; and, finally, a transfiguration phase in which learning becomes an
ongoing process at all levels in response to changes in the external environment.
The first three stages reflect progressively enhanced individual learning capabilities, while the last two stages reflect organizational learning.

The learning company (Pedler *et al.* 1997) is characterized as adopting particular practices:

- a learning approach to strategy; participative policy formation;
- 'informating', a term used to describe internal dialogue facilitated by information technology;
- formative accounting and control providing feedback from which individuals can learn;
- exchanges of personnel between departments;
- systems to reward learning and sharing knowledge;
- enabling structures to facilitate learning;
- boundary workers who act as environmental scanners;
- benchmarking for development in line with best practice;

- a culture supportive of shared learning from experience;
- processes supporting individual self-development.

Stahl *et al.* (1993: 52) argue that the learning organization 'turns the strategy, structure and culture of the enterprise into a learning system. The transformation of the whole system is the goal of learning enterprises, and management development is transformed into a self-learning, self-management process.' To achieve this transformation, the enterprise must implement the following changes:

- decentralization of decision-making, responsibilities and quality assurance;
- integration of functions at the workplace especially re-integration of 'brain and hand' in enlarged and enriched working fields;
- flattening of hierarchical structures, along with moderating, coaching and guidance roles for management;
- lateral networking instead of hierarchical control.

The learning organization may be perceived as an ideal state that is unattainable in so far as it addresses development to meet unknown future needs. Reminiscent of religious concepts like the messianic era and the holy grail, perhaps the power of the learning organization is in the development which accompanies the journey and the struggle in pursuit of the unattainable. The test of the utility of the approach is the extent to which the adoption of learning organization principles leads to improvements in BP. While none of the organizations studied made any claims to be learning organizations, the cases where the most impressive improvements in BP were apparent shared some of the characteristics identified above.

Business performance outcomes

The extent to which MD had contributed to improvements in BP was explored in the sixteen organizations studied for the competence-based management development project (Winterton and Winterton 1996). The sixteen cases were ranked according to the robustness of evidence that MD had contributed to improvements in BP using the the key criteria identified in the report of the study group (Leman *et al.* 1994):

- improvements in business performance can be demonstrated (and linked to MD and the use of the Management Standards);
- improved returns on staffing costs can be demonstrated;
- the organization has increased market share;
- share prices have increased for the organization.

Overall, the cases were ranked against these criteria along a continuum according to the extent of improvements in BP and the robustness of evidence identified. The ranking was undertaken by independent consultants on the basis of the validated case reports and written evidence.

The organizations which were ranked highest displayed quantified, written and corroborated evidence of improvements in BP, and respondents were unequivocal that MD had improved all prime measures of business efficiency. In cases which were ranked lower than the best, evidence was provided of specific improvements in BP, which were largely attributable to MD activities. In the cases which were ranked below these, organizations had generally made little attempt to evaluate the effect of MD on BP, or improvements were difficult to attribute, although in most cases management believed that MD had contributed to improved BP to some extent. For cases at the bottom of the hierarchy, there was either little evidence of improvements in BP, or any improvement was not attributable to MD.

In the cases where improvements in BP were identified with the most robust evidence, the contribution of MD to improved BP was clearly charted, while in the weaker cases, there was little measurement of outcomes and only circumstantial attribution. Problems of measurement of BP were most serious in the weaker cases, and largely arose from the interaction of other factors affecting BP, while difficulties of attribution were a consequence of being unable to produce counter-factual evidence of what would have been the BP outcome in the absence of MD initiatives. The evidence of improvements in BP draws upon the ten best cases, while the problems of measurement and attribution also include details from the remaining six cases.

The evidence is presented under four headings:

1   major improvements in BP attributed to MD;
2   moderate improvements in BP attributed to MD;
3   the contribution of MD;
4   problems of measurement and attribution.

Major improvements in BP attributed to MD

The five organizations which were ranked highest displayed quantified, written and corroborated evidence of improvements in BP, and respondents were unequivocal that MD had improved all prime measures of business efficiency. In one case, it was claimed that the organization would not exist in its present form today without MD.

Senior management in the retail company viewed efficiency or BP in terms of the degree to which company strategy had been achieved and how far the development of strategy involved company personnel. Reductions in arrears and stock holding are regarded as good indicators of improvements in staff performance which have had a direct financial advantage to the company. For example the percentage of arrears on overall income level more than halved in 18 months, and stock holding was reduced by 26 per cent in the same period, as members of staff became fully trained and able to operate the new computerized stock holding system. The rental market is the most profitable part of the retail business, and between 1988–9 and 1994–5, the company increased the number of rental units by 50 per cent, increasing share in a highly competitive, declining market. The retail company was making a steadily increasing profit; turnover had grown by 57 per cent in the last five years and rental income by 58 per cent. The clearest evidence of the importance of the contribution that MD makes to BP is that whereas in the past it took a new store at least two years to reach financial viability, MD has ensured this target is now achieved in one year (case 3).

In the insurance company, senior strategic managers identified various aspects of BP which are measured in the organization, such as 'subscriber numbers, earned income, underwriting ratio and renewal rate'. Since the creation of the autonomous business units, many of the BP measures are relevant to the business units (BUs), which have been treated as departments in this case. The underwriting ratio, the percentage of premium income paid out in claims, is seen as the primary measure of BP. Improvements in BP over the past three years were cited, especially in areas which are intimately related to MD: 'there has been a 40 per cent improvement in delivered quality and a 50 per cent increase in productivity', while 'staff turnover has fallen from 66 per cent to 2.5 per cent'. There have been substantial improvements in productivity and important quality improvements, as well as an improved claims to income ratio. In terms of the all-important solvency measures, the DTI requires a minimum volume ratio (free reserves as a percentage of exposure to risk, in terms of total premium income) of 20 per cent. The organization had a volume ratio of '35 per cent ten years ago, which rose to 50 per cent last year despite investment income losses on the stock exchange, and although this has now fallen to 40 per cent it is still double the minimum requirement' (case 7).

In the galvanizing company, three broad areas of BP are measured: overall productivity, market position and profitability. Productivity, in terms of output per man hour, is 48 per cent higher than in 1978. Market share has increased from 2.9 per cent to 4.6 per cent, in a highly competitive context in which price-cutting is commonplace, largely through the company becoming acknowledged as the highest quality galvanizer in the UK. Output has increased by 67 per cent, productivity has increased by about 32 per cent, zinc efficiency has improved by 17 per cent and market share has risen by 27 per cent. The QA system is reviewed annually and at March 1995, sixteen formal complaints had been recorded against 10,800 orders processed, a complaints rate of approximately 0.15 per cent (case 2).

The BP measures used in the engineering company include profits, return on capital, ability to generate new business and to develop overseas markets, and the capacity to develop management teams within the company. The finance director reported that overall performance has improved over the last year: sales and profits had grown, and targets relating to internationalization had been met (case 5).

In the Magistrates' Courts, senior strategic managers described the four principal organization-wide 'performance indicators' in the MIS as measures of BP: 'weighted case load; average time to complete case; fine enforcement; and quality of service'. In terms of the MIS statistics, there have been improvements in BP, but these should be interpreted with caution. Weighted case load has increased since 1990, and 'although there have been definition changes in that period', the 'historic picture is one of improvement in position in the league table of MCCs'. The time to complete cases has been reduced, and this is thought to be 'a fair indicator of performance', especially since 'waiting times have been reduced'. Fine enforcement has improved, but the key issue is the 'speed of getting information to the police', since after that, enforcement is a police issue (case 9).

Moderate improvements in BP attributed to MD

In the five cases which were ranked next highest in terms of evidence of improvements in BP, evidence was provided of specific improvements in BP, which were largely attributable to MD activities, but there were greater difficulties of measurement or attribution than in the organizations higher up the ranking.

In the aeroplane components company, overall productivity and sales growth were viewed as the major measures of BP. Total sales in 1988 of £14 million were achieved with 515 employees, while estimated total sales in the current year of £19 million are being achieved with 274 employees, so sales per employee have increased from £27,000 to £69,000 (case 12).

In one of the NHS Trusts, business performance is very much linked to performance against the contracts held with its purchasers, which in turn are linked to activity levels. Productivity and competitiveness are measured but market share is not. The organization is not profit-oriented but focuses on the provision of quality services – although it clearly has to do this within the internal market structure of the NHS. Specific examples of improvements in business performance included cost reductions and improved project management (case 11).

Senior strategic managers in the newspaper organization described efficiency or BP in terms of the 'key indices for publishing: profit and return on sales (profit to turnover)', and explained that each title is measured for gross margin. A monthly financial report is prepared for each title, from which the crucial measures of net profit and return on sales are calculated. Market share is measured by comparing the yield of each title in terms of advertising revenue per page with the estimated yield from competing titles, given the audited VFD (verified free distribution) service figures. Over the past two or three years, there has been some growth in VFD/pagination, and market share has increased by 1–2 per cent. Profits increased by 20 per cent last year, and over two years, if the effects of changed titles are removed, there has been a sustained improvement of 5 per cent per annum in revenue and profit (case 10).

In the oil company, the Director of Technical Operations identified a number of different measures of BP, including cash flow, rate of return on investment, production, safety, exploration success, control of staff numbers. Off-shore performance can be measured through norms for jobs. Decreasing unit cost has assumed critical importance as a measure of success since the company has moved from a project phase into one of managing a reducing resource. According to this indicator, BP has improved steadily since 1989–90 (case 4).

In the footwear company, BP is measured by what the factory manager termed 'the cost of productivity', i.e. the cost of a standard minute (SM) (the unit of time used in work measurement). The number of SMs per pair had decreased from 31 to 28.5 between 1994 and the first quarter of 1995, an improvement of 8 per cent, pairs per employee per week had increased from 88.6 to 90.7 (2 per cent) in the same period, but cost per SM had only fallen from11.44p to 11.4p, less than 0.5 per cent improvement. The factory manager stated that it was difficult to say whether the market share of the unit had improved. The overall performance of the whole company was down on last year. Trading profit at the time of the study stood at £3.8 million compared with £8.4 million in the previous year, representing £3.3 million down in the UK and £1.2 million down overseas on the previous year (case 15).

The contribution of MD

Respondents reported wide-ranging improvements in BP, which they broadly associated with MD initiatives, but they were also asked to demonstrate specifically how, and to what extent, MD had contributed to these business benefits. The evidence is considered below, in order of the importance given to MD in achieving the improvements.

In four cases, MD was seen as the crucial determinant of improved BP. According to the managing director of the retail company, the organization would not exist today in its present form without MD: 'you have to develop managers at the same pace as you wish the company to develop; if you didn't do this the company would be unable to operate'. Line managers similarly felt that it would have been impossible to sustain the type of growth experienced by the company without MD which has played a vital role in achieving this success, encouraging all staff to develop to their greatest potential, 'if we weren't developing our staff we couldn't be expanding' (case 3). In the engineering company, senior managers believed that the company would not have held its market share without the significant investment it had made in training but stressed that MCI was only one strand of this (case 5).

The chief executive of the aeroplane components company believed that MD had contributed to sales growth, because this had only occurred since the BPR and the MD associated with the changes. Before these initiatives, the average customer response time for the sales team was 30 days, and it is now 5 days. The improvements in BP 'would have been impossible without MD, without multi-skilling at all levels, which had resulted in ownership by the workforce'. Managers believed MD was 'the major factor' accounting for improved performance, and as a result, the company wins more business because of the quality of proposals and produces more with fewer engineers (case 12). A chief executive in the newspaper organization commented that 'we would not have achieved what we have without investing in these people and assessing the value of that investment with them'. The senior financial manager noted improvements in BP arising from the new management which had established 'a mission statement, road shows and investment in training' (case 10).

In two organizations, MD was seen as a necessary factor, in association with other changes, which had led to improved BP. Despite important caveats concerning difficulties of measuring BP in the Magistrates' Courts, senior strategic management believe that MD has led to improvements in BP as measured by the increased throughput with reduced staffing (case 9). The chief executive of the insurance company argued that 'MD *alone* would have made no contribution to the improvements in business performance, but we could not have made these improvements without it'. Another senior strategic manager attributed the productivity increases primarily to BPR, but concluded similarly that 'MD has made a major contribution because the change cannot happen without it'. The senior financial manager thought that MD 'was not the only factor but was a major contributory factor' to significant improvements in BP (case 7).

In two cases, the contribution of MD to BP was implicit, but the link could not be established with certainty. In the oil company, there was a strong commitment to MD and now attempts were being made to justify this investment and to demonstrate the business benefits of their competence improvement efforts. Following an evaluation study, the business benefits of the Certificate in Management Programme were estimated at £380,000 by participants and £550,00 by their managers. One operational department also believed that they were able to quantify the results of workshops on team working and problem-solving in terms of drilling progress (case 4). All prime measures of business efficiency in the galvanizing company have shown improvements since MD activities with MCI were established early in 1989. The observations of improved BP were broadly supported by written evidence, although the specific improvements in the period which could be attributed to MD were less dramatic (case 2).

Problems of measurement and attribution

While most organizations had a plethora of measures of BP, and could demonstrate improvements, these were often difficult to attribute unambiguously to MD, and overall few systematic attempts were made to evaluate the effect of MD on BP.

In two cases, extraneous factors made it difficult to measure BP in a meaningful way. The BP measures in the Magistrates' Courts are 'susceptible to external influences beyond the control' of the Magistrates' Service. Weighted case load especially is affected by factors such as the economic climate, human behaviour and policing policy. There are also difficulties with the throughput measure of time to complete cases, since 'the concept of justice constrains throughput: it is said that "justice delayed is justice denied", but it is equally true of "justice hastened"' so it is essential that throughput is not increased at the expense of the quality of justice. Similarly, fine enforcement is also not only influenced by the efficiency of the Magistrates' Courts administration, but by wider social factors affecting people's ability to pay, and the efficiency of the police (case 9). Similarly, different companies within the engineering group identified problems with various measures of BP. For an offshore subsidiary, overall productivity is not a good measure of BP because extraneous factors, such as the weather, are out of the company's control. Competitiveness is also very difficult to evaluate and there are problems with getting a clear objective view of market share. For a logistics subsidiary, the most useful indicators of performance were probably lack of complaints and cost over-runs, along with market feedback and customer retention (case 5).

In two organizations there had been few attempts to quantify the business benefits of investment in MD. In the oil company, to achieve and to demonstrate business benefits resulting from MD activities was likely to be a 'real long-haul exercise' (case 4). Respondents in the engineering company similarly questioned whether it was worthwhile to attempt to quantify results, since it could cost more to monitor and evaluate the impact of the MCI programme than to run the programme itself (case 5).

In three cases, MD was thought to have brought additional improvements, but other factors were held to be more important by some respondents. The senior financial manager in the aeroplane components company, for example, thought that the improvements in BP 'could have been done without formal MD, given the same people involved', although he acknowledged that MD contributed to their improved performance (case 12). Similarly, little of the improvement in BP in the mining company to date could be attributed to MD, because 'capital investment' has been the major source of improved BP, although 'MD has already added some value to that investment, and more is expected' (case 1). In the government agency, an area manager believed that MD had made some contribution to improvements in BP, but thought that 'it was more the Hawthorne effect'. Showing interest in employees was thought to be more important than the MD itself: 'it's this that gives you the results' (case 6).

In a further three organizations, respondents found it difficult to attribute improvements in BP unambiguously to MD. The senior financial manager in one NHS Trust expressed the hope that MD had directly contributed to an improvement in business performance, but he was unsure how this could be demonstrated. There has been a substantial financial commitment made to MD, which has been channelled particularly towards developing middle management and improving the general management structure in the Trust. 'MD has certainly improved control in the Trust and this might have improved performance' (case 13). In another NHS Trust, very few examples were given of improvements in BP due to MD, and one of the top managers interviewed did not believe that there had been any improvements in BP because of MD (case 16). Interviewees had difficulty in identifying clear links between improvements in BP as a result of MD in the charity. Although it was claimed that there were ongoing improvements in relation to most of the relevant performance indicators, these improvements could not be specifically attributed to MD (case 8).

Summary and conclusions

The objective of this chapter was to investigate the link between MD and improvements in performance at the level of the organization as a whole. The elements of business success were examined .The meaning of the learning organization was explored and outcomes of MD in terms of improvements in BP were analysed. Finally, this chapter reviewed the evidence of improvements in BP arising out of MD in the sixteen organizations studied. In the organizations where there was most robust evidence of significant improvement in BP attributed to MD, the improvements most often mentioned included the following:

- increased turnover and profit;
- sales and revenue growth;
- increased market share and competitiveness;
- higher productivity and efficiency;
- improved quality;
- decreased unit costs;
- reductions in arrears and stock holding;
- shorter waiting times and queues;
- reduced staff turnover.

Where significant improvements in business performance were identified, the extent to which these were attributed to management development initiatives varied as follows:

- improvements would have been impossible without management development;
- management development was the major, but not the only, contribution to success;
- management development was a necessary factor, in conjunction with other changes
- the contribution of management development was implicit.

There were major difficulties of measurement of business performance and of attributing improvements to management development in the organizations which provided less robust evidence. The main difficulties identified were as follows:

- extraneous influences affected business performance;
- few attempts had been made to measure the impact of management development;
- other factors were more important than management development;
- improvements could not be attributed unambiguously to management development.

9   Conclusions

The purpose of this chapter is to draw together the empirical findings discussed in Chapters 4–8 and to offer overall conclusions in relation to the five hypotheses outlined in Chapter 1. The research produced extensive evidence of improvements in performance which are attributable, in varying degrees, to CBMD in the sixteen organizations studied. In this chapter, these findings are analysed to offer both explanations for the patterns of variation between the cases and strategic recommendations relevant to public policy.

The chapter is organized into three sections:

1   an overview and review of the evidence from the case studies that CBMD improves performance;
2   a discussion of the relative importance of factors explaining variation in performance improvements arising from CBMD;
3   strategic policy recommendations to increase the business benefits of CBMD and suggestions for further research.

Evidence that CBMD improves performance

In all sixteen organizations selected for case study, a significant amount of MD was undertaken, and this was largely competence based. In organizations which had not adopted the MCI Standards, it was more difficult to establish the extent to which the MD was competence based. For the purposes of this study, any MD initiatives which were described as competence based by respondents were accepted as such, and the distinction between CBMD and MD was blurred in practice because MD was directed at raising competence. In this section, the evidence is reviewed for the three performance measures separately, and then for overall performance.

Individual performance

The review of the literature in Chapter 6 identified the strategic role of MD in the renewal of individuals and the improvement of their performance. Best practice involved the devolution of MD to line management and the development of both technical competences and generic management skills. Few examples exist in the literature of empirical evidence of improvements in IP which are measurable and attributable to MD initiatives.

In this study, however, significant improvements in IP, attributed to MD, were identified in the cases described in Chapter 6. These improvements included greater self-confidence, personal competence and better understanding of the organization, and specific skills such as interviewing, delegating, communicating and problem solving. As well as individual career advancement, MD had empowered middle management, and contributed to more effective development and motivation of team members. In the most robust examples, the MCI Standards had provided a framework to structure CBMD, through which its impact on performance could be tracked in relation to specific competences. Problems of measurement and attribution were apparent in all cases, but were most pronounced in cases where MD activities were either recent in origin or undergoing profound change.

Organizational performance

In the literature, OP is often related to OD and MD initiatives designed to improve group performance. Best practice examples combined individual development with improvements in organizational effectiveness, often with a focus on team working and self-managed teams. Despite widespread consensus of the value of team working and other group developmental activities, there is little empirical evidence supporting the claims made in the literature.

In this study, however, there were significant improvements in OP attributed to MD in the cases described in Chapter 7. These improvements included improved quality of service, cost reductions and efficiency gains, more focus on customer needs, reduced queues, better procedures and monitoring of actions, improved debt control, telephone standards and customer relations. In the most robust examples, significant improvements in OP were attributed to management development initiatives designed to promote more effective team performance. In the weakest cases, however, the difficulties of measuring OP and attributing improvements to MD were particularly pronounced, and it proved difficult to isolate OP and to identify anything other than anecdotal and impressionistic evidence.

Business performance

The literature reveals substantial problems in attributing improvements in BP to MD because of the wide variety of influences on BP which are unrelated to any HRD issues. Accounts are largely anecdotal with relatively few examples of systematic empirical research linking business improvements to MD.

In this study, however, significant improvements in BP are attributed to MD in the cases described in Chapter 8. These improvements included increased turnover, profit, sales and revenue, market share, productivity and efficiency, quality improvements, decreased unit costs, reductions in arrears and stock holding, shorter waiting times and reduced staff turnover. In the cases which exhibited the most robust evidence, MD was shown to have played a crucial role in achieving concrete, measurable business benefits. Problems of measurement of BP and attribution of improvements to MD initiatives were common and particularly acute in the weakest cases.

Overall performance

The organizations were evaluated on the basis of the case reports and written evidence by independent experts on the Management Standards who had not been involved in the case studies. The cases were then ranked in terms of the two defining characteristics relevant to the conditional hypotheses: the degree to which MD was linked to OS and the extent to which the Management Standards had been adopted in HRD systems and processes. The cases were also ranked according to the extent of improvements in IP, OP and BP attributable to MD, taking into account the robustness of the evidence, against the criteria outlined in the report of the study group. Table 9.1 summarizes the ranking of cases in terms of performance measures and other characteristics.

In the absence of direct quantitative measures, which would provide cardinal data capable of parametric statistical testing, the ranks provide ordinal data which can be analysed using non-parametric statistical techniques. Had there been direct quantitative measures of individual, organizational and business performance, which were consistent between cases, then such cardinal data would have been amenable to statistical testing for correlation, assuming that the variables were normally distributed. Such measures do not exist for comparing performance between organizations, and there is no way of quantifying the extent to which CBMD is linked to OS, nor of the extent to which the Management Standards have been adopted. Parametric statistical methods cannot, therefore, be employed.

The cases were, however, examined by independent experts and ranked according to the performance criteria and according to the criteria relating to the conditional hypotheses. These ranks provided ordinal data which are more powerful than mere nominal (classificatory) data since they were amenable to analysis using non-parametric statistical techniques. The value of such an analysis is crucially dependent upon the quality of the rankings, hence the importance of using experts who have not been involved in the fieldwork, so are independent of the case reports. The experts discussed the cases and agreed a single ranking against each criterion amongst themselves, but had more time been available each could have undertaken an individual ranking and the concordance between the different judges calculated as a measure of reliability.

The agreed rank order of cases according to the different measures was correlated to establish whether there was a significant association between the different factors being investigated, although of course, as with a conventional correlation, association does not prove causality. The two statistical tests of rank

Table 9.1 Ranking of cases

Case	P rank	OP rank	BP rank	OS rank	HRD rank
1	14	7	12	12.5	8.5
2	5	11	3	1	1
3	1	3	1	6.5	2.5
4	6	14	9	3	5.5
5	4	1	4	3	5.5
6	10	10	13	8	8.5
7	8	9	2	9	4
8	12	13	16	12.5	7
9	2	2	5	6.5	2.5
10	7	8	8	5	11
11	3	6	7	3	11
12	9	4	6	10.5	15.5
13	16	16	14	15	11
14	15	12	11	16	13.5
15	11	5	10	10.5	15.5
16	13	15	15	14	13.5

correlation used are the Spearman's rank correlation coefficient, which is used when two rankings are being compared, and Kendall's coefficient of concordance, which is a measure of the agreement between more than two sets of rankings.

In the case of Spearman's correlation coefficient, $R_s = 1$ when the rankings are identical and -1 if one ranking is the reverse of the other. When there are more than ten cases being ranked, the significance of R_s can be assessed from t tables since:

$$t^2 = \frac{R_s^2 (n-2)}{(1-R_s^2)} \quad \text{with } (n-2) \text{ degrees of freedom.}$$

In the case of Kendall's coefficient of concordance, $(\omega = 1$ when the rankings are identical and cannot be less than zero because if more than two sets of ranks are involved the rankings cannot all disagree completely. The significance of Kendall's coefficient is assessed from tables of S (rather than ω), where S is the sum of squares of the observed deviations from the mean rank, and the number of ranks, k, and number of items ranked, n, define the critical values of S.

$$\omega = 12S/k^2 (n^3 - n)$$

The rank order of cases according to the different measures could therefore be correlated to establish whether there is a significant association. Despite the measurement difficulties associated with performance, and especially OP, there was found to be a high degree of overall concordance in the ranking of cases according to the three performance measures, suggesting that these measures are very significantly correlated.

The overall coefficient of concordance between the rank orders of IP, OP and BP is significant at the 1 per cent level (Kendall's $\omega = 0.796$), showing that the rank position of an organization in terms of one performance measure is similar to its rank position for another performance measure. Moreover, Table 9.2 shows that each pair of performance measures correlates at the 5 per cent level or better, especially in the case of IP and BP (Spearman $R_5 = 0.797$). Of the three performance measures, OP was found to be the most problematic, but the significant rank correlation coefficients suggest that OP can be 'captured' adequately by IP and BP measures.

In the table, correlation coefficients in bold are significant at 1 per cent, others are significant at 5 per cent, (results in brackets are not significant at the 5 per cent level).

These results are highly significant, first, because they show a very high correlation between the two extreme performance measures, IP and BP, and a significant correlation of each with the intermediate performance measure, OP. Moreover, they demonstrate a very high correlation between the extent to which CBMD is linked with OS and improvements in IP and BP, and a significant correlation between the extent to which HRD systems and processes are based on the Management Standards and improvements in IP and BP.

Factors explaining variations in performance outcomes

As was explained in Chapter 3, the case study approach was adopted for this illustrative, exploratory research which investigated the processes by which CBMD translates into business benefits. It was important in selecting cases not only to identify organizations in which CBMD initiatives were taking place, but also which were representative of the four possible combinations (A, B, C, D) defined by the conditional hypotheses relating to OS and HRD. When the cases were re-coded following evaluation by an independent consultant, it was found that fewer cases were of type A (where CBMD is linked to OS and HRD systems and processes are based on the Management Standards) than originally assumed, and that there were no cases of type B (where CBMD is *not* linked to OS and HRD systems and processes are based on the Management Standards).

Table 9.2 Spearman rank correlation coefficients

	factor	*OP*	*BP*	*OS*	*HRD*
IP	0.635	**0.797**	**0.863**	0.611	
OP		**0.650**	(0.411)	(0.170)	
BP			**0.658**	0.548	
OS				0.575	

Note:
For 14 degrees of freedom,
$Rs_{(0.01)} = 0.645$
$Rs_{(0.05)} = 0.456$

In addition, the cases were deliberately chosen to provide a range of organizations of different sizes and from different economic sectors, since *a priori* reasoning suggested that size and sector could also influence the results. While the case study approach does not permit systematic testing of size and sector influences, the range of cases was adequate to explore whether these factors were more or less important in explaining the variance in performance than the two factors relating to OS and HRD systems and processes, which are the focus of the conditional hypotheses. Therefore, this section explores how performance measures vary with size, sector, OS, use of the Management Standards, and the characterization of cases as types A, C, and D.

Size and performance

Table 9.3 shows the average ranking of cases grouped according to five size categories (in employment terms). The size of organization appears to account for some of the variance in evidence of performance outcomes of MD.

Among the cases studied, evidence of improvements in OP and BP was demonstrated far more conclusively in organizations with 201–499 employees than in other size categories. Improvements in IP were demonstrated most effectively in organizations with 201–1,999 employees. Overall, taking IP, OP and BP together, the most robust evidence of performance improvements was found in medium-sized organizations (201–499 employees). The next most robust results were in large organizations (500–3,999 employees, two groups in the table which are not significantly different).

For small (up to 200 employees) and very large (4,000 employees or more) organizations, the evidence of performance improvements is substantially weaker than in the medium and large organizations. The small organizations may face resource difficulties whereby management are prevented from behaving strategically and devoting sufficient time or finance to MD initiatives because of the need to address more immediate issues. The very large organizations may have problems in establishing structures for MD because of their complexity. These are plausible explanations but suggest the need for further systematic investigation into how organizational size affects the performance improvements arising from MD activities.

It is important that there is little evidence that size affects the average ranks

Table 9.3 Average ranks by size of organization

size range:	< 201	201–499	500–1,999	2,000–3,999	> 3,999
IP	11.25	6.00	6.00	7.67	10.67
OP	8.75	5.33	7.67	7.33	13.33
BP	9.00	3.00	9.00	9.33	12.00
OS	10.00	8.67	7.83	6.83	8.67
HRD	9.63	7.33	9.00	7.83	8.33

for OS and HRD, since this shows that the OS and HRD dimensions are not functions of organizational size and suggests that size influences performance outcomes of MD independently of the OS and HRD dimensions. Small organizations, however, generally exhibited lower rankings in both dimensions, which may again reflect the special difficulties facing SMEs in linking MD to OS and in adopting the Management Standards.

Sector and performance

Table 9.4 shows the average ranking of cases grouped according to five broad sector categories. The sector of organization appears to exert a small influence on variations in evidence of performance outcomes of MD.

Overall, taking IP, OP and BP together, the private service organizations demonstrated the most robust evidence of performance improvements attributable to CBMD, while the health sector organizations provided the least significant evidence. The cases grouped under manufacturing showed the next most significant evidence of performance improvements, followed by public services in terms of IP and OP and the primary sector in terms of BP.

The differences between sectors are not a function of size since each sector group contains a wide range of different sized organizations (although all the health sector organizations have over 1,000 employees). While there is no evidence from these results that sector is a major source of variation, further systematic investigation would be necessary to investigate conclusively whether sector affects the performance improvements arising from MD activities.

Significantly, the order of sectors in terms of their average performance rank corresponds closely with their order in terms of OS and HRD average rank. Thus the public services group which shows the most evidence of performance improvements also has the highest average rank for OS and HRD, suggesting that these factors are more important than sector in explaining the patterns of variance.

Organizational strategy and performance

Chapter 4 demonstrated the importance of linking MD with OS and of altering the emphasis of MD from the individual to the organization. While MD is frequently shown to be divorced from strategic planning, there is evidence that

Table 9.4 Average ranks by sector

sector	primary	manufacturing	private services	public services	health
IP	10.00	8.80	5.33	8.00	10.67
OP	10.50	6.60	6.67	8.33	12.33
BP	10.50	6.80	3.67	11.33	12.00
OS	7.75	8.20	6.83	9.00	10.67
HRD	7.00	10.20	5.83	6.00	11.83

organizations are increasingly integrating MD with OS.

The cases described in Chapter 4 provided empirical support for the importance of linking MD with OS. In the cases which exhibited the strongest link
between OS and MD, there was a clear perception of how MD supports OS to
achieve commercial objectives and the MCI Standards were shown to play a key
role in this process. By contrast, in the organizations where MD was weakly linked
to OS, there were inconsistencies and ambiguities in management perceptions.

In Chapter 4, the cases were ranked according to the extent to which MD is
linked to OS. In general, there was a significant degree of linkage between MD
and OS in the majority of cases. For the purposes of exploring the conditional
hypothesis that MD is more likely to improve IP, OP and BP if linked to OS, the
ranking of that link is more useful than a simple dichotomy of 'linked' or 'not
linked'. To test the hypothesis, the rank order of OS is compared with the
ranking for IP, OP and BP.

From the Spearman rank correlation coefficients reported in Table 9.2, it is
clear that the correlations also provide support for the conditional hypothesis
that MD is more likely to improve performance when it is linked with OS. The
Spearman rank correlation coefficients between OS and both IP and BP are
significant at the 1 per cent level. Paradoxically, there is no significant correlation
between OS and OP, which may reflect the difficulties of measurement and
attribution already identified with OP. In the case of IP and BP, these results
offer unambiguous support for the importance of linking MD to OS in order to
realize business benefits.

Human resource development processes and performance

Chapter 5 demonstrated the value of a framework of support to promote self-
development in which HR needs are defined strategically. The Management
Standards developed by MCI were shown to provide a means for basing HRD
systems and processes on a common, coherent integrated set of competence
statements.

The cases described in Chapter 5 provide substantial evidence of the value
added by the use of the Management Standards. In the organizations where the
Standards had been adopted comprehensively, MD was entirely competence
based, the MCI framework was central to most HRD processes and MD
appeared to deliver business benefits more effectively. At the other extreme,
where organizations had not adopted the Management Standards to any meaningful extent, the coherence of HRD systems and processes was less apparent.

In Chapter 5, the cases illustrated variations in the extent to which HRD
processes are based on the Standards. Overall, four organizations had adopted
the Standards comprehensively, and in another three cases, the Standards were
partially used. For the purposes of exploring the conditional hypothesis that MD
is more likely to improve IP, OP and BP if HRD systems and processes are based
on the Standards, the ranking of the extent to which the Standards have been
adopted is more useful than a simple dichotomy of 'MCI user' or 'non-user'. To

test the hypothesis, the rank order of HRD (systems and processes based on the Management Standards) is compared with the ranking for IP, OP and BP.

From Table 9.2, it is clear that the results of the rank correlation also provide support for the conditional hypothesis that MD is more likely to improve performance when HRD systems and processes are based on the competence statements in the MCI Standards. The Spearman rank correlation coefficients between HRD and both IP and BP are significant at the 5 per cent level, although again there is no significant correlation between HRD and OP. In the case of IP and BP, these results again offer support for the importance of developing MD around the Management Standards in order to realize business benefits.

Organization characteristics and performance

Table 9.5 shows the average ranking of cases grouped according to the organizational characteristics established in Chapter 3. These statistics confirm the importance of the two defining characteristics upon which the conditional hypotheses are based (the link between CBMD and OS, and the adoption of the Standards in HRD systems and processes). Type A cases rank significantly higher in terms of performance improvements by all three measures, and especially by the more reliable measures IP and BP. The performance rankings for type A organizations are significantly better than for type C organizations, but these in turn are very substantially better than for type D organizations.

Notwithstanding the limitations of the case studies, these results are highly significant, since they again provide support for both of the conditional hypotheses. It is clear that CBMD improves performance by all measures, and especially in terms of IP and BP, much more effectively when linked with OS, and that using the Management Standards as a framework for HRD systems and processes brings additional benefits.

The average ranks for OS and HRD are included to demonstrate the validity of the characterization of cases as types A, C and D. Thus there is little difference between type A and type C cases in terms of the OS dimension, but they are quite distinct in terms of the HRD dimension. Similarly, there is little to distinguish type C and type D cases in terms of the HRD dimension, but they are quite distinct in terms of the OS dimension. The classification A, C, D is therefore meaningful in the analysis.

Table 9.5 Average ranks by organizational characteristics

characteristics	type A	type C	type D
IP	4.00	7.14	14.00
OP	6.25	6.86	12.60
BP	2.75	8.14	13.60
OS	5.75	6.14	14.00
HRD	2.50	10.36	10.70

Strategic recommendations and policy implications

Three strategic recommendations can be made on the basis of the above conclusions, relating to the performance measures which should be used to monitor the business benefits of MD, linking MD to OS, and adopting the Management Standards.

1 The performance measures which are most reliable for monitoring the business benefits of MD are IP and BP, which correlate with, and therefore probably also incorporate, the less tangible OP measures. The strength of the link between MD and both IP and BP suggests that MD should be promoted with the message that *developing human potential contributes to business success*.
2 Performance benefits are more likely to arise from MD where this is strongly linked with OS. The link between MD and OS should be seen as complementary to the value of developing people since this is the mechanism through which the development of individuals contributes to business performance. In policy terms, these findings provide further support for the *Investor in People* approach, through which development is linked to business strategy.
3 Performance is improved additionally where organizations adopt the Management Standards as a framework for development within HRD systems and processes. The additionality is important and provides support for policies to promote further marketing of the *MCI Standards*, encouraging their adoption by organizations to provide coherence in CBMD and to support mobility within the managerial workforce.

Further research

Within the limitations of a case study approach, a high degree of confidence can be attached to the conclusions from this research, but further investigation would provide an opportunity to corroborate, or modify, our findings in relation to the business benefits of CBMD. In particular, three complementary studies would provide a rigorous test of the conclusions reached in this research.

Ideally, a linear tracking study could be organized as a follow-up, revisiting the fifteen remaining organizations after a suitable period had elapsed for MD initiatives to become more embedded, and using the same case study protocol. Second, a survey of a stratified sample of organizations, using a postal or telephone questionnaire, could explore the extent of MD and associated IP improvements, and how far such improvements correlate with *Investors in People* and the adoption of the *MCI Standards*. Third, a replication study could be undertaken using a different set of organizations but with the same case study protocol. Until such further research is undertaken to replicate the study and to develop the analysis further, the hypotheses cannot be regarded as conclusively proven. Nevertheless, on the basis of this research, the evidence is overwhelming that MD improves IP and that this translates into improvements in BP. Equally, the organizations studied clearly demonstrate the value of linking MD with OS and of incorporating the Management Standards in HRD systems and processes. These findings are sufficient for management to be confident that working towards *IiP* status and signing up with the MCI will increase the value added from MD.

Case 1

Tin mine

Background

The tin mining operation began production in the first half of the nineteenth century. In the 1960s, the company became a wholly-owned subsidiary of an overseas syndicate, and in the 1980s was acquired by a major transnational mining corporation. In 1985 the price of tin dropped dramatically in world markets following the collapse of an international agreement and the suspension of trading for four years. Mines were closed, operations rationalized and employment reduced, with the DTI financing some of the restructuring. In 1988 the business and assets of the group were purchased from the transnational by a management buy-out, and in 1991 the DTI stopped all further support of capital projects. Labour costs were reduced and a small rise in metal prices allowed the mine to continue operating at a small loss, through the sale of surplus land and redundant assets. A share issue was launched to create a new undertaking in 1994, and the DTI and the transnational corporation subsequently wrote off their loans. In June 1995 the holding company raised substantial private funding to accelerate a major capital investment programme designed to increase productivity and raise efficiency.

The metal market and the exchange rate created a precarious environment for the organization because market regulation made prices artificially high leading to over-capacity and the 1985 crisis in which prices collapsed well below production costs. Stockpiles were reduced and excess mine capacity was taken out of production globally, leaving only higher grade, low-cost mines in operation.

In such circumstances business success was defined in terms of survival and as the *only* successful UK operation of its kind, began to consider developing HRD processes to support organizational strategy. The key focus was on team building and the development of intermediate skills for front line supervisors and line managers at NVQ3 and NVQ4 levels, and the company was preparing to apply for *Investor in People* status, at the time of the study.

Organizational strategy

Recently, the company undertook an organization and management review of the 'development and use of the resources in each part of the organization', in order to support departmental strategic objectives. For each department, the review considered the following:

- the strategic objectives of the department for the period, reflecting its role in achieving business objectives;
- a SWOT analysis of what the department faces in the light of the strategic objectives;
- the tactical plan for achieving these objectives, including deployment of resources, recruitment, training and development.

The strategic objectives of the Milling Department, in relation to *Investors in People*, for example, were 'to promote the development and training of all people in the department in line with these objectives', and 'to restructure work practices in the department so that decisions are made as close as possible to the activity'. The SWOT analysis for the Milling Department contrasted the technical strengths of the team with the 'lack of training and morale within the whole workforce', and identified an opportunity to raise productivity through improving morale.

According to the managing director, OS began to influence the company's MD strategy once the management team began 'looking to a more strategic, long-term approach'. For the senior financial manager, OS and MD were linked implicitly as part of the *IiP* approach: 'profitability is a function of efficiency and this in turn is a function of management capabilities'.

Line managers were generally doubtful about the extent to which OS influenced MD. One noted that 'up to 1990, business strategy influenced MD', but since then 'the business plan has been much looser, focused on short-term survival'. Another line manager thought that MD had not been influenced by OS until the company 'cut back so that responsibility and decision-making were pushed downward', which exposed significant training needs. Meeting these training needs, brought a 'culture change away from an autocratic management style'. The managing director explained that they were using *IiP* as a 'tool' to link MD more closely with OS, which would involve 'front-line supervisors making decisions'. The training manager believed that departmental strategies also influenced MD 'in principle', and that this would increasingly be the case with the *IiP* strategy, but line managers noted that MD was 'moving at different paces depending upon individual departmental managers'.

Team members regarded past training and development as 'entirely experiential'; and one individual spoke of '15–20 years of on-the-job training'. Recent initiatives in connection with the *IiP* project, however, entailed 'various aspects of basic training', including a 'supervisors' course' and team members generally believed that MD had become more effective. One individual thought that the supervisor training was 'not a great benefit', after 'fifteen years' experience as a supervisor'. A newcomer who had been 'thrown in at the deep end', however, claimed to have 'learnt more here in two months than in three years working in a South African gold mine', because he had been 'given more responsibility'. This emphasis on devolving managerial responsibility to first line supervisors appeared to provide both the necessity and opportunity for extensive MD.

HRD systems and processes

The training manager explained that the organization was moving towards a competence approach to MD, especially with the adoption of NVQs, but they had not considered using the Management Standards in any HRD processes. In place of the Standards, job descriptions were used based on an analysis of the tasks and competences required to fulfil a particular role. Appraisal was first introduced for senior managers, then managers and was to be introduced for supervisors.

Line managers emphasized the 'technical competences' in their own job descriptions, such as 'metallurgical competences and engineering knowledge' supported by an 'appreciation of what the job requires', the practicalities of applying the technical knowledge in the context of a working mine and manage-ment skills developed experientially. One manager commented that he did not have an adequate job description, partly because of the flexibility of job roles dictated by the environment. Technical competences were emphasized in all jobs, but there was 'more emphasis on man-management at higher levels', and the company objectives, broken down into departmental objectives, constituted a 'tactical plan' for MD to achieve the required competences.

Team members had job descriptions to varying degrees. The mine areas of responsibility, included 'production, rostering and safety', as conventional in the industry. One shift boss had a 'very loose-fitting job description', but such ambi-guity was 'inevitable given the need for flexibility'. A former shift boss had written his own job description 'because none existed before', and contrasted this lack of focus of job roles unfavourably with an equivalent job in South Africa. It was thought that the adoption of clearer job profiles would facilitate more strategic behaviour among front line supervisors.

An appraisal system had been introduced, with regular performance reviews of all employees by their immediate superior. Before the appraisal, the appraisee listed the key tasks of their job, what they achieved and what they failed to achieve in the period under review. The manager's preparation form explored the appraisee's previous goals and achievements/failures in the period under review and any events which constrained their work, as well as suggesting three goals for the individual during the next period in the light of the company's objectives and the person's strengths. The main issues discussed at the appraisal meeting were recorded, and an appraisal action list drawn up, summarizing agreed goals and actions which each would undertake in the next period.

Line managers viewed the six-monthly appraisal as an opportunity for 'feedback in two directions', a chance 'to make clear what are the individual's goals and "to clear the air"', an 'open opportunity to discuss any problem'. Team members welcomed the introduction of appraisals and viewed them as having twin objectives: 'getting some direction and feedback from management', and identifying strengths and weaknesses…training and development needs', with the manager acting in 'a supportive role'.

The training manager explained that responsibility for MD rested primarily with the line managers, while the individual was also responsible for 'adopting a questioning attitude'. In the words of one line manager, the individual and their manager 'should determine what training is needed in a one-to-one session'. Two other managers, however, believed that the MD initiative instigated by the managing director was only just 'starting to filter down to other management', who were 'accepting responsibility for developing the supervisors'. At the time of the study, 21 out of 50 supervisors were undergoing training to NVQ3.

Team members generally emphasized the responsibilities of individuals and line managers for MD, which until recently had not been pursued 'in a structured way'. Line managers were seen as being 'responsible for training their subordinates', while the managing director was responsible for facilitating 'external courses' and identifying the 'objectives of introducing NVQs'.

While all managers were expected to take advantage of the opportunity to participate in MD activities, the managing director recognized that in practice some managers, such as those 'approaching retirement', would have little interest in career development. Line managers offered some contradictory views but accepted that they had some responsibility for their own development.

According to the managing director, although the MD strategy is currently 'concentrated on the management team, including supervisors' with NVQ 3, 4 and 5, a more structured approach to mining training was anticipated with development 'all the way down the line'. Line managers accepted a major role in MD of their subordinates, and articulated this with obvious enthusiasm, especially the development and training of management immediately below Section Heads, who were to take on wider responsibilities. Given that there is extensive technical competence (a legal requirement for underground working), another priority mentioned was 'developing man-management skills of the new technical management and facilitating inter-departmental, cross-functional movement'.

Team members saw their role in their own development as being to identify their capabilities and to decide what opportunities they wanted to take up. Development was viewed as crucial for five shift bosses who had been recently appointed, all of whom had at least fifteen years' mining experience but no training in supervisory management.

The training manager explained that normally an 'individual would identify both the need for MD and the training opportunity', although sometimes this 'may come from above', a view reinforced by line managers. Team members unequivocally viewed decisions about MD as coming from the 'management team', 'senior management' or the 'mine superintendent'.

Line managers either believed that the achievement of management competence was 'not rewarded at all', or that the rewards were 'other than financial', such as a 'sense of achievement'. One had no experience of managers failing to attain the required competence, and of the others, one thought 'support, rather than criticism' would result, while the other suggested that 'managers who don't perform are fired'. Team members were equally clear that competence was not rewarded through remuneration, which was seen as 'inevitable given the market situation', and 'the economics of tin'. Supervisors thought that in place of higher earnings, the achievement of competence resulted in some 'improvement in status', or 'more responsibility'.

Individual performance

As part of the *IiP* programme senior management were undertaking a 'review of company objectives', which were to be broken down into departmental and section objectives, with individual performance measured against these targets. Line managers referred exclusively to departmental performance, as did most team members. One supervisor commented that in addition to the performance of their department, they were also judged on 'man-management and communication with other people', while another believed that 'individual performance could be measured but isn't'.

Neither the managing director nor the training manager thought that improvements in IP to date could be attributed to MD activity, but anticipated that the MD strategy would do this in the future. One line manager, however, recognized that MD had led to 'dramatic improvements with first line supervisors', because 'individuals were now aware of production targets' providing an 'opportunity for strategic thinking'. Managers recognized that the development of the shift bosses was allowing them to use more effectively the considerable tacit knowledge which they had accumulated experientially, and 'supporting them with technical services training'. The NVQ programme was expected to complement this with training in supervisory management.

All first line supervisors had followed the 'course on basic introductory supervisory management', and agreed that there were direct improvements in IP as a result. Individuals who had been given greater responsibility clearly valued this, and believed they were working much harder as well as experiencing greater job satisfaction, but there was a criticism of a lack of transparency: 'empowerment results from turning information into knowledge'. One supervisor felt 'management is too focused on immediate demands' to develop a longer-term strategy for MD. A head of section, immediately senior to shift bosses, with extensive experience that was clearly invaluable to the organization, was keen to take responsibility 'for more strategic long-term planning', but there was little prospect for him to be promoted to Mine Superintendent because this position is traditionally reserved for graduate Mining Engineers.

Organizational performance

According to the managing director, part of the *IiP* programme would involve senior management in a 'review of company objectives', which would be broken down into departmental and section objectives, in three areas: production tonnage; service standards; and unit rates of development. The measures of OP varied between departments and line managers described measures of OP relating to their own departments. In the mine, the key performance measures are 'tonnage and advance', and the 'grade' of the metal mined, which is compared with the estimated grade of the vein being worked, this estimate being 'refined by an iterative process' of sampling along the lode. Safety performance, measured as the 'lost time accident frequency rate', was also monitored. In the mill, the percentage of metal recovered is monitored, which is 'a measure of technical competence and team working'.

The line managers' responses in relation to OP measures were paralleled by those of the first line supervisors. In the mine, the main measures are 'tonnage', specified as targets such as '4,000 tonnes per week at 1.4 per cent of grade', and 'metres advanced for development'. It was suggested that sometimes the pursuit of productivity, measured in tonnes per manshift, caused the 'quality of work to suffer because men cut corners'. In the mill, three key targets were identified: grade or quality: 'the sample analysis of the product, monitored at 5 minute intervals'; recovery: 'the percentage of metal extracted'; and tonnage per hour: 'the tonnes of ore processed per plant hour'.

Written evidence demonstrated that major improvements in OP had occurred. In the mine, for example, the monthly average development rate had trebled in three years while tonnage had increased by 8 per cent on the previous year. In the mill, recovery had improved from 82 per cent to 86.5 per cent and concentrate grade had steadily increased from 37.6 per cent to 57.8 per cent.

The senior financial manager thought that as a result of MD 'there is more strategic behaviour, better relationships and more transparency'. The training manager cited the dramatic improvements in productivity: 'we are now producing more with 200 mine employees than we were with 750 workers'.

Two line managers cited improvements in OP as a result of MD designed to promote team working, and noted relations between the mining and engineering departments had improved because engineering staff were involved in production target meetings. Another manager anticipated significant improvements in team working following the development of shift bosses. Team members cited 'better liaison between the engineering and mining departments' as a result of MD initiatives. Two supervisors were unable to comment on improvements in OP as it was 'too soon' to find any evidence, although one believed that MD will improve OP.

Business performance

The managing director described break-even as 'the crucial overall global measure' of BP, and the senior financial manager explained the need to reduce break-even as low as possible. The break-even is influenced by production rates and by geology: 'all we can affect are our inputs'. The key input is productivity, measured in 'tonnage/manshift and tonnes of metal /man-month'. Output per manshift is 'built in to the contract bonus system', both in terms of tonnages and development rates. Market share is irrelevant as a measure of BP since the company has 1 per cent of world production and 100 per cent of UK production. Profit is determined by break-even, metal prices and exchange rates, and the two external factors are beyond the organization's control. Like all commodities, the world price for tin is determined by supply and demand, through the London Metals Exchange.

There had been dramatic improvements in productivity, which 'doubled between 1988 and 1992 in response to international competitive pressure'. Manpower was reduced from 680 employees in 1985 to 180 in 1991, and the grade of tin mined increased at the same time as output per manshift. The company financial accounts improved correspondingly, and break-even was 'reduced from £12,000 per tonne to £4,000 per tonne', in constant cost terms. Over a shorter period, the senior financial manager referred to a reduction in break-even from £7,000 per tonne to £4,500 per tonne, so that break-even was 'approaching the tin price' and there was every prospect of 'long-term improvement in profitability over the next ten years'.

Written evidence demonstrated a steady decline of break-even, from £8,730 per tonne in 1984 to £3,685 in 1992, after which it increased to around £4,764 partly as a result of a 33 per cent increase in labour costs per hoisted tonne in 3 years. Nevertheless, the break-even was showing convergence with the market price of tin.

The managing director believed that little of the improvement to date could be attributed to MD. The senior financial manager noted that 'capital investment' had been the major source of improved BP, but 'MD has already added some value to that investment, and more is expected.' All respondents commented on the precarious nature of the industry and commodity markets. Optimism based on major improvements in BP which had been achieved was tempered by the recognition that the tin market or exchange rate movements could easily make these improvements irrelevant.

Conclusions

While little of the improvements in performance at the time of the study could be attributed to MD, the managing director recognized that there was 'a need to focus on man-management, training and development'. Two priorities for these developmental activities were clear: team building and supervisory/intermediate skills. The training manager noted that the improvements in productivity derived from a variety of factors, such as 'working longer hours', concentrating production on 'the best seams', and 'the introduction of long hole stoping' [a new mining method]. Nevertheless, MD had made '*some* contribution, particularly in raising commitment of those in supervisory grades'. The senior financial manager recognized the difficulty of attribution and the importance of capital investment, but believed that there had been some 'additionality' from MD which had contributed to the performance improvements.

One line manager, in the mine, believed that evidence for the effects of MD on performance was apparent from 'feedback in the production target meetings'. There had been a 'qualitative change' in the input from shift bosses, which had led to 'refinement of the production schedule', and this change was not just as a result of fear of job insecurity. Another line manager in the mill attributed all of the improvements in OP to 'technical competence, not MD'.

Team members established a link between MD and improved performance because 'the [supervisory management] course was followed by the improvements', and 'the management style has become more transparent, so we get more feedback'. One individual contrasted the earlier improvements, which were a consequence of 'fear of redundancy', with more recent improvements, where people felt 'less threatened'. There was widespread confidence that 'the company will become profitable', and that the modernization would also facilitate improvements in work organization. At the same time, there was some anxiety that the inevitable neglect of training and development in the past presented a challenge for the future, especially with respect to succession planning. The age structure of shift bosses and skilled workers in the engineering department was cause for concern and suggested a need to target resources on developing younger employees, perhaps through accelerated learning, as well as on enhancing work organization to retain the essential skills and experience of the older workers.

Following a steady rise in the value of sterling, the mine closed in 1998.

Case 2

Galvanizing factory

Background

The company undertakes hot dip galvanizing of products after fabrication, specializing in structural steelwork up to 16m in length and weighing up to 4 tonnes. Hot dip galvanizing involves chemically cleaning iron and steel products and dipping them into a bath of molten zinc at 450°C, at which temperature the zinc forms an alloy with the ferrous material to create a protective anti-corrosion layer on the metal surface, preventing rust. The factory is located in the West Midlands, where there are forty-six small firms undertaking similar jobbing work. There is an obvious economic advantage in being close to the customer to reduce transport costs and time, so the spatial concentration is a function of the location of engineering companies. The company has 103 employees and is owned by a holding company which employs a total of 330 people in five companies including this case. This organization, specializing in processing larger items such as factory gates and crane jibs, is the largest in the group, while the holding company represents the second largest galvanizing concern in the UK.

In twenty years, the company increased output fourfold, while employment more than doubled, and such growth in a highly competitive industry was attributed to the quality and service focus which was adopted from 1978. All work is undertaken to BS729:1971, the technical quality standard for hot dip galvanizing. In 1985 the company achieved BS5750 (ISO9002) accreditation for its quality management arrangements. Although the company retained its BS5750 accreditation, senior management believed that such an approach was 'superfluous to a properly integrated management system and simply creates unnecessary bureaucracy', so intended to adopt a strategy of developing their management system 'to ensure that quality performance is continually enhanced'.

The major expansion occurred at the end of the 1980s, and the success of this expansion programme depended upon adequate HRD; in October 1991 the organization achieved *Investor in People* status in recognition of its achievements in this area. Written evidence demonstrated the company's commitment to MD in the number of individuals who had achieved NVQs: out of a management team of nine, seven have qualified to NVQ 3, and one each to NVQ 4 and 5. Supervision was organized around the shift system, and training for supervisors was found to be inadequate. All training for galvanizers has been on-the-job; the general engineering training organized by EITB and EnTra was found to be insufficiently specialized, although training for supervisors through the Engineering Employers' Federation was found to be more useful. In 1994 the company gained a National Training Award for its staff development activities.

Organizational strategy

In 1989, the company operated a double day shift and planned expansion through introducing three-shift working. Staffing increased by 40 per cent between 1989 and 1991, so the sales volume had to be won to justify this. The market expanded because of quality improvements which made it necessary to focus on training and development to ensure that standards were maintained while production and employment increased.

MD was therefore influenced by OS, in that it was designed to meet business needs, and through *IiP* the linkage was strengthened so that the 'Business Plan drives personal development'. In the *IiP* submission, the company identified 'personal competence and technical capability, properly assessed and continuously enhanced' as the key to achieving its objective of progressively increasing market share.

Line managers confirmed the link between OS and MD, and generally thought that it could not be strengthened. The 'scale of business failures' in the area over the past decade had demonstrated the 'need for competent people' to ensure the survival of the business. The industry is very competitive, with 'short lead times' so the immediate focus of development was on 'cost and quality'. Because the company grew by acquisition, managers were 'encouraged to develop within job roles to be ready for new opportunities'.

Team members at supervisory level viewed MD as organized 'from the top' and described such examples as achieving NVQ 3 in supervisory management using portfolio evidence. The arrangements for MD were thought to be 'quite effective' in so far as shift foremen had been developed via NVQ 3 to take on a shift manager role.

HRD systems and processes

MD was described as 'entirely competence based' by the director with responsibility for HRD, with additional 'academic top-up' where necessary. The Management Standards were adopted in 1989, since when they had been used in all HRD systems and processes except recruitment and remuneration. The Standards were not used in recruitment because the company 'only recruit to production level jobs', supervisors and managers are developed internally 'from within' the existing workforce. The reward system is not built around the Standards because 'competence is the standard for the job', although there is additional remuneration for production workers who achieve NVQ 2. The Standards are the 'very foundation' of training and development, and targets for personal development are 'related to the MCI Standards'.

The business expansion was built on management competence, through a competence-based approach which involved adopting the MCI Standards and using Accreditation of Prior Learning (APL) as the foundation of a training needs analysis. The company helped to pilot the M1 Standards (NVQ 4) via the Engineers Employers' Federation, through which two individuals had been developed: a works engineer with no previous management training; and another individual who had joined the company 'unqualified' from a maintenance background in the steel industry and is now the works manager for another company in the group. Foremen were replaced by supervisors who were assessed using APL and developed in the workplace and through C&G 7281 to the M1S (NVQ 3) Standards, and as Trainer/Assessors through the D31 and D32 units.

Key management were developed using the M2 (NVQ 5) Standards. The same approach was used with training production workers: line managers and supervisors were trained to generic standards in the company, and they were then given responsibility for developing training for production workers. The personal development of the production manager had been integrated into other MD to NVQ 5, which has involved the Institute of Management Diploma in Operations Management, completed wholly on an open learning basis. That individual was developing NVQ 3 with other managers and assembling the supporting documentation, while the organization was working with EnTra to develop an NVQ 2 in galvanizing at the time of the study.

Line managers explained that the competences outlined in their job descriptions were based upon 'the job itself' and 'the tasks performed' as they related to the Management Standards. These competences were identified by senior management and the incumbents, but rather than rigid job descriptions, there were 'flexible responsibilities' arising out of the 'organic management structure'. At supervisor and shift manager level, the competences were identified by the production manager and senior management, and again related to the Standards.

Line managers explained that they were 'not appraised formally', but there was a 'continuous process' of informal appraisal by the senior manager, who had a very close understanding of every manager's activities. At shift manager level, the process involved regular discussion with senior management throughout the day, while supervisors saw the appraisal as 'an opportunity to identify further training needs'. Operators were formally appraised by a visiting EnTra official, which 'gives a good understanding of people in the team, addresses their weaknesses and leads to developmental opportunities'.

The director responsible for HRD described MD as the responsibility of 'everyone': individuals, line managers and the HR function. The MD strategy was developed from above and devolved responsibility to line managers and individuals. Line managers agreed with this perspective, noting that the director was the 'main instigator' who 'set the agenda' for MD, while managers were responsible for 'developing team members'. All individuals, including line managers, were seen as having a responsibility for 'developing their own competences' and participating in training, including 'investing their own time in preparing portfolios of evidence'. Supervisors had a similar view of senior management with HRD responsibilities identifying 'individuals', 'opportunities' and 'what can be done'. The line manager's role was seen as one of providing a lead and support, while the individuals' main responsibility was 'working on portfolios'.

The director with HRD responsibility noted that all managers are expected to participate in MD activities for their own development. Line managers described their responsibilities for self-development in terms of 'working towards NVQ 5', 'performing', 'doing the job' and 'developing a portfolio for NVQ 3'.

The director with HRD responsibility explained that line managers had a vital role to play in the development of their staff. Line managers also acknowledged these responsibilities to develop their staff by assisting supervisors to 'achieve NVQ 3' and providing opportunities for shift managers to be trained as NVQ assessors. The appraisal process was seen as the major vehicle for identifying MD needs, but it is 'difficult to find the opportunity for moving people around: it takes time but we do it'. Supervisors defined their role in their own development in terms of 'preparing portfolios', for which some had 'to learn new areas' of competence.

All parties were agreed that the decision on what MD is appropriate for an individual manager is taken by the director with HRD responsibility. In the words of one line manager, he 'identifies the potential of an individual and then works with them'. One supervisor believed that the director had identified the 'wrong course' in his case, because he had 'no involvement in discipline or recruitment', two areas where he needed to demonstrate competence against the Standards.

According to the director with HRD responsibilities, the goals of MD are a result of the 'perception of what is required to achieve quality' or other objectives. In assessing an individual's 'ability to manage people', the Standards proved an invaluable discipline. For the production manager, the goals of MD were established 'broadly, in terms of creating a reservoir of competences to support the business strategy'. One shift manager saw the goals as 'flexible', but related to the 'targets established under NVQ 3', while another believed there were 'no particular goals, no pressures' and individuals were simply encouraged 'to have a go'. At supervisor level, the goals of MD were interpreted as 'NVQ and MCI targets', rather than explicitly linked to OS.

The production manager believed that the reward for achieving management competence was in 'performance improvement', which in turn could have a positive influence on the 'salary review', but there was 'no mechanistic link' between achieving an NVQ award and remuneration. Shift managers, however, saw the achievement of competence as leading to 'merit pay increases and promotion' as well as wider 'recognition'. For one individual, there had been 'increase in salary and additional responsibilities on achieving the Standard'. At supervisor level, the reward was 'in the achievement', and there was 'no expectation of increased pay', although there might be 'future job opportunities'.

The production manager explained that there had been no experience of line managers failing to achieve the required competence, since the qualification had been achieved through APL. However, it was assumed that in such a situation the solution would be to identify 'a developmental opportunity to remedy the problem'. Shift managers had experienced difficulties in attaining competence, and senior management had provided 'support' and given 'advice on interpreting the documentation'. For supervisors, the failure to achieve competence similarly resulted in 'assistance from senior management' and an attempt to find 'new developmental opportunities'.

Individual performance

The director with HRD responsibilities emphasized appraisal as a key tool for monitoring IP among operatives, while managers' portfolios represented one way of crediting competence. The production manager explained that IP involved 'all aspects', including 'attitudes, decision-making and strategic thinking'. There were no specific individual targets and the portfolios were 'only a developmental tool', of limited value for monitoring performance. Given the informal structure and the small management team, the works director was able to monitor IP informally on a day-to-day basis. Shift managers tended to view IP in terms of the production levels of the shift for which they had responsibility; this was monitored daily by senior management, with whom they had 'regular discussion', and their portfolios were 'evidence of effectiveness'. The IP and effectiveness of supervisors were assessed from 'feedback from customers and the shop floor', which was relayed via the production manager.

The director with HRD responsibilities gave no estimate of the contribution which MD had made to improvements in IP. The production manager believed MD had led to 'improved understanding' and had helped him develop a 'more methodical and structured approach' to his work. Shift managers also noted how MD had given them 'increased awareness of their responsibilities' and helped to 'structure the way experience has developed the individual'. Most significantly, MD had 'improved the quality of our documentation, in both production and training'. Shift managers had established a training programme for all operatives and developed all the supporting documentation: 'the loss of apprenticeships had left little training of operatives; we have now developed a reputation as a company with good training, and our workers will accept responsibility'. The individual at supervisor level could identify no improvements in IP in their present job as a result of MD, but anticipated that there could be benefits if they were promoted to shift manager.

Portfolios of NVQs from levels 3 to 5 show how the developmental needs of individuals have been identified by senior management. The claim that MD had improved operator training was supported by written evidence: from 1990, when the documentation was developed, detailed training records demonstrate what competences individuals have achieved and show how this has been supported by assessor training.

Organizational performance

The director with HRD responsibilities identified several measures of OP relevant to departmental and team targets against which departments are assessed. Materials consumption is an important consideration because zinc is an expensive metal, and maintaining quality standards is crucial to the success of the business. At the time of the study, customer complaints, including a proportion which prove unjustified (typically arising out of deficiencies in the components supplied by the customer) were running at 0.15 per cent of turnover, while those which involve compensating the customer for faulty galvanizing amounted to about 0.07 per cent of turnover. Health and safety statistics are also important in an industry which has a worse record than mining or deep sea fishing.

The production manager explained that tonnage was a 'crude measure of OP', because of the different sizes of objects galvanized. Clearly, a large structural item would represent the equivalent tonnage of thousands of smaller items, which would entail substantially more person-hours per tonne to galvanize. Nevertheless, provided departments received a similar mix of work, tonnage figures supplemented by 'close personal knowledge and value judgements' gave a measure of OP. Quality assessment is a more exact science, and is 'a major measure of performance' against technically defined standards. In addition to the internal quality control, customer complaints are monitored and 'fed back to individuals'.

Shift managers noted a '40 per cent increase in tonnage', reiterating the crudeness of tonnage as a measure of performance and noting that it is 'not really related to profitability', but is some indication of how much each shift is handling. Quality reject rates were seen as a better measure of performance, but it was thought that 'customer complaints were not normally attributable to one shift'. At supervisor level, OP was monitored by 'the efficiency of yard operations' and 'customer complaints'.

The director with HRD responsibilities identified no direct links between MD and improvements in OP. The production manager, however, believed that as a result of MD the organization operated more effectively because 'we are more structured in our organization of work and have a greater understanding of the way we work'. Shift managers noted that MD had 'highlighted their responsibilities and increased their involvement'. Moreover, it was felt that 'the shifts are now more keen to work flexibly'. A supervisor who was interviewed was unable to identify any improvements in OP, nor any arising out of MD activities that had taken place up to the time of the study, but they did not exclude the possibility of benefits eventually becoming apparent.

Business performance

The director with HRD responsibilities outlined three broad areas of BP which are measured: overall productivity, market position and profitability. Productivity, in terms of output per man hour, had increased by 48 per cent in eight years. Market share had increased from 2.9 per cent to 4.6 per cent, in a highly competitive context in which price-cutting is commonplace, largely through the company becoming acknowledged as the highest quality galvaniser in the UK. The company's net profit had grown and its financial contribution to the group had increased making it the major contributor to the return on capital employment of the holding company. The production manager elaborated on these improvements, and noted that all prime measures of business efficiency had shown improvements since MD activities with MCI were established early in 1989: 'output has increased by 67 per cent, productivity has increased by about 32 per cent, zinc efficiency has improved by 17 per cent and market share has risen by 27 per cent'.

These observations of performance improvements were broadly supported by written evidence, although the specific improvements in the period which could be attributed to MD were less dramatic. At the end of 1989, six months from the first MD activities, annual tonnage was 27 per cent higher than in the previous year, and in the year ended March 1995 it was 33 per cent higher than during the first year of MD. Notwithstanding the limitations of tonnage as a measure of output, the increase is impressive, particularly given that since 1988 heavy structural work has decreased as a proportion of the total. Productivity invariably fluctuates as a result of the changing composition of work, and the statistics show that it decreased between 1988 and 1991, but subsequently increased to 1995. Taking the first quarters of 1988 and 1995, productivity had increased by 22 per cent in terms of tonnes per factory hour and by 29 per cent in terms of tonnes per direct man hour.

A measure of how far quality standards have being maintained can be gained from the damage loss bonus paid to employees, which represents half the difference between the amount budgeted for customer credits and the amount actually refunded (the other half returning to the company). After a downturn in 1991, the bonus increased to a peak in 1993, then fell back slightly; in the first quarter of 1995 it was 8 per cent higher than in 1988. The QA system is reviewed annually and at March 1995, 16 formal complaints had been recorded against 10,800 orders processed, a complaints rate of approximately 0.15 per cent.

Conclusions

While attribution is inevitably difficult, the director with HRD responsibilities believed that the benefits of MD were apparent because 'the condition of the business now is a function of the way it has been managed'. Hence, the improved OP and BP were taken as evidence of the success of MD in

developing the appropriate competences of management, and the value of operator training and development. The production manager noted that there had
been some technical plant changes which had contributed to improved performance, but 'these had been managed effectively', and MD has been 'a significant
factor, otherwise we would not have invested time in it'. Shift managers identified
the benefits of MD in relation to their own effectiveness and the quality of operator training, but questioned how OP and BP improvements could be attributed
to MD as opposed to other factors. The individual at supervisory level was
unable to attribute any performance improvements to MD.

Case 3

Electrical rental and retail company

Background

Founded as an independent company in 1969 with a shop in Stockport selling and renting 'brown' electrical goods, the core of the company's business became rental of television, video, audio and satellite equipment. By 1989 there were twelve shops and the company had found a niche market for brand-named, quality products at low prices having by then become Air-Time Agents for Vodafone and Cellnet and added cellular telephones to its product list. The mobile phones operation expanded rapidly to involve 200 staff and by 1990 the communications company became independent of the retail company.

The twenty-five showrooms operated on a profit/loss basis by a manager, assistant manager, and on average, four sales staff, are open 6 or 7 days a week. Extended opening hours and rapid expansion highlighted an acute shortage of trained staff and a lack of a coherent training strategy to fill this gap. Traditional 'sitting with Nelly' training and promotion related to length of service were inadequate as the company was transformed from a small family business to a larger and more dynamic organization.

When a training officer was appointed in 1988 turnover among showroom staff was running at 30 per cent, a serious problem in a sector where a high level of product knowledge is essential. Training needs analysis identified the need for a comprehensive training programme for staff at all levels and a new training centre was established to begin training managers, many of whom had been employed by the company for fifteen years without any HRD, and to institute induction courses for new staff. New HRD systems and skills had to be developed in a relatively short period of time, including appraisal schemes and interviewing.

The Training and Development Policy established the principle of providing facilities and developmental opportunities for all employees to perform their jobs effectively; to enjoy full job satisfaction, to maximize performance to achieve company objectives and allow them to develop preparation for future responsibilities.

All staff are now able to work towards a National Qualification in-house, as the company is an approved Training Provider. The company won a National

Training Award for the effectiveness of its training and obtained ISO9000, and BS5750 Quality Awards. The company was in the process of applying for *IiP* status at the time of the study.

Organizational strategy

All senior and line managers believed that OS influenced MD. The MD programme was closely linked to expansion through succession planning and the development of management for the future of the organization.

Organizational strategy is limited by the competences of staff, so identifying strengths and weaknesses of individuals is essential for the development strategy to support the strategic goals of the organization. Team working is encouraged by the Training Department through providing managers with team briefing notes and in-house programmes.

The company expansion plan is published annually and all staff are aware of the targets that they and the company will have to meet, and all management agreed that departmental strategies influenced MD. Restructuring and rationalization of the service/distribution function demanded a new range of skills from staff and MD played a key role in equipping them with the required competencies.

The majority of managers thought that MD could not be linked more closely with departmental strategy: 'we are very strong on MD…We all have a common theme throughout the organization.' The consensus was that managers outside the organization employed in comparable organizations do not have the same opportunities for development as those employed in the company. The area manager of the Yorkshire Region, in charge of a multi-million pound operation, started his working life with the company on a YT scheme and took up all the development opportunities provided by the company. The MD needs of individual managers are identified as part of the formal annual appraisal process.

HRD systems and processes

The majority of HRD systems and processes were competence based; all training programmes had been reviewed and focused on key tasks in line with MCI Standards and the company had become an Accredited Competence Centre. Nevertheless, line managers were unable to identify what the competences outlined in their job description were based upon: 'I don't know, they came from personnel and are based on performance measures and specific tasks that need to be achieved.' The team members interviewed had even less idea than their line managers about the source of the competences required of them.

Two line managers believed appraisal was the primary process for identifying the competences required for particular functions. An individual's level of competence is measured against the requirements of the job and when someone fails to demonstrate the required competence, this would emerge during the appraisal process and remedial action could be taken. Two other line managers viewed appraisal as a flexible system, which needed to be constantly amended in the light of changing organizational needs and resulting changes in competences needed.

Team members were not convinced that the competences required for particular functions had always been identified except that if an individual was not performing their job competently, then line managers would identify this and seek to remedy the situation.

Appraisal systems were designed to support the achievement of the MCI Standards, and new appraisal criteria were being developed that are directly linked to the Management Standards. The new format separated personal and managerial skills and placed far more emphasis on appraising the strategic aspects of a manager's performance, focusing on how an individual manager monitors and controls the resources for which they are responsible, for example.

Line management felt that the primary purpose of the appraisal was to explore how an individual was currently performing in their job, to identify strengths and weaknesses and to develop a positive action plan for the next year. Team members regarded the primary purpose of individual appraisal as a private means of assessing IP and determining any training and development needs, providing an opportunity for those involved to express their opinions fully and frankly, without affecting their position in the organization or their job security.

The new system included provision for a personal action plan to identify areas for development and to detail how this will be achieved. Personal development objectives were not fully defined in terms of the Standards, as these are agreed with line managers who may not all be familiar with MCI. The senior HR manager believed that the revised appraisal would help to overcome these difficulties.

The company also uses upward assessment as a means of appraising staff performance; no one is exempt from this process, even the managing director is involved. Managers are given their average scores in each area appraised and are able to compare themselves with other managers at the same level. The head of HRM produced profiles of the ideal manager at each level surveyed and managers found this helped them to make an informed judgement about their own current performance.

MCI Standards are not used in recruitment and selection of managers although they are in the recruitment and selection of other members of staff, largely because the company has a policy of promoting from within the organization. Some managers feared that the staff currently employed were insufficient to satisfy the company's future HR needs and others believed that fresh blood could promote innovation.

Managers and staff at all levels acknowledged that individuals had a responsibility for their own development typically through Personal Development Plans. The Training Department viewed their role in MD as an enabling one, encouraging development of managers and providing them with the necessary time to acquire skills: 'We give them the opportunities, but they must transfer and build on the skills which we have provided.' Managers endorsed the notion of individuals applying skills acquired: 'sending someone on half a dozen courses doesn't make them a good manager, they need to develop these in the field'. Team members saw the role of the Training Department as providing the theoretical underpinning to be developed in the practical environment of the store.

The major developmental role of line managers was in identifying the development needs of staff and ensuring that the strategic objectives of the organization would be operationalized. Team members viewed the line manager's role in MD as one of facilitation, identifying individual developmental needs through appraisal. Senior managers emphasized that managers were expected to participate in their own development and line managers accepted this through identifying opportunities and producing portfolios of evidence for NVQ assessment.

Company policy also expects all line managers to contribute to the development of their own staff, identifying staff needs and providing appropriate opportunities for development. Team members generally felt part of their role in MD was to keep abreast of company development, 'you have to be committed to the company; you can't develop if you aren't interested'.

According to the senior HR manager, MD is not a prescriptive process, but it involves staff at all levels and programmes are developed through consensus. Line managers placed differing emphasis on the importance of the parties involved in deciding what MD was needed by an individual, but all agreed that the process involved the individual, their line manager and the HRD specialists. Most team members thought that the line manager decided on the MD most appropriate for them; only one felt that they had more influence in determining appropriate development.

A small one-off payment was made to those managers attaining NVQ levels 3 and 4, but senior management thought the reward for attaining competence lay in obtaining a nationally recognized qualification and having the opportunity to develop with company support. Line managers believed the reward for achieving competence was in increased promotional opportunities in the smooth running of their departments.

Team members felt that competence was not rewarded through remuneration but through personal achievement, the satisfaction of performing well, increased responsibility and career progression. Team members reported that those failing to achieve the required level of competence were given counselling, extra training and peer support, but individuals failing to progress could be offered a lower position.

Individual performance

The senior HR manager identified a number of areas where managers' IP was measured, including people-management and communication skills. The adoption of the MCI Standards encouraged managers to re-examine their performance against new criteria. The senior HR manager saw the Standards as a way of developing individuals in all aspects of their role and providing guidance by producing a yardstick for best practice. Appraisal had formerly been a top-down process and the Standards encouraged the adoption of upward assessment.

The managing director focused on the ability of individuals to meet targets, which line managers elaborated in terms of sales targets, number of complaints, arrears and rental growth, with staff development, training and competence targets as secondary measures of performance.

Team members highlighted a variety of IP measures, including team work skills, ability to work under pressure, accuracy of records, stock control and supervisory skills. One member of the team believed there was no measurement of their operational skills and another was unaware of any performance criteria which were being applied.

The senior HR manager explained that the difficulty in separating individual targets from team targets led the company to focus on team targets but individuals also have performance objectives, in relation to sales and rentals. While IP is monitored on a branch basis, team performance is the most important measure of success, and team members did not feel they had to achieve IP targets.

Senior management had no doubt that MD had improved IP: the managing director believed 'there would be no development without MD'. The senior HR manager believed MD had given managers increased competence, confidence and awareness of responsibilities. For line managers the benefits in their performance attributed to MD were numerous: 'it made me stand back and look at my performance more carefully to find out what I am doing right, what I am doing wrong and what I could be doing better'; 'the contribution has been awesome. I have been given a helping hand all the way'; 'I could never have done this without MD'; 'working to MCI competence Level 4 helped me in every aspect of management from handling employees to handling finance, it even helped me in my personal life and totally changed my outlook'.

All team members equally felt that their performance had improved because of MD. Team members had been given more responsibility, taught how to manage themselves, and encouraged to take a wider view of issues: 'I don't just look at what I have to do, but at what everyone has to do.'

Organizational performance

The senior financial manager felt that almost every aspect of team performance was measured against the designated budgets for each area; for example, sales and expenditure were compared against budgets under various headings. As a result, the company gained a higher level and quality of management information. The production of more detailed accounts and improved monitoring of company finances allowed tighter control of budgets and increased efficiency in monitoring the company's overheads; budgets were delegated to a dozen different cost centres and individual managers. Having followed the MCI development programme, managers are able to identify weak performance and keep a branch and its staff on track. The senior HR manager also mentioned debt control, service delivery and first time fix on repairs as elements of OP monitoring.

Line managers were mainly concerned with the achievement of store targets, and achieving a consistent level of profitability. Team meetings within each store are an inherent part of maintaining a profitable organization; 'We have a team meeting every Friday night...We have store target sheets and we monitor the team's performance against these.'

MD was necessary to facilitate the introduction of a computerized stock system which cut costs enormously, allowing purchase ordering, preventing deliverers off-loading stock and allowing automated stock count.

The monitoring of arrears levels in each store and levels of customer complaints are important indicators of OP. Arrears and customer complaints data are available from the computer information system and monthly reports are prepared for senior management. Monitoring customer complaints is an inherent part of the company's quality assurance system; a 3–4 day complaints monitoring system is in place in the company with computer summaries passed to the training manager, for quality assurance, and to senior management as well as to the branch for the team to act upon. If a branch has a high level of unresolved complaints on a regular basis, then advice or corrective action is provided, but it is the responsibility of the line manager to ensure that arrears and customer complaints do not reach unacceptable levels. Having been as high as 22 per cent of customers during 1993, complaints were brought below the target of 5 per cent in 1995.

In the opinion of the senior HR manager, team performance is a direct function of a manager's IP: 'the more competent the manager, the more competent the team; they set the standards for others and this is how we achieve quality of operations'. Team members felt that MD had improved team performance: 'MD motivates people and makes them more aware of the direct importance of company profits to each individual and how they can work together as a team to improve them.'

Business performance

According to the managing director, the major measure of efficiency or business performance was the degree to which company strategy had been achieved and how far feedback had been received from company personnel in developing that strategy. The senior financial manager emphasized the importance of two specific measures of BP, percentage arrears and stock holding, followed by supplementary measures of unit growth and cash sales.

Productivity was taken to be a measure of BP, and computerization was acknowledged as a source of productivity and efficiency as well as a mechanism for closely monitoring arrears. The managing director was dubious of the efficacy of productivity as a measure of BP: 'productivity could have increased 20 per cent, but perhaps the potential increase could have been 80 per cent'.

It was difficult to ascertain the market share held by the company, which is the third largest in the sector. The senior financial manager stated that the company 'keeps an eye on what other people are doing on an annual basis', but was circumspect concerning the nature of that monitoring. As the last independent company to maintain a substantial share of the market, its senior strategic managers aimed to increase market share by expansion rather than acquisition.

Reductions in arrears and stock holdings arising out of improvements in staff performance had a direct financial advantage. The percentage of arrears on overall income level, measured by the number of days rental to which this would equate, more than halved between August 1993 and February 1995, and stock holding was reduced by 26 per cent in the same period, as staff became fully versed in the computerized stock holding system.

The most profitable part of the retail business was the rental market, and in five years the company increased the number of rental units by 50 per cent which represents an increasing share of a declining market. The retail company was not growing at the same rate as the communications company, but was making a steadily increasing profit: turnover increased by 57 per cent over five years and rental income by 58 per cent. The managing director was interested in developing the company, not just in profitability, and expansion had a negative impact on company profits. The senior financial manager noted: 'if we opened no shops at all our profits would be much greater'. In five years ten new shops were opened and two more planned, net assets increased by 111 per cent, and in the same period pre-tax profits increased by 52 per cent.

According to the managing director, the company would not exist today in its present form without MD: 'you have to develop managers at the same pace as you wish the company to develop; if you didn't do this the company would be unable to operate.' For the senior financial manager, MD provided the impetus to drive the company forward, whether it was MD of his immediate staff which made them more sensitive to 'accounting in the real world', or with shop managers who were using the new computerized information systems to improve shop performance.

Conclusions

For line managers the evidence of the success of the company lay in its rapid expansion in recent years, the improved quality of its staff, its increasing market share in a declining market and the increased productivity of all employees. Managers believed it would have been impossible to sustain the type of growth experienced by the company without MD which has played a vital role in achieving this success, encouraging all staff to develop to their greatest potential: 'if we weren't developing our staff we wouldn't be expanding.' Although operating in a competitive, shrinking market, through a combination of good management, MD and training, the company management has been able to cope with market pressures, whilst stabilizing the workforce with a reduction in labour turnover from 30 per cent to 18 per cent.

Working towards *IiP* status complemented these processes, by identifying staff training needs. The reduction in labour turnover made investment in human resources far more cost-effective, and produced a workforce which was more confident, self-motivated and aware of organizational needs. Increasing sales and rentals, coupled with a decline in customer complaints and the level of arrears, are proof of this success. Team members also identified the importance of working towards Quality Awards as an inherent part of MD, which ensured that all staff work to the same set of procedures. Staff had to undergo a substantial amount of training but the overall result of the standardization and the supporting MD was a general improvement in the quality of business performance. The development of a consensual form of management had integrated and utilized the skills and opinions of all the team, producing further efficiency gains.

The most robust evidence of the importance of the contribution that MD makes to BP was provided by the senior HR manager. For a new store to become established as financially viable, at least 2,000 rental accounts are needed, since rental customers are the 'bread and butter' of the business. In the past it took a new store at least two years to reach this level of performance, but this target is now attained in one year. The improvement was attributed to the extensive programme of MD for new store managers and the extended period of training and development for all new store staff, undertaken during the two months prior to opening the new store.

Case 4

Oil and gas exploration company

Background

Part of a large transnational engaged in oil, natural gas, chemicals, coal and other businesses, the company had over 4,000 employees and an annual turnover of over £2.5 billion at the time of the study. It is divided in terms of its organizational structure into seven directorates: Production, Finance, Natural Gas, Technical Operations, Personnel & Administration, Development and Exploration. The Production Directorate constitutes 70 per cent of the company.

The staff interviewed were employed in three Directorates: Development, Technical Operations, and Personnel & Administration and located at a range of levels within the company from director to junior manager. All management training and development is contracted out rather than provided in-house. Two staff are responsible for planning and coordinating this and for contracting with suppliers. Technical training is managed separately and some of this is delivered by the company's own staff. The Group takes responsibility for development of the company's senior managers and also sets the parameters within which staff development takes place, particularly in relation to those designated as 'high-fliers'.

In spite of its heavy investment in training and development, and the extensive use of quality standards, the company has sought neither *Investor in People* accreditation nor BS5750 and managers expressed scepticism about the additional benefits that these might bring.

Organizational strategy

Senior staff believed that the company's business strategy had a general influence upon its approach to MD. Various aspects of OS were viewed as having an impact on the company's MD activities. For example, the increased use of outsourcing placed heavier demands upon company supervisors and was a major driving force behind the company's competence-based Certificate and Diploma in Management programmes. Second, the devolution of commercial management of contracts to a lower level in the organization necessitated training to raise managers' commercial awareness. Third, the adoption of management by process rather than management by 'silo' required managers to take a long term view and to operate across departmental barriers. Finally, the increasing importance of change management and the ability to work in teams presented new MD needs. These developments were seen as supportive of broad-based MD such as the company's two MCI-based programmes which were specifically intended to facilitate flexible use of staff in line with the company's needs.

The personnel director suggested that the link between OS and professional development was closer than that between OS and MD, probably because senior managers had usually attained their positions on the basis of technical skills. Most senior staff interviewed also acknowledged that 'the join between MD and OS was not seamless'. Directors indicated that the link between OS and MD seemed more tenuous at senior management level, particularly in relation to structured training. The technical operations director thought the company had not 'adopted such a systematic broad approach to MD as some think'. If MD were to be linked closely to OS this 'would require each of us to analyse what are the real requirements that I need to bring to this particular job to maximize bottom line results'. It would also be necessary to examine what constituted a good management team rather than trying to develop similar qualities or competences in all managers.

In some instances departmental strategy was not made explicit or was unclear but the staff appraisal system was helping to strengthen the influence of departmental strategy on individual development by measuring performance against work targets.

The re-definition of core business had led to development programmes emphasizing management skills seen as critical to the success of the new strategy.

HRD systems and processes

Recruitment and selection processes were not based on MCI or other management competences. Job descriptions are worded in terms of accountability rather than competences. For a number of years the company has operated a highly structured system of staff appraisal or performance review, carried out by the appraisee's immediate supervisor on an annual basis and supplemented by quarterly reviews of progress. The system is intended to monitor and record performance and progress, improve performance, develop employee competence, assist with planning future career development and reward performance and results.

The first section of the appraisal form focuses on appraisal against both work performance and competence development targets, thereby cascading down the business plans of the company into quantifiable targets for individual staff. Competence in the appraisee's present job is assessed by comparing the level of competence displayed in each area with the level required for the job. Four gradings ('below', 'fulfils', 'exceeds' and 'high') are used rather than 'competent' and 'not yet competent'. Appraisal is intended to throw up shortcomings in competence which are having a detrimental effect on work performance or preventing improvement in this. Competence development targets relating to skills, abilities and knowledge are then agreed and ways of meeting these identified.

Responsibility for MD was seen to rest primarily with individuals, and their supervisors. Individuals assisted with the identification of development needs during the appraisal process and might be expected to undertake study in their own time. The supervisor was responsible for conducting the appraisal, for identifying development targets and ways of meeting these and ensuring follow-through. The Training Department's role was primarily that of provider but training staff would also be involved if there was a dispute about access to programmes.

Career planning was described as 'playing a very significant role in driving the organization'. 'Current estimated potential' was described by the director of personnel as being 'the biggest driver behind all MD' because of its critical importance in determining access to career development opportunities for which a training programme was specifically developed.

In February 1990 the company introduced an academically-based and certificated MCI 1 programme for newly appointed first line supervisors, but the programme only ran for one year and in 1993 the company re-started its structured management programmes with a new supplier and eighty-seven staff had gained a level 4 management VQ at the time of the study. The level two programme, aimed at more senior and experienced managers, started in June 1994 with an intake of thiryt-eight and leads to a VQ at level 5.

Registration for both programmes is voluntary. Allocation to level depends primarily on the applicant's job grade and the opportunities that their current role provides for gathering evidence against the competences. Applications must be supported by the candidate's line manager and a learning or development contract is drawn up between the two, identifying those MCI competences which should be the focus for development during the programme.

Several respondents pointed out that employees' access to MD opportunities varied a great deal according to their position in the company and their potential as perceived by their line manager. Notwithstanding the advent of the two MCI-based programmes, systematic MD for both senior managers and for junior supervisors was viewed by some respondents as very patchy.

As a highly technically oriented company which made extensive use of technical standards as a framework for assessing and developing staff, the company was aware of the gap in standards for management. In line with its decision in 1993 to use the MCI Standards for its structured management training programmes, the Standards were introduced as a tool for assessing competence, both managerial and personal, within its appraisal system.

For the purposes of appraisal, MCI competences are not explicitly linked to particular work roles, but for many managers MCI supplements their technical standards because there is a large technical or safety component to their work.

A review of the effectiveness and usage of MCI Standards in the Staff Reporting process was carried out in August 1994, and found the prime area of weakness in appraisal to be assessment of 'competence shown in present job'. Of the sample of thirty-five staff interviewed, 73 per cent confirmed that they had used the MCI Standards to some extent and most said that they would again.

The director of technical operations suggested that the use of the Standards 'is very fragmented', largely because they were 'not user-friendly, they put people off', and were 'too detailed to use as a tool for analysis for the staff report'. Some managers nevertheless found the Standards helpful as a framework for the staff report and for structuring the development of staff.

Individual performance

The primary tool for measuring IP is appraisal and the work targets set within this process. At the time of the study efforts were being made to develop harder performance indicators as a supplement to targets that otherwise tend to be stated in terms, for example, of carrying out projects satisfactorily and within time-scales. For very senior managers, such as the director of technical operations, hard financial targets, i.e. bottom-line business achievements, are the critical measure.

The annual appraisal was intended to be supplemented by quarterly reviews at which progress is monitored and targets – both work and development ones – adjusted as necessary. Reviews did not appear to be mandatory in the same way that appraisals were. Depending on the nature of the work being undertaken, progress against targets would be monitored more frequently than this. For example, the major target for an Operations Support Supervisor was to ensure that everybody on the offshore platform met a legal deadline for verification of technical competence, a target monitored by monthly reports because of its critical importance.

The review of the Staff Reporting System indicated that it was too early to determine whether the use of the MCI Standards had had a significant impact, either on IP or on the conduct of appraisal. Informal feedback on the competence improvement workshops, which are cross-referenced to the standards, was positive. One interviewee commented that the team work planning workshop had been particularly helpful for planning workload.

Participants on the Certificate in Management Programme felt that they had significantly improved their skills across a wide range of the MCI Standards with most improvement in the 'soft' or 'people management' areas and least in the management of finance. Manager and mentor respondents largely agreed with this but also identified other areas of improvement: personal development, contributing to meetings/problem solving discussions and communication.

Individuals noted improvements in relation to individual course participants including leading and formalizing meetings, managing time and presentation skills. The director of technical operations commented that individuals on both management programmes appeared to be working much more efficiently with in-trays being managed much faster. In more general terms there was a feeling that the programme had helped to broaden horizons.

One interviewee pointed out that since the intakes for both programmes consisted primarily of experienced and already competent staff, gains in competence as a result of the programme were likely to be incremental rather than significant.

Organizational performance

As with measurements of IP, the extent to which departmental performance can easily be measured depended on the 'hardness' or 'softness' of the targets appropriate to the nature of the work. In some instances it was the individual's performance that was measured rather than that of teams. In the IT section efforts were made to measure the effectiveness of training in softer areas linked to the vision statement, such as managing the cultural and political aspects of change effectively. The results were inconclusive although the training did lead to a greater awareness of the section's role in driving change within the organization, an acknowledgement of the need for internal support groups and to managers feeling more in control of such change efforts.

At the organizational level the impact of participation in the MCI programme was regarded, not surprisingly, as harder to identify than the benefits accruing to individuals. More efficient use of meetings, the most frequently cited benefit to individuals, clearly also had benefits for a wider range of staff. Interviewees also felt that it was too early to say whether use of the Standards had improved the appraisal process since they had not been in operation for sufficient time.

Business performance

According to the director of technical operations, a number of different measures of BP were used including cash flow, rate of return on investment, production, safety, exploration success and control of staff numbers. Off-shore performance was measured through norms for jobs. Productivity was not directly measured for the company as a whole, and neither was market share, but competitiveness was evaluated using benchmarking studies, for example, on competitors' unit costs. Decreasing unit cost had assumed critical importance as a measure of success since the company moved from a project phase into one of managing a reducing resource. According to this indicator, BP had improved steadily during the 1990s.

There had been few attempts to quantify the business benefits of investment in MD. The company's director of personnel suggested that the MD programme in its broadest sense (not just the certificated courses) had been instituted and was being supported because of a strong commitment to MD 'in the broad, generic, personal sense'. Attempts were now being made both to tighten up on the justification for this investment and to demonstrate the business benefits of their competence improvement efforts.

An evaluative study carried out on the company's Certificate in Management

Programme estimated the business benefits to be £380,000 by participants and £550,00 by their managers. Examples of actual benefits achieved were given such as 'managing the shutdown of the operations department so that the unit was brought back on-line three days ahead of schedule which gave a cost saving of £240,000'. In this instance no evidence was supplied of the causal link between attending the programme and making this saving. However, other examples did attempt to provide more of an explanation of the process, attributing cost savings associated, for example, with contract negotiations, to increased financial awareness resulting from the programme. One operational department also believed that they were able to quantify the results of workshops on team working and problem-solving (which were not MCI based) in terms of drilling progress.

Realistically, however, achieving and demonstrating business benefits resulting from MD activities were likely to be a 'real long-haul exercise'. A major reason for this was the perceived lack of investment in senior management training and the feeling amongst many of this rank that their own effectiveness as managers had been limited by a lack of structured development opportunities. Because 'the behaviour of the organization is a mirror of direction from the top', attitudes such as this were likely to limit the potential for introducing new ways of working at lower levels. It would take 5–10 years, therefore, for the junior managers, who were the chief recipients of the company's current MD efforts, to come up through the system.

Conclusions

There was a general link between the company's business strategy and its commitment to broad-based MD and education. Several changes in the company's environment and its *modus operandi* highlighted the importance of enhanced management skills as a critical ingredient in success. In particular, it was a business imperative that managers are equipped to cope with uncertainty and to manage change.

The link between OS and MD was seen to be looser than that between business strategy and the company's investment in professional technical development. There appeared to be a consensus that MD efforts lagged behind professional development activities in terms of both the level of investment and the extent to which such investment was explicitly focused on meeting business objectives. In particular, the business strategy appeared to imply the need for considerably more MD at senior level than was taking place at the time of the study.

The extent to which broad-based management training enabled specific company objectives to be achieved was also an issue. As one interviewee put it, 'there is an act of faith in allowing individuals to make this link'. This was perhaps especially the case in an organization which places considerable stress upon career development for a selected elite and where such planning is strongly driven by the company's business strategy. At the level of individual staff the relationship between MD and OS appears stronger because of the efforts currently being made to link individuals' targets more closely to business needs via the appraisal system. The MCI Standards are playing a role in this process.

The introduction of the two structured MCI-based programmes clearly raised the profile of MD within the company and was seen to have had a positive impact both by the participants themselves and by other managers interviewed. Aside from this, access to MD opportunities was viewed as patchy at senior management level and even seen as unnecessary. Access to systematic development at junior supervisory levels was also viewed as patchy despite heavy investment in traditional training programmes.

The MCI Standards were contributing to assessment of staff competence and to the setting of competence development targets but were doing so in the context of the Group's approach to appraisal, which involved the assessment of staff against generic, non-job-specific competences. The company's commitment to broad-based MD and its expectation that staff should improve their level of competence beyond that required for their current job suggested the need to maintain a generic concept of competence for appraisal purposes, and the MCI Standards were being used in this way across jobs of varying levels of seniority. On the other hand, the view was expressed by several interviewees that the MCI Standards were too detailed and precise to be used for systematic assessment of the competence of all staff.

Assessment for career planning purposes was separated out within the appraisal process from assessment of current competence or work performance. The MCI Standards played no role in either assessment of Current Estimated Potential or in identifying development needs emerging from this. Since this assessment has a crucial influence on individuals' promotion prospects, the impact of other assessments which do involve the MCI Standards is necessarily reduced.

Since the Standards had been used within management training and appraisal only from mid-1993 and the end of 1993, respectively, it was premature at the time of the study to expect hard evidence of any benefits resulting from their use. Nevertheless there was anecdotal evidence of improvements in the 'softer' areas of management and a perception that some cost savings had accrued from the Certificate in Management programme. Senior managers expected a time-lag of 5–10 years in realizing the full benefits of MD, by which time, the current generation of junior managers will have reached key positions in the company. Until then the company would, continue to be constrained by its past failure to develop the current generation of senior managers.

In the longer term it seemed unlikely that the benefits of systematic CBMD would be realized in full unless and until the organizational culture of the company accords MD equal value with professional development, places a stronger emphasis upon interpersonal skills and ties in the achievement of competence more closely with other reward systems.

Case 5

Energy technology service

Background

One of the UK's leading indigenous energy service companies with over fifty subsidiary companies and over 3,000 employees, the company provides a global engineering and high technology service to offshore oil, power generation and general industrial markets. The Group is committed to continuous development and to internationalization of its services: over £50 million was invested over five years in strategic acquisitions, joint ventures and research and development programmes. The Group has only a small team at headquarters and is highly decentralized in the management of its subsidiary companies, some of which employ less than a hundred workers.

An ongoing quality culture programme, involving major investment in quality and safety systems, personnel development and the environment was adopted and some, but not all, of its subsidiary companies achieved British and International Standards for quality systems. One company registered its intention to achieve *Investor in People* status but has not progressed further with this due to resource constraints – another is currently exploring accreditation. At least one company is seeking to achieve BS7750, the standard for environmental management systems.

All offshore supervisors working on one major project are expected to undertake the SVQ 3 MCI qualification in supervisory management which is awarded by META (the Marine and Engineering Training Association). On shore, twenty-eight staff from one subsidiary company commenced the same SVQ in February 1995 supported by in-service sessions organized by the Group's Training Centre and a leading management training provider. Some of the charge-hands were aiming for unit accreditation rather than the whole SVQ where this was not appropriate for their job. At levels 4 and 5 all staff working towards MCI qualifications will also complete a linked academic qualification delivered by a local university.

A total of thirty-six staff were working on level 4 and the Certificate course at the time of the study, and the first group of level 5 candidates was about to begin the SVQ and Diploma.

Organizational strategy

The Group's organizational strategy was described as influencing its MD activities in three distinct ways. First, outsourcing responsibility for project management to Group companies created MD needs. Second, recognizing the importance of management in service industries demonstrated the need to provide career pathways to retain and develop good managers. Third, offshore safety issues highlighted the importance of demonstrating competence to potential customers in order to retain a competitive edge.

Increased investment in systematic MD via the route of MCI certification was attributed by senior managers to the fact that 'the market has changed in a revolutionary way'. Most significantly, customers were increasingly outsourcing responsibility for managing the whole project so that Group companies were forced either to recruit managers from outside or to develop their own management capabilities. Associated with these changes was the introduction of contracting on a 'zero profit' basis, whereby payment is made for completion of the task or project rather than for the time of the contractor's employees.

More generally, the Group's primary role of servicing the oil industry highlighted the importance of management skills; the size of the workforce fluctuates according to demand and heavy reliance is placed on core staff to manage temporary and contract labour.

MCI qualifications provided a mechanism both for improving management skills and for developing the career pathways needed to retain managers. The difficulty, risks and potential costs (resulting from 'mistakes') of appointing senior managers from outside the company were highlighted by at least two respondents.

The North Sea oil industry is also subject to special requirements for accreditation and certification under the Safety Case Regulations 1992, which requires companies to provide an 'auditable trail of competence' in management and supervisory skills as well as technical skills for all their offshore staff. The need for companies to demonstrate that they are using competent individuals to perform safety critical roles, demanded an extensive rolling programme of SVQ certification for the Group. Although demonstration of management competence, much less MCI certification, is not mandatory onshore, this was seen as a way of demonstrating competence across all the Group's activities.

The Group is very decentralized, and it was thought to be very difficult to achieve a closer link between OS and MD, since each company had its own approach to implementing the MCI Standards. Furthermore, the volatility of the markets in which some of the Group's companies were located required continuous adjustment of OS with little lead-time to develop appropriate MD. Some respondents felt that the link between OS and MD would be improved by a more specific link to the individual companies' development needs.

HRD systems and processes

MD is competence-based in the Group in the sense that MCI is the basis of most management training apart from high-level courses, although some subsidiary companies, continue to second staff to MBA programmes.

Other MD and training with a specific focus take place on the job, and are not specifically related to MCI qualifications or Standards but emerge from changing market and operational conditions. For example, the rapid expansion of the workforce in one company created a need for a higher level of competence in industrial relations.

Many managers appeared to regard MD as synonymous with management training and, indeed, with MCI, and it was suggested that prior to the introduction of MCI there had been little systematic MD. Technical staff promoted into management positions were expected to develop management skills on the job but with the introduction of MCI more attention was focused on training needs.

The MCI Standards were not used in recruitment and selection (except in the sense that possession of an MCI qualification would be seen as a positive indicator). Job descriptions were linked to duties and responsibilities as defined by management systems and kept as flexible as possible. Person specifications would prescribe minimum qualifications and level of experience rather than being based on competences.

The Group had an appraisal system which individual companies adapted involving an annual review when personal development objectives and targets were set and progress against these reviewed. Most respondents viewed the primary purpose of appraisal as diagnostic and developmental, although it was also seen as a formal communication tool for 'letting people know where they were going in the company'. The criteria or categories specified on appraisal forms in use were not explicitly linked to MCI competences. The Group's form was revised in order to fit better with MCI Standard and the benefits of linking appraisal to MCI were seen to be enabling gaps in competence to be identified and training needs more clearly articulated.

Responsibility for MD was seen by most respondents as shared between the manager and their supervisor, with senior managers placing more emphasis upon their own responsibility. The appraisal process and routine monitoring by Managers are the main means by which MD needs were identified. Individual managers were expected to contribute to identifying their own training needs, to keep up to date with relevant professional developments and, in the case of staff compiling MCI portfolios or undertaking distance learning, to do some of this in their own time. Line managers were expected to undertake appraisals and identify training needs for the staff that they supervise, in some instances taking on the role of mentor.

The Group's central training department buys in and organizes training on behalf of subsidiary companies and provides advice and guidance on selecting programmes as well as promoting company policy on training, especially in relation to MCI.

Achievement of the Standards was not explicitly linked to reward, although most companies in the Group tended to recognize the achievement of MCI qualifications in terms of enhanced status and better promotion prospects. Bonuses were paid for achieving work goals or meeting targets ahead of schedule, usually to teams rather than individuals. Senior managers were more likely to receive performance bonuses as individuals but these were also related to contracts and profitability.

Individual performance

The primary means for monitoring IP was appraisal which included measuring the extent to which work targets had been met. Where profitability and productivity could be traced back to a project manager, this aspect of management performance was also measured. For example, one engineering manager working in design reported targets for utilization of personnel and equipment. In one company working in the logistics field, the volume of customer complaints/service failures was measured and attributed to specific managers.

Measurement of the impact of MCI was viewed as premature and thought to be more difficult than SVQs in technical areas which Group companies were using. Systematic evaluation of the impact of MD on IP would require, as the finance director pointed out, taking a base-line measurement by appraising individuals against the Standards to identify competences not yet acquired, providing learning opportunities and then re-assessing them against these same outcomes at a later date.

Evidence of the link between participation in MCI and improvements in IP was therefore necessarily anecdotal and derived from respondents' own perceptions that the two were related. All the respondents believed that use of MCI had already had, or would have, a positive impact on performance.

Several managers made reference to the way in which undertaking the programme had resulted in new ways of thinking about their work. The managing director of one company believed that MCI helped them 'to acquire an understanding of issues that are normally dealt with at a higher level'. One senior manager referred to a broadening of staff's knowledge base and to staff being less blinkered. For mentors also, involvement in MCI had focused the mind on fundamentals. One manager undertaking level 3 said: 'I'd been doing the job for the last seven years in the same way – it becomes second nature but it might not be the best way of doing things.' Another said: 'It's given me my first opportunity to look at myself as a manager.'

Along with a general increase in self-confidence as managers, some respondents were able to cite examples of specific areas in which they had developed knowledge or skills, such as developing budgets, reading company accounts, representing the company at meetings and selecting the right information for presentation to potential customers.

The MCI programmes were also thought to have changed employees' attitudes to their own development, to the company and their role. A Group board member felt that the MCI approach encouraged staff to take personal responsibility for their own development and strengthened their commitment to the company. A senior manager with HRD responsibilities thought MCI had increased people's confidence and willingness to put themselves forward for promotion. Benefits in terms of the opportunities for career progression that MCI opened up were clearly of major significance for several participants in the programme. Findings from a recent study undertaken by a local university on the business benefits of the Certificate in Management (MCI level 4) were broadly in line with those identified above but also cited development of skills in a larger number of specific areas such as communication, delegation, motivating and relating to staff, and stress management, as well as in financial budgeting and control. An increased awareness of the importance of strategic planning and marketing linked to specific projects undertaken in this area was also cited.

Organizational performance

Organizational and departmental performance is measured by means of contractually specified milestones (deadlines for completion of stages of the project), productivity and other types of targets, which are cascaded down to teams from project level. On some contracts reduction in the number of safety incidents or in waste may be used as indicators. In the field of engineering design, repair and overhaul, the number of instances of complaints or non-conformance with quality standards was an important measure of performance. The previous year's performance was also used as a base-line for comparison. Monitoring of performance on contracts is normally undertaken on a weekly or monthly basis, with information collected via time sheets and cost reports.

The caveat above concerning the short time that MCI has been in use within Group companies applies, if anything, more forcefully to any attempt to identify improvements in organizational or team performance resulting from its use. The small number of managers undertaking level 4 within any one company is also likely to limit the impact of MCI at levels beyond that of IP.

However, three respondents from two different Group companies independently cited improvements in internal communications as a result of participation in MCI. For example, in one company working in the logistics field, safety records of drivers were poor for reasons that established communication channels had failed to identify. One of the MCI students identified deficiencies in communication procedures, which resulted in the procedures being changed so that drivers now attend safety meetings.

In one of the engineering companies two respondents reported that communication had improved greatly because they were now making more use of written documentation. Initially this development had been prompted by supervisors and charge-hands collecting written evidence for portfolios, and the practice was continuing because the benefits of written records had become evident. Verbal instructions for minor jobs which previously might have been forgotten about were now noted down in a diary which was accessible to everybody at shift hand-overs.

Another respondent described how the programme had made him more aware of his legal responsibilities in relation to health and safety and prompted him and his employees to check that their facility was meeting company requirements. An example was also given of the MCI Standards and performance evidence collected by one manager being made available to supervisors who reported to him. The manager concerned believed that the unit on enhancing subordinates' performance had had a direct impact on his supervisors. Since becoming more aware of the importance of the environment they had worked at weekends in order to paint the building!

The university study, which was based on interviews with senior supervisors and managers, reported that respondents attributed increased efficiency and direct cost savings to the Certificate programme. Examples given included improved procedures for controlling and handling materials as well as the identification of potential areas for improvement in the future such as in relation to information systems. Several of their respondents also suggested that heightened awareness of the importance of maintaining and developing the customer base had improved relationships with customers.

Business performance

The finance director reported that for the Group as a whole, BP was measured using the following yardsticks: profits, return on capital, ability to generate new business and to develop overseas markets and ability to develop management teams within the company.

At the level of individual companies, such measures may be less useful. The managing director of an offshore subsidiary suggested that, in the case of his company, overall productivity was not necessarily an accurate measure because of factors outside the company's control, such as the weather. Competitiveness was also very difficult to evaluate. Similarly, company financial accounts might not give a true picture of performance because of the degree of obscurity permitted in statutory accounts.

There were also problems with getting a clear objective view of market share, and customer output of oil was thought probably the most appropriate. For the logistics company the most useful indicators of performance were probably lack of complaints and cost over-runs along with market feedback and customer retention. The Group finance director reported that overall performance had improved over the previous year, sales and profits had grown, while targets relating to internationalization had been met.

In view of the short period that MCI Standards had been adopted, respondents' views on their business benefits were, inevitably, more of an expression of what the Group hoped to achieve by their introduction than a statement of what had actually been achieved to date. Some respondents doubted whether it was worthwhile to attempt to quantify results and a board member noted that investment in MD was not being justified in these terms. It was possible that it would cost more to monitor and evaluate the impact of the MCI programme than the programme itself was costing.

Introduction of MCI could reasonably be expected to result in improved retention and reduced recruitment from outside but quantifying the resulting savings was likely to be impossible. Similarly, the cost of wrong appointments can be very high but no attempt was made to measure this. One of the companies within the Group attempted to project the productivity benefits and reduced recruitment costs which would accrue from improving the appraisal system and associated training and development activities. The projected reduction in recruitment costs was relatively small and most of the savings resulted from productivity gains based on 'guesstimates'.

A senior manager with HRD responsibilities suggested that the visibility of MCI qualifications 'demonstrates a major commitment by the company to the long-term future of its employees'. There was also some anecdotal evidence that individual managers participating in the MCI programme had been prompted to review marketing strategies and invest more effort in gaining new customers but no hard evidence of results was available. One senior manager believed that his company would not have held on its market share without the significant investment it had made in training but stressed that MCI was only one strand of this.

Conclusions

There is a general link between the Group's OS and MD in the sense that certain aspects of the former provide a rationale for investment in MD activities. The influence of strategy and of certain aspects of the Group's market environment (such as the need to meet the requirements of Offshore Safety Case Regulations) could also be seen in the decision to opt for highly visible nationally accredited qualifications. However, the link between the two is not specific in the sense that strategy determines the goals or content of MD. Since MCI accredits all-round competence and the primary purpose of the programme is certification, MD activities do not necessarily focus on those aspects of competence that are critical for a particular company.

Closer or more specific links between OS and MD would suggest the need to target specific areas of expertise, for example, financial budgeting and control or marketing, which were critical to the company's success. Such a focus might be instead of, or in addition to, the development of the 'rounded' manager with broader vision which appeared to be a major aim of the programme.

The MCI programme clearly raised the profile of MD within the company. Interviewees who were participants in the programme believed that training and certification were providing opportunities for focused and systematic learning which were previously unavailable. At the same time MD became equated with MCI certification and with formal academic management training and such a perspective could conceivably result in an under-emphasis on identifying and meeting training or development needs for managers that arise from changing market and operational conditions. It might also lead to a down-grading of MD activities which focus on teams rather than individuals.

Little use had been made of the MCI Standards for other HRD processes, although the benefits of integrating the Standards within the appraisal process were acknowledged. Such an approach would enable weaknesses in relation to specific competences to be identified and addressed through appropriate personal development objectives. Use of the Standards for other HRD processes had received less consideration.

Individual participants believed that through MCI they were acquiring new knowledge and skills and significantly increased opportunities for career development and progression. There was little hard evidence of improvements in BP from MCI despite the volume of anecdotal evidence of improvements in both IP and OP. Business benefits anticipated from using the MCI Standards relate to the messages which the qualifications give both to customers and their own staff. To customers the MCI route demonstrates both the competence of the Group's managers and its commitment to staff; for its own employees the opportunities that certification presents act as a motivating force generating loyalty and commitment. Of equal significance is senior managers' belief that the programme will foster the development and retention of a pool of competent managers upon which companies can draw.

As one of the Group's board members put it: 'In a sense, MCI is about expressing commitment to people – it strikes the right theme – it's for self-starting people who will do a lot for themselves.' From this perspective especially, quantifying the return from the adoption of MCI certification as the Group's strategy for MD may not be as crucial as fostering the organizational culture that the Group believes to be critical for its success.

Case 6

Government agency

Background

The organization is one area of a government executive agency, which delivers a service through its network of 455 local offices, each employing around 60 to 70 staff, and organized into 159 districts. The Agency deals with approximately 22 million callers a year and in 1995–6 anticipated a substantial growth in demand for its services.

In order to support that level of provision, the agency had an administrative budget allocation of £2.5 billion, intended to cover all running costs, including staff costs, new policy developments and improvements to the organization's infrastructure. A new management structure was also created with the introduction of the agency; a chief executive was appointed in late 1990 and a selection exercise held to appoint district managers and area directors. The organization was restructured prior to the emergence of the agency and the number of staff employed fell from 100,000 to approximately 68,000, which involved a high degree of upskilling for the remaining employees. Formal strategic and business planning was introduced for all business units.

In order to cope with a four-year change programme, which involved widespread de-layering of management, MD was employed across the agency, dealing with those managers who were feeling vulnerable, displaced and not capable of taking on the financial roles required of them. MD also concentrated on upskilling senior management, in recognition of the fact that these managers form a focal point of the organization.

At the time of the study, the agency was seeking to develop staff in order to deliver a 'one stop' service to all its customers, through an integrated benefit delivery system. Although the agency overall had not applied for *Investor in People* status, some individual districts had already achieved *IiP* and others were in the process of working towards *IiP* status. Senior management preferred individual districts to apply so that the agency would not have to wait for the 'slowest' before achieving overall *IiP*. The agency has a well established in-house 'Quality Framework', which is extremely robust and has been recognized in Britain as well as Europe: '*IiP* is very much tied to this Quality Framework'. The senior manager with responsibility for staff development explained that overall in the agency 18 out of 154 units had achieved *IiP* and 60 more were working towards it. It was anticipated that application for *IiP* might become mandatory in the agency and some individuals believed that a corporate application might be the best way to proceed. The in-house training provider had achieved a National Training Award.

Organizational strategy

All districts of the organization have a business plan which reviews performance during the previous year and sets out the strategy to be followed in the coming year. One district business plan focused on the service delivery and financial and milestone targets set by the Secretary of State and laid out a detailed strategy of how these targets would be achieved in the district, explored the means by which the work programme, already in progress, could be 'taken forward', how staff could be best supported to deliver these services direct to customers and the best methods of progressing the agreed market testing programme.

The area director felt that OS influenced MD and that MD had firm links with OS. The senior area management team and the district managers were all good at delivering current business, but were less confident regarding the business aspects of their role, and MD had been used to raise business awareness.

The senior staff development manager believed OS 'probably' influenced MD, but could only speak about his own area of responsibility, where there is a well-developed HRD strategy. In his view, the agency should only train and develop in areas that would help the organization attain its business objectives. A training specialist explained that strategy outlined at the top of the organization tends to become diluted as it percolates down. Line managers had diverse views concerning the extent to which OS influenced MD. OS was described as imposing a structure that required managers to acquire competence, which was seen to link business needs with strategy.

The area director thought that MD could be more closely linked with OS, but saw dangers in this connection: 'an organization needs to have a very clear view of the future and aim to develop a broad range of competences, which must be constantly reviewed. If an organization's strategy is wrong you could find yourself tied to something that doesn't work.'

The senior staff development manager thought departmental and local strategies influenced MD, but to date these were a function of corporate strategies, such as *IiP* or the NVQ programme. Line managers also felt that departmental strategies influenced MD, in so far as these strategies focus on the business plan. The link could be more effective: MD is needed to develop staff at local level 'to know what we are working towards', simply empowering managers is not enough. Moreover, resource constraints mean 'you haven't always got the time to allow your staff to develop'.

One team member thought MD had been organized 'sketchily' in their local office; there was no proper MD structure in place, and new roles had evolved virtually of 'their own accord, instead of through managed change'. Another team member thought that 'for those that are keen and have potential MD is quite effective'; but the management team is largely static, and some managers have no desire to be developed.

HRD systems and processes

Training and development in the agency were designed 'to support the delivery of service to customers', so included technical training as well as training in management and business planning. The introduction of a Management Development Scheme in 1993 offered the opportunity for up to sixty managers to develop competencies needed for the agency in the future, without any guarantee of career progression.

An active NVQ programme was begun in 1993 following the establishment of a Vocational Qualifications Support Service (VQSS) in 1992 to design, develop and implement a national programme of NVQs/SVQs. VQSS had created a framework to deliver the programme and at the time of the study were waiting for this to be validated by MCI, BTEC and ScotVEC. A senior management development programme was also created by the Cambridge Management Centre, focusing on personal development for senior managers to increase their effectiveness as individuals and team leaders.

At the time of the study less than 20 per cent of MD was competence based, although there was a commitment to adopt a competence-based system and integrate this with the appraisal and recruitment processes. The agency was in the process of developing in-house competence-based standards, but only 3–4 per cent of the training products were MCI approved, and massive investment would be involved in validating them all. The senior staff development manager explained that there was a general lack of appreciation of what 'MCI did and can do for an organization'. Products and systems developed independently around in-house competence standards could just as easily have been based on MCI Standards.

MCI Standards were used by the organization for VQs and a 'watered-down version' was used for senior management development workshops, but the application of the Standards to HRD systems was limited. Recruitment and selection criteria related to traditional civil service competences, but the whole HRD system was under review and consideration was being given to basing systems, including the revised appraisal system, on the MCI Standards. MD was developing a stronger link to the Standards, but establishing a broader relationship between HRD systems and the Standards was seen as a major problem.

Managers and team members had key work objectives, which are not competence based, rather than formal job descriptions. The appraisal system is concerned with monitoring individual performance against key work objectives and acting as a developmental tool. Traditionally pay was a function of performance, rated as part of the appraisal process, and the two have become inextricably linked. MD goals were established through the appraisal process but line managers had widely differing standards, and the whole process was seen as extremely subjective.

Line managers found it difficult to explain how MD goals for individual managers were established, and focused on work objectives rather than MD goals for specific training events organized outside the immediate workplace. The management team felt that MD goals 'weren't really established at all' or confused MD goals with work objectives. Through the appraisal system weaknesses in a manager's performance have to be addressed by further development within a specified time period.

Individuals are expected to take a proactive role in their own development through agreeing a personal development plan (PDP) linked to an action plan based on business unit objectives. The role of HR staff is a strategic one, ensuring that all agency staff are given the opportunity to develop. Line management's role is as a catalyst to ensure that MD occurs and their staff adopt a PDP, linking individual and business needs. MD for team members was traditionally viewed as an exercise in passivity: 'staff historically sat there and let MD be done to them'.

Individual performance

Appraisal through the Assessment of Professional Performance (APP) is the major means of assessing individual performance. The APP is carried out by the job holder's line manager and a reviewing manager (usually the appraiser's line manager), who is responsible for monitoring standards and training. The area manager explained that IP measurement is 'all based around the appraisal process', with each individual manager expected to contribute to the targets for their business unit.

The monitoring of performance, through achievement of individual targets, was thought to be more difficult the more senior the manager. At an operational level, managers have delivery targets, but the attainment of policy or strategic objectives is much harder to measure. Appraisal was the major means available of measuring managerial performance on an individual basis, but the line managers interviewed emphasized the inadequacy of these arrangements. Operational targets were monitored on a regular basis and there were thirty-six of these in place, but systems were not in place to monitor individual contribution to the overall targets.

According to the area manager, the contribution MD had made to IP varied considerably and was a direct function of 'what an individual manager wants for themself'. It was thought to be relatively easy to improve an individual manager's skills and knowledge, but changing attitudes was qualitatively different, depending upon an individual's willingness to change and the MD available. The senior staff development manager similarly noted that 'some managers have developed an enormous amount, whilst no amount of MD results in an improved performance from other individuals; the success of the process depends on the attitude of the manager.'

Line managers believed that MD had improved IP, although in varying degrees. One line manager cited the case of a manager who, after following an NVQ, had developed the necessary competence to deal with a site that was riddled with problems and turn it into a viable operational unit. Another manager felt that there had been 'considerable' improvement in IP, as a result of which 'managers were far more willing to openly discuss their development needs'. A third line manager believed that MD only improved IP in certain circumstances: 'there is a nucleus of managers who aren't prepared to be developed'.

Three of the five team members interviewed felt that MD had made a positive contribution to IP. Secondment, job shadowing, opportunities to work on detached duties and training courses had enabled individual managers to develop in ways that they had never previously thought possible, with MD geared to individual needs.

Organizational performance

The Quality Framework was launched in May 1993 and had enabled all parts of the agency to monitor progress towards improving quality, had consolidated performance in new target areas and had improved the accuracy of payment. The Quality Framework is broken down into twelve criteria (one being development) based on core values of customer service, caring for staff, bias for action and value for money. In order to support an improved quality service to customers, training and development of staff were targeted to identify key performance areas in need of improvement. The Quality Framework was expected to be an inherent part of the strategic planning process and all existing initiatives such as *IiP* and the total quality approach were complemented by the framework.

To monitor customer service standards, a team of outside researchers was hired to visit or phone an office for advice or information and then rate their performance against various criteria, such as how long it took for the telephone to be answered, and the quality of information provided. The 'Mystery Shopper' scheme was not always well received by staff, some of whom felt it, 'smacked of sneakiness' and took up 'valuable time which could be used by a genuine customer'.

Team targets were measured by computer monitoring of budgets, delivery, quality and time. Team productivity and effectiveness were monitored by comparing local performance against nationally established criteria. Other performance measurements focus on teams' work commitments, over and above their everyday work allocation, and what competences are being demonstrated in excess of the basic requirements for that job. The training manager explained that there had been some tension between team and individual objectives so district targets were introduced to encourage team working within a district.

One line manager commented that team and individual targets were the same, but that the achievement of these had to be shared. In one line manager's opinion, the introduction of new schemes had a detrimental effect on improvements in OP, as these are being introduced without any corresponding increase in resourcing.

Team members felt that team performance targets did not really exist, instead various IP measures were amalgamated at district level. One team member felt that team working could be far more effective in terms of improving organizational performance; there was a huge amount of scope for rationalization because of the duplication of certain processes, on a number of sites in a specific district, which could be centralized: 'we need to encourage cooperation between sites rather than competition.'

In the opinion of the senior staff development manager, MD had made a special contribution to OP, and without MD, the agency would have needed to employ at least another 15,000 staff to deliver the required level of service. MD had developed and trained staff to provide a more efficient level of service than ever before. The training manager also thought MD had significantly improved OP: 'the improvements are maybe not quite as great as people wanted, but progress has definitely been made'.

Line managers were less certain that OP had been improved by MD 'if it has, it's by accident'. It was acknowledged that MD had allowed teams to develop a common purpose, and developed manager's 'people-related skills', which helped to motivate the workforce and give them leadership. The development of combined team working was identified by team members as a major MD initiative, which had a positive effect on team performance. Managers were thought to be more flexible, empowerment having given them more time to manage. A change in organizational culture had been achieved through MD, and empowerment had produced a more efficient and effective team.

Business performance

All offices were expected to meet Secretary of State targets in the following areas:

- clearance times for benefit claims;
- accuracy of benefit payments;
- customer satisfaction with the level of service;
- benefit control and financial recovery targets;
- management of resources allocated;
- milestones relating to significant business developments.

Targets on clearance time, accuracy, customer satisfaction and benefit control and financial recovery were measured on an agency-wide basis and the degree of conformity to these targets explored in detail at district and area level. Failure to comply with targets had to be fully explained and action plans prepared in order to ensure targets would be met in the future. Under the new structure, the agency achieved efficiency savings of £267 million in the first three years, and coped with a workload which four years previously would have required another 15,000 staff, as well as operating with management overheads reduced by 25 per cent. Market testing had been introduced on an agency-wide basis and at the time of the study £180 million of business had been successfully market tested.

The agency was measured by how well district offices performed to targets, which are nationally determined. Attempts were being made to introduce productivity measures as performance indicators and a project in operation at the time of the study was exploring unit costing in terms of inputs and outputs. Major problems had been encountered in reducing cases to inputs and outputs, as each case required a different number of actions to complete.

The market share of the agency was fairly secure, but respondents recognized that the situation could change in the future. The agency had been judged to be very successful in a prior options review and given another five year framework, but an internal structural review was underway at the time of the study. Outsourcing had not been introduced because adjudication has traditionally been conducted by an employee of the Secretary of State, but at the time of the study pilots were testing the removal of adjudication from the benefit process and giving this responsibility to another agency. Office services had been outsourced following market testing and a total facilities management contract had also been won by a private bidder.

The area manager believed that MD had made some contribution to improvements in BP, but attributed this to the 'Hawthorne effect'. Showing interest in employees was thought to be more important than the MD itself: 'it's this that gives you the results'. This phenomenon applied to all levels of managers, since it was untrue that 'the higher up the organization you go the less nurturing you need'.

Conclusions

The area manager did not believe that MD alone had improved BP, but felt that demonstrating interest in managers was the key issue to improving performance. Also, mechanistic MD alone could be a waste of time, and the importance of internalizing MD was emphasized. Some managers were thought to be too results-orientated and needed to trust the MD process more and give people the space to develop: 'It is important to balance what you need to deliver and how you are going to deliver it with MD, so that the development aspects are not lost in this process.'

The training manager thought that a good example of improved BP arising indirectly from MD was the 'drastic reduction' in the number of people involved in checking, which had been achieved by team working, itself a function of MD. Equally, the shift to the provision of more customer-focused services could not have been made without MD, coupled with the introduction of the Quality Framework. The important influence of the quality initiative was confirmed by the senior staff development manager, who explained that the introduction of the Quality Framework had resulted in an increasing emphasis on the importance of competence to achieve the quality service required by the agency; this had raised the profile of the PDP as a vehicle for raising competence and hence quality.

According to line management, the agency had experienced massive organizational changes over the past four years, but the focus of development was mainly at staff rather than managerial level: 'MD has been a case of self-development rather than a structured approach to the issue.' Nevertheless, it was acknowledged that MD must have had some effect, because the agency was having to meet the same targets as in the previous year, with fewer staff, including 30 per cent fewer managers.

Team members, in general, found it hard to identify specific benefits of MD. Their opinion was that it would take time for MD initiatives to feed into performance outcomes. MD has to relate to the agency's core business, but at the time of the study improvements in, for example, customer relations targets, could not be directly attributable to MD. One team member explained, 'my gut feeling is I'll be disappointed if it doesn't succeed in improving performance....I'm sure it will work and we will get something out of it.' Management attitudes had been changed by MD: 'managers are now more man-management orientated; they know how to handle staff and lead staff', but the issue for team members was how far this change would feed directly into improving district performance and quality of service. There was a consensus that there had to be some tangible pay-back or there was no point in undertaking MD. The problem was that MD might not be reflected in outputs, but it certainly was in terms of its impact on a well-established, strictly hierarchical, civil service culture, which was gradually changing into a far more flexible, devolved organization.

Case 7
Specialist insurance

Background

This specialist insurance company evolved out of a working people's hospital fund established in 1901. The Provident Fund, as it became known, continued after the NHS was established, facilitating the purchase of private rooms for contributors. Paradoxically, the restrictions on private beds in NHS hospitals imposed by Labour governments in the 1960s increased demand for the organization's services. Prices and incomes policies in the 1970s also increased demand for private health insurance because companies offered this as part of a remuneration package to executives. A further stimulus to growth was provided by tax concessions in the 1980s.

The pace of the growth in business was phenomenal. In 1960 the organization's turnover was £50,000 per annum; by 1970 this had increased to £50 million, with an annual growth rate of 30 per cent for five years. To cope with this growth in business, the organization employed more people but retained the original working methods established by the 'charitable' people who ran this as a welfare provision from the 1940s.

Every operation was manual, with multi-coloured forms completed on manual typewriters; the organization had the dubious honour of being the largest consumer of multi-coloured correction fluid in the UK! The chief executive estimated that 35 per cent of the floor space was taken up with paper and 25 per cent of staff were engaged solely on moving files. There was only one PC in the organization and a mainframe computer to print cheques to claimants; salary cheques were written by hand. Claims would be paid to clients who were in arrears with their premiums, the premium owed being deducted from the payment made. The four telephone lines were inadequate to cope with the level of demand, bad debt and customer complaints were increasing and staff turnover had reached 68 per cent.

When the new chief executive arrived in 1987, the situation was chaotic and critical. In an attempt to improve customer response, 100 telephone lines were introduced, which allowed more subscribers to contact the organization, while employees were unable to respond adequately because the process was so bureaucratic. The organization could not survive on that basis.

After the changes, the organization achieved a range of awards in recognition of its achievements in training, technological development and quality. At the time of the study it was the only UK insurer to have achieved *Investor in People* status and in addition to winning three Information Technology awards, has been certified to BS5750 parts 1 and 2.

Organizational strategy

The necessary dramatic improvement could only be accomplished by completely transforming the elements of the business: people, technology and processes. People were seen as the priority, since without human resource stability other changes could not be effectively made. To restore morale and build staff commitment, salaries were increased, a communications programme was established and a training strategy developed to raise skills. To increase operational efficiency, a network of PCs was installed, which improved communications and reduced paper handling through image processing.

These technological developments were the catalyst for business process re-engineering (BPR) which entailed restructuring operations around multi-disciplinary customer-service teams, instead of sequential processing by specialist departments. The transformation of work organization was based upon the strategy pioneered by Volvo at their Kalmar plant, where work teams took responsibility for complete production instead of fragmented tasks on the track. Stand-alone business teams were established to operate as autonomous units and new customer-concentric systems combined activities formerly undertaken by separate departments.

Each autonomous Business Unit (BU) created in this new flatter structure, is headed by a General Manager, and responsibility is devolved for writing their own business plans, establishing their own objectives and managing their staff. As a result, most HRM activities, including MD initiatives, are devolved to the BUs. The BPR allowed staffing levels to be reduced from over 400 to 250, while the volume of business increased.

All senior strategic managers agreed that OS 'fundamentally' influences MD. The flatter structure and empowerment of teams through BPR demanded various MD initiatives. Most line managers shared this view: 'the emphasis on quality and excellence in the strategy led to training to install that ethos within managers'. One manager believed MD was 'too focused on short-term goals, reacting to the market', while a senior strategic manager thought that MD could be linked more closely with OS by using MD to pursue long-term goals.

Senior strategic management noted that departmental strategies also influence MD since autonomous BUs develop annual business plans and identify appropriate training plans with the HR staff to support these. Line managers commented that following the directors' strategy meetings, all staff were involved in developing plans to achieve the objectives. Line managers believed that time constraints limited the scope for making the link stronger: 'the necessity to react to short-term issues makes it difficult...but it would be helpful'.

Team members described their experience of MD in terms of on-the-job (OTJ) coaching and designed courses: 'new team leaders are trained in appraisal by HR [department] then given guidance in preparing and executing appraisal'. Team members' views on the effectiveness of MD in their department varied widely. One individual commented that their training and development needs had not been identified recently other than *ad hoc* consideration around the introduction of a new process. Another noted that when developments are put in place, they are not always followed through as they should be, and this has an impact on morale. There was also some concern that 'de-layering reduces opportunities for promotion and change, and promotes a feeling of insecurity'.

HRD systems and processes

The HR manager described MD as competence based 'in the sense that all managers have a list of competences against which they are appraised'. Competences had been established at all levels to meet OS, but job performance was related to OS only 'in part'. Almost all HRD systems and processes were based on the Management Standards developed by MCI, which had been adopted 18–24 months before the study. Thus recruitment, selection, appraisal and personal development objectives are all couched in terms of the Standards.

The organization's Management/Supervisory Competence Standards and Staff Competence Standards, contextualized and modified forms of the Management Standards, are employed in the construction of job profiles and to define required competence. Line managers and team members defined the competences outlined in their job profiles in task terms, derived 'from the job as it exists today, and as it evolves with the department'. Job profiles and competences, initially identified from 'an analysis of job tasks', were regularly reviewed.

For line managers, appraisal in the organization was seen as two-way communication, an opportunity both to offer 'feedback to the individual and to plan for individual development'. Team members were equally clear about the two purposes of appraisal in the organization: 'feedback in both directions', involving a 'review of performance', and 'identify future training, development and prospects'.

Responsibility for MD is shared between the individual, the HR function and line managers. All individuals are responsible for self-improvement, while the HR function provides a TNA service, identifying gaps where training and development are needed and maintaining an overview of opportunities for MD. Line managers believed individuals needed to show willingness to engage in MD, while the HR role was seen as one of facilitating this. Team members similarly emphasized the responsibilities of line managers over HR specialists.

Senior strategic managers were emphatic that all managers were expected to be proactively involved with MD: 'all managers take responsibility for developing themselves', and 'those who do not take responsibility for their own development are unlikely to have a future'. MD was seen as a line function: 'all managers are expected to contribute to the development of their staff'. Line managers take these responsibilities seriously, starting with anticipating what MD is needed to support the business plan: 'it is necessary to interpret company strategy because roles are changing in the future'.

According to the HR manager, the goals for MD are derived from what is necessary to achieve the business plan. Line managers confirmed that the goals of MD are determined from the objectives of the business plans, and established as part of the process of identifying MD needs.

Most line managers felt that the achievement of management competence was rewarded for junior management by 'open recognition, salary increases and perks', and that '*ad hoc* recognition is more effective than PRP'. Compared with junior management, some managers felt that recognition was 'lacking for line managers', especially in terms of 'promotion opportunities', although 'PRP and bonuses' were thought to be available for 'higher management'. Where people fail to achieve defined goals, the reasons are explored through appraisal, support provided and appropriate remedial action taken: 'ultimately, the organization is not reticent about removing managers who fail to achieve'.

Individual performance

Senior strategic management explained that individual performance at supervisor level had been measured using a Management Information and Control System (MICS) which 'recorded individual work performance' against targets set for 'individuals and teams'. In addition to these productivity and quality measures, 'innovation and motivation' were assessed through appraisal. Because the MICS is 'very focused on individual performance', it is being replaced with 'customer facing standards', known as Customer First, which relate more to organizational or team performance. Appraisal is the 'foundation of individual performance assessment', providing a mechanism through which 'performance is monitored against competences' and an individual's deviation from the standard is discussed with their immediate superior.

Line managers generally equated their own individual performance with that of their team or department, since 'ultimate responsibility is with the manager'. Nevertheless, individuals within their department had 'tasks to be achieved weekly', which the managers monitor routinely. Appraisal was not thought of generally as a mechanism for monitoring performance because it is retrospective: 'any performance problems are dealt with immediately', although it provided a formal opportunity to examine and discuss performance trends.

The chief executive believed that MD had improved IP, because 'managers are now able to manage'. The senior manager responsible for human resources believed that MD had given individuals 'a better understanding of management' and made them better equipped for 'coping in today's business world'. Managers were unanimous in attributing improvements in IP to MD activities. A director cited as an example of self-development: 'I have applied what was learnt from case studies encountered in my Diploma in Leadership...I now brief people more clearly and have eliminated unnecessary activities.' A line manager commented that leadership training had made them 'recognize the "soft side"', provided a means of identifying potential, and changed their behaviour towards managing supervisors'. As a result of 'one-to-one coaching', managers had developed the 'skills and confidence to make client presentations at the highest level'. Line managers cited their application of skills developed through 'coaching on disciplining staff', 'interviewing' and 'presentation skills'. The benefits of various courses were also cited, including training in 'leadership, which helped me to understand people and taught me how to manage upwards'. Competence-based training for account managers was reported to have improved their performance, while 'team management was developed from situational learning and MD arranged by consultants'.

Team members similarly gave examples of improvements in IP arising out of MD activities. In addition to the value of specific training, in telephone techniques and appraisal, for example, individuals referred to wider benefits: 'I gained experience of the broader business environment through my BTEC course and this enhanced my ability to take on my new role.' A multiplier effect was cited in relation to coaching practice: 'I learnt coaching skills from my own manager and used these to develop a new member of staff at a junior level who was very bright and enthusiastic.' The development of supervisory level staff has meant that they are increasingly 'contributing to the management of others'.

Organizational performance

The senior financial manager referred to the importance of 'strict measures of performance in the operating areas'. Departments and teams have clear targets which must be met, such as 'claims must be turned round in 10 days'. Measures of productivity and effectiveness are monitored for each business area, especially 'internal customer standards' which are considered at monthly business managers' meeting. Negative measures of performance are also monitored: 'the organization pays £25 compensation if a claim is not dealt with in 7 days', and the incidence of such payments is monitored. Complaints are followed up and analysed, and, for example, 'if a telephone call has not been returned, the individual responsible may be dismissed'.

Another senior strategic manager explained how the MICS was being dismantled and replaced by Customer First, which focuses on the achievement of team targets agreed in the annual plan, in accordance with defined 'standards of service to achieve the mission', which are measured daily and monitored monthly. For the BU reports, 'performance indicators are required of every department'. The Executive (CEO and Directors) agree a strategic approach for the coming years and based on this, each BU produces an annual plan, converting the agreed strategy into actions and anticipated bottom-line results. These plans are subject to half-yearly review, accounting for what has been achieved and making modifications in the light of the experience of the six months. At the end of the year, the next annual plan is formulated and performance over the year reviewed against the targets that had been set.

Line managers placed great emphasis on the standards of service as key measures of departmental performance. Customer service standards are used in the BUs while in service units, such as accounts, there are reciprocal service standards which relate to the relationships with internal customers, the BUs. Departmental productivity measures define work load and turn-round time, so a given volume of work must be processed in a defined period.

Team members confirmed the volume and quality measures of OP. In addition to volume targets, the 'daily and weekly performance standards', include quality measures incorporated in 'Customer First', such as 'turnaround times' and 'telephone standards'. These measures are combined into a departmental quality index (DQI), which 'reports on business produced within standard and within quality'. In an area where it is expected that 85 per cent of business will be produced within standard and within quality, the DQI is 'usually around 96 per cent'.

The senior financial manager believed that MD had made a significant contribution to improving quality throughout the organization. The senior HR manager noted that MD had led to improved OP because 'all managers have expanded their knowledge base and built effective teams'. Line managers identified several areas in which MD had led to improved OP. Several managers mentioned the impact of team building courses which created 'identity and bonding' within departments, and allowed people to 'share information about successes'. Some team members referred to improvements in OP from MD initiatives which were highly specific: the fact that 'more schemes are now being sold with medical underwriting' necessitated 'training assessors to know what to look for'. Other comments were of a more general nature: 'as I develop, in turn I develop the team'; 'identifying training needs by comparing competences required with those acquired, helps to identify relevant OTJ training'. One team member thought that 'pressure has brought the team together, but this cannot be attributed to MD'.

Business performance

Senior strategic managers identified various aspects of BP which are measured in the organization. Since the creation of the autonomous BUs, many of the BP measures are relevant to the BUs, which were treated as departments in this case. The BU Reports for each unit detail 'subscriber numbers, earned income, underwriting ratio and renewal rate'. The underwriting ratio, the percentage of premium income paid out in claims, is seen as the primary measure of business performance.

The senior financial manager explained that the business measures such as ROCE are 'highly regulated by the Insurance Companies Acts and by the DTI', so that in an insurance company 'the ultimate objective is to out-achieve the solvency margins'. Productivity measures are a poor guide to BP unless the volume takes account of quality and time. Market share is not regarded as relevant; the organization has about 6.5 per cent of the total market but has adopted a niche marketing strategy where 'competitiveness is based on quality – we aim to exceed our customers' expectations'. ROCE is monitored for each BU and all costs are allocated to business divisions, whereas the performance of service departments is assessed against the budget allocated.

Senior strategic managers cited improvements in BP over the past three years, especially in areas which are intimately related to MD: 'there has been a 40 per cent improvement in delivered quality and a 50 per cent increase in productivity', while 'staff turnover has fallen from 66 per cent to 2.5 per cent'. There have been substantial improvements in productivity and important quality improvements, as well as an improved claims to income ratio. The different BUs 'have different profit rates, the bottom line is knife edge, but the investment return is good'. In terms of the all-important solvency measures, the DTI requires a minimum volume ratio (free reserves as a percentage of exposure to risk, in terms of total premium income) of 20 per cent. The organization had a volume ratio of '35 per cent 10 years ago, which rose to 50 per cent last year despite investment income losses on the stock exchange, and although this has now fallen to 40 per cent it is still double the minimum requirement'.

The chief executive believed that 'MD *alone* would have made no contribution to the improvements in business performance, but we could not have made these improvements without it.' Another senior strategic manager attributed the productivity increases primarily to BPR, but concluded similarly that 'MD has made a major contribution because the change cannot happen without it.' The senior financial manager thought that MD 'was not the only factor but was a major contributory factor' to the major improvements in BP.

Conclusions

For the chief executive, it is impossible to attribute the improvements in performance to MD as opposed to other factors, although the effects of MD are apparent at the level of individuals and teams. Nevertheless, MD was clearly seen as a necessary, but not sufficient, cause of improvements in BP and unambiguously linked to the transformation of HR statistics such as staff turnover. The improvements in IP are self-evident, and while recruiting 'the right people' was thought to be crucial, their further development has clearly been a result of a successful MD strategy. The senior financial manager believed that the role of MD should be considered as a part of the organization's wider HR philosophy of recruiting 'good people' and providing 'in-house and external training', to assemble a highly qualified team: 'people are "incentivized" here, not by money, but from the commitment to MD which comes from the top'.

Some line managers were confident in linking improvements in IP and OP to MD: 'all the evidence of rising productivity and falling complaints has coincided with MD activities'. Others felt 'intuitively that MD has contributed to the success', and observed how 'individuals are not daunted by challenges *because* MD has provided the competences to cope with new demands'. To support the changes under BPR, 'MD was essential – we could not have done it without

MD'; 'the changes are important, but MD supported their achievement'; 'MD was a major factor in the improvements'. While all had provided specific examples of improvements arising out of MD, some had reservations about how overall improvements could be attributed to MD: 'MD is tied to strategy, but attribution is difficult'; 'MD cannot be isolated from other factors, such as recruitment'; 'it is difficult to prove MD is having an effect…it has contributed but is not a panacea and drive or ambition is more important'.

Team members were unanimous and confident in attributing improvements to MD, since they invariably referred to improvements in IP relating to themselves and the staff for whom they were responsible: 'the effects of coaching can be clearly traced'; 'the immediate impact is obvious from the improvement in performance of all individuals'; 'the standard is established, and MD designed so that it can be met, so when the standard is achieved we can say that the MD has been effective'; 'I could not have known how to do this without having taken the NVQ route'. At the same time, there are signs that work pressure is 'stretching resources and making it difficult to train newcomers, so there is a need to develop training away from the job, even though people within the department are capable of delivering the necessary training'.

Case 8

Charity organization

Background

As a major charity providing a total of sixty different services to blind and partially sighted people throughout the UK, the organization has a large potential customer/client group: one million people in the UK are blind or partially sighted, of whom more than 90 per cent are aged 60 and over.

The organization's vision is to work for 'a world in which people with a visual impairment enjoy the same rights, freedom, responsibilities and quality of life as people who are fully sighted'. Their mission is 'to challenge blindness by empowering people with a visual impairment, removing the barriers they face and helping to prevent blindness'.

Four 'Strategic Priorities' were established to guide the organization's work until the end of the decade which entailed challenging blindness, extending services to more people, giving priority to older blind and partially sighted people, and improving the quality of services to users and supporters.

Since its foundation in 1868 the organization has grown into one of the largest employers in the voluntary sector with a current workforce of some 2,300 paid staff, and over 10,000 volunteers. The organization is structured into three external and two internal service divisions. The external divisions are concerned with education and training, vocational services and technical consumer services. The internal divisions are concerned with finance and administration and external relations. In addition, there is a small Directorate which includes the Director General and support staff as well as teams working in key strategic areas, including corporate planning.

The organization's income comes from a small statutory grant from central government, the sale of products and services to individuals, contracts with other organizations (such as local authorities) for the provision of services to particular groups, and donations, of which 70 per cent are legacies.

Staff development in general is given high priority within the organization's strategy, a review having concluded that

'investing in training and development is of critical importance. It improves both the way we listen and respond to users and the quality of the services we offer them. We will increase spending on training and development by 20 per cent over the next six years.

Management development, however, is relatively recent in the organization. A post with specific responsibilities for MD was created and the organization established corporate MD so that at the time of the study a strong commitment to MD was claimed, although it was also recognized that restricted resources limited what could be achieved.

Formal MD provision involved both internal courses run by the personnel department and opportunities to take part in a range of external, certificated programmes. MD was seen by all interviewees to equate with the provision of training via these internal and external courses. The organization does not have national accreditation/recognition for any aspects of its training and development in general, or MD in particular. However, one department is currently working towards *Investor in People* status.

Organizational strategy

The existence of clear links between OS and MD was vigorously asserted by senior managers, and was reflected in the organization's strategy document. The four Strategic Priorities were supported by a series of 'Resource Objectives' relating to the development of human, physical and financial resources, including a target that, by 1999 100 per cent of managers would, within six months of appointment, meet the required level of core competences.

Interviewees gave examples of how OS influenced MD. For example, the strategic priority to expand the customer base translated into the need to improve marketing skills at all levels of management. The review of the organization's services and development of its strategy led to large-scale internal reorganization: 'much of the internal management training provision has aimed to support and enable the management of change – courses have covered areas such as team leadership, consultancy skills and presentation skills'.

Departmental strategies and objectives were taken directly from OS and appeared to have a definite link to MD, although one interviewee indicated that departments also set other objectives which are not linked to corporate strategy. Some of the more junior managers interviewed felt that the links between corporate and divisional strategies and MD were less clear, doubting that comprehensive MD existed in the organization.

There was also a feeling that the organization does not have a strategy for developing its managers, with apparently *ad hoc* allocation of places on courses and no systematic, strategic approach to developing either individuals or groups of managers. The lack of any pathway for progression within the organization was commented on by a number of interviewees, together with the lack of encouragement to develop careers either within the organization or outside it. Some junior staff felt that while the organization was committed in principle to MD, a shortage of financial resources and a lack of willingness on the part of some managers to support the development of their staff were impeding its implementation in practice.

Higher levels of management also acknowledged that resource constraints were hampering progress in terms of putting plans for MD into practice. A Management Competency Framework (MCF) had been approved by senior management a year previously, but the development programmes which would support the achievement of those competences by the organization's managers had not yet been established.

Another concern common to a number of the more junior managers was that their management role and responsibilities were not clearly defined and that there was no standardization of what was expected of managers in different parts of the organization, suggesting that knowledge of the MCF was limited.

HRD systems and processes

The MCI Standards were first considered three years prior to the study but were not found to meet the organization's needs. Instead, the MCF based on the MCI Standards, reflected working practices within the organization. The MCF includes thirty-eight competences, half of which equate to some degree with MCI elements of competence from the level 5 NVQ/SVQ.

There were plans to use the MCF in a number of ways throughout the organization in the future, but at the time of the study its use was limited and it had not been widely disseminated.

Although the MCI Standards are not used explicitly in the organization's in-house management training courses, it was claimed that the development provided would enable managers to meet the Standards in areas such as recruitment and selection. Of the external courses used by the organization, the Certificate in Management Studies (CMS) is based on the underpinning knowledge requirements of the MCI Standards, and 10 per cent of managers had been through this programme.

There was unanimity that all individual managers have a key role to play in their own MD, identifying their own training needs (both via the annual appraisal process and on an ongoing basis) and requesting places on training courses. Some felt that the process of identifying training needs was individual interests and motivation rather than being guided by what the organization expects of its managers. The organization's Staff Development Policy outlines the roles and responsibilities of individuals for development in general.

Line managers' responsibility for the development of their staff was described as identifying needs (again, via the appraisal process), approving training courses and funding individuals' training from their departmental budgets.

Inconsistent approaches to MD in different parts of the organization were reported, with some managers being very supportive and others showing little interest in, or commitment to, the development of their teams. Line managers were seen to be powerful 'gatekeepers' to development opportunities, so the amount and type of development which an individual could access were dependent on the attitude of their manager.

The role of the central personnel department was generally seen as providing a range of courses, identifying other training provision and strategic planning of MD, ensuring it supports the corporate strategy. Personnel staff regarded the organization's appraisal system as designed to support achievement of the MCF as there is a direct reference to the framework in the appraisal documentation. When agreeing managers' objectives and personal development plans, reference is made to the MCF in order to describe outcomes and acceptable standards. The majority of interviewees saw the purpose of appraisal as being to review performance and achievement of objectives over the past year and to plan future work and personal development.

According to interviewees, personal development objectives were not expressed in terms of the MCI Standards or the organization's MCF, although the appraisal policy states that they should be. The appraisal process was nevertheless seen as the main vehicle for identifying these needs and discussing personal development issues.

According to personnel staff, the Management Standards were used in recruitment and selection procedures, but their use seemed to be limited to that central team, rather than being widespread throughout the organization. When questioned about job descriptions, the majority of interviewees felt it was up to individual managers to decide what was required of posts within their teams/departments and did not refer to any central guidance or framework on which job descriptions should be based. Two interviewees were aware of the existence of the MCF but did not feel that it was being widely used. Reward systems in the organization are not linked to achievement of the MCI Standards or the organization's own MCF.

Individual performance

The main vehicle for measuring and monitoring IP was the appraisal system with its annual review of progress and achievement. Many of the interviewees also mentioned monthly reviews of targets and objectives. There was a cascade process to target setting: corporate objectives feed into departmental and team objectives which then feed into the objectives for individual managers. A number of interviewees felt that the objectives tend therefore to relate mostly, if not entirely, to the operational/service delivery side of managers' roles, rather than the people management aspects. Examples of areas of performance which were set as objectives/targets included: 'the number of customers accessing/using their service or product'; 'financial targets – related to both expenditure and income'; and 'output targets'.

Some interviewees mentioned that aspects such as personal effectiveness, managing your own work, managing the work of a team and staff turnover were included in their targets. For example, one manager had a target of 'having a settled and effective team', although they were unsure how possible it was to measure its achievement.

A number of improvements in IP as a result of MD were cited by interviewees. The interviewee from central personnel had witnessed the promotion and career development of managers who had taken part in the CMS programme, and believed this was at least in part due to their participation. The same interviewee also believed that better recruitment decisions were being made as a result of the training which managers had received in this area. One of the more senior managers believed his own management practice had improved greatly as a result of following a number of courses up to and including one at degree level. One interviewee had found the in-house time-management course very helpful and as a result of it believed that her work performance was more effective and efficient; she was also taking part in the CMS programme and was finding that useful in a range of areas including marketing, developing service indicators and team working and motivation.

A second participant in the CMS course also found that it had improved performance through becoming able to identify areas for change within their area of responsibility and to implement those changes. The manager also felt better able to assess the needs and capabilities of staff. One interviewee knew two other managers who were taking part in MBA programmes claiming that they found the courses very useful, and that their performance as managers was improving, although this could not necessarily be attributed to the MBA. No written evidence was produced to support these claims.

Organizational performance

As noted above, team and departmental performance targets were very much linked to individual targets at the organization and some interviewees found it hard to separate the two. A number of interviewees referred to the relatively new system of Service Delivery Planning (introduced about a year before the study was undertaken) and the associated performance indicators which are set for each team's work and which relate to a wide range of cost, quality, output and other measures, such as numbers of customers served and the speed of response to letters and phone calls. There are over 1,000 such indicators across the organization's 60 services, so the aspects of performance which are measured and monitored therefore varied from team to team, depending on the nature of the service they were providing. Managers were expected to collect basic data relating to the performance indicators for their service and this data was then analysed and evaluated across the organization as a whole by the Corporate Planning Unit.

Improvements in team or departmental performance resulting from MD were difficult for interviewees to identify. The most common example was that particular teams were seen to function more effectively after their managers had been through a particular course or development programme: therefore the improved IP of the manager resulted in improved team performance.

Others mentioned broad improvements in areas such as marketing, public relations, recruitment and selection, appraisal, team building and public speaking across the organization as a whole following training in those areas. Fund-raising income was claimed to have increased by 40 per cent over the past few years following extensive training of all levels of staff in relevant skills.

However, one interviewee was more aware of the lack of MD than of its success in improving performance, feeling that morale was low in the organization due to recent restructuring and that this low morale could have been alleviated if more MD had taken place. Again, no written evidence was available to support the claims of improved performance.

Business performance

The performance indicators referred to above were also seen to be one way in which BP is measured. More specifically, levels of income from different sources were measured (voluntary, legacy, investment and service), as are levels of expenditure. It was emphasized though that as a charity, the organization was not a 'finance-led' organization: it does not exist to earn ever higher profits. Rather, it is 'service-led' and works to reach as many people as possible with its products and services. However, it was also pointed out that the charity sector is becoming increasingly competitive and that more MD is needed to enable the organization to maintain and expand its levels of service.

In terms of improvements in BP as a result of MD, interviewees again found it difficult to identify clear links between the two. Although it was claimed that there were ongoing improvements in relation to most of the relevant performance indicators, these improvements could not be specifically attributed to MD. One senior interviewee believed that the organization is now producing better quality products and services, but that there had not been an improvement in 'bottom line' performance because of their status as a charity rather than a commercial organization.

Conclusions

All interviewees felt that MD was just one factor amongst several which can impact on performance. Other factors which were seen to affect performance included the following:

- skills learnt elsewhere (e.g. a single parent had learnt coping and 'juggling' skills from that experience which could be applied to the management role);
- experience gained from doing the job for longer;
- teams getting to know each other and their respective roles better;
- managers being given the opportunity to extend their work roles and thus learn from new experiences.

The MCI Standards themselves were judged to be inappropriate to the needs of the organization and established working practices, so the alternative MCF was developed by adapting and expanding some aspects of the MCI Standards. However, this MCF was still not widely used at the time of the study although there were plans for it to be fully implemented by the end of the decade.

Some of the external management training provision used by the organization was based on parts of the MCI Standards, but relatively few managers had taken part in these external programmes. It was therefore concluded that the majority of managers in the organization do not take part in development activities based on the MCI Standards.

Some MD is provided, even if its extensiveness was questioned by some of those interviewed, and the majority of respondents believed that it did improve the performance of individuals. Nevertheless, MD was seen by all to be just one factor amongst several which have an impact on managers' performance, and it was difficult to say whether development based on MCI Standards would lead to clearer or more easily attributable improvements. As for the impact of MD on team and departmental performance, this was more difficult for interviewees to identify although it was generally felt that a more effective manager leads to a more effective team. The links between MD and improved BP were even harder to identify, particularly given the organization's focus on service rather than profits. It was generally acknowledged that MD does improve performance, although this was more of a view based on knowledge and experience of the organization rather than something which could be verified with documentary evidence.

The extent to which MD is linked to OS was another issue on which respondents expressed differing views. The more senior managers believed that there were very strong links between the two, and the strategy document and staff development policies supported this view. However, the more junior managers seem to be unaware of the links.

The extent to which HRD systems and processes, particularly appraisal, were based on the MCF was again something on which those interviewed did not agree. Knowledge of the Framework's existence was patchy, particularly at lower levels of management, and it appeared that its implementation would be welcomed by those who wanted some guidelines as to what the organization expects of its managers.

Finally, there were other factors affecting the success of MD in the organization, beyond its links to OS and other HRD processes. These factors included:

- a lack of resources to implement planned MD;
- differing levels of commitment to staff development by line managers;
- limited information (to junior managers in particular) about what MD is aiming to achieve, for whom and how;
- a lack of time and support for managers to fulfil their management responsibilities (given the pressure to achieve service/operational objectives);
- managers not having enough time (because of work and home pressures) to complete assignments and projects required by external management programmes.

Case 9

Magistrates' Courts

Background

The organization comprises all the Magistrates' Courts in a region of England. The employing organizations are eight Magistrates' Courts Committees (MCCs), which are made up of Magistrates elected annually by the bench. The MCCs, which elect a chairman, perform roles analogous to a company board of directors:

- they appoint Justices' Clerks and their staff;
- they determine necessary court house infrastructure;
- they establish courses of instruction and training for Magistrates;
- they authorize costs, allocate and control budgets;
- they oversee personnel administration.

Each of the 105 MCCs in England and Wales is a legal entity which estimates the financial resources required for its operations over the coming year; the local authority pays 20 per cent and the Lord Chancellor's Department (LCD) 80 per cent of the sum requested. The 105 MCCs are served by seventeen Regional Training Units (RTUs), headed by a Regional Training and Development Officer (RTDO), which deliver and facilitate training and development and are responsible to all the MCCs in their region. Often a Clerk of the Justices at a major Magistrates' Court assumes line management responsibility for the RTU, which also liaises with the Training Branch of the LCD.

The RTDO in the region studied has been especially active in promoting MD, for example through facilitating opportunities for individuals to qualify for NVQ at levels 3, 4 and 5. There are currently 130 staff in the region working towards NVQs out of 560 employees in total, and 195 employees have gained nationally recognized qualifications through the RTU since it was formed in May 1990. Similarly, significant commitment to MD has been demonstrated by senior management in the MCCs in the region, which are treated as a sub-unit of analysis in this case, analogous to divisions of an enterprise.

Within each MCC there is a number of Courts, each containing four departments: Courts (dealing with the activities within the court room); General Office (administrative functions divided into Pre-Court Administration and Post-Court Administration); Accounts Office (dealing with fixed penalties, fines and fees, maintenance and domestic finance and fine enforcement), and a Computer Section.

In administering justice, the Magistrates' Courts serve several client groups, as well as society at large: the police and their administration; the Crown Prosecution Service (CPS); the Probation Service; the Crown Court; lawyers and solicitors; the Prison Service; victim and witness support groups; social workers; and the public, including claimants, witnesses and defendants.

The organization had made commitment to achieving *Investor in People* status and an application was in progress for a National Training Award (NTA) at the time of the study. Senior strategic managers noted that MD activities in each MCC would 'feed into the *IiP* initiative in the region' and that the MCCs would in time also achieve *IiP* status and apply for NTAs.

At the time of the study, however, the strategic priority was restructuring. Having been in existence for over 600 years, the Magistrates' Courts underwent significant changes prior to the study. In the late 1980s a rationalization of the 105 courts in England and Wales was proposed, bringing the local MCCs under the control of a national operation from the Home Office.

Organizational strategy

Performance targets were introduced in 1986 and since 1992 there have been cash-limited budgets. Public finance constraints, coupled with the devolution of budgets and a statutory requirement for MCCs to produce Business Plans, were the stimulus to a change in managerial philosophy away from the paternalistic, hierarchical traditions. In the resultant flatter structures, a team approach was emphasized, in which responsibility was devolved, creating a need for more MD. In view of the changes, actual and proposed, senior management took a proactive approach to developing appropriate strategies. These strategies have been underpinned by MD: 'our managers could not have coped with the changes without MD because now our legal administration heads are strategic managers'. As in any organization, 'the change process is managed more effectively when managers are supported, developed and equipped to deal with change'.

In 1990 the Training Policy Committee of the LCD issued guidelines in the *Management Competences and Training Strategy*, which established a basic framework for the development of all levels of managers. Funding from the LCD for MD within the MCCs was to focus on work which fitted within this framework. Written evidence from the Action Plan of one MCC shows how strategic objectives, linked to senior management indicators, were mapped onto senior management performance standards.

Senior strategic managers, one a Justices' Chief Executive and another Clerk to the Justices, confirmed that OS influences MD. The RTDO explained that the Magistrates' structure had always required most senior managers to have a law qualification, and because managers are now required to 'write strategic plans and business plans for the MCC', the need for MD has been recognized. Individuals in various line management positions gave examples of how OS influences MD: 'developing team work to put the strategy into effect'; 'the skills required for career development in line with the business plan'.

Senior strategic managers believed MD could be linked more closely with OS because the organization is 'very localized, making MD slow and haphazard'. The RTDO, however, believed that MD could not be linked more closely with OS because 'MD is now linked into NVQ standards and competence must be demonstrated against the needs of the organization'.

If the MCCs are regarded as the departments within the region, then their strategies very much influence MD activities. Specific MD is designed for particular courts to support 'translating the strategic plan into individual business plans'. Line managers gave specific examples of the link between departmental strategies and MD. For the courts to work as a whole together, 'MD strategy had moved from "go on this course", to the policy of basing training and development on NVQs in order to get staff involved in MD'. The link between MD and departmental strategy could be strengthened, and was expected to be, because 'under the restructuring, everyone will have a development plan related to the Business Plan'. As two managers explained, the 'Action Plan is doing this by translating aims into targets' through which MD needs are identified.

There was universal support for MD initiatives among the team members interviewed. One described it as 'brilliant' in the way that 'MCI Standards have been adopted and given a qualifications structure to MD'. Another thought that MD was 'very successful and very effective' but noted the difficulty in 'finding time to operationalize' it.

HRD systems and processes

The RTDO described the approach to MD in the organization as '100 per cent competence based'. Most HRD systems and processes are based on the MCI Standards, which were adopted in 1991. The MCI developed a guide to the Management Standards for the Magistrates' Courts Service in October 1992, which outlines the framework of MD in the Magistrates' Courts, how the Standards are to be used and the Senior Management Development Initiative, a development and accreditation process central to MD in the Service.

Some courts are using the Standards in recruitment and selection and they form the fundamental framework for MD and training. Moreover, PDPs are work-related and linked to the achievement of Standards. Appraisal systems were not yet in place at the time of the study, but it was intended to build them around the Standards once in operation. Competence, within the context of the Magistrates' Courts, has been defined as 'the demonstrated ability and willingness to perform a task to the standard required by the organization'. Among line managers, current job descriptions were seen as inadequate: 'a list of tasks, not linked to competences'; although it was recognized that in the future, they would be linked to the MCI Standards.

The Magistrates' Courts Service guide to MD noted that 'roles and responsibilities in MD need to be defined and agreed locally'. Responsibilities for MD were described in terms of collaboration between the individual, RTDO and line manager. The RTDO outlined a 'triangular model of MD' and explained that the goals of MD for individuals are 'negotiated between the line manager, human resource specialist or tutor and the individual learner'. Line managers described goal setting as part of the process of identifying MD needs and opportunities. The goals stem from the management team's objectives; these are recommended in the Division Business Plan to the MCC, who 'decide what is achievable and what targets are set for improvement'.

The individual and their line manager should work together to assess current competence and to complete a personal development plan (PDP). Line managers were seen as helping clarify MD needs with the individual, and providing 'support and encouragement' as well as acting in a 'mentoring role'. The RTDO was seen both as a 'facilitator', providing 'training and facilities for MD', and in a strategic role, 'linking MD to the Business Plan' and 'putting forward ideas to the MCC'.

Senior strategic managers acknowledged that although all managers are expected to contribute to MD of their staff, 'not all are doing so'. At present, managers' involvement in MD for staff is 'left to the individual', but the adoption of PDPs was expected to ensure managers take responsibility for staff development. Line managers accepted their role in developing staff, and some related this to OS. Team members commented that all MD is agreed 'for a certain purpose', and demonstrated how the organization's objectives and the individual's development were matched. Two individuals described their role in relation to the activities undertaken in pursuit of a Management NVQ 5.

The achievement of managerial competence is usually 'not directly rewarded', in as far as there is 'no remunerative advantage, with the exception of Trainee Court Clerks'. Improvements in performance lead to further opportunities for development, and in some cases there are resource implications for attaining organizational objectives.

Individual performance

According to senior strategic managers, the traditional 'authoritarian style' of management in the Magistrates' Courts has given way to 'the empowerment of middle management'. As a result, IP is 'measured by self-empowerment' and there is less need for line managers and senior managers to intervene. There are specific targets for the organization, but the monitoring of IP for managers is mainly through the appraisal process, just as the organization 'is currently appraising Magistrates using a competence-based approach'. The RTDO explained how the functional model and the personal competence model from the Management Standards were used in MD to trace personal development through a 'log book, counter-signed and corroborated by a third party, showing both functional and behavioural achievements'.

Individual targets were sometimes set for managers from the Business Plan. The individual managers' log books and portfolios of evidence are primarily used for 'qualification and assessment of NVQ levels 4 and 5, or supervisor awards ISM, BTEC, and CMS', but in addition they may be monitored by the line manager.

Line managers noted that OP measures were more significant than IP measures. On the court clerking side, 'office statistics are interpreted by local managers to identify bad practice and to monitor IP'. In general, IP is monitored through 'observation by line managers and mentors in various sections'. In Court administration the achievement of individual targets was 'part of the action plan currently being developed by supervisors'. The portfolios of managers working towards NVQs 'can be used as a reference document for improving IP'. Two team members were unable to identify any aspects of IP which were measured, although a third noted that the 'analysis of corporate targets led to a focus on IP'. The work of court clerks is overseen routinely, and if the work of the management team or the legal advisor to the Magistrates is 'done badly, the Magistrates complain, or it may involve the Appeal Court'.

Senior strategic managers believed that MD had contributed to improved IP, for example in improving the 'consultative style' of managers and gaining a 'better understanding of the needs of the organization'. In one case, the MCC had explicitly 'acknowledged the improved performance of the chief executive and other individuals'. The RTDO explained how 'linking MD to Standards has given benchmarks and criteria for individuals to perform to, and has structured recruitment and selection'.

Line managers cited a wide range of ways in which MD had contributed to improved IP. At the individual level, MD had 'boosted confidence' and made managers 'more aware of their potential'. Gaining qualification to NVQ level 5 had brought 'recognition of achievements', which made one individual 'more motivated to continue to improve performance'.

Improved IP had come from gaining a better 'appreciation of their role in the organization' and 'understanding the organization's objectives.' Several mentioned the 'demonstration value' of their MD achievements, the 'knock-on effect in encouraging other staff' and their improved role in MD activities, such as 'assessing other people's work'.

Team members also mentioned general benefits of MD such as 'improved perception of themselves', 'better understanding of the job' and 'pride from recognition of achievement'. One individual commented how their own development had led to 'changing the work organization of the department through job rotation'.

Organizational performance

The RTDO explained that 'objectives are set and agreed between the Management Board and the MCC' and that OP is measured in terms of 'achievements against these objectives'. While performance within the magistrates' Courts is most closely measured, monitored and analysed at the level of OP, these measures are complicated by diverse national targets and the impact of other parties involved in the administration of justice; new Police Standards, for example, have slowed down the performance of Magistrates' Courts. Nevertheless, there are targets established in terms of 'volume of processing' and 'response rates', as well as customer service measures.

Line managers described the monitoring of OP through official MIS statistics, which are considered as measures of BP, and measures of 'inter-departmental effectiveness'. The MIS statistics are used to judge the effectiveness of departments, as is inter-departmental feedback. Cases are entered into the computer and 'at each phase in the process there are time limits' for processing the case, since 'any delays have a knock-on effect in other departments'. Feedback from adjacent departments provides a measure of internal customer satisfaction, while quality of service measures include 'waiting time' on the day of a court appearance and customer service issues discussed by all agencies involved in a quarterly forum of court user groups (youth, adult and family). In addition, there is a complaints procedure and HMI inspection every four years. Team members commented on the relative absence of OP measures, other than the MIS overall measures of BP.

The RTDO believed that 'groups of people working on the Standards together raises awareness of the constraints and pressures on colleagues', which improves OP. Line managers cited various improvements in OP arising from MD activities, such as a 'recognition among staff that the administrative side is not just there to "open up the shop"'. Improved team performance was obvious to another manager, and attributed to MD; while a third cited 'a team development project to produce a guidance manual' which resulted in increased 'team awareness and effectiveness'.

Team members explained how job rotation had resulted in 'better team working: individuals will automatically move to help where there is workload pressure'. As a result of MD activities, quality improvements were also evident. In another Court, the administration was faced with the problem of using magnetic tape returns to issue DVLA endorsements in place of the manual system: 'how this should be introduced was discussed with the team and as a trial run parallel systems were brought in and after 6 weeks we had transferred to magnetic tape only'.

Business performance

Senior strategic managers described the four principal organization-wide 'performance indicators' in the MIS as measures of BP: 'weighted case load; average time to complete case; fine enforcement; and quality of service'. About 35 per cent of the MIS is based on weighted case load, which therefore has most impact on the budget. However, this indicator is particularly 'susceptible to external influences beyond the control' of the Magistrates' Service, such as the economic climate, human behaviour and policing policy. Moreover, since the budget is based on *previous* weighted case load, fluctuations in activity can be problematic for the Service. In one Court, for example, the weighted case load had increased by 10 per cent compared with the same quarter of the previous year. There are also difficulties with the throughput measure of time to complete cases, since 'the concept of justice constrains throughput: it is said that "justice delayed is justice denied", but it is equally true of "justice hastened"', so it is essential that throughput is not increased at the expense of the quality of justice. Also, inefficiencies of solicitors and the fact that some Magistrates are slower than others in their deliberations are extraneous factors affecting this statistic. Fine enforcement is not only influenced by the efficiency of the Magistrates' Courts administration, but by wider social factors affecting people's ability to pay, and by the efficiency of the police. Quality of service measures contribute to 5 per cent of the budget, but in the past these have simply been concerned with court facilities rather than customer perceptions. As one respondent commented, 'by the very nature of their activities, the Magistrates' Courts have considerable capacity for customer *dissatisfaction!*'

In terms of the MIS statistics of BP, there have been improvements, but these should be interpreted with caution. Weighted case load has increased since 1990, and 'although there have been definition changes in that period', the 'historic picture is one of improvement in position in the league table of MCCs'. The time to complete cases has reduced, and this is thought to be 'a fair indicator of performance', especially since 'waiting times have been reduced'. Fine enforcement has improved, but the key issue is the 'speed of getting information to the police', since after that, enforcement is a police issue. The quality of service measures used by the MIS have shown little change because they are concerned with facilities, but the MCCs recently developed Service Charters, explaining what court users are entitled to expect from the Service and outlining the complaints procedure.

Despite these caveats, senior strategic management believe that MD has led to improvements in BP as measured by the increased throughput with reduced staffing. Senior management have seen the changes as opportunities rather than threats and acted to take advantage of them.

Conclusions

Senior strategic managers believed that the benefits of MD were evident in the changes in their own behaviour, and identified a 'direct link between MD and improved performance'; also MD had proved an 'impetus to other developments', and had 'removed the fear of change'. Another senior manager cited 'evidence from improvements in behaviour' and believed that MD 'has been a significant factor' contributing to this and to building confidence. The RTDO acknowledged that causality cannot be attributed unequivocally to MD but believed that 'MD is a contributory factor, which cannot be isolated' and suggested that by considering the counter-factual, what does not happen in the absence of MD, its impact could be assessed.

Line managers agreed in the difficulty of attributing causality, especially since in many areas 'the action plan has only just started' but most were nevertheless 'personally convinced', and believed that monitoring and measurement would provide concrete evidence in the future. There was a 'change in individuals' attitudes and behaviour: they see the job differently'. People were said to be more motivated, 'despite the prospect of cuts' as a result of budgetary constraints, because they are 'more aware of the problems'. Certainly performance improvements were 'nothing to do with money!' and 'increased motivation and involvement was associated with MD' activities. For example, 'there had been increased remuneration in 1992 and no improvements in performance, whereas since individuals had begun working towards NVQs they had demonstrated increased motivation', despite increased workload. The qualification of the administrative side was seen as having 'important demonstration value' in breaking down the 'historic division between the administrative and legal functions'.

For team members, the key to attributing improvements to MD was their temporal coincidence: 'the improvements only began when MD started to happen, not before'; 'I have been in the post for 23 years and improvements, like MD, have been recent.' For example, the skills developed in interview training were 'put into practice immediately' and the improvements in interviewing were 'evidenced by *feedback* from the agency providing youth trainees'. In another case, 'team working only improved because of the developmental activity'. Top management were thought to be 'seeking improvements and raising standards', and MD was seen to play a vital role in enabling individuals to cope with the reorganization and in 'making the new organization suit middle management aims'.

Case 10

Regional newspaper

Background

The organization represents one region of a major regional newspaper publisher employing 3,200 people in the group overall. In this region, 460 employees (FTE) work on 38 titles, 29 of which are free papers, providing saturation coverage in the area with almost 1.8 million copies per publishing day. One title represented one of the largest free distribution papers in the UK.

There was a slight decrease in circulation revenue in 1995, but this was still above the 1993 level, which had itself been a 60 per cent increase on the previous year. Over the previous three years advertising revenue had represented a constant 91 per cent of total revenue (97 per cent if leaflets are included). Other revenue sources, such as package travel services for readers, more than compensated for loss of revenue from declining circulation, and a diversification strategy was introducing further new revenue sources. The increasing cost of newsprint had a major impact on the whole newspaper industry and a further contraction of circulation and reduction of titles was thought to be inevitable, leading to intensified competition as publishers of free papers target competitors' titles for closure.

The organization was widely characterized as being dynamic and committed to HRD. Since June 1993 they had been working towards *Investor in People* status and had implemented NVQs to a significant extent. The *IiP* status was not being pursued for the value of the award itself, but in order to deliver HRD benefits for the business.

The purpose of the organization has been defined as being 'to provide our communities with valuable, up-to-date information on which they can rely to help make decisions and enrich their lives'. Among the values and beliefs under-pinning this purpose, two are of particular significance for MD:

- we value highly the enthusiasm, commitment, knowledge, skills, team work and integrity of our colleagues, recognizing that our future is built on these qualities;

- we are committed to providing training and feedback to allow each individual to bring added value to their role, and to help them realize their full potential.

In fulfilling this purpose, the organization's mission is 'to publish the region's acknowledged brand leaders supplying local information in each of the communities we serve'. One indication of achieving the mission was thought to be that 'our employees will say this is the best company they have worked for and we will feel that our colleagues are the best we could have'.

Organizational strategy

The OS reflects the purpose and mission of the organization and involves a range of cost control measures including integration and rationalization of certain operations and cost reduction through cutting back some distribution. Credit management targets include maintaining the days outstanding for debts to below 36, keeping bad debt at below 1 per cent of revenue, and maintaining a pre-paid ratio of 2.6 per cent. Technological changes in progress at the time of the study were substantial, involving an upgrade of equipment and an integrated database as well as more extensive use of labour.

The Business Plan identifies key tasks with targets for market share growth in each marketplace, and a private advertising strategy to increase the customer base and revenues. Management development was cited as an area for further action in the Business Plan, with key tasks focused on appraisals, in-house programmes and conferences and seminars.

The extent to which OS influences MD was a matter of some debate among senior strategic managers interviewed. A managing director believed that OS did not really influence MD because of the devolved autonomy of operations, although a developing influence from the group was acknowledged. Two other directors believed OS influenced MD and each cited investment in new technology, such as the direct input system, which was a key part of OS and which created new training and development needs. New technology radically altered the process, changing roles, staffing levels and the required competences, all of which had implications for MD. A fourth director was more circumspect, suggesting that OS influenced MD 'to a degree' and citing the shift from a hierarchical structure to a more project-based structure, which had created the need for MD to improve team-building skills.

One line manager agreed that OS influences MD 'to some extent', and noted that MD gave individuals a better idea of the business aims. Other line managers were unequivocal that OS influences MD, and gave various examples:

- the key tasks set at the beginning of the year lead directly to identifying MD needs;
- training culture and commitment to MD are implicit in the Business Strategy;

- top management produce the vision and management seminars delegate and empower managers.

The apparent difference in perceptions between senior strategists and line managers is explicable in terms of their different levels of awareness of OS. The senior strategists were most familiar with the overall strategy so could identify areas which were not reflected in MD activity, whereas line managers tended to respond in relation to areas OS had influenced MD for themselves or their team members.

Only one senior strategic manager thought that MD could not be linked any more strongly with OS because 'the culture of the company is one of HRD'. Others thought the link could be stronger: 'it would be good to do this and would require all managers to understand the organization's strategy'. The influence of OS on MD would be felt more in this period of change and with increasing harmonization within the group, and the *IiP* initiative was expected to help in that process.

Line managers thought that the extent to which departmental strategies influenced MD varied between different departments and most thought MD could be more effectively linked with departmental strategies by utilizing more training opportunities.

HRD systems and processes

According to the senior manager involved, HRD processes were not exclusively competence based, and the Management Standards had not been adopted. While ability to do the job is the key criterion, functional competences are only part of the MD in the organization, which is also concerned with developing behavioural skills, most obviously through the Coverdale team working training programme.

Each department maintains up-dated HRD documentation defining training responsibilities devolved to named line managers, and detailing all individuals undergoing training and development. Job descriptions are 'reviewed and re-visited' through appraisal, which is the key opportunity for Training and Development Review (TDR). The TDR process in all cases includes a pre- and post-course evaluation.

In place of the Management Standards, HRD processes are centred on job descriptions which define the scope of each job, its key elements and lines of reporting. The appraisal system operates in accordance with standards of performance which are defined around key elements of the job. Reward systems are not linked to performance, except for incentive payments in the sales department. Training and development are not related to specific competences or performance standards, but arise from TNA with individuals, and familiarity with particular courses, such as the Ashridge leadership and Coverdale courses. The organization had not considered basing HRD systems and processes on the Management Standards.

Appraisal, via an annual management and career development review, centres on a report on performance and development. An individual's senior manager comments on their 'strengths and areas for improvement/development' and makes 'career development recommendations' in three areas: 'next job steps; formal training; and secondment'.

Line managers viewed the appraisal system first as an opportunity 'to review progress' and 'to get feedback in a structured way'. Second, the appraisal system is 'developmental, growing people in line with their aspirations', since part of the purpose of 'identifying strengths and weaknesses' is to match 'training and development to individual needs'. For team members, the appraisal process is primarily a developmental activity: 'to identify skills to be developed'; 'to harmonize the goals of an individual with those of the organization'; and 'to see where an individual's direction is within the company'.

Responsibility for MD is largely devolved to the individual and their line manager. Individuals are responsible for identifying training and development needs and influencing what is delivered, while their managers are charged with identifying people to develop and making it happen in line with corporate strategy. The HR function is responsible for managing the HRD process, but this represents only 10 per cent of the activity. This devolution of responsibility for HRD is apparent in the consensus of those interviewed at all levels. The HR role is variously described as 'small' or 'minor' and one senior strategic manager commented on the significance of not having a training manager. Some managers mentioned the involvement of others, such as the managing director's budgetary role and upward appraisal by staff.

Senior strategic managers confirmed that all managers were expected to promote their own MD via career development reviews. All managers were also expected to contribute to the MD of their staff and line managers were clear on their responsibilities towards subordinates. Team members saw their role in MD as having two elements: demonstrating their potential and identifying specific skills to be developed.

Line managers reported that the achievement of management competence was rewarded mainly through 'recognition' or some form of 'acknowledgement', such as a letter from the managing director, rather than through remuneration. Where individuals fail to achieve the required competence, then 'training is requested or recommended at the review stage'. Where there is an 'identifiable training need or systematic under-performance, this is addressed through the appraisal mechanism', and 'once problems or difficulties have been identified', appropriate 'remedial action is taken', but 'there is a limit to how many opportunities an individual is given'.

Individual performance

Senior strategic managers explained that the measures of IP depend upon the areas of activity involved. Thus in sales, performance is measured in terms of revenue targets, in distribution by distribution effectiveness and in editorial against the objectives set by the sort of newspaper the organization wanted to publish. In addition to the obvious 'financial performance against targets', individuals had 'communication-based objectives, such as consistency in weekly team meetings, production of minutes, etc.'. For all managers, performance was reviewed and individual targets are set in 'weekly one-to-one meetings', while in sales, performance was reviewed monthly in terms of 'sales volume, revenue and yield', and 25 per cent of remuneration derives from a performance bonus.

For line managers, IP was measured against 'key tasks', mutually agreed during appraisal, which are related to their particular departments, and may equally be considered as departmental measures of OP. In the editorial department, for example, the key tasks against which the performance of the manager responsible was measured were 'papers out on time, avoiding litigation, no mistakes and work within budget'. In distribution, the manager's key tasks were defined in terms of 'sales finance and the quality and effectiveness of distribution'. Appraisal was the major mechanism for regular monitoring of IP, although for managers preparing NVQ portfolios, these could also be used evidentially.

Team members similarly described measures of IP which related to the attainment of departmental targets. Thus in sales, 'sales revenue is monitored for each team leader and their team'. Individuals have targets to attain, typically 'key tasks established every three or four months, or even monthly'. The key tasks may include 'deadlines and revenue targets', as in sales, or 'the quality of newspapers produced in terms of stories, features and competitive position', as in the editorial department. A weekly assessment is made of the quality of newspapers, through '*ad hoc* meetings with the directors at which comparison is made with competing titles'. Performance is monitored over six months and reviewed in appraisal, then 'new key tasks are established for the next six months'. In sales there is a scheme of 'sales person of the month' for those who most exceed their target, while in distribution there is a bonus related to financial budgets and the attainment of key tasks.

The chief executive explained that MD made a significant contribution to IP not only through developing existing staff, but also because the organization 'attracts good people because of its reputation for MD'. Senior strategic managers involved in HRD were convinced that MD had been 'a major source of improvements in IP' and gave examples of how MD initiatives had 'hugely enhanced and "focused" individuals', providing them with an underpinning of confidence which led to 'major improvement in their performance'. An example was given of one individual with no newspaper background who had been developed through three significant training events and had been appointed as 'distribution manager, replacing a manager with thirteen years' experience'.

Line managers cited various examples of how MD had contributed to improvements in IP. Specific training, in interviewing skills, for example, had resulted in 'demonstrable improvements in interview technique' and better outcomes associated with the interviews. Editors are typically chosen from editorial staff for their 'management potential' and then developed within the organization. The opportunity to 'learn other aspects of the business' through

MD initiatives has 'increased cross-departmental activity and improved communications'. The NVQ open learning exchanges have 'enabled managers to identify best practice', and as a result 'management skills have improved'.

Team members cited examples of MD initiatives which had led to improvements in IP: 'computer training increased my effectiveness'; 'a presentation skills workshop improved every aspect of my work and presentation'; 'training has ensured that I am able to improve distribution'; 'the Coverdale course influenced my behaviour, especially with respect to risk taking'; 'Coverdale training encouraged me to adopt a systematic approach and made me more effective'.

Organizational performance

A senior financial manager explained that one measure of performance common to all departments was the comparison of 'actual overheads and salaries against budgeted costs'. In addition, all departments have 'key tasks, some of which are also financial'. Productivity or effectiveness measures are used, such as 'rate/page, which determines performance in revenue/page', as are negative measures, such as 'keeping credits within 1 per cent for advertising'.

Senior managers with responsibility for HRD mentioned both financial measures of departmental performance and 'key tasks' such as 'time targets' for editorial departments, and 'effectiveness of delivery' for distribution, which define the success factors – 'what must be achieved'.

Team members cited a variety of measures of OP relating to their own departments. In sales, the key tasks relate to 'sales, training and development and new operations': 'calls handled and revenue' are monitored for each team. The measurement of OP is through 'computer-based monitoring of sales and tally sheets of calls', and departmental productivity is assessed in terms of the 'call rate', and the 'achievement of objectives of calls'. Negative performance measures include 'customer complaints' and 'credits for incorrect advertisements', both of which are 'monitored against individuals and teams'. In distribution, as well as budgetary constraints, the main performance measures are 'the audited VFD [verified free distribution] service figures', and, as negative measures, 'complaints of delivery quality, or non-delivery'. In the editorial departments, 'the quality of the newspaper' is the over-riding measure of OP, and this involves three areas which are monitored: editorial content is assessed through a 'weekly product review with reporters', 'deadlines must be met for copy', and inaccuracies and defamation must be avoided to minimize 'legal action and complaints'.

Senior managers with responsibility for HRD believed that there were 'indications that MD has delivered benefits' in OP, but noted that these are 'less dramatic' than improvements in IP 'because more effective team working is difficult to identify'.

According to line managers, the improvements in OP as a result of MD initiatives are visible in the changes in team behaviour. In advertising, for example, 'MD taught the team how to plan to achieve targets and improve features', while in the editorial department there is greater 'team involvement and commitment: a feeling of pride in the product'.

Team members reported improvements in OP resulting from MD in most departments. In sales, training had 'enabled the team to perform better on features', although one team member believed it was difficult to identify improvements in OP in the sales environment. In distribution, after seventeen years of 'authoritarian management', the new manager introduced 'improved communication and team working', and the team demonstrated 'increased confidence and performance improvements within six weeks'. In the editorial department, 'weekly news meetings improved performance through better communication and getting the team to take responsibility for generating new ideas'.

Business performance

Senior strategic managers described efficiency or business performance in terms of the 'key indices for publishing: profit and return on sales (profit to turnover)', and explained that each title is 'measured for gross margin'. A monthly financial report is prepared for each title, providing a 'profit and loss statement, and an analysis of revenue, variable costs and overheads directly attributable to the title', from which the crucial measures of net profit and return on sales are calculated. Productivity is only monitored for efficiency in 'pre-press' (the stages before printing), but elsewhere it is 'not amenable to measurement'.

A calculation is made of 'VFD × titles × pagination/people employed', as a measure of performance, but this is not viewed as productivity. Market share is measured by comparing the yield of each title in terms of 'advertising revenue per page' with the estimated yield from competing titles. In making such comparisons, there is an acknowledged space ratio of '80 per cent advertising to 20 per cent editorial'. Competitiveness is assessed through 'anecdotal evidence from customers' and from 'good intelligence and communication'. Competitiveness of advertising rates is easily assessed and the mix of advertising is crucial to the revenue of a title because different rates are charged for different categories, such as 'motor' and 'classified'.

Over the past two years, there had been 'some growth in VFD/pagination', despite a deliberate policy of targeting distribution more specifically, and reducing VFD to offset the escalating costs of newsprint. Market share had 'increased by 1–2 per cent over the last three years', and significantly rose from 44 per cent to 46 per cent recently with no change in distribution area. It had recently been reported that two opposition titles would no longer be published and another competitor was to reduce distribution of one of its titles. Profits had increased by '20 per cent last year', although during the year in which the study was conducted the improvement was expected to be more modest owing to the costs of newsprint. Over two years, profits had improved by 11 per cent, 'partly due to changed titles', but ignoring these, there had been a sustained improvement of '5 per cent in revenue and profit'.

The chief executive commented that 'we would not have achieved what we have without investing in these people and assessing the value of that investment with them'. The senior financial manager identified improvements in BP arising from the new management which had established 'a mission statement, road shows and investment in training'.

Conclusions

The chief executive commented on the difficulty of attributing improvements in IP and BP to MD, as this is 'a question of philosophy: human resources are to be developed'. While noting that there was 'an element of economic recovery' behind the improved BP of the organization (a growth in job advertisements with increased recruitment, for example), the senior financial manager believed that MD had also contributed: 'empowerment, team building and responsibility have resulted in higher sales and better performance'. Senior strategic managers with responsibility for HRD were unequivocal in attributing improvements in IP and OP to MD, since this is demonstrated in the 'quality of performance of people: they are more effective after MD'. While major management changes and other actions were clearly also having an impact, the 'review process would show if MD was not delivering' the intended improvements in performance.

Line managers cited cases where improved performance could be attributed to MD without ambiguity. For example, 'an individual who had worked for three years as a reporter and assumed that this was as far as she would go, was developed to be chief reporter and took to the responsibility so well that we developed her to news editor and then editor. This individual was nurtured by MD and *only MD has done this* since in its absence, she would have stayed as a reporter.'

Team members noted that the effects of MD were 'clearly identifiable' and apparent in 'improved management decision-making', which brought benefits at all levels in implementing effective change. Individuals could identify the benefits of MD from 'comparison of performance before and after training on features', for example. Team performance had improved after individuals had undergone MD 'which focused on motivating…and training to approach different situations', and 'morale and motivation are higher'.

Case 11
Eastern NHS Trust

Background

The organization became an NHS Trust in April 1993 and at the time of the study provided over forty services in a number of locations; employing some 1,400 people. The Trust's purpose was described as: 'to help people be healthy and to provide local and specialist care' for the communities in the region. In pursuing this purpose, its objective is: 'to provide excellent services which are appreciated by the community we serve and by our purchasers and which represent good value for money'.

The health care services which it offers are divided into: local health services, specialist health services and social care services (residential places with integrated day care support for adults with learning disabilities). In addition, the Trust provides some 'employment and organization services' (such as training) and 'facilities and estates services' (such as cook chill) to outside organizations in order to generate income. The proposed key areas for strategic development were those of primary care and specialist health services.

The range of MD included formal provision in the shape of national accredited programmes and in-house workshops, facilitated learning sets, mentoring, on-the-job training, project work, development centres, organizational development activities and career support services. Some of the managers interviewed argued that MD can and should include the development of 'management' skills in all staff groups, for example, all workers are responsible for some form of resources and should therefore know how to manage those resources.

The major learning and development opportunities offered to managers within the Trust were:

- MESOL (Management Education Scheme by Open Learning);
- Health and Social Services Management (HSSM), leading to a Diploma in Management or NVQ 5;
- Managing Health Services (MHS), leading to CMS or NVQ 4 ;
- Workshops, offered by the Trust's Development and Training Agency (DTA);
- Learning Sets (bringing together managers from different teams).

Organizational strategy

All managers reported very close links between OS and MD. It was also clear from answers to related questions that all interviewees were aware of the close link. The Trust's draft Strategic Direction document states that all of its support departments (including human resources and other areas such as communications and finance) have the strategic objective of providing 'responsive high quality services which directly support the front line provision and development of patient services and meet the corporate needs of the Trust'.

A number of MD documents reflect the link to business objectives and strategy. The internal discussion paper on the Senior Managers' Development Programme, for example, notes that:

> The programme needs to be seen in the context of the fast-changing environment that the Trust finds itself in....The continuing development of a more business-like, flexible and user-focused approach to its operations is reflected in the needs of its managers....It is important that [the programme] is linked to the business objectives of the Trust and seen in relation to other initiatives, such as *Investors in People*.

The paper outlining the services which DTA will provide for the Trust during 1995–96 adds a financial argument: 'It is important to ensure that the investment made in staff and organizational development is locked into the Trust's business plan and supports the management of change to achieve the objectives around the strategic fronts.'

The processes by which MD needs are identified, and by which provision is planned to meet those needs, also mean that it is influenced by OS. Drafts of the Trust's business plan are analysed to identify ongoing and future needs, managers are consulted both formally and informally and, once developed, the MD strategy must be approved by the Trust's board.

Links between team/departmental strategies and MD were also identified. Although there is a less formal process for feeding team needs into the planning and provision of MD, suggestions from managers are checked out against the Trust's business plan and if the link is not clear then further clarification is sought of the need and the reasons for it.

HRD systems and processes

Some of the learning and development opportunities offered to managers at the Trust were based on the Management Standards, but the majority of provision was not. The national MESOL programmes to which some managers have access have some links to the MCI Standards, particularly the HSSM programme. However, this programme has only been running for a year. The Trust's in-house programme has been redesigned to fit the Standards but this new programme is not in use yet as the DTA is awaiting accreditation as a centre to offer management NVQs.

The setting of personal development objectives and the appraisal process are inter-linked but neither make use of the Management Standards, except in the case of some managers who are on the MESOL NVQ programmes. Appraisal and personal development planning look at how individuals are contributing to the business plan and objectives of the Trust. The appraisal process provides a forum for individuals and line managers to review and discuss progress against past objectives, set new objectives and agree future training and development which will meet both individual and organizational needs. All interviewees made explicit reference to the requirement to link organizational and individual goals via the appraisal system.

All interviewees believed that individuals had a key role in their own development as managers and that this was embedded within the Trust's objective setting and review process. This process involved setting individual objectives, identifying strengths and weaknesses and additional skills needed to do the job effectively, prioritizing development needs and working out a development plan to meet these needs.

Most of the managers interviewed felt that individuals' line managers are closely involved in this process and that decisions are taken jointly. Line managers' input is important because the constraints of time, budget and practicalities have to be taken into account and because of the line manager's role in coaching, mentoring and appraising their staff on an ongoing basis. The central human resources function (specifically the Training and Development Agency) was seen to have a strategic role of identifying needs at the organizational level and designing, developing and providing interventions to meet both organizational and individual needs.

Standards are not used in recruitment and selection. Job descriptions are based on the key tasks, duties and responsibilities of the job and include both managerial and clinical or other specialist/professional roles. The job description is supplemented by a person specification which identifies the essential and desirable skills needed for the post.

Reward systems do not make use of the Management Standards. The Trust has a system of objective setting and review (OSR) for staff in management and supervisory positions and those on individual PRP. For those managers who are eligible for PRP, a 'banding framework' has been developed to enable decisions on pay to be based not only on whether objectives have been achieved, but also how they were achieved, wider job performance and any special contributions which individuals have made. Ratings are given to seven aspects of performance: pace; volume of work; standard of work; leadership; communications; managing people; and managing change.

The use of the MCI Standards in areas other than MD has not been considered at the Trust, and it was thought that systems based on the Standards would be unlikely to succeed.

Individual performance

The main vehicle for measuring and monitoring IP was the objective setting and review process mentioned above. Other ways in which managers got feedback on their performance was via various management fora, clinical audit and patient satisfaction surveys on their services.

Interviewees identified a number of areas where objectives may be set, including service viability and activity levels – related to contracts; innovation in service provision; quality of care; budget management; cost improvements (e.g. via less use of agency staff); project management (e.g. achieving project outcomes to time and budget); inter-personal relations with staff; team morale (e.g. sickness and absence levels); and handling of complaints.

Most interviewees believed that MD in its broadest sense had led to improved IP; some interviewees were even surprised that the question needed to be asked. Of those managers involved in programmes using the MCI Standards, it was claimed that some found them useful and made them more reflective about their jobs, whereas others found them of no help: 'a waste of time'. Similarly, the value to individuals of specific training events provided by DTA varied, though mostly they were found to be useful and positive.

A number of examples of improvements in IP as a result of MD were given. Personal confidence and competence had improved because of the development undertaken: one individual's 'idiosyncratic' management style had been replaced by one in which outcomes were achieved more quickly and with fewer mistakes. Specific skills had improved, such as negotiating, managing change, project management, and these skills could be applied to situations which managers encountered as part of their normal work. It was claimed that more effective decisions were being made. As well as learning better ways of doing things, managers understand the reasons why particular approaches are important and successful. One manager thought they had developed a better management style, based on team building, facilitating and enabling people to manage their own performance, rather than on solving problems for them.

The interviewee from the DTA claimed to have seen individuals develop as a result of structured programmes and training; although this development might have happened without the formal inputs, it would probably have been a longer and more difficult process. One line manager noted that there is a noticeable change in approach from people who have taken part in HSSM, MHS, MBA or other similar programmes, for example, they are able to bring out policy issues in discussions, understand and explain statistics, as well as quote management theory.

Preliminary observations on the HSSM programme made by the National Institute for Social Work (NISW) is a first look at the outputs (such as specific areas of learning, completion of assignments and development of broad competence) and outcomes (actual achievements in the workplace) achieved by participants. In terms of workplace outcomes, the report noted that both networking and paperwork/record-keeping had improved. It also noted that 'the twin NVQ disciplines of applying measures of quality and seeking for evidence – rather than working on assumptions – are quickly being transferred to a range of work areas'.

Organizational performance

The Trust's business planning system was the means by which team or departmental performance is measured against agreed objectives in areas such as service development, cost efficiency and overall budgeting/financial performance. There was a formal half-yearly report with ongoing, monthly monitoring and review. Business planning also fitted very much into the objective setting and review process for individual managers as many of their objectives related to the performance required of the service or department for which they were responsible. Both quantity and quality of service were measured and monitored against the requirements of the contracts which the Trust holds with its purchasers. Clinical audits and surveys of patients, relatives and carers are also important in monitoring the quality of services provided and the degree to which they meet the needs of service users.

In relation to improvements in team performance as a result of MD, some interviewees gave examples of several managers from the same department undertaking development activities at the same time, and therefore being able to work better as a team. One management team had all started in post at about the same time and as they all developed and learnt together, so their effectiveness as a team improved. One interviewee stated that being on the same development programme as her peers enabled them to use actual, current organizational and service issues as 'case studies' for their development, devising solutions which could be applied back in the workplace. Three managers from one area followed the MHS programme at the same time and as a result felt that the hospital had benefited a great deal as they were better able to work together and move forward as a team. Each became more aware of the others' roles. With the skills gained from their MD, the team was able to take forward and implement a new 'patient-focused care' initiative. One interviewee felt that in general, managers who have been through some form of structured MD are more likely to place importance on the development of their teams, both as individuals and as a group, and that this would therefore lead to better team performance.

A number mentioned the strong management skills which have been developed in the Trust's middle management team. Many of this group see their primary role as a professional/clinical one and they have only recently had to take on a managerial role, following the reorganization of management structures. Training and development were a key factor in enabling these managers to cope with the new structure and their new role.

Examples of service improvements were also described. One manager stated that the service now had a reduced length of stay, an increased number of finished customer episodes, a higher rate of bed occupancy and was working in a more effective, multi-disciplinary way because of the new facilitating and enabling management style. Services are now more targeted on what patients need and want and quicker discharges are possible because of better 'patient management' skills. Interviewees found it difficult to provide more specific examples of improvements in team performance and no written evidence was provided.

Business performance

The Trust's business performance is very much linked to its performance against the contracts held with its purchasers, which in turn are linked to activity levels. Productivity and competitiveness are measured but market share is not. The organization is not profit-oriented but focuses on the provision of quality services, which it clearly has to do within the internal market structure of the NHS.

The business skills which have been needed by the Trust's managers since the organization became a Trust, such as contracting and business planning, were certainly seen to have improved. Managers are now able to develop new ideas and market them effectively to purchasers because a 'business case' approach has been developed. This has led to increased business for the Trust.

Specific examples of improvements in business performance included cost reductions and improved project management. Reductions in cost were achieved through a ward closure which was planned and implemented by managers from that service (rather than imposed by top management), MD had enabled the managers to look at the needs of the service and identify the most cost-effective way in which it could be provided. Project management skills have improved greatly meaning that projects can be delivered to time and budget. One interviewee believed that MD in its broadest sense had made a major contribution to the growth of the Trust from a small geriatric hospital to a reasonable-sized community hospital. Again, specific improvements were hard to find and no written evidence was given.

Conclusions

The provision of learning opportunities by formal and informal means was seen by all interviewees to be just one factor which contributes to improved management performance. Other factors identified included: the flow of 'new blood' into the organization bringing new ideas, new approaches and new enthusiasm, and experiential learning. Individuals' own interest in, and commitment to, developing themselves was seen as crucial for the success of MD. Organizational restructuring at the Trust has had a big impact on the way in which managers operate, their accountability and their effectiveness. Team performance was seen as greatly affected by the ability and willingness of team members to work together to improve services. Finally the appraisal and objective setting and review processes were thought to have played a vital role in focusing management activity and development.

Some of those interviewed also recognized that the scope and achievements of MD were limited by the resources available and the time which managers could find for formal development. There was often a conflict between the pressure to 'get the job done' and the time needed for development. Development therefore had to become an integral and integrated part of managers' work which was well planned and clearly focused on achieving relevant outcomes.

As noted above, the MCI Standards were only used in a small proportion of the development offered to the Trust's managers. While further provision based on the Management Standards had been developed it was not yet on offer at the time of the study. The conclusion therefore is that the majority of managers at the Trust do not take part in development activities based on the MCI Standards. However, a wide range of MD opportunities were provided, ranging from formal, structured courses and workshops to on-the-job development through mentoring and project work.

All interviewees clearly believed that MD has a very positive influence on the performance of individuals and they were able to quote a number of examples, although no written evidence was available to support their claims. Specific improvements in team/departmental and business performance were harder to identify, although again it was believed that MD does have a positive effect.

However, all interviewees recognized that many other factors also impact on management performance and that MD does not, and cannot, work in isolation. The Trust had been through major change over the past few years, with the move to Trust status and entry to the 'internal market' in health care, and the subsequent reorganization of management structures. These changes in turn meant that management roles and responsibilities have changed significantly, in order both to work within the new business environment and 'contract culture' and to provide efficient and effective management of services within the new structure. The Trust believed that it has the structures and systems in place which will allow managers to be effective and accountable. MD enables and supports managers to work competently within those new structures and systems. The effectiveness of MD also depends on the resources available – not just money but also the time which individuals can devote to development given the constant pressures of the service. Individual interest and commitment also play a big part.

There was a lot of evidence to show that MD at the Trust was closely linked to OS, both from the interviews and the written materials. This link was seen as an essential precursor to successful MD. The interviewee from the DTA believed that the move to Trust status has enabled them to focus far more closely on organizational needs and that this has made a big difference to the effectiveness of the development opportunities provided. Part of the 'focusing' has involved targeting the right development at the right groups of managers.

HRD processes were not based on the MCI Standards, but were linked to the needs and goals of the organization. So although there was no 'common, integrated set of competence statements' to link the different HR systems and processes, a unifying theme was provided by the link to the organizational strategy.

Case 12

Aeroplane component manufacturer

Background

The company, formerly part of a large UK electronics and engineering group, is a specialist manufacturer of aeroplane windshields, involving a high-technology process. With a UK market share of about 40 per cent, and a world-wide share of about 18 per cent, the company is a technological leader with respect to advanced composite manufacture and metal coating.

In 1988, in the face of 'increasing warranty claims and failures causing huge losses', the parent company planned to sell the factory and a new management team was brought in 'to re-engineer the business using Parnaby's principles' to make it more attractive for sale. An attempted management buyout was rejected in 1992 but went ahead in 1993. Before the buyout the total workforce of 320 at the company's single factory comprised 160 direct workers (involved in manufacturing activities) and 160 support workers (research, design, managerial, white-collar and ancillary activities). As a result of business process re-engineering (BPR), total employment was reduced to 274 by 1995.

The factory was about 75 per cent unionized, with membership evenly split between the TGWU, AEEU and MSF, which organized, respectively, production workers, craft workers and staff, although the jurisdiction and demarcation between the unions was not rigid and single-table bargaining had been established. Labour relations were good and union courses were opened up to cell leaders, not only irrespective of union office (some cell leaders are lay officials), but even irrespective of union *membership*, demonstrating a high-trust relationship. Sickness absence was rare, and labour turnover was under 2 per cent, having been above 10 per cent ten years previously, although it was acknowledged by some managers that this also reflected lack of alternative employment.

The quality of the organization's training and development strategy was acknowledged by a National Training Award in 1990, and the attainment of *Investor in People* status in 1992. Having won the British Quality Award in 1990 for the total quality culture which had been implemented, this was followed by ISO9001 certification in 1992 and the company became the first manufacturing enterprise to achieve the environmental standard BS7750 in 1996.

The new management team introduced computer aided design, integrated with production, and following the BPR exercise restructured the business into Business Development Groups (BDGs). Multiskilling and team working were introduced, and work was re-organized into cells having 95 per cent ownership of work including responsibility for the quality of work produced. Before BPR, the order administration procedure entailed twenty internal ownership changes involving accounts, quality, despatch, production engineering, contracts and production control. The process was re-designed and simplified so that 95 per cent of the ownership of the task was given to the order administration module.

After the management buyout, PRP was dropped in favour of an annual profits-related plan, and shareholding was opened up to all employees. Quality has increasingly been emphasized in all aspects of the business, from customer relations to production, and training, re-training and MD are an intrinsic part of the BPR and quality developments.

Organizational strategy

The chief executive explained that MD was intimately related to OS. MD initiatives derive from the broader human resource objective of the company: 'to recruit the best people we can afford and to develop and maximize the ability of those in the organization'. The functional structure of the company was altered through BPR and as a result of 'giving ownership for business to the BDGs and cells', it became necessary 'to train team people with appropriate leadership skills'.

'Task forces' were established comprising 'cross-functional teams working on specific projects', which both demanded and promoted flexibility, but some individuals were unable to 'make the change'. Both HRD specialists believed training and development was more focused on business needs and elaborated on how OS influences the MD strategy. For example, the new 'customer-focused, team-based organization' made it necessary for thirty managers to be trained in 'team working, and compliance with customer requirements'.

Of seven line managers interviewed, five identified clear linkages between OS and MD: the 'competitive action plan is tiered down to individual MD needs'; business objectives were said to 'cascade down to the individual through developmental appraisal'. Several managers saw a particular relationship between BPR and MD: 'reorganization into product-based teams necessitated a broader awareness of business needs'; 'customer needs and quality issues mean that cell leaders need to be sensitive to customer requirements'.

The chief executive thought that MD could be linked more closely with OS, but the company 'is not ready for this yet, because the development of OS via the Task Force is ongoing'. The training and development manager acknowledged that 'not all training is strategic, but the purpose is to make all training focused on strategic vision'. The HR director noted the difficulty of measuring how closely MD is linked with OS, but believed that there would be 'further MD opportunities as new business is acquired'.

According to the HR director, at departmental level also, business strategies influence MD 'indirectly', since the strategies developed by BDGs create MD needs. The Training Manager explained that to launch the Continuous Improvement Initiative, for example, 'all employees in departmental groups of twelve are involved in operationalizing the business plan'. Most line managers noted that departmental strategies influenced MD: the strategy 'cascades down to MD requirements'; and 'departmental objectives for the year lead to training and development needs of individuals'.

All the line managers interviewed thought that MD could be linked more effectively with departmental strategy. Two managers thought that departmental strategies were 'starting to influence' MD more, although another noted that 'business pressures impose limitations'. Although acknowledging that the 'emerging strategy was in its infancy', two managers emphasized the importance of linking MD more closely with departmental strategy 'in the long term'. Two managers saw appraisal as a weak link in the relationship between departmental strategy and MD because 'progression is weaker than remedial emphasis' and 'insufficient attention was given to developmental issues', as a result of which 'MD is not entirely congruent with what needs are identified in appraisal'.

HRD systems and processes

The HR specialists agreed that MD was, for the most part, competence-based, in that they 'only train in the skills needed to support the business strategy'. While MD was geared to business needs, some less specific training, such as 'general people management', was not linked to specific activities but concerned with developing key competences. The HRD systems and processes 'satisfy ISO9001' but the organization decided against adopting the Management Standards: the training and development manager believed that 'our best practice delivers anything that MCI can'. In place of the MCI Standards, 'competence standards have been identified within the company', based on the experience of HR staff and the incumbents in particular posts. These internal competence standards are used in recruitment, appraisal and all HRD processes, which have been 're-designed along with the business using Task Forces to identify best practice'.

The appraisal process is pivotal, and provides the opportunity for the training and development manager 'to analyse what is the *purpose* of any proposed developmental activity', so that MD is kept focused on developing competences to support OS. Line managers saw the appraisal process as fulfilling several roles in the organization: as a review process, as a communication system, and as an opportunity to discuss a person's 'attitudes to work in a formal situation'. Most line managers thought appraisal 'should be about employee development' and 'should not be about remuneration'. Typically, appraisal provides an opportunity for a TNA, in which the Departmental Plan is compared with the individual's profile. At the same time the goals of MD are established as part of the process of identifying what MD is appropriate for an individual.

Line managers explained that job descriptions and job profiles had been discarded because of the restructuring of work organization, and because job descriptions 'stifle flexibility'. Some cell leaders thought that a job description had existed for the new post, but others noted the 'job specification for cell leaders is still being elaborated'.

Senior HR managers saw the responsibilities for MD as amounting to a 'partnership' between the individual and their line manager, with responsibilities shared between individuals focusing on 'personal ambitions and identifying areas for improvement' and line managers addressing the MD equation from the 'business plan and what development is necessary to achieve the departmental plan'. The HR role is a minor one, a 'business responsibility' to implement ways of identifying what MD is needed and to establish the necessary structure.

Senior strategic managers agreed that all managers are expected to actively participate in MD. Similarly, all managers are expected to contribute to the development of their staff, although the chief executive noted that in practice there had been some problems, for example with appraisal. Line managers were all enthusiastic about their role in developing their staff, which involved identifying the needs of the department and the individual, and establishing MD to reconcile these.

Individual performance

The chief executive explained that individual performance is measured against the achievement of targets. For example, the executive board had six key points to meet and these cascaded down to the departments. The individual's performance and contribution to attaining these targets are monitored formally every six months through appraisal. Both HR specialists cited 'performance against agreed objectives and budgets' as measures of IP. The HR director argued that appraisal was concerned with MD, 'not monitoring performance', for which reason the appraisal had been 'de-coupled from pay and made voluntary'.

Several line managers conflated IP measures with OP measures on the grounds that the performance of their department was the best measure of their performance in managing it. Those managers who cited specific IP measures emphasized the 'achievement of objectives' or 'attainment of targets'. Typical targets included those established under the Business Plan, such as 'stock levels, cost reductions and "people management" issues', and various 'project-related targets' such as 'to establish a materials database', or 'to introduce a system like MRP'. For cell leaders, IP was measured both indirectly through team performance and directly through 'communication at meetings' and the 'line manager's perception' of the cell leaders' success in achieving individual tasks. Similarly, for the development engineer, IP was measured against the achievement of 'milestone targets' which relate to project teams.

The chief executive believed that IP improved as a result of putting individuals into BDGs, the management equivalent of the cellular manufacturing previously introduced on the shop floor, and the MD necessary for the BDGs to operate. The HR specialists cited specific examples of improvements in IP as a result of MD. In general, customer awareness training had instilled a 'clear understanding of customer needs' in individuals, and given them a 'sense of purpose'.

Line managers cited examples of how MD had improved IP for themselves and for members of their departments. One manager had changed their behaviour 'as a result of a continuous improvement group which focused on HR issues', which raised the motivation of their staff, while another 'developed computing skills through open learning which improved their presentation skills in project groups'. An engineering manager explained that he had previously worked on the shop floor and 'began qualifying in his thirties, attaining NVQ 5 in Operations Management', without which he 'could not have done this job'. In the second category, audit training for quality systems was stressed: under the 'delegated authority' arrangements, individuals were trained externally on 'lead assessor' courses, and this had increased the range of products and the scope of repairs for which the organization obtained the approval of the Civil Aviation Authority and the US Federal Aviation Authority.

Cell leaders cited several ways in which their IP had improved directly as a result of MD initiatives. A team working course had given one cell leader 'greater confidence and a better understanding of the work of other departments'. Another had developed 'better planning of workflows' and recognized the need 'to be prepared for problems' because of OTJ experiential MD.

Organizational performance

The senior financial manager noted the difficulty in separating departmental measures of OP from the measures of BP. The Annual Business Plan 'sets the financial objectives of the company' from which 'departmental budgets and targets' are derived. Departments are monitored in terms of 'spend, sales and manufacturing output' as well as a variety of 'cost control measures', including 'scrap, customer returns and credit notes raised'. OP in manufacturing operations 'is easily measured through benchmarking', while the project management systems 'monitor all performance'.

Line managers outlined how OP was measured in each department against fixed objectives and targets outlined in the Departmental Plan, which reflects the impact of business objectives on the 'functional requirements of the department'. Output targets in operational areas were 'defined to support business aims', such as the pursuit of competitive advantage. In operations, OP measures were moving from 'cost per hour' to 'sales per employee', as a value-added approach was being adopted. Sales targets were used in the BDGs, while in the engineering group, OP was 'measured against the objectives set by the engineering manager and the chief executive'. In supplies, OP is measured in terms of 'stock levels and cost reduction'. The quality department's OP is assessed against such objectives as 'to achieve BS7750 environmental management, reduce scrap and reduce energy consumption'.

In customer support, OP is measured against the business objectives 'to maintain a credible presence in the aerospace industry by providing a quality product' and 'to ensure the organization becomes a first-class industry supplier' which is monitored through 'customer perceptions'. All customer complaints are 'logged, actioned and closed off'; these are 'analysed for trends and audited using fault tree analysis'. In supplies, 'overdue orders' are similarly analysed.

Cell leaders defined OP in terms of 'delivery compliance', which is monitored routinely each week and analysed for the previous month when the next month's targets are set. While weekly delivery compliance is the primary measure of cell performance, in addition the effectiveness of cells is measured by 'standard hours as a percentage of actual hours', and the teams are 'encouraged to find ways of reducing standard hours' as well as minimizing overtime. Negative measures of OP for the cells included 'scrap, customer returns, re-tooling and re-work costs', although it was noted that a relatively small proportion of scrap is due to operator error compared with 'material failures and process problems'.

The senior financial manager noted difficulties in relating improvements in OP to MD. The Task Forces determined business strategy, which had led to MD, but the process was 'so informal: MD arose out of the need to be competitive and from BPR and the associated changes'. The HR director related MD to OP because of the role which MD played in 'restructuring operations to reduce ineffective working and the focus on environmental issues'. The training and development manager saw MD as 'fundamental in making people feel part of a team and involved in decision-making'.

Line managers universally noted improved team performance, such as more 'flexibility and commitment', although two managers believed that this was a result of 'start-up meetings' and 'improved communications', rather than MD. For the majority of managers, however, improvements in OP, such as 'reduced direct labour costs per hour', were attributed to the 'effectiveness of training cell leaders'. As part of the BPR, half of the twenty-eight former supervisors were returned to manufacturing, working on products, while the other half were trained as cell leaders, in 'problem solving, setting objectives and meeting targets'. The transparency associated with moving to BDGs had 'worked well, in that people are now more involved and see the whole picture', and MD was necessary for individuals to make use of the statistics and information available. The success of the team which prepared the organization for BS7750 accreditation was, in part, a result of 'courses on environmental systems and environmental auditing' that they had attended.

Cell leaders explained how OP had improved following the establishment of cells four years ago: as a result of 'multiskilling, involving training and MD', all tasks were undertaken within the cells. Evidence was cited of 'more effective team working' and of 'more co-operative relationships between teams', which was attributed to 'team working courses for department heads and cell leaders'.

Business performance

The chief executive emphasized overall productivity and sales growth as the major measures of BP. In addition to productivity measures such as 'output hours for manufacturing' and market measures such as the 'value of sales per employee', the senior financial manager elaborated on detailed measures of BP from the management accounts: 'ROCE is the major measure of BP', and in addition, the company monitors profit, cash budget and sales budget.

As a measure of the extent of improvement in overall productivity, the chief executive demonstrated that total sales in 1988 of £14 million were achieved with 515 employees, while estimated total sales of £19 million during the year of the study were being achieved with 274 employees. Thus sales per employee had increased from £27,000 to £69,000. Profit before investment and tax 'increased from £1.4 million in 1993–94, to £1.8 million in 1994–95 and is projected to be £2.2 million next year'; growth of 10 per cent per annum is necessary, however, 'to satisfy the banks'. The senior financial manager cited significant improvements since August 1993 when the company became an independent business: 'overall productivity has increased, as have sales per employee', while ROCE which was 29.8 per cent in 1993–94 was in 'excess of 30 per cent for 1994–95'.

The chief executive believed that MD had contributed to sales growth, because this had only occurred since individuals were in BDGs. Before the MD initiatives 'the average customer response time for the sales team was 30 days, and it is now 5 days'. For the senior financial manager, the improvements in BP 'could have been done without formal MD, given the same people involved', although he acknowledged that MD contributed to their improved performance.

Conclusions

The chief executive had no hesitation in attributing improvements in IP, OP and BP to MD, noting that 'the improvements would have been impossible without MD, without multiskilling at all levels, which had resulted in ownership by the workforce'. The training and development manager similarly believed MD was 'the major factor' accounting for improved performance. As a result of MD, the company 'wins more business because of the quality of our proposals'; 'more production with fewer engineers has been facilitated by multiskilling and a successful transformation has been made to a "process-driven organization"'. The HR director was more circumspect, believing that the transformation 'could have been done without MD, but the support of MD made it easier for individuals to contribute to this success', and overall productivity increased only because 'individuals were developed to do the task'. The senior financial manager was sceptical of the contribution made by MD: 'recruiting the right people is the main issue, the impact of formal MD has been less significant than the individuals recruited'.

For almost all line managers, MD was inseparable from the BPR, and had been an essential part of 'equipping individuals to take on new roles': the 'MD period was critical' in involving everyone in the change; 'MD has been part of re-engineering the whole process'. The link between MD and performance is clear because 'the MD programme has a clear purpose and a clear effect'. One manager explained that while 'the critical factor in transforming the business was the introduction of 10–15 dynamic young managers', they had been 'brought along by the business and MD was the key'. Only one line manager believed that MD had played a 'minor role in the success of the business', which he attributed to improved communications, and another manager noted that 'some of the improvements in motivation were a result of a recent round of redundancies'. The overwhelming view, however, was that 'we could not have done this without MD'; 'if we had not engaged in MD individuals could not have taken on the new roles'; 'MD, as part of BPR, clearly brought 80–85 per cent of the improvements'.

Cell leaders also acknowledged the 'redundancy factor', but saw a distinct 'contribution from MD'; 'MD was a major factor contributing to success.' People were 'more focused on customer needs', and had a 'better understanding of what needs to be done'. Moreover, as part of BPR, 'MD had made delegated authority possible, and significant performance improvements had resulted from this'. The development engineer similarly accepted the 'significant contribution of MD' to the success of BPR which had 'turned the business around'.

Case 13
Northern NHS Trust

Background

The Trust was formed in 1991 and until 1993–94 comprised four hospitals. During this time the Trust has undertaken a substantial development programme involving a number of its hospitals. The first year of the Trust proved to be successful in terms of financial results, expansion and clinical excellence. Financial success lay in the fact that in the first year the Trust managed to break even, which was a vast improvement on previous financial performance. The Trust's expansion was guaranteed by receiving approval for an £11 million expansion of facilities at one hospital and securing £72 million for the redevelopment of another, a project that has been delayed since the late 1970s. Clinically, the Trust is well known for being at the forefront of practice in a number of areas.

A day case unit was developed under trust status and the number of day cases treated rose from 86 in 1990–91 to 1,500 in 1991–92 reducing the waiting list for operations by half. A major new initiative has begun to improve the management of beds throughout the Trust. Bed shortages continually disrupt patient care and the Trust was making every effort to balance the needs of the emergency/acute cases, which utilize 70 per cent of the beds available, with the needs of those patients waiting for less urgent treatment. In 1991–92 the Trust employed more than 5,000 staff and was one of the largest employers in the city; 75 per cent of the employees are women and 46 per cent are employed on a part-time basis. This figure had increased to almost 6,000 by 1992–93 and exceeded this in 1993–94.

The Trust has a reputation for excellence within the health service and was featured in the previous government's response to the Health Service Select Committee and noted for 'ward housekeeping, improved supplies, services and better communications'. It was one of the first health service employers to become committed to the *Investors in People* initiative, supported by the most senior level of management. To this end, an extensive MD programme was established, but the initial enthusiasm has not been translated into the achievement of *IiP* status. Also, to date, the organization's MD, or broader training and development strategy has not been recognized by any training awards, although the Trust may apply for a NTA in the future. The Trust personnel director (PD), while applauding the principles and spirit of *IiP*, did not feel it was appropriate for the organization because 'it would lock us into something that would not fit our organization; our performance management systems are far broader than those encompassed by *IiP* and we would want to do better than *IiP*'.

Quality has always been a major concern of the hospitals and the medical audit has traditionally been used to compare actual with best practice. The Patient's Charter has become a 'useful focus' for quality development; there is now a full-time audit person in each unit and the Trust is striving to achieve the highest quality standards by preparing its own charter, which is even more demanding than the Patient's Charter and will set standards that exceed those required by the government. With regard to Quality Awards, the senior HRM manager explained: 'competences need to be built around what is important for the organization and a lot of these quality standards are very bureaucratic; they can get in the way of development. Standards need to be developed to meet our own organizational needs.'

Organizational strategy

Organizational development in the Trust is based on a series of principles, including: shared values, meeting the needs of patients and customers, multi-disciplinary team work, full participation, genuine communication, individual liberation, and self-discipline. The objective of this approach is to encourage all staff within the organization to work with a common sense of purpose.

Business process re-engineering (BPR) was being widely applied at the time of the study in order to modify hospital processes, utilizing 'change management skills'. Process mapping is the major diagnostic tool of BPR, which is suited to ensuring 'efficient multi-disciplinary' hospital processes. The assistant personnel director explained that only five years ago the driving force behind the development of OS was the achievement of trust status, and MD is the tool by which the organization can enhance the changing culture of the Trust.

All line managers interviewed agreed that OS influences MD. Its main thrust is to support the strategic objectives of the organization: 'management need to be a step ahead to help the organization get where it needs to go'.

Personnel specialists agreed that MD could be linked more closely to OS: the HRD plan is not really linked to the Business Plan for the organization and this is something they will work towards over the next couple of years. New performance management systems were being developed to enable the individual manager to contribute to organizational success, although the competences that determine this had not been agreed. The senior financial manager believed that MD could be more closely linked with OS and felt that MD ought actually to be driven by that strategy. The organization should be identifying its skills gaps and after such a skills audit should decide what the current position is in terms of skill levels and what the organizational requirements for the future are.

In the past, professional MD focused very much on acquiring the clinical skills necessary to reach the top of a specified profession and this was achieved by established traditional career routes. Today the situation is very different and top posts no longer require purely clinical skills, but also demand competence in a wide range of areas, as managers increasingly manage across functions; these necessary skills can be acquired in a number of ways, one of the most recent innovations being secondment as a means of MD.

HRD systems and processes

Senior management believed that competences 'should increasingly be used as an integral part of managing and developing individual and team performance' and that organizational objectives could be achieved 'by enhancing effective performance and continuous improvement'. The Trust's model of competences is expected to contribute to the management of achievement-oriented performance. Competences are being identified in role profiles and use the level 2 and 3 Management Standards.

Views on the extent to which MD is competence based differed considerably between the senior HRM managers interviewed. The personnel director did not feel that MD was competence based yet, whereas their assistant believed MD was 'very heavily' competence based, as did the project development manager, who described it as 'a very unimaginative and boring approach to MD and does not develop the mind of an individual manager to self-learn'.

The organization was involved in the original MCI pilots for Management levels 1 and 2 and modified versions of these were still used in the organization and closely conformed to the MCI Standards. The Trust originally offered NVQ 4, but this was scrapped in favour of an in-house development programme accredited by a local university because assessment was extremely bureaucratic, bore no relationship to an individual manager's work, and did not contribute to the development of the manager.

The competences outlined in the job descriptions of two of the three line managers interviewed were based on MCI Standards. Of the team members interviewed, only one specifically related the competences outlined in their job description to MCI Standards.

Line managers believed that the formation of an individual manager's personal development plan (PDP), as part of the Individual Performance Review (IPR), was the responsibility of each individual manager. Nevertheless, although the Trust employs a large number of highly motivated managers, there is still a large number of managers who need to develop an understanding of the concepts and practice of self-managed learning.

All members of the team felt that individual managers had a personal responsibility for MD, and line management were expected to nurture their teams, at the same time ensuring that the needs of the organization were being met. All managers were expected to contribute to the MD of their staff, but this was not the case across the Trust; at two hospitals 90 per cent of the staff had not been involved in MD.

The specific MD for an individual manager was decided by a combination of departmental and individual development agendas. The decision regarding what MD is appropriate for an individual manager was often a joint one made between the individual manager and their senior manager. The goals of MD may be established as part of an appraisal plan, by a personnel and training department on an in-house programme, or by involving the team leader, personnel and training, line manager and individual managers. According to team members, goals of MD are established through the IPR, during which a PDP is established for each manager by joint discussion between the reviewer and reviewee. The PDP encompasses professional development as well as MD and has to relate to team and organizational development plans.

Individual performance

A new performance review process was being piloted in the Trust at the time of the study, as the existing IPR system was proving unsatisfactory for the organization's needs. Appraisal was considered to be a key process in managing workplace performance and the new performance management system was expected to create a more structured approach to developing effective performance (DEP). Each individual line manager will be expected to 'instigate DEP in their area and conduct the DEP discussion', and must attend training courses to ensure that the system is implemented properly.

A performance rating system was also designed, with managers placed in one of five categories: outstanding, very good, good, satisfactory and unacceptable. Two Performance Management pilot projects had been run in the Trust, involving wide consultation with the parties involved. The standards of performance against which individual managers will be judged have been developed integrating the views of the senior management team regarding the priorities of the organization. In the assistant PD's opinion, MCI Standards focus on functional competences which are insufficient for the needs of the organization; the Trust is seeking to broaden the original MCI Standards by integrating a wider range of behavioural requirements into the standards they are developing in-house. Budgetary performance was the key measure of IP mentioned by all the management team members; other IP measures were related to the objectives that had been set for each individual manager at appraisal.

There was some difference of opinion regarding the contribution that MD had made towards improvements in IP. A project development manager expressed the view that the contribution of MD to IP was enormous: 'the biggest contributory factor', but qualified this by explaining that no written evidence existed. The personnel director also felt that MD had profoundly improved IP, especially for female managers who had 'translated MD into career progression'. The assistant personnel director was more cautious, noting that in some cases MD had improved IP and in others had very little effect.

Line managers felt that MD had improved IP in some cases, such as those managers who had been involved in a long-term development programme.

Another manager felt that managers were generally more motivated and that this was a direct result of MD and a third line manager argued that MD made people more aware of their role within the wider organization, noting that how they performed in their jobs had a knock-on effect on other managers in the organization, producing a corresponding improvement in the IP of those managers.

According to team members, MD makes managers more aware of their own role as individual managers and as team members, developing a manager's ability to manage their teams, write reports, and participate in meetings more effectively.

Organizational performance

Teams work towards a set of objectives, which have both an individual and team dimension to them. There are no explicit standards of performance measurement, other than meeting deadlines and producing work of an acceptable standard in what is often a very limited timescale. The senior financial manager felt that this lack of standards was problematic and that it was difficult to achieve detailed meaningful performance measurement of management teams.

The Trust was trying to introduce a team working system throughout the organization and attempting to develop a systematic form of measuring team performance. Monitoring of achievement of team targets had traditionally, 'not been done very well' because targets were not well integrated into OS. The Trust established a project development officer, who initiated the development of thirty-five clinical area teams, each working towards the same 'shared objectives', according to a 'coordination model'. The project development officer's role is to facilitate the introduction of this model, set team objectives and measure team performance against these objectives. At present most teams set their own objectives and review themselves against internally agreed targets.

Line managers mentioned various measures of OP, such as the delivery of contract within budget. Specific performance measurements mentioned for particular teams included quantity of tests undertaken in a given period, research activity, research grants received, amount of teaching and income generation. Departmental productivity and effectiveness are measured in numerous ways such as waiting lists, the diagnostic quality of testing, and complaints monitoring.

Team members explained that OP was monitored in terms of milestones representing the progress made towards achieving team objectives. Measurement generally involved self-monitoring. Measures of departmental productivity and efficiency appeared to be departmentally specific: achievement of financial targets; absence of complaints letters; number of operations performed; how many case notes were missing at the clinic; how many home visits are made, for example.

The senior financial manager believed there was no concrete evidence to demonstrate that MD had improved OP, despite instinctively feeling it had. The

Trust had been able to meet financial targets without any drastic cuts to service, such as ward closures. For the PD, similarly, it was not obvious how MD had improved OP, although the assistant PD thought the organization had been transformed by team working, which could not have been achieved without MD.

One line manager claimed that MD had enabled managers to work as a team and perform far more effectively than they had as individuals, and another manager believed team working had been essential for the Trust. Team members were divided on the issue of whether MD contributed to improvements in OP, some believing communication had vastly improved and that managers generally had a much better idea of what goals they were working towards, and others noting that there had been nothing comparable in place before MD and the development of team working.

Business performance

Financial performance was measured in terms of income against expenditure or expenditure against budget and productivity was not monitored. The price and quality of health provision is what makes the Trust competitive; although the price of provision can be measured objectively, this is not true of quality and competitiveness is directly related to the reputation and quality of provision.

Measures of productivity were inadequate and it was recognized that these needed to be developed. Taking the total number of patients treated in relation to cost as a crude measure of productivity, in 4 years productivity had increased substantially.

The Trust has to achieve three financial targets: to live within the external financing limit; to break even on a recurring basis; and to earn a return on capital assets. In 1991–92 the Trust remained within their external financing limit and also achieved this in 1992–93 despite a substantial investment through the Trust's capital programme, as well as in 1993–94. In 1991–92, the Trust as a non-profit-making organization not only balanced their income and expenditure, but generated a surplus of almost £2.81 million, in 1992–93 this fell to £1.9 million, which was not really surprising in the light of major expenditure on the capital programme. In 1993–94 the net surplus achieved was £34,000, this reduction in the income/expenditure reserve was the result of a technical adjustment, arising from the change in definition of capital from items costing over £1,000, to items costing over £5,000 and did not reflect on Trust performance.

During 1991–92 total income was £128.266 million, which increased to £141.5 million in 1992–93 and continued to rise, reaching £150.3 million in 1993–94. Trusts are expected to earn a 6 per cent return on capital assets: during 1991–92 the organization earned 8.7 per cent; in 1992–93 this fell to 5.5 per cent, but this was as a result of a revaluation of the Trust's fixed assets; and in 1993–94 the return was 5.8 per cent.

A comparative review of contract prices in the Trust with other major teaching hospitals in the area found that the Trust generally had lower than average in-patient prices in 32 per cent of nineteen specialities considered and higher prices in 68 per cent. When examined in relation to the average in the Regional Health Authority (RHA), the Trust's position was relatively better, having prices lower than the RHA in 53 per cent of specialities and higher than average in 47 per cent. In terms of day cases, out of eighteen specialities the Trust had lower than peer group average prices in 67 per cent and higher in 33 per cent and when compared with the average prices in the RHA, lower than average in 78 per cent of specialities and higher in 22 per cent.

The senior financial manager expressed the hope that MD had directly contributed to an improvement in BP, but was unsure how this could be demonstrated. There had been a substantial financial commitment to MD, which was channelled particularly towards developing middle management and improving the general management structure in the Trust: 'MD has certainly improved control in the Trust and this might have improved performance.'

Conclusions

The benefits of MD could be identified in the development of a new organizational culture of shared goals and values. The commitment to CBMD was an inherent part of achieving this goal and the development of the performance management system, team working and multiskilling were all contributing to the new Trust culture. The focus on core competences is expected to help the Trust deliver an increasingly efficient and effective service and MD should facilitate the empowerment of individuals and teams to achieve this goal to the best of their abilities.

Increased management control is the major consequence of MD that had obviously succeeded in the Trust. Development was rooted in the needs of the job with the objective of developing the competences necessary as an individual manager or team member. Such MD facilitates the achievement of OS which is geared to moving away from a centralized form of control towards a set of independently operated units.

Line managers felt that one of the obvious benefits of MD was that IP improved; managers were more focused on meeting their objectives and targets so progressed more quickly through the organization. Teams that had undergone MD often changed their style of management, delegating more and enhancing the development of other members of the group.

Another line manager felt that MD had fostered a business approach to the operation of internal markets in the NHS. Their department had completely changed the approach to purchasing equipment, with a strategy of diversifying sources.

One line manager argued that in general terms, MD had benefited the Trust directly by changing the culture of the organization, and this could not have been achieved without MD: 'People grew in their jobs. They didn't just have the ability to do the job, the competence, there was a qualitative change in them because of the MD experience.' The new culture emphasized the value of each individual member of staff, yet individuals still felt undervalued, especially junior members of staff.

Some team members expressed reservations in attributing improved individual and team performance specifically to MD. One team member argued that in their clinical role the immediate benefits of developing competence could be seen, as it was possible to judge the success of one method, as opposed to another, by the use of comparative data. Management, by contrast, was viewed more as a function of an individual's ability to deal with people, which need not be a competence-based quality. 'I get very nervous with people just extolling the virtues of one approach; we need to cherry pick and use the best parts of different approaches to management and MD.' Another team member felt that there was no perceptible change that could be attributed specifically to MD; 'one of the great problems of MD is that the habits of a lifetime don't change because of a few days training here or there and if you haven't altered a manager's attitude to life, you've not cracked it.'

Case 14
Clothing manufacturer

Background

The organization is one division of a clothing manufacturing company, founded in 1885. By the 1960s, the company had expanded significantly and increased its product range to include menswear, ladies wear, children's wear and uniforms. The factory studied, the manufacturing unit for uniforms and corporate wear, was opened in 1979, and employed approximately 170 workers at the time of the study. The group has six operating divisions and an annual turnover of approximately £250 million. Its commitment to quality has been recognized by the Quality award BS5750.

The mission statement of the company is 'to become the dominant supplier of uniforms in our chosen market sectors by offering standards of excellence not achieved by our competitors'. In order to meet these objectives, senior management believe it is imperative to have the total commitment of all employees to the company's objectives; this will be achieved by providing all employees with relevant information on all issues related to the operation of the business and establishing channels of communication to allow individual employees to have a direct input into the strategic decision-making process, which influences business performance.

A flexible workforce is the cornerstone of company strategy; to be competitive the business must be able to respond quickly to the changing demands of the market. This heightened responsiveness can only be achieved by employees of the company being willing and able to undertake a wider range of tasks than ever before. The achievement of TQM is another strategic goal of the organization, which is committed to an ongoing process of improvement in three areas: 'fitness for purpose', 'to specification', and 'on time'. A number of principles have been identified and adopted as core company values which will enable the enterprise to become a 'company of excellence', providing standards of achievement which cannot be matched by competitors in the same market. For example, 'we are committed to develop an open management style which has the ability to respond quickly to change. Our management is based on leadership within an atmosphere of trust, openness and fairness' and 'we will continually mould a lean healthy business where ability is more important than status. We provide effective training and encourage people to realize their full potential and develop their careers. Wherever possible, we will promote internally.'

Organizational strategy

In the past, OS had little influence on MD in the organization. While this was not true of the group as a whole, it was felt that this branch of the company had become separated from mainstream company policy on MD, an issue that was being addressed with some urgency at the time of the study in order to bring the Uniforms Division in line with company policy. The group had an overall policy of divisionalization and strategic planning has become increasingly important in this context. A business strategy was developed for the Uniforms Division and strategy meetings were an established means of managing the organization.

Departmental strategies do not influence MD in the company and there was some difference of opinion regarding whether they would do in the future. The factory manager felt that the company strategy was the most important factor in relation to MD; a number of teams had been set up to take forward these strategies drawing expertise and problem-solving skills from a cross-section of departments. Another manager had a different vision of the future for MD and felt that the strategies of the production team, the quality team and sales team were to some extent departmentalized and would therefore influence MD. This manager thought that MD could be linked more closely with departmental strategy.

All senior managers shared the view that MD could be linked more closely with OS; strategy development was still in its infancy in the company. In the past the company had not had a coherent business strategy universally acknowledged and understood by all staff in the organization, let alone any MD strategy linked to this. Effective communication was perceived as a key strand of OS, providing the means by which all employees are made aware of what the company needs from each member of staff in terms of their own IP and how this relates to investment and growth decisions and overall company performance in the market place. Communication is perceived as a two-way process concerned both with disseminating relevant information to all levels of the organization, and with eliciting ideas from staff and integrating these into the development strategy for the company. Team briefings formed an inherent part of this process and were focused on creating a working environment in which individuals had both responsibility for, and ownership of, the quality and volume of the work produced. This initiative is supported by a company commitment to standards of excellence and innovative approaches to working methods.

Although the management team were expected to develop and change in accordance with the shifting demands of the business, in the past there had been no formal mechanism for MD. Managers had recently been given the opportunity to attend various courses to enhance their levels of competence in line with company developments. A strategic management workshop had been provided for all managers, which was followed up with regular strategy meetings, run outside regular working hours every 6–8 weeks. The strategic management workshop had a number of specific objectives:

> to develop an understanding of the management concepts used to prepare a strategic plan for business; to examine the type of information required to facilitate the preparation of the plan to present a tried and tested methodology for preparing a business strategy and to introduce the vocabulary of strategic planning to ensure a common understanding of that vocabulary; to explore how investment and the cost drivers of a business unit can be managed to ensure a consistency with the strategic plan for the business; and to apply this strategic management framework to prepare a prototype strategic plan for each business unit within the organization.

HRD systems and processes

At the time of the study none of the HRD systems were based on national occupational standards and the company had not considered doing this. Although the senior HR manager recognized the importance of having a 'competent' management team, there was little concrete evidence to suggest that MD was competence based, other than in relation to the performance criteria demanded by a specific job. None of the managers interviewed had formal job descriptions, although the senior HR manager explained that managers now had much more clearly defined roles than previously. Appraisal systems had not been introduced, although some form of monitoring of management performance had existed including an annual interview for each manager with the Managing Director.

There were no recruitment and selection criteria for managers, although there were policy statements for the company as a whole. New recruits were expected to meet specific job criteria and have 'potential for future progression', as the company has a policy of promoting internally whenever possible, making training and development crucial.

Line managers had no responsibility for their own MD, nor officially for the development of more junior staff, although they played an informal role in this process. The senior HR manager explained that MD was in a very early stage of development in the company, but recognized the need to explore with each manager on an individual basis what they felt they needed individually for their own personal development and what the company needed in terms of performance improvements. The strategy group meetings were providing the basis for these developments and the company was keen to promote 'on the job training' for managers.

MD in the company is still perceived as very much the property of senior management, none of the staff interviewed felt that MD was the responsibility of the individual manager. The personnel departments tend to focus on the personnel and training issues related solely to operatives and had no responsibility for MD. The corporate division had an established tradition of MD, and the factory manager was responsible for developing managers in order to operate the new, slimmer organization.

One manager mentioned that the company was promoting the importance of managers' role in MD, but felt that development initiatives did not always work in practice. For example, the company was promoting team working but 'we don't work as teams, we don't help one another, although the factory manager wants to change this'.

According to the senior HR manager, the decision about what MD is appropriate for an individual manager was not really made on a systematic basis in the company. One manager reiterated that there was no MD within the company, while others referred to the role of senior management in MD. Individual managers had no goals for MD formally established, but individuals felt that there were implicit goals related to performance.

Individual performance

The IP of managers, according to the senior HR manager, was measured in relation to efficiency and general performance of the department, quality, absenteeism, time standards and costs: 'managers have total control of their departments in the areas specified and it is up to them to improve the performance of their team in each of these areas'. Historically, improvements were rewarded by the payment of a bonus to successful managers on an individual basis, but it was planned to award future bonuses on a team basis because the individual incentive 'does not encourage team working'. Line managers felt that behavioural performance was also measured, since individual managers needed to know 'how to handle people', and 'lead by example'. Such assessment of managerial performance was not based on any written criteria and tended to be subjective. Line management also confirmed that individual mangers had to demonstrate technical knowledge, and attain both production and quality goals.

Two of the three team members interviewed felt that individual performance measurement focused on productivity, quality and workflow; whilst the third member of the team seemed unsure about which specific aspects of their performance were actually being measured. Managers could in theory achieve a £300 bonus every three months, '£100 if I meet my daily production target, £100 if I have no time off and £100 if I manage to reach the required quality standards; but in practice it is almost impossible to achieve these three targets.'

The senior HR manager explained that each manager involved in the production side of the business had specific targets relating to efficiency, excess cost, performance, absenteeism and quality. Team members confirmed these targets and explained that, depending upon the complexity of the product, the target varied from 750 to 400 jackets per week. 'Production sheets are completed on an hourly basis and we monitor what we are achieving compared with the targets set.' The trouser department had a higher weekly production rate, but this target was expected to increase. Managers were not undertaking NVQs and therefore portfolios of evidence were not considered when judging an individual manager's performance. Since no formal systems of appraisal were in place in the company, this process also played no part in an individual manager's performance appraisal.

In the view of the senior HR manager, MD in the form of strategy meetings had improved IP considerably: 'managers now know what is happening in the company, in financial, sales and production terms. They know what the company plans are for the future and have input into these plans.' This input gives those individuals ownership of OS and empowerment, as responsibility for carrying out these strategies is increasingly developed. Line managers felt that MD had not yet had a significant impact on managerial performance, whereas team members believed that IP had undoubtedly improved through the introduction of computerized systems. Managers had to be trained for the new system, which operated with a slimmer team, increasing efficiency. Another member of the team was not convinced that they had received any MD:

> managers would like to go on a training programme; we've been managers for eight years and never been on a training programme. We had a strategy group meeting with the managing director, who asked if any of us had been on a MD programme; when he discovered none of us had, he said it must be looked into.

Organizational performance

According to the senior financial manager, team performance was monitored monthly. Annual budgets covering all aspects of the business, sales, production and overheads, were produced and monthly performance assessed in relation to last year's performance and the cumulative annual performance goals. The senior financial manager also produced forecasts which updated the accounts in relation to current performance and the wages system requires a daily monitoring of factory performances.

The senior HR manager explained that team results are arrived at by individual effort and although team targets are the major performance measures, managers need to be aware of an individual operative's contribution to those targets. Line management also focused on the monitoring of production targets and quality control targets as the major means of monitoring team performance. Two of the three team members were unable to separate IP and OP, while a third team member was unsure what aspects of team performance were being measured.

Departmental and team targets were very specific and related to the throughput of garments; in the trouser room for example it was the manager's responsibility to ensure that the section averages 400 pairs of trousers per day and 54 each hour. The piece work system was being phased out in the factory, although a 'room' bonus had not proved entirely successful. Nevertheless the company is determined to introduce team incentives in order to promote the team working spirit in the factory, and the new bonus scheme will be calculated on contracted efficiency (taking absenteeism into account) based on perfect garments produced by each section of the factory. Productivity and quality are monitored; all faults are recorded and if the proportion exceeds 1 per cent of production, strategies to reduce the level of errors are discussed with team members and the senior manager for quality standards. Analysis of quality cost reports is an important part of the new company strategic plan and aims to reduce the number of time-consuming and costly recuts.

The senior HR manager believed that MD had been extremely important in encouraging management staff to work together as a team, 'although this process is in its early stages and we have a long way to go'. Direct business benefits had been derived from bringing together twenty-five managers from all areas of the company to discuss a wide range of issues at the strategy meetings. Line managers also felt that the impact of the strategy meetings was to some degree limited because MD was in its infancy.

One manager explained how the new strategy group had been broken down into four major areas; productivity, finance, sales, and quality, with teams consisting of four or five members. This particular manager was part of the productivity team and had become increasingly aware through team meetings how their own decision-making affected not only their immediate team, but also the other management teams in the strategy group. 'I have realized that I need to discuss my decisions with others before putting my ideas in to practice; you need a general consensus to innovate and other people's point of view can only help.' Regular team meetings were having a knock-on effect throughout the factory; people on the shop floor had come to know each manager's role, how the business was performing, whether the company was losing or increasing profits, and what was happening in the group in general. The new strategy was producing a 'better informed' workforce.

Business performance

For the senior financial manager, sales were a major measure of efficiency. All sections of the factory were under pressure to increase their standards of efficiency. The jackets section was operating at 68 per cent efficiency at the time of the study, having increased by 10 per cent over the previous two months, but the aim was to reach 80 per cent within six months. Absenteeism was running at 8 per cent against a target of 4 per cent, excess costs were running at 31 per cent against a target of 20 per cent and standard performance was averaging 102 per cent compared with 110 per cent previously attained. The trouser section was operating at 80 per cent efficiency against a target of 87 per cent, absenteeism was 9 per cent against a target of 4 per cent, excess costs were 25 per cent against a target of 15 per cent and the standard performance was averaging 109 per cent, the normal standard.

Maintaining and expanding market share was proving a challenge for the company and formed an inherent part of the strategy being developed. The organization's two major customers were the Ministry of Defence and the Police, where all contracts are won by tendering, which was becoming increasingly competitive. The company had a policy of tendering for the highest possible number of contracts beyond factory capacity, outsourcing excess production to Romania.

Company turnover over the previous five years peaked in 1993 and by 1995 had declined by 29 per cent and pre-tax profits followed a similar pattern. The ratio of overheads to labour increased as sales steadily declined. The company held 32 per cent of the police uniform market, and 10 per cent of the military market, and was aiming to increase market share of the much larger military market.

The company has always competed on quality rather than cost, regularly winning contracts from competitors, who could undercut the company's prices, but who were unable to produce uniforms of the same high quality standard. Government cut-backs squeezed margins, changing the emphasis in contract from quality to price.

The senior financial manager believed that MD would in the future help to improve BP significantly: 'The company is a small set-up employing people who are skilled through experiential learning and can do a good job – we've been lucky; but now managers need to have the qualities to be a good manager.' Part of the MD involved weekly meetings to monitor levels of excess costs, efficiency, absenteeism and performance and to develop action plans to deal with problems. These meetings resulted in general improvements which contributed to an overall improvement in BP.

A major cause of poor performance was the company's failure to provide a consistent work flow of garments through the factory. Empowerment following the strategy meetings brought information on production priorities to all levels of management, so junior management would know what production was expected each week and had time to plan production and improve line balancing. Empowerment had also led to the development of communication skills for managers which reduced delivery inefficiencies.

Conclusion

In the past the company had little need for MD, according to its most long-serving line manager because the business was expanding and profits continued to increase. This situation had altered and the organization was fighting to maintain its share of a declining market, where profit margins were continually eroded. In this situation it became essential to develop company management in order to give the business a competitive edge in the market. Change was inevitable and staff had to be prepared for this change. MD was seen as the ideal vehicle to facilitate this preparation and develop a more highly trained, efficient and flexible management. One example was the need to develop market research skills as the company planned to diversify from tendering for established markets to penetrating new markets. Developing computer skills allowed the company to shed staff and therefore reduce labour costs in certain areas, without experiencing any reduction in productivity.

Strategy group meetings appeared to be the most carefully planned and widespread vehicle for MD. These meetings were welcomed by junior management as a means of resolving recurrent production problems but they also exposed large gaps in MD that needed to be addressed. Junior management were demanding individual development that would allow them to become more effective managers. Empowerment alone did not naturally develop all the skills necessary to become the new type of manager needed by the company.

There is no doubt that the importance of training and development has been recognized by the organization at the highest level of management. Plans were in hand to improve BP and the new proposed management structure was one means by which this could possibly be achieved, at the same time giving MD a much higher priority in the company. However, since overheads were high it was doubted whether the increased efficiency of functions can justify the expense involved.

Turnover had increased and the number of direct employees was to be correspondingly increased, reducing the overhead to labour ratio and enhancing the possibility of returning the company to a more profitable trajectory. Whether this improvement would be sufficient to increase investment in training and development substantially was uncertain at the time of the study.

Case 15
Shoe factory

Background

The factory is part of the international division of a shoemaking business, founded in 1825, which markets a range of quality branded shoes. The company's productive capacity is concentrated in twenty-two factories, fifteen of which are in Europe, two in North America and five in Australia.

The factory was opened in 1961 in a converted warehouse and recruited local labour to produce a limited range of children's shoes. Operatives were trained at a neighbouring factory to produce two main styles of shoes. As output expanded to meet growing demand, production was moved into purpose built-premises. The workforce, which was under 100, expanded rapidly to approximately 280; and two extensions were added to the factory in the 1970s.

The factory's main focus remained children's shoes, but infants and ladies styles were also produced as the demand for children's shoes began to decline. This development was not entirely successful, as operatives were expected to deal with finer leathers, paler colours and finer stitching, with which they were unfamiliar. Eventually, this part of production was returned to the women's division and in 1988 the factory lost its status as a cut-box resourcing unit and became a cut-close resourcing unit. This decision effectively downgraded the factory, which lost the independent status it had enjoyed for twenty-seven years as a cut-box factory. The downsizing resulted in the factory site being too large for the productive capacity required and to reduce overheads the factory moved to its new smaller site.

Following the move the number of operatives employed fell by almost 50 per cent from approximately 270 to 130 employees. The closing department subsequently expanded, bringing the number of operatives employed in the factory up to 164. The year target for number of shoes produced at the time of the study was 835,000 pairs and company turnover was estimated to be approximately £1.5 million.

The company provided the opportunity to attain NVQ 2 and wished to introduce NVQ 3, but had not anticipated higher level NVQs. Head Office had *Investor in People* status, but this did not include the site studied.

Organizational strategy

For the company the critical success factors are the following:

- to attract and retain more loyal and delighted customers profitably;
- to launch more innovative products and to innovate in all we do;
- to make available the first choice of shoes;
- to improve the consistency of the brand experience every time, everywhere;
- to grow our brands in world markets;
- to eliminate waste of time and cost;
- to unlock the potential of our people.

Although the managerial structure of the company was traditionally hierarchical, the number of managers employed in the factory has been greatly reduced and teams are being developed to incorporate self-management and to promote a team vision. This vision is based on introducing a culture of continuous improvement in response to customer needs: value for money, quality, delivery, flexibility and innovative products and processes. Teams need to be able to prevent or resolve interpersonal problems relating to such issues as conflict, attendance and performance. MD is regarded as a key building block of team working, providing the vehicle for developing the competences that managers need to acquire to attain organizational goals.

OS and MD are very closely linked, as the HRD specialist explained: 'we are having to manage a huge culture change in the organization and management must develop the skills necessary to manage this change'. The company is gradually moving from piece work to team working and each manager must now run their team as if it were their own business, developing an understanding of for example, how the whole business is run, costs and a whole range of other areas of knowledge and skills which have never previously been required.

The factory manager felt that MD could be linked more closely with OS: the development of people needed to be more systematic, the operating unit strategy needed to be more closely linked to people, and MD should be sharply focused to generate business advantage as well as advantage to the individual.

One manager thought departmental strategies did not influence MD: 'in the past we used to have our own departmental budgets and quotas, now we are measured on overall performance'. Line managers were divided on the issue of whether MD could be linked more effectively with departmental strategy. They explained that company training and development were good and that it was directed towards acquiring the competences needed to perform their managerial role more effectively. Managers noted 'what made good sense whilst you were away on a course was often extremely difficult to put into practice when you returned to work at the factory'.

HRD systems and processes

The HR specialist explained that 'all MD is entirely competence based' in the company. Moreover, 'all management training and development is geared to the organizational objectives of the factory'. However, none of the HRD systems and processes in the company are based on MCI Standards. Recruitment, selection and appraisal systems are all based on in-house standards and the reward system is based on the Hay grading system. Nevertheless, it was emphasized that competence was the most important criterion for recruitment and selection of managerial candidates. There was no evidence that the unit had considered basing its HRD systems and processes on the Management Standards.

Job descriptions had become redundant as managerial responsibilities vary with the changing needs of the company and all jobs are fluid. The competences required for particular managerial responsibilities are a function of the degree to which operative teams are empowered. How much of the managers' role will remain after this process is complete is unknown: 'At present managers all require four basic competences, coaching ability, shoemaking knowledge, industrial engineering knowledge and process improvement skills, but these will change as organizational strategy develops.'

According to line managers, the primary purpose of appraisal is to provide a means by which an individual manager can review their performance over the last few months, their strengths and weaknesses, and identify what they wish to achieve in the future. For junior managers, appraisal was likened to 'a "stock-take" of an individual's skills'; it was the opportunity to discover 'how you have progressed over the last few months, what are your strengths and weaknesses, and what skills you should develop for your own future progression'.

The factory manager has the major responsibility for MD recognizing the skills, knowledge and competences that each manager will need to achieve the organization's strategic objectives. Individuals also have some responsibility for their own MD, 'first to be honest in their performance review, so we are tackling the right issues and second, to commit themselves fully to an agreed training programme'.

Line managers and team members recognized their own responsibilities for MD: identifying what they need to learn and being increasingly empowered to create their own MD programme. Team members perceived the personnel department as having a minor role to play in their MD. Senior strategic managers confirmed that all managers are expected to participate in MD activities and to contribute to the MD of their staff. One line manager felt that a programme for MD was arrived at through joint discussion at the appraisal meeting, whereas another felt that this was much more of a prescriptive process, with the factory manager advising the line managers regarding what skills they needed to acquire from a position of superior knowledge.

The goals of MD were established as part of the appraisal process through a two-way discussion between the line manager and the factory manager, or between team members and their managers. Personal development was very closely tied to team goals and focused on such issues as coaching, learning to deal more effectively with others, initiating change and empowering your team.

The performance review mechanism involved reviewers commenting on the achievements of each individual manager during the review period, how the reviewee communicates, delegates, develops subordinates and relates generally to colleagues on a personal and professional level. Half of the review form was devoted to an individual action plan, including training and development plans. The factory manager introduced a separate staff appraisal and review procedure, on an experimental basis. Under this scheme, each individual manager was required to self-assess themselves under four major headings: departmental performance; individual performance; future development; and value to the company.

One junior manager felt that in the last twelve months their MD had been exceptional, whereas the other manager at this level was more reserved in their judgement. It was explained that MD was good in terms of developing managers to have the 'right' skills for the job, but that MD was not always well structured and that the onus was on the individual manager to make senior management aware of their MD needs. Also MD did not appear to be linked to any career structure in the company; even the graduate training scheme no longer existed.

Individual performance

The Factory Manager explained that there was very little measurement of individual performance: he normally asked each individual manager their own opinion regarding the adequacy or inadequacy of their own performance. A manager's individual performance tends to be measured mainly in the light of their department's performance. Attainment of individual goals, for example to develop a specific department, may be measured in terms of milestones of achievement or a manager may have behavioural goals. The appraisal is the main means of measuring an individual manager's performance and the criteria applied are those detailed earlier in the revised performance review document, e.g. departmental performance, their own perception of their individual performance and their unique contribution to the company.

The HR specialist noted the difficulty of measuring IP, as opposed to team performance: 'process improvement can be measured…but an individual may have the ability to be an excellent team leader and be highly skilled and be doing a good job yet the team he is managing may not be developing as required'. Nevertheless, the performance of line managers is measured on the results of their departments and the relationship with their teams, such as good industrial relations. They are judged on the 'quality, costs, delivery time and output' of their team and given weekly feedback on their team's performance.

Team members identified productivity results as a major, measured, indicator of their individual performance. Other areas of managerial performance which were measured were their abilities in the areas of coaching and communication and ability to deal with problems under pressure and to initiate change. Appraisal reports were identified as the main method of measuring IP and the extent of MD that had taken place during a specified time.

Junior managers have a performance review with the factory manager three times a year; at this meeting an action plan for future development is formulated for each individual. Managers felt that the initiative for MD was very much in their own hands at these meetings; they had to express what they felt they needed in terms of skills and experience. The review meeting also provided the individual manager with the opportunity to discuss the training needs of other members of the team in order to enable the team to function more effectively.

The factory manager felt that MD had made a significant contribution towards improvements in IP. For example, an industrial engineer who had to acquire competence in areas where he had not received any previous training now performs well in a managerial capacity. The HR specialist believed the contribution of MD to IP had been mixed in the factory; in some cases it had made a noticeable difference, in others it had no effect whatsoever.

One line manager was unable to comment on the question of whether MD had improved IP. Others believed MD had improved their ability to interact with other people which improved their managerial performance. Team members felt that MD had made a significant contribution to their IP, providing 'the competences necessary to leave the shop floor and assume a managerial role and to perform well in this role'.

Organizational performance

Team working was perceived as the key to improving OP, making the company competitive and staying in business. The introduction of team working had varying degrees of success, depending on the make-up of the team, and the organization was still exploring the best combinations of workers to form into teams. Team working was expected to vastly improve productivity, and 'quick response' had been introduced to improve the quality of the finished product. Every employee was being developed to strive for the highest standard, monitoring the quality of the product. Improvements in quality were planned to free more person hours and allow more effective utilization of machinery, making the whole process far more cost-effective. At the time of the study it took 5 days to replace retailers' stock and the company was aiming to reduce this to 1 day. Efforts had been made to introduce team working throughout the organization, but the major focus was on the shop floor and the success with the management team had been limited.

The HR specialist explained that teams were expected to achieve a range of productivity and efficiency targets, such as a 0.5 per cent level for recuts and errors. To monitor their own performance, teams needed the skills to self-manage in line with the OS of empowerment. The company wanted all employees fully committed: 'We don't want them to have their brains on hold when they walk through the factory doors; they have the answers to a lot of our problems, people are flexible, not like robots and they can think for themselves.'

Line managers explained that every morning a production meeting is held at the factory, where the output of each department is examined and the management team try to resolve some of the problems that have caused bottlenecks in production. Each individual manager then discusses these issues with their departmental team.

One team member commented that there was no performance measurement of the management team: instead targets focused on output, cost efficiency and throughput in the factory overall. Teams did not feel that they had ownership of these targets.

According to the HR specialist, team performance had benefited directly from MD. Developing team working rather than the traditional piece work was seen as the key to improving the factory's efficiency and was expected to improve performance significantly, but at the time of the study there was no evidence of its effect.

MD had allowed the development of team working among line managers which 'unleashed a huge potential on this site', according to one line manager. Another line manager commented that in twelve months time it would be possible to identify the effect on the management team, but the beneficial effects of shop floor team working on productivity were obvious. Under the piecework system it took 7–8 days to produce an upper, which under team working conditions can be produced in one day. This 'quick response' means that customers can now receive a much better service, ordering a pair of shoes on Friday and receiving them on Monday. MD enabled managers to develop the skills necessary to form and motivate the teams to pull together and vastly improve their performance and hence the performance of the factory.

Business performance

The most important aspect of BP was what the factory manager termed 'the cost of productivity'. There is no point in counting the number of uppers that come out of the factory, as this will differ considerably depending on the complexity of the work involved. Other measures of efficiency are attendance, availability to fulfil customer requirement throughout the year, overhead cost of a standard minute, quality, delivery and throughput time. Overall productivity is measured by the cost of a standard minute (SM). The number of SMs required to complete an upper will vary depending on the complexity of the upper. The factory had the capacity to produce approximately 21 million SMs and needed to produce these at the lowest cost per SM possible.

The overhead costs per SM had been too high in the factory and the overhead cost, on average, doubles productive costs. The company was aiming for an overhead cost of 9p per SM through the introduction of team working. In 1993 the overhead cost per SM was approximately 13p, in 1994 it was 12.5p and it was 11.9p at the time of the study, so the factory was gradually moving towards this target.

The more complex the shoe, the more labour-intensive it is to produce and the higher the cost per SM, which has led to the more complex shoes being manufactured abroad. Moves to produce simpler styles at the factory would help but the company aimed to produce complex styles at 9p/SM, which was feasible in the light of the fact that some teams were already operating at below 9p/SM. A saving of 1p/SM represented £200,000 if extrapolated over a whole year.

The number of SMs per pair had decreased by 8 per cent, and pairs produced per employee per week had increased by 2 per cent, but cost per SM had only fallen by 0.5 per cent. The job rate of teams was far lower than that of piece workers: the closing room rate was 0.3 per cent compared with a team rate of only 0.1 per cent and recuts of teams in closing were six times less than those of piece workers in general.

The factory manager stated that it was difficult to say whether the market share of the unit had improved. The overall performance of the whole company was down on the previous year in terms of trading profit partly because of hot weather, which focused demand on cheap, seasonal items and slowed 'back to school' demand. Generally, over the past three years turnover had steadily increased by approximately 5 per cent, whereas trading profit had only increased 0.2 per cent. The factory manager believed that the transition from piece working to team working could not possibly have been achieved without MD and without this change the factory would have had no future.

Conclusions

As part of the International Division, the factory was required to compete against manufacturing units abroad with lower labour costs. 'Quick-response', was the only strategic tool available to domestic units to give them the competitive edge over foreign factories, and this could not have been developed so cost-effectively in the company without MD. Time is of the essence in this process and the company had to adopt a 'quick-response' mode for the factory to stay in business. In the past children's footwear was considered to be the most profitable part of the International Division and central to the production strategy of the company. As a result, there was a marked reluctance to source too much of this production abroad for fear of losing control of a key part of the business but inevitably more production was being shifted outside the UK.

The introduction of team working in the factory had proved costly, and the support cost of teams, for example, was running at 10 per cent higher than for piece workers in the closing room. It was anticipated that it would take at least 9–12 months to achieve these levels from team start-up and it is at this point that inroads can be made into depreciation costs of the new machinery necessary for team working.

Team working, which will result in flexibility, increased productivity and a higher quality product will also involve the empowerment of the smaller multiskilled teams. This empowerment was regarded as a mixed blessing by some managers. MD had developed those managers who were capable of developing team working, and part of this process involved the empowerment of operatives in the team. Increasingly, therefore, team performance would be less tied to the skill of the manager and would become a function of the skill of the team member, who is being developed in the first instance to self-manage. This strategy begs the question, 'what will be the manager's future role?', or indeed, 'will there be a future role for managers?' and will the company 'just have MD for operatives?'

As for the future of the company in the UK, the managing director wrote in the company newspaper: 'If we get quick response, flexibility and lower overheads in our factories, this probably means more, not less factories in the United Kingdom. However, each unit is quite likely to be smaller.'

Case 16

Southern NHS Trust

Background

The NHS Trust in the South of England offers a wide range of community health services in a large area. It had Trust status from April 1993 and at the time of the study provided services from over sixty different sites, including small clinics, health centres and community homes and larger hospital sites. The total workforce numbers approximately 1,400, of which by far the largest proportion are nurses. The Trust states its purpose as being: 'to provide a wide range of high quality community care services which will enable people to lead as independent a life as possible, and have meaningful choices'. The core values of the Trust are: 'valuing the people who use our services; valuing our partners in other organizations; valuing each other as colleagues; social responsibility'.

As well as the changes brought about by the move to Trust status, the Trust had recently been through a restructuring exercise which involved reallocating responsibilities within and between its directorates. The restructuring also involved reducing the senior management tier and devolving responsibility for a range of areas (such as budgeting and staffing) to 'front line' care professionals. Further change was brought about by short-term moves within the senior management team due to secondment and maternity leave. The Trust's activities were split between six directorates: community services; learning disability services; mental health services; service development; finance and information; and personnel.

Training and development, originally the responsibility of the District Health Authority, were taken on shortly before the organization became a Trust and were restructured to provide a better service. A MD strategy was produced and a MD programme established to cover all levels of management, but it became outdated and was discontinued. The Trust was preparing new strategies for training and development in general and MD in particular at the time of the study.

Training provision for managers included a range of in-house workshops, such as finance for managers, management of change, facilitation skills and recruitment and selection. A three-day introduction to management was also offered for new first-line managers. Other training sessions were provided to support the implementation of new corporate policies and systems, such as sickness absence and appraisal.

Some managers were supported in undertaking external, accredited programmes such as MBAs, although the opportunity to take part in such programmes varied across the organization. Others were involved in job-shadowing activities with colleagues from other directorates in order to gain a broader knowledge and understanding of the services offered by the Trust and the links between them. The first use of the MCI Standards at the Trust was taking place in the Learning Disabilities Directorate where a group of sixteen home leaders were taking part in a pilot scheme offering the level 4 management NVQ. The Trust did not yet hold *Investor in People* status, but was in the process of applying for it.

Organizational strategy

There were mixed responses from interviewees regarding the links between MD and OS. Some felt that there were clear links between the two, although these links had only recently become more formal. The new Appraisal and Development Scheme linked MD to organizational and departmental objectives: individuals needs are identified in relation to their individual objectives, which in turn are based on organizational objectives. All objectives and related training needs should therefore be defined in line with OS.

The training and development implications of the Trust's long-term strategy and annual business plans were considered when the senior management team defined additional skills (including management skills) needed to achieve the agreed plans, and how those skills would be acquired. The links were seen by some to be somewhat *ad hoc*, reacting to particular issues and objectives rather than planned as part of ongoing strategy. This was partly due to the lack of a MD strategy for the Trust, the revision of which was expected to address longer-term OS.

Some examples of how MD has been provided to support specific organizational and departmental goals were given. Over the previous year the Trust had introduced a new Sickness Absence policy in order to monitor and manage work days lost through sickness absence; to support its implementation, all managers were obliged to attend a one-day training event. A new strategy for mental health services was about to be implemented and specific training and support were to be provided for individuals appointed to new management positions in connection with this.

Other interviewees felt that while in theory MD was supposed to be linked to organizational and departmental goals, in practice it did not work that way. Development opportunities available to managers were seen to depend on where individuals worked since there was no coordinated approach to MD.

Closer links between MD and OS were thought to be both possible and desirable, but a lack of time and resources to invest in development and patchy 'ownership' of MD in the Trust as a whole were blocks to achieving effective development. For example, releasing ward staff to take part in training events caused logistical problems in terms of cover as services still had to be provided to clients.

The NVQ scheme was quoted as a good way of linking development to the needs of the organization, and also an example of development which was well thought out and properly targeted. The scheme would not only change work practices and improve client care, but would also give participants a national qualification.

Written materials provided some evidence for the intended links between organizational goals and MD. The Appraisal and Development Scheme Course Manual also made reference to the need to set individual objectives which support organizational and departmental goals, although it provided no guidance on how to identify development needs and relevant learning opportunities which link to these objectives.

HRD systems and processes

No use was made of the MCI Standards in management training and development in the organization apart from in connection with the pilot NVQ 4 programme. The majority of this programme was planned and provided by a local college rather than the Trust's own training and development team. It was claimed that much of the training provided in-house was nevertheless focused on competence requirements: what people need to be able to do, rather than being knowledge or theory-based.

All interviewees believed that individual managers have a high degree of responsibility for their own development: some felt that they have the major responsibility, particularly at more senior levels of management, to identify training needs and find suitable ways of meeting those needs. Decisions on MD should be made jointly as a result of two-way discussions, with the Appraisal and Development Scheme providing the main framework and forum for these discussions and decisions to take place. Some line managers were felt to be far more committed to this role (and to the importance of training and development in general) than others, with a consequent imbalance between different teams and directorates in the amount of development which individuals can access.

The central personnel department were seen to have a supporting, advising and enabling role in relation to MD. For example, they advise on the Appraisal and Development Scheme and can propose potential options for development. MD courses were planned and provided by the training and development team within the Personnel Directorate who are also able to provide information and advice on possible development opportunities.

The MCI Standards were not used as a basis for setting objectives, identifying development needs or monitoring management performance. The new Trust-wide Appraisal and Development Scheme was the main, formal means by which these activities took place and there was widespread support for the scheme. Most interviewees linked its main purpose to training and development, to the setting and monitoring of objectives linked to those of the department and organization and to the review of IP, strengths and weaknesses. It was generally seen to be a constructive scheme which enabled time to be put aside for one-to-one discussion between managers and their staff and for feedback to be given by both parties.

The MCI Standards were not used in any other areas of HRM in the organization, and the content of job descriptions was thought to be based on historical practice, Whitley Council gradings, the current and future needs of teams and departments, and key roles and responsibilities. There were no plans to use the MCI Standards more widely as they had not been considered in detail by the HRM teams, but would be considered in the future.

Individual performance

The main means of formally measuring and monitoring IP was the Appraisal and Development Scheme. Through this scheme, objectives were set for individuals via a process of negotiation with their line manager. The objectives should relate to the overall objectives of the team/department, and hence to those of the Trust as a whole. Both quantitative and qualitative objectives may be set in areas such as budget management, standards of care, team management, project management and service development.

The Trust's Appraisal and Development Scheme was relatively new and there was therefore little firm evidence about its operation in general and, particularly, concerning its role in improving IP. Evaluation of training and development was recognized as an area which had not yet been fully developed. Although participants on in-house courses were asked for immediate feedback at the end of an event ('happy sheets'), there was no further follow up to find out what impact the training had on an individual's performance at work.

On the whole, interviewees found it hard to think of improvements in IP due to management training and development. Examples of specific management skills which had been achieved or improved were given by some interviewees. The in-house training provided for new managers (introduction to management, finance/budget management and recruitment and selection) had enabled them to take on new responsibilities.

In particular, training and development had given front-line care professionals the new skills they need to take on managerial responsibilities for the first time. Managers' ability to monitor and manage sickness absence was seen to be much improved by training in the new Sickness Absence Scheme.

Other interviewees felt that the main benefits of MD were in raising awareness of the business culture within which the Trust now operates and the reasons why contracting, audits and objective setting were needed. Managers could implement new policies and practices more effectively, as a result of involvement in the NVQ 4 pilot programme. The managers on the NVQ pilot were proving better able to manage and implement change than they were prior to the programme.

In general terms, MD was also seen to give a broader outlook, new ideas and new approaches to problem solving together with a new way of thinking in terms of customer/client needs and how to meet them. It was also seen to have brought about a new 'management culture' in the organization by increasing managers' confidence, enabling them to understand their role within the Trust as a whole and empowering them to take decisions. No written materials were available to support or refute claims of improved IP.

Organizational performance

Measures for team or departmental performance were in some areas similar to those for the managers of those teams/departments. They link very much to the requirements in terms of quantity and quality of service specified in the contracts held with the Trust's purchasers. Budget performance is another main area which is monitored, as are waiting lists/waiting times and levels of complaints.

Improvements in performance across teams or departments as a result of MD were even harder for interviewees to identify. One interviewee felt that their team worked better and was better managed due to the development which their line manager had undertaken. Handling of complaints had improved across the organization as a whole following training provided to managers, and targets in this area were being met Trust-wide. One interviewee stated that the team's budget management skills had greatly improved: they had come in on target with their budgets for three years running and even had some underspend.

It was claimed by one of the top managers interviewed that specific changes in service provision were in large part due to MD. Two examples given were continuing care services and a day hospital for the elderly. Both of these services had been substantially changed to better meet client needs; both in terms of what was provided and how it was provided. MD had helped those responsible for the services to take a broader view of client needs and to identify flexible and new ways in which those needs could be met.

One of the more senior managers interviewed felt very strongly that all training and development should have a benefit beyond the particular individual involved. In their area, anyone who goes on a course or conference is expected to share their learning in some way with colleagues, or use it to make clear improvements to services. For example, a person who recently took part in a counselling course might start to train others in the team in counselling, or may offer a counselling service to clients. Again, no written evidence was provided in relation to improved team or departmental performance.

Business performance

Very few examples were given of improvements in BP due to MD. One of the top managers claimed that the Trust's high success rate in gaining contracts from GPs in the area and in neighbouring areas was a sign of improved performance which was in large part due to the attitude, approach and capability of the Trust's managers, brought about by MD. However, another of the top managers interviewed did not believe that there had been any improvements in BP because of MD. No written evidence was available in this area.

Conclusions

Use of the MCI Standards was limited at the Trust at the time of the study, being restricted to one group of sixteen managers from the Learning Disabilities Directorate who were involved in a pilot level 4 management NVQ programme. Therefore the vast majority of the Trust's managers were not involved in development activities based on the MCI Standards. It was, however, claimed that the in-house provision was 'competence based' in that it focused on what managers needed to be able to do.

Some improvements in the performance of individuals, teams and the organization as a whole were identified by interviewees, although they tended to find it difficult to give specific examples of where there was an explicit link between development activities and improved performance.

Other factors were identified which had also impacted on management performance, particularly the organizational restructuring which had taken place and the devolution of management decision-making and accountability. It was felt by some that even though improvements might have happened anyway over time, they happened more quickly when training was given, individuals have more confidence to try new approaches and are more sure of their role and responsibilities.

There were differing views from individuals about the extent to which MD is linked to OS, although the majority felt that strategy does influence MD. There were some sceptics who believed that MD opportunities were not offered equitably throughout the organization and that in practice the development available depends more on individual personalities than OS.

HRD processes were not based on the MCI Standards or on any other explicit, organization-wide definition of what is required and expected of managers in the Trust. However, the new Appraisal and Development Scheme was designed to ensure that all training and development undertaken would contribute to achieving the Trust's objectives.

References

Abrams, M. (1981) 'A manager's view of management development', *Management Education and Development*, 12, 2: 113–15.

Adair, J. (1986) *Effective Teambuilding*, Aldershot: Gower.

Aguren, S., Bredbacka, C., Hansson, R., Ibregren, K. and Karlsson, K.G. (1984) *Volvo Kalmar Revisited*, Stockholm: Efficiency and Participation Development Council.

Ahlstrand, B.W. (1990) *The Quest for Productivity: A Case Study of Fawley after Flanders*, Cambridge: Cambridge University Press.

Alderson, S. (1993) 'Reframing management competence: focusing on the top management team', *Personnel Review*, 22, 6: 53–62.

Alexander, G.P. (1987) 'Establishing shared values through management training programs', *Training and Development Journal*, 41, 2: 45–53.

Andreu, R. and Ciborra, C. (1996) 'Organisational learning and core capabilities development: the role of IT', *Journal of Strategic Information Systems*, 5, 2: 111–27.

Andrews, K.R. (1965) *The Concept of Corporate Strategy*, Homewood, IL.: Irwin.

Ansoff, H.I. (1965) *Corporate Strategy*, Harmondsworth: Penguin.

Aoki, M. (1986) *The Co-Operative Game Theory of the Firm*, Oxford: Clarendon Press.

Argyris, C. (1962) *Interpersonal Competence and Organizational Effectiveness*, Homewood, IL: Dorsey.

—— (1982) *Reasoning, Learning and Action: Individual and Organizational*, San Francisco, CA: Jossey-Bass.

Argyris, C. and Schön, D. (1978) *Organisational Learning: A Theory of Action Perspective*, Reading, MA: Addison-Wesley.

—— (1996) *Organisational Learning II: Theory, Method and Practice*, Reading, MA: Addison-Wesley.

Armstrong, M. (1987) 'Human resource management: a case of the emperor's new clothes?', *Personnel Management*, August, 30–5.

—— (1989) *Personnel and the Bottom Line*, London: Institute of Personnel Management.

Arthur, J.B. (1994) 'Effects of human resource systems on manufacturing performance and turnover', *Academy of Management Journal*, 37, 3: 670–87.

Arthur, M.B. and Kram, K.E. (1989) 'Reciprocity at work: the separate yet inseparable possibilities for individual and organizational development', in M.B. Arthur, D.T. Hall and B.S. Lawrence (eds) *Handbook of Career Theory*, Cambridge: Cambridge University Press, 292–313.

Ashton, D. and Easterby-Smith, M. (1979) *Management Development in the Organization: Analysis and Action*, London: Macmillan.

Ashton, D., Easterby-Smith, M. and Irvine, C. (1975) *Management Development: Theory and Practice*, Bradford: MCB.

Ashton, D., Green, F. and Hoskins, M. (1989) 'The training system of British capitalism: changes and prospects', in F. Green (ed.) *The Restructuring of the UK Economy*, Hemel Hempstead: Harvester Wheatsheaf, 131–54.

Atkinson, J. (1984) 'Manpower strategies for flexible organisations', *Personnel Management*, August, 28–9.

Baker, D.P. and Salas, E. (1992) 'Principles for measuring teamwork skills', *Human Factors*, 34, 4: 469–75.

Bal, S. (1995) *The Interactive Manager*, London: Kogan Page.

Barlow, A. and Winterton, J. (1996) 'Restructuring production and work organization', in I. Taplin and J. Winterton (eds) *Restructuring within a Labour Intensive Industry: The UK Clothing Industry in Transition*, Aldershot: Avebury, 176–98.

Barnard, C.I. (1938) *The Functions of the Executive*, Cambridge, MA: Harvard University Press.

Barney, J. (1991) 'Firm resources and sustained competitive advantage', *Journal of Management*, 17, 1: 99–120.

—— (1995) 'Looking inside for competitive advantage', *Academy of Management Executive*, 9, 4: 49–61.

Bartram, S. and Gibson, B. (1997) *Training Needs Analysis*, 2nd edition. Aldershot: Gower.

Becker, B. and Gerhart, B. (1996) 'The impact of human resource management on organizational performance: progress and prospects', *Academy of Management Journal*, 39, 4: 779–801.

Beer, M., Spector, B., Lawrence, P.R., Mills, D.Q. and Walton, R.E. (1984) *Managing Human Assets*, New York: Free Press.

Beer, S. (1959) *Cybernetics and Management*, London: English Universities Press.

Belbin, M. (1981) *Management Teams: Why they Succeed or Fail*, Oxford: Butterworth-Heinemann (1987 edition).

Berry, J.K. (1990) 'Linking management development to business strategies', *Training and Development Journal*, 44, 8: 20–2.

Binsted, D.S. (1980) 'Design for learning in management training and development: a view', *Journal of European Industrial Training*, 4, 8: whole issue.

Boak, G. (1991) *Developing Managerial Competences: The Management Learning Contract Approach*, London: Pitman.

Boak, G. and Joy, P. (1990) 'Management learning contracts: the training triangle', in M. Pedler, J. Burgoyne, T. Boydell and G. Welshman (eds) *Self-Development in Organizations*, London: McGraw-Hill.

Boak, G. and Stephenson, M. (1987) 'Management learning contracts: from theory to practice, Part II, Practice' *Journal of European Industrial Training*, 11, 6: 17–20.

Boam, R. and Sparrow, P. (1992) *Designing and Achieving Competency*, London: McGraw-Hill.

Bols, R., van Bree, J., Bolton, M. and Gijswijt, J. (1995) 'Emerging issues in assessment and development', in M. Bolton (ed.) *Assessment and Development in Europe*, London: McGraw-Hill, 99–112.

Bolton, M. and Moreira, H. (1995) 'Assessing and developing people: the background', in M. Bolton (ed.) *Assessment and Development in Europe*, London: McGraw-Hill, 1–18.

Boutall, T. (1997) *The Good Manager's Guide*, London: MCI.

Boyatzis, R. (1982) *The Competent Manager: A Model for Effective Performance*, Chichester: Wiley.

Boydell, T. and Pedler, M. (1981) *Management Self-Development*, Westmead: Gower.

Braham, B.J. (1995) *Creating a Learning Organisation*, London: Kogan Page.

Brooks, A. (1992) 'Building learning organizations: the individual culture interaction', *Human Resource Development Quarterly*, 3, 3: 323–35.

Brooks, A. (1994) 'Power and the production of knowledge: collective team learning in work organizations', *Human Resource Development Quarterly*, 5, 3: 213–35.

Brown, R.B. (1993) 'Meta competence: a recipe for reframing the competence debate', *Personnel Review*, 22, 6: 25–36.

Brown, R.B. (1994) 'Reframing the competency debate: management knowledge and meta-competence in graduate education', *Management Learning*, 25, 2: 289–99.

Brown, W. (1993) 'The contraction of collective bargaining in Britain', *British Journal of Industrial Relations*, 31, 2: 189–200.

Bundy, R. and Thurston, R. (1990) 'Transferring supervisors into coaches and advisors', *The Journal of Quality and Participation*, June, 46–50.

Burgoyne, J. (1988a) *Competency Based Approaches to Management Development*, Lancaster: Centre for the Study of Management Learning.

Burgoyne, J. (1988b) 'Management development for the individual *and* the organisation', *Personnel Management*, June, 40–4.

Burgoyne, J. (1989a) *Management Development: Context and Strategies*, Aldershot: Gower.

Burgoyne, J. (1989b) 'Creating the managerial portfolio: building on competency approaches management development', *Management Education and Development*, 20, 1: 56–61.

Burgoyne, J. and Hodgson, V.E. (1983) 'Natural learning and managerial action: a phenomenological study in the field setting', *Journal of Management Studies*, 20, 3: 387–99.

Burgoyne, J. and Stewart, R. (1976) 'The nature, use and acquisition of managerial skills and other attributes', *Personnel Review*, 5, 4: 19–29.

Butler, J. (1990) 'Beyond project-based learning for senior managers and their teams', *Journal of Management Development*, 9, 4: 32–8.

Callendar, C., Toye, J., Connor, H. and Spilsbury, M. (1993) *National and Scottish Vocational Qualifications: Early Indications of Employers' Take-up and Use*, Brighton: Institute of Manpower Studies.

Campbell, A. and Sommers Luchs, K.S. (1997) *Core Competency-Based Strategy*, London: Thomson.

Campion, M.A., Medsker, G.J. and Higgs, C.A. (1993) 'Relations between work group characteristics and effectiveness: implications for designing effective work groups', *Personnel Psychology*, 46, 4: 823–50.

Cannell, M. (1993) 'Team working in the UK garment industries', *Textile Outlook International*, March: 62–75.

Canning, R. (1990) 'The quest for competence', *Industrial and Commercial Training*, 122, 5: 12–16.

Cannon, T. (1994) *Working Party Report: Developments since Handy and Constable: Management Development to the Millennium Research*, Corby: Institute of Management [see Institute of Management (1994)].

Carter, P. and Lumsden, C. (1988) 'How management development can improve business performance', *Personnel Management*, October, 49–52.

Casey, D. and Pearce, D. (eds) (1977) *More than Management Development*, Farnborough: Gower.

Cheetham, G. (1994) *The Development Effectiveness of the Management Standards and Associated NVQs: An Examination of the MCI Approach to Management Development*, Sheffield: Employment Department Learning Methods Branch R&D Series, No.19.

Claydon, T. (1989) 'Union derecognition in Britain in the 1980s', *British Journal of Industrial Relations*, 27, 2: 214–24.

Clement, R.W. (1981) 'Evaluating the effectiveness of management training: progress during the 1970s and prospects for the 1980s', *Human Resource Management*, Winter, 20, 4: 8–13.

Cockerill, T. (1989) 'The kind of competence for rapid change', *Personnel Management*, September, 52–6.

Cohen, M.D. (1996) 'Individual learning and organizational routine: emerging connections', in M.D. Cohen and L.S. Sproull (eds) *Organizational Learning*, London: Sage Publications, 188–94.

Cohen, M.D. and Sproull, L.S. (eds) (1996) *Organizational Learning*, London: Sage Publications.

Collin, A. (1989) 'Managers' competence: rhetoric, reality and research', *Personnel Review*, 18, 6: 20–5.

Collin, A. (1997) 'Learning and Development', in I. Beardwell and L. Holden (eds) *Human Resource Management: A Contemporary Perspective*, 2nd edition, London: Pitman, 282–344.

Collis, D. (1991) 'A resource-based analysis of global competition: the case of the bearings industry', *Strategic Management Journal*, 12, Special issue, Summer: 49–68.

Confederation of British Industry (1989) *Towards a Skills Revolution*, London: CBI.

Constable, C.J. (1988) *Developing the Competent Manager in a UK Context*, Sheffield: Manpower Services Commission.

Constable, J. (1991) 'A Management Charter or a Chartered Manager?' in M. Silver (ed.) *Competent to Manage – Approaches to Management Training and Development*, London: Routledge, 228–32.

Constable, J. and McCormick, R. (1987) *The Making of British Managers*, London: British Institute of Management.

Coopers and Lybrand Associates (1985) *A Challenge to Complacency: Changing Attitudes to Training*, London: MSC/NEDO.

—— (1992) *Meeting the Management Challenge*, London: CLA.

Corlett, S. (1992) *Analysis of Managers' Views on the Potential Business Performance Benefits of using Competence-Based Standards*, Washington (Tyne & Wear): Northern Regional Management Centre.

Cotton, J.L. (1993) *Employee Involvement: Methods for Improving Performance and Work Attitudes*, Newbury Park, CA: Sage.

Critten, P. (1993) *Investing in People: Towards Corporate Capability*, Oxford: Butterworth-Heinemann.

Crowley-Bainton, T. and Wolf, A. (1994) *Access to Assessment Initiative*, PSI report RM.4, Sheffield: Employment Department.

Currie, G. (1994) 'Evaluation of management development: a case study', *Journal of Management Development*, 13, 3: 22–6.

Currie, G. and Darby, R. (1995) 'Competence-based management development: rhetoric and reality', *Journal of European Industrial Training*, 19, 5: 11–18.

Cutcher-Gershenfeld, J.C. (1991) 'The impact on economic performance of a transformation in workplace relations', *Industrial and Labor Relations Review*, 44, 2: 241–60.

Dale, M. (1993) *Developing Management Skills: Techniques for Improving Learning and Performance*, London: Kogan Page.

Dale, M. and Iles, P. (1992) *Assessing Management Skills*, London: Kogan Page (1996 edn).

Day, M. (1988) 'Managerial competence and the Charter Initiative', *Personnel Management*, August.

Dechant, K., Marsick, V. and Kasl, E. (1993) 'Toward a model of team learning', *Studies in Continuing Education*, 15, 1: 1–14.

De Geus, A. (1988) 'Planning as learning', *Harvard Business Review*, 66, 2: 70–4.

Deming, W.E. (1993) *The New Economics*, Cambridge, MA; MIT Center for Advanced Study.

Dence, R. (1995) 'Best practices bench marking', in J. Holloway, J. Lewis and G. Mallory (eds) *Performance Measurement and Evaluation*, London: Sage, 124–52.

Department for Education and Employment (1998) *The Learning Age: A Renaissance for a New Britain*, Green Paper, Cm.3790, London: HMSO.

Department of Trade and Industry (1994) *Competitiveness: Helping Business to Win*, White Paper, Cm. 2563, London: HMSO.

—— (1995) *Competitiveness: Forging Ahead*, White Paper, Cm. 2867, London: HMSO.

DiBella, A.J., Nevis, E.C. and Gould, J. (1996) 'Organizational learning style as a core capability', in B. Moingeon and A. Edmondson (eds) *Organizational Learning and Competitive Advantage*, London: Sage, 38–55.

DiPietro, R.A. (1993) 'TQM: strategic significance for management development', *Journal of Management Development*, 12, 7: 11–18.

Dodgson, M. (1991) 'Technology learning, technology strategy and competitive pressures', *British Journal of Management*, 2, 3: 132–49.

—— (1993) 'Organizational Learning: A review of some literatures', *Organization Studies*, 14, 3: 375–94.

Donnelly, E. (1991) 'Management Charter Initiative: a critique', *Training and Development*, April, 43–5.

Downham, T.A., Noel, J.L. and Prendergast, A.E. (1992) 'Executive development', *Human Resource Management*, 31, 1–2: 95–107.

Doyle, M. (1995) 'Organisational transformation and renewal: a case for reframing management development?', *Personnel Review*, 24, 6: 6–18.

Doyle, M. (1997) 'Management development', in I. Beardwell and L.Holden (eds) *Human Resource Management: A Contemporary Perspective*, London: Pitman, 399–476 (second edn).

Doz, Y. (1997) 'Managing core competency for corporate renewal: towards a managerial theory of core competencies', in A. Campbell and K. Sommers Luchs, *Core Competency-Based Strategy*, London: Thomson, 53–75.

Drew, S.A.W. and Davidson, A. (1993) 'Simulation-based leadership and team learning', *Journal of Management Development*, 12, 8: 39–52.

Dreyfus, H.L. and Dreyfus, S.E. (1984) 'Putting computers in their proper place: analysis versus intuition in the classroom', in D. Sloan (ed.) *The Computer in Education: A Critical Perspective*, New York: Columbia Teachers College Press.

Dreyfus, H.L., Dreyfus, S.E. and Athanasion, T. (1986) *Mind over Machine: The Power of Human Intuition and Expertise in the Era of the Computer*, New York: Free Press.

Driskell, J.E. and Salas, E. (1992) 'Collective behaviour and team performance', *Human Factors*, 34, 3: 277–88.

Easterby-Smith, M. (1994) *Evaluating Management Development, Training and Education*, 2nd edition, Aldershot: Gower .

Easterby-Smith, M., Braiden, E. and Ashton, D. (1980) *Auditing Management Development*, Farnborough: Gower.

Eccles, R.G. (1991) 'The performance management manifesto', *Harvard Business Review*, January–February: 131–7.

Edmonds, T. (1988) 'Competence based management training', *The Administrator*, October: 10–12.

Edwards, P. (1985) 'Myth of the macho manager', *Personnel Management*, April, 32–5.

Egan, G. (1993) *Adding Value – A Systematic Guide to Business-Driven Management and Leadership*, San Francisco: Jossey-Bass.

Eisenhardt, K.M., (1989) 'Building themes from case study research', *Academy of Management Review*, 14, 4, 532–50.

Eisenstat, R.A., and Wessel, J.R. (1993) 'Implementing strategy: developing a partnership for change', *Planning Review*, 21, 5: 33–7.

Elkin, G. (1990) 'Competency-based human resource development', *Industrial and Commercial Training*, 22, 4: 20–5.

Emery, F.E. and Trist, E.L. (1960) 'Socio-technical systems', in C. W. Churchman and M. Verhust (eds) *Management Science, Models and Techniques*, vol. 2, Oxford: Pergamon, 83–97.

Employment Department (1989) *Employment for the 1990s*, White Paper, London: HMSO.

—— (1990) *What is an Investor in People?*, London: ED.

Employment Department and NCVQ (1991) *Guide to National Vocational Qualifications*, Sheffield: ED.

Endres, G. and Kleiner, B. (1990) 'How to measure management training and effectiveness', *Journal of European Industrial Training*, 14, 9: 3–7.

European Commission (1994) *Growth, Competitiveness, Employment: The Challenges and Ways Forward into the 21st Century*, White Paper, Luxembourg: EC Publications Office.

—— (1996) *Teaching and Learning: Towards a Learning Society*, White Paper, Luxembourg: EC Publications Office.

Evans, L. and Kerrison, S. (1994) *MCI Personal Competence Model: Uses and Implementations*, Sheffield: Employment Department Learning Methods Branch R&D Series, No. 24.

Fairbairns, J. (1991) 'Plugging the gap in training needs analysis', *Personnel Management*, February, 43–5.

Fayol, H. (1949) *General and Industrial Management*, New York: Pitman.

Finegold, D. and Soskice, D. (1988) 'The failure of training in Britain: analysis and prescription', *Oxford Review of Economic Policy*, 4, 3: 21–53.

Fiol, C. and Lyles, M. (1985) 'Organizational learning', *Academy of Management Review*, 10, 4: 803–13.

Fitts, P.M. (1962) 'Factors in complex skills training', in R. Glasser (ed.) *Training Research and Education*, Pittsburgh: University of Pittsburgh Press, 177–97.

Fletcher, S. (1991) *NVQs, Standards and Competence: A Practical Guide for Employers, Managers and Trainers*, London: Kogan Page.

Fonda, N. (1989) 'Management development: the missing link in sustained performance', *Personnel Management*, December: 50–3.

Forrester, J.W. (1961) *Industrial Dynamics*, Cambridge, MA: Productivity Press.

Fowler, A. (1991) 'How to identify training needs', *Personnel Management Plus*, 2, 11: 22–3.

Fox, S. (1989) 'The politics of evaluating management development', *Management Education and Development*, 20, 3: 191–207.

Fryer, R.H (chair) (1997) *Learning for the Twenty-First Century*, First Report of the National Advisory Group for Continuing Education and Lifelong Learning, London: NAGCELL.

Fulmer, R.M. (1992) 'Nine management development challenges for the 1990s', *Journal of Management Development*, 11, 7: 4–9.

Gall, G. and McKay, S. (1994) 'Trade union derecognition in Britain, 1988–1994', *British Journal of Industrial Relations*, 32, 3: 433–48.

Garratt, B. (1987) *The Learning Organisation and the Need for Directors who Think*, Aldershot: Gower.

—— (1990) *Creating a Learning Organisation: A Guide to Leadership, Learning and Development*, Cambridge: Director Books.

Garvin, D. (1993) 'Building a Learning Organization', *Harvard Business Review*, 71, 4: 78–91.

Gilliland, N. (1997) *Developing your Business through Investors in People*, Aldershot: Gower.

Goold, M., Campbell, A. and Alexander, M. (1995) 'Corporate strategy: the quest for parenting advantage', *Harvard Business Review* , March–April: 120–32.

Granovetter, M. (1985) 'Economic action and social structure: the problem of embeddedness', *American Journal of Sociology*, 91, 3: 481–510.

Grant, R.M. (1991) 'The resource-based theory of competitive advantage: implications for strategy formulation', *California Management Review*, 33, 3: 114–22.

Graves, D. (1976) 'The manager's job and management development', *Personnel Review*, 5, 4: 11–16.

Guest, D.E. (1989a) 'Personnel and HRM: can you tell the difference?', *Personnel Management*, January: 48–51.

—— (1989b) 'Human resource management: its implications for industrial relations and trade unions', in J. Storey (ed.) *New Perspectives on Human Resource Management*, London: Routledge, 41–55.

Guest, D. and Peccei, R. (1994) 'The nature and causes of effective human resource management', *British Journal of Management*, 32, 2: 219–42.

Guzzo, R.A. and Dickson, M.W. (1996) 'Teams in organizations: recent research on performance and effectiveness', *Annual Review of Psychology*, 47: 307–38.

Hackman, J.R. (1987) 'The design of work teams', in J.W. Lorsch (ed.), *Handbook of Organizational Behavior*, Englewood Cliffs, NJ: Prentice-Hall.

Hague, H. (1973) *Management Training for Real*, London: Institute of Personnel Management.

Hales, C. (1986) 'What do managers do? A critical review of the evidence', *Journal of Management Studies*, 23, 1: 88–115.

Hall, D.T. (1984) 'Human resource development and organisational effectiveness', in C. Fombrun, N. Tichy and M. Devanna (eds) *Strategic Human Resource Management*, New York: John Wiley, 159–81.

Hamel, G. (1994) 'The concept of core competence', in G. Hamel and A. Heene (eds) *Competence-Based Competition*, New York: Wiley, 11–16.

Handy, C., Gordon, C., Gow, I., Maloney, M. and Randlesome, C. (1987) *The Making of Managers: A Report on Management Education, Training and Development in the USA, W. Germany, France, Japan and the UK*, London: National Economic Development Office.

Handy, C., Gordon, G., Gow, I. and Raddlesome, C. (1988) *Making Managers*, London: Pitman.

Harbridge Consulting Group (1991) 'Management training and development in large UK business organisations', *Journal of European Industrial Training*, 15, 7: 22–4.

Harri-Augstein, S. and Webb, I.M. (1995) *Learning to Change*, London: McGraw-Hill.

Harris, P.R. (1989) 'Developing the learning manager', *Journal of Managerial Psychology*, 4, 1: 17–21.

Harrison, R. (1992) *Employee Development*, London: Institute of Personnel and Development.

Hartle, F. (1995) *How to Re-engineer your Performance Management Process*, London: Kogan Page.

Hay, J. (1990) 'Managerial competences or managerial characteristics?', *Management Education and Development*, 21, 4: 305–15.

Hayes, C. (1982) *Training for Skill Ownership: Learning to Take it With You*, Brighton: Institute of Manpower Studies.

Hayes, R.H., Wheelwright, S.C. and Clark, K.B. (1988) *Dynamic Manufacturing: Creating a Learning Organization*, New York: Free Press.

Hedberg, B. (1981) 'How organizations learn and unlearn', in P. Nystrom and W. Starbuck (eds) *Handbook of Organizational Design*, vol. 1, Oxford: Oxford University Press, 3–27.

Henderson, I. (1993) 'Action learning: a missing link in management development?', *Personnel Review*, 22, 6: 14–24.

Hendry, C., Arthur, M.B. and Jones, A.M. (1995) *Strategy through People: Adaptation and Learning in the Small-Medium Enterprise*, London: Routledge.

Herriot, P. and Pemberton, C. (1995) *Competitive Advantage through Diversity*, London: Sage.

Herriot, P., Pemberton, C. and Pinder, R. (1993) 'Misperceptions by managers and their bosses concerning the managers' careers', *Human Resource Management Journal*, 4, 2: 39–51.

Higgs, M. (1988) *Management Development Strategy in the Financial Sector*, London: Macmillan.

Hirsh, W. (1989) *Defining Managerial Skills*, IMS Report No.185, Brighton: University of Sussex: Institute of Manpower Studies.

Hirsh, W. and Bevan, S. (1988) *What Makes a Manager?*, Report No.144, Brighton: Institute of Manpower Studies.

Hirsh, W. and Strebler, M. (1994) 'Defining managerial skills and competences', in A. Mumford (ed.) *Gower Handbook of Management Development*, Aldershot: Gower, 79–96.

Hoerr, J. (1989) 'The pay-off from teamwork', *Business Week*, 10 July: 56–62.

Holes, G. and Sugden, A. (1991) *Interpreting Company Reports and Accounts*, London: Woodhead-Faulkner.

Holmes, L. and Joyce, P. (1993) 'Rescuing the useful concept of managerial competence: from outcomes back to process', *Personnel Review*, 22, 6: 37–52

Holyfield, J. and Moloney, K. (1996) *Using National Standards to Improve Performance*, London: Kogan Page.

Honey, P. and Mumford, A. (1992) *Manual of Learning Styles*, 3rd edition, London: Peter Honey.

Hornby, D. (1991) 'Management development – the way ahead', in M. Silver (ed.) *Competent to Manage – Approaches to Management Training and Development*, London: Routledge.

Huselid, M.A. (1995) 'The impact of human resource management practices on turnover, productivity and corporate financial performance', *Academy of Management Journal*, 38, 3: 635–72.

Hussey, D.E. (1988) *Management Training and Corporate Strategy: How to Improve Competitive Performance*, Oxford: Pergamon.

—— (1996) *Business Driven Human Resource Management* , Chichester, Wiley.

Hyman, J. (1992) *Training at Work: A Critical Analysis of Policy and Practice*, London: Routledge.

Iles, P. (1993) 'Achieving strategic coherence in HRD through competency-based management and organization development', *Personnel Review*, 22, 6: 63–80.

Institute of Management (1994) *Management Development to the Millennium: The Cannon and Taylor Working Party Reports*, London: IoM.

Institute of Personnel Management (1984) *Continuous Development: People and Work, the IPM Code*, London: IPM.

—— (1992) *Towards a National Training and Development Strategy*, London: IPM.

Investors in People UK (1995) *The Investors in People Standard*, London: IiP UK.

Jackson, S. and Kulp, M.J. (1979) 'Designing guidelines for evaluating the outcomes of management training', in *Determining the Payoff of Management Training*, Washington, DC: American Society for Training and Development, 7–8.

Jacobs, R. (1989) 'Getting the measure of management competence', *Personnel Management*, 21, 6: 32–7.

Janes, J. and Burgess, C. (1992) *Applying the Management Standards within Organisations*, Sheffield: Employment Department Learning Methods Branch R&D Series, No. 8.

Johnston, R. and Sampson, M. (1993) 'The acceptable face of competence' *Management Education and Development*, 24, 3: 216–24.

Jones, A.M. and Hendry, C. (1992) *The Learning Organisation: A Review of Literature and Practice*, London: Human Resource Development Partnership.

Jones, B. (1993) *The Management Standards and Coping with Contingencies*, Sheffield: Employment Department Learning Methods Branch R&D Series, No.15.

Jones, S. (1996) *Developing a Learning Culture*, London: McGraw-Hill.

Kanter, R.M. (1989) *When Giants Learn to Dance: Mastering the Challenges of Strategy, Management and Careers in the 1990s*, London: Unwin.

Kaplan, R.S. and Norton, D.P. (1993) 'The balanced scoreboard – measures that drive performance', *Quality and Productivity Management*, 10, 3: 47–54.

Kay, J. (1993) *Foundations of Corporate Success – How Business Strategies Add Value*, Oxford: Oxford University Press.

Keep, E. (1989) 'Corporate training strategies: the vital component?', in J. Storey (ed.) *New Perspectives on Human Resource Management*, London: Routledge, 109–25.

Kelleher, M. (1996) 'New forms of work organisation and HRD', in J. Stewart and J. McGoldrick (eds) *Human Resource Development: Perspectives, Strategies and Practice*, London: Pitman, 138–57.

Keller, D.A., Campbell, J.F. and Lake, D.A. (1992) 'Building human resource capability', *Human Resource Management*, 31, 1–2: 109–26.

Kelly, J. (1987) 'Trade unions through the recession 1980–1984', *British Journal of Industrial Relations*, 25, 2: 275–82.

Kern, H. and Schumann, M. (1987) 'Limits of the division of labour: new production concepts in West German industry', *Economic and Industrial Democracy*, 8, 2: 151–70.

Kilcourse, T. (1988) 'Making management development a co-operative venture', *Personnel Management*, August, 35–8.

—— (1994) 'Developing competent managers', *Journal of European Industrial Training*, 18, 2: 12–16.

Kim, D.H. (1993) 'The link between individual and organizational learning', *Sloan Management Review*, Fall, 37–50.

King, S. (1993) 'Business benefits of management development', *Management Development Review*, 6, 4: 38–40.

Kirkpatrick, D. (1967) 'Evaluation of training', in R. Craig and L. Bittell (eds) *Training and Education Handbook*, New York: McGraw-Hill, 18.1–18.27.

Kirkpatrick, D.A. (1983) *A Practical Guide for Supervisory Training and Development*, Reading, MA: Addison-Wesley.

Knights, S. (1992) 'Changing spaces: the disruptive impact of a new epistemological location for the study of management', *Academy of Management Review*, 17, 3: 514–36.

Kolb, D.A. (1983) *Experiential Learning*, New York: Prentice Hall.

Kolb, D.A., Lubin, S., Spoth, J. and Baker, R. (1986) 'Strategic management development: using experiential learning theory to assess and develop management competencies', *Journal of Management Development*, 5, 3: 13–24.

Kolb, D.A., Rubin, I.M. and MacIntyre, J.M. (1984) *Organizational Psychology: An Experiential Approach*, 4th edition, New York: Prentice-Hall.

Lawrence, H.V. and Wiswell, A.K. (1993) 'Using the work group as a laboratory for learning: increasing leadership and team effectiveness through team feedback', *Human Resource Development Quarterly*, 4, 2: 135–48.

Lee, G. and Beard, D. (1994) *Development Centres: Realising the Potential of your Employees through Assessment and Development*, London: McGraw-Hill.

Lees, S. (1992) 'Ten faces of management development', *Management Education and Development*, 23, 2: 89–105.

Legge, K. (1989) 'Human resource management: a critical analysis', in J. Storey (ed.) *New Perspectives on Human Resource Management*, London: Routledge, 19–40.

Leman, S. (1994) 'NVQs, SVQs and occupational standards: how employers and candidates see them', *Competence and Assessment*, Issue 25, Sheffield: Employment Department.

Leman, S., Mitchell, L., Sanderson, S., Sturgess, B. and Winterton, J. (1994) *Competence-Based Management Development: Methodologies for Evaluation*, Sheffield: Employment Department.

Levitt, B. and March, J.G. (1988) 'Organizational learning', *Annual Review of Sociology*, 14: 319–40.

Lippitt, G. (1982) 'Management development as the key to organisational renewal', *Journal of Management Development*, 1, 2: 21–30.

Mabey, C. (1994) 'Organizational learning', in C. Mabey and P. Iles (eds) *Managing Learning*, London: Thomson, 3–4.

Mabey, C. and Iles, P. (1993) 'Strategic integration of assessment and development practices', *Human Resource Management Journal*, 3, 4: 16–34.

——. (eds) (1994) *Managing Learning*, London: Thomson.

McBeath, G. (1990) *Practical Management Development: Strategies for Management Resourcing and Development in the 1990s*, Oxford: Blackwell.

McClelland, S. (1994) 'Gaining competitive advantage through strategic management development', *Journal of Management Development*, 13, 5: 4–13.

MacDuffie, J.P. (1995) 'Human resource bundles and manufacturing performance: organizational logic and flexible production systems in the world auto industry', *Industrial and Labor Relations Review*, 48, 2: 197–221.

Magistrates' Courts Service (1994) *A Framework for Management Development*, London: Lord Chancellor's Department.

Management Charter Initiative (1992) *Management Development in the UK 1992*, London: MCI.

—— (1993) *Management Development in the UK 1993*, London: MCI.

—— (1997) *Management Development in the UK 1997*, London: MCI.

Manpower Services Commission (1981) *The New Training Initiative: An Agenda for Action*, Sheffield: MSC.

—— (1986) *SASU Note 16: Guidance on Designing Modules for Accreditation*, Sheffield: Standards and Assessment Support Unit. MSC (mimeo).

Mansfield, B. and Mathews, D. (1985) *The Job Competence Model: A Description for Use in Vocational Education and Training*, Coombe Lodge: FESC.

Mansfield, B. and Mitchell, L. (1996) *Towards a Competent Workforce*, London: Gower.

Manwaring, T. and Wood, S. (1984) 'The ghost in the machine: tacit skills in the labour process', *Socialist Review*, 74, 57–86.

Manz, C.C. and Sims, H.P. (1987) 'Leading workers to lead themselves: the external leadership of self-managing work teams', *Administrative Science Quarterly*, March, 106–29.

March, J.G. and Olsen, J.P. (1975) 'The uncertainty of the past: organizational learning under ambiguity', *European Journal of Political Research*, 3, 2: 147–71.

Marchington, M., Goodman, J., Wilkinson, A. and Ackers, P. (1992) *New Developments in Employee Involvement*, Research Series No.2, Sheffield: Employment Department.

Marchington, M. and Wilkinson, A. (1996) *Core Personnel and Development*, London: Institute of Personnel and Development.

Margerison, C. (1985) 'Achieving the capacity and competence to manage', *Journal of Management Development*, 4, 3: 42–55.

Margerison, C. (1991) *Making Management Development Work*, London: McGraw-Hill.

—— (1993) 'Improving and reviewing manager performance', *Management Development Review*, 6, 3: 15–20.

Marsh, N. (1986) 'Management development and strategic management change', *Journal of Management Development*, 5, 1: 26–37.

Marsick, V. and Watkins, K.E. (1996) 'A framework for the learning organization' in K.E. Watkins and V.J. Marsick (eds) *Creating the Learning Organization*, Alexandria, VA.: American Society for Training and Development.

Mathewman, J. (1995) 'Trends and developments in the use of competency frameworks', *Competency*, 1, 4: whole issue.

Maznevski, M. (1994) 'Understanding our differences: performance in decision-making groups with diverse members', *Human Relations*, 47, 5: 531–2.

Megginson, D. and Pedler, M. (1992) *Self-Development: A Facilitator's Guide*, London: McGraw-Hill.

Michael, J. (1993) 'Aligning executive training with strategy', *Executive Development*, 6, 1: 10–13.

Miller, E.J. and Rice, A.K. (1967) *Systems of Organization: The Control of Task and Sentient Boundaries*, London: Tavistock.

Miller, L. (1991) 'Managerial competences', *Industrial and Commercial Training*, 23, 6: 11–15.

Miller, P. (1991) 'A strategic look at management development', *Personnel Management*, August, 45–7.

Millward, N. and Stevens, M. (1986) *British Workplace Industrial Relations 1980–84*, Aldershot: Gower.

Mintzberg, H. (1980) *The Nature of Managerial Work*, Englewood Cliffs, NJ: Prentice-Hall.

—— (1987) 'Crafting strategy', *Harvard Business Review*, July–August: 65–75.

—— (1989) *Mintzberg on Management: Inside our Strange World of Organizations*, New York: Free Press.

Mintzberg, H. and Waters, J. A. (1985) 'Of strategies deliberate and emergent', *Strategic Management Journal*, 6, 3: 257–72.

Mitrani, A., Dalziel, M. and Fitt, D. (1992) *Competency Based Human Resource Management*, London: Kogan Page.

Moingeon, B. and Edmondson, A. (1996) *Organizational Learning and Competitive Advantage*, London: Sage.

Molander, C. (1986) *Management Development*, Bromley: Chartwell Bratt.

Molander, C. and Walton, D. (1984) 'Getting management development started: the manager as trainer' in C. Cox and J. Beck (eds) *Management Development: Advances in Practice and Theory*, Chichester: Wiley.

Molander, C. and Winterton, J. (1994) *Managing Human Resources*, London: Routledge.

Mole, G., Plant, R. and Salaman, G. (1993) 'Developing executive competencies: learning to confront, confronting to learn', *Journal of European Industrial Training*, 17, 2: 3–7.

Moorby, E. (1996) *How to Succeed in Employee Development: Moving from Vision to Results*, London: McGraw-Hill.

More, C. (1980) *Skill and the English Working Class, 1870–1914*, London: Croom Helm.

Morgan, G. (1988) *Riding the Waves of Change: Developing Managerial Competencies for a Turbulent World*, Oxford: Jossey-Bass.

Morgan, G. (1997) *Images of Organization*, London: Sage.

Mullen, T.P. (1992) 'Integrating self-directed teams into the MD curriculum', *Journal of Management Development*, 11, 5: 43–54.

Mumford, A. (1988a) 'What managers really do', *Management Decision*, 26, 5: 28–30.

—— (1988b) 'Learning to learn and management self-development', in M. Pedler, J. Burgoyne and T. Boydell (eds) *Applying Self-Development in Organizations*, New York: Prentice Hall, 23–7.

—— (1989) *Developing Directors: The Learning Process*, Sheffield: Manpower Services Commission.

—— (1993a) *Management Development: Strategies for Action*, London: IPD.

—— (1993b) *How Managers can Develop Managers*, Aldershot: Gower.

—— (1994) 'Effectiveness in management development', in A. Mumford (ed.) *Gower Handbook of Management Development*, Aldershot: Gower, 3–20.

National Advisory Council for Education and Training Targets (1996) *Skills for 2000: Report on Progress Towards the National Targets for Education and Training*, London: NACETT.

Newstrom, J.W. (1985) 'Management development: does it deliver what it promises?', *Journal of Management Development*, 4, 1: 3–11.

Nordhaug, O. (1993) *Human Capital in Organizations: Competence, Training and Learning*, Oslo: Scandinavian University Press.

Nyhan, B. (1991) *Developing People's Ability to Learn: A European Perspective on Self-Learning Competency and Technological Change*, Brussels: EUROTECNET Technical Assistance Office on behalf of the CEC.

Oram, M. and Wellins, R.S. (1995) *Re-engineering's Missing Ingredient: The Human Factor*, London: Institute of Personnel and Development.

Otter, S. (1994) *Higher Level NVQs/SVQs – Their Possible Implications for Higher Education*, Further and Higher Education Division, Sheffield: Employment Department.

Parker, T.C. (1973) 'Evaluation: the forgotten finale of training', *Personnel*, December, 61–3.

Pate, L. and Nielson, W. (1987) 'Integrating management development into a large-scale, change programme', *Journal of Management Development*, 6, 5: 16–30.

Pearn, M., Roderick, C. and Mulrooney, C. (1995) *Learning Organizations in Practice*, London: McGraw-Hill.

Pedler, M. (1986) 'Developing within the organisation: experiences with management self-development groups', *Management, Education and Development*, 17, 1: 5–21.

—— (1996) *Action Learning for Managers*, London: Lemos and Crane.

Pedler, M., Boydell, T. and Burgoyne, J. (1988) *Learning Company Project Report*, Sheffield: Training Agency.

—— (1989a) 'The learning company', *Studies in Continuing Education*, 11, 2: 91–101.

—— (1989b) 'Towards the learning company', *Management Education and Development*, 20, 1: 1–8.

Pedler, M., Burgoyne, J. and Boydell, T. (1986) *A Manager's Guide to Self-Development*, 2nd edition, London: McGraw-Hill.

—— (1997) *The Learning Company: A Strategy for Sustainable Development*, 2nd edition, London: McGraw-Hill.

Pedler, M., Burgoyne, J., Boydell, T. and Welshman, G. (1990) *Self-Development in Organizations*, London: McGraw-Hill.

Peel, M. (1984) *Management Development and Training*, London: British Institute of Management/Professional Publishing Limited.

Pendleton, A. and Winterton, J. (eds) (1993) *Public Enterprise in Transition: Industrial Relations in State and Privatized Corporations*, London: Routledge.

Peregrine, P. (1994) *Effective Practice in Assessment against the Management Standards*, Sheffield: Employment Department Learning Methods Branch R&D Series, No. 25.

Peters, T. (1992) *Liberation Management: Necessary Disorganization of the Nanosecond Nineties*, London: Macmillan.

Phillips, J.J. (1990) *Handbook of Training Evaluation and Measurement Methods*, Houston: Gulf.

Piore, M. and Sabel, C. (1984) *The Second Industrial Divide*, New York: Basic Books.

Pont, T. (1995) *Investing in Training and Development*, London: Kogan Page.

Porter, M.E. (1985) *Competitive Advantage: Creating and Sustaining Superior Performance*, New York: Free Press.

Prahalad, C.K. and Hamel, G. (1990) 'The core competence of the corporation', *Harvard Business Review*, May–June, 79–91.

Preston, D. and Smith, A. (1993) 'APL: current state of play within management education in the UK', *Journal of Management Development*, 12, 8: 27–38.

Proctor, R.W. and Dutta, A. (1995) *Skill Acquisition and Human Performance*, London: Sage.

Purcell, J. and Ahlstrand, B. (1993) *Strategy and Style in Employee Relations*, Oxford: Oxford University Press.

Rae, L. (1997) *How to Measure Training Effectiveness*, 3rd edition, Aldershot: Gower.

Rainbird, H. (1990) *Training Matters: Union Perspectives on Industrial Restructuring and Training*, Oxford: Blackwell.

Randlesome, C. (1990) 'The business culture in Germany', in C. Randlesome, W. Brierley, K. Bruton, C. Gordon and P. King (eds) *Business Cultures in Europe*, London: Butterworth-Heinemann, 1–85 (1993 edition).

Raper, P., Ashton, D., Felstead, A. and Storey, J. (1997) 'Towards the learning organisation? Explaining current trends in training practice in the UK', *International Journal of Training and Development*, 1, 1: 9–21.

Revans, R. (1971) *Developing Effective Managers*, New York: Praeger.

—— (1983) *ABC of Action Learning*, Bromley: Chartwell-Bratt.

Rix, A., Parkinson, R. and Gaunt, R. (1994) *Investors in People: A Qualitative Study of Employers*, Sheffield: Employment Department, Research Series No. 21.

Robinson, D.G. and Robinson, J.C. (1989) *Training for Impact*, San Francisco: Jossey-Bass.

Robinson, G. (1994) 'Management development and organization development', in A. Mumford (ed.) *Gower Handbook of Management Development*, Aldershot: Gower, 366–83.

Russ-Eft, D., Preskill, H. and Sleezer, C. (1997) *Human Resource Development Review: Research and Implications*, London: Sage.

Salem, M., Lazarus, H. and Cullen, J. (1992) 'Developing self-managing teams', *Journal of Management Development*, 11, 3: 24–32.

Sashkin, M. and Franklin, S. (1993) 'Anticipatory team learning', *Journal of Management Development*, 12, 6: 34–43.

Schein, E.H. (1978) *Career Dynamics, Matching Individual and Organizational Needs*, Reading, MA: Addison-Wesley.

—— (1985) *Organizational Culture and Leadership*, San Francisco: Jossey-Bass.

Schroder, H.M. (1989) *Managerial Competence: The Key to Excellence*, Iowa: Kendall-Hunt.

Schuler, R.S. and Jackson, S. (1987) 'Linking competitive strategies with human resource management practices', *Academy of Management Executive*, 1, 3: 209–13.

Senge, P.M. (1990a) 'The leader's new work: building learning organizations', *Sloan Management Review*, 32, 1: 7–23.

—— (1990b) *The Fifth Discipline: The Art and Practice of the Learning Organization*, New York: Doubleday.

Senge, P.M., Kleiner, A., Roberts, C., Ross, R.B. and Smith, B.J. (1994) *The Fifth Discipline Fieldbook*, London: Nicholas Brealey.

Senker, P. (1992) *Industrial Training in a Cold Climate*, Aldershot: Avebury.

Shea, G.P. and Guzzo, R.A. (1987) 'Group effectiveness: what really matters?', *Sloan Management Review*, 28, 3: 25–31.

Simmons, J. and Blitzmann, G. (1986) 'Training for self-management teams', *Quality Management Journal*, December, 18–21.

Sink, D.S., Tuttle, T.C. and DeVries, S.J. (1984) 'Productivity measurement and evaluation: what is available?', *National Productivity Review*, 3, 3: 265–87.

Sisson, K. (1994) 'Personnel management: paradigms, practice and prospects', in K. Sisson (ed.) *Personnel Management*, 2nd edition, Oxford: Blackwell, 3–50.

Smith, A. (1993) 'Management development evaluation and effectiveness', *Journal of Management Development*, 12, 1: 20–32.

Smith, B. (1993) 'Building managers from the inside out: competency based action learning', *Journal of Management Development*, 12, 1: 43–8.

Smith, P. (1993) 'Outcome-related performance indicators and organizational control in the public sector', *British Journal of Management*, 4, 3: 135–51.

Smith, P. and Morton, G. (1990) 'A change of heart: union exclusion in the provincial newspaper sector', *Work Employment and Society*, 4, 1: 105–24.

—— (1993) 'Union exclusion and the decollectivization of industrial relations in contemporary Britain', *British Journal of Industrial Relations*, 31, 1: 97–114.

Snape, E., Redman, T. and Bamber, G. (1994) *Making Managers: Strategies and Techniques for Human Resource Management*, Oxford: Blackwell.

Snyder, A. and Ebeling, H.W. (1992) 'Targeting a company's real core competencies', *Journal of Business Strategy*, 13, 6: 26–32.

Spencer, L.M. (1995) *Reengineering Human Resources*, New York: Wiley.

Spencer, L.M. and Spencer, S. (1993) *Competence at Work*, New York: Wiley.

Spender, J.-C. (1996) 'Competitive advantage from tacit knowledge? Unpacking the concept and its strategic implications', in B. Moingeon and A. Edmondson (eds) *Organizational Learning and Competitive Advantage*, London: Sage, 56–73.

Spilsbury, M., Simkin, C. and Toye, J. (1994) *Employers' Needs for Information, Advice and Guidance when Implementing NVQs*, Report 276, Brighton: Institute for Employment Studies.

Stahl, T., Nyhan, B. and D'Aloja, P. (1993) *The Learning Organisation: A Vision for Human Resource Development*, Brussels: EUROTECNET Technical Assistance Office on behalf of the CEC.

Stammers, R. and Patrick, J. (1975) *The Psychology of Training*, London: Methuen.

Starkey, K. (ed.) (1996) *How Organizations Learn*, London: Thomson.

Stemp, P. (1987) 'Improving management effectiveness: a strategic approach', *Management Education and Development*, 18, 3: 175–80.

Stewart, J. and Hamblin, B. (1992a) 'Competence-based qualifications: the case against change', *Journal of European Industrial Training*, 16, 7: 21–32.

—— (1992b) 'Competence-based qualifications: a case for established methodologies', *Journal of European Industrial Training*, 16, 10: 9–16.

Stewart, J. and McGoldrick, J. (1996) *Human Resource Development: Perspectives, Strategies and Practice*, London: Pitman.

Stinchcombe A.L. (1990) *Information and Organizations*, Berkeley, CA: University of California Press.

Storey, J. (1989a) 'Introduction: from personnel management to human resource management', in J. Storey (ed.) *New Perspectives on Human Resource Management*, London: Routledge, 1–18.

—— (1989b) 'Management development: a literature review and implications for future research. Part I: conceptualisations and practice', *Personnel Review*, 18, 6: 3–19.

—— (1990) 'Management development: a literature review and implications for future research. Part II: profiles and contexts', *Personnel Review*, 19, 1: 3–11.

Storey, J., Edwards, P. and Sisson, K. (1997) *Managers in the Making*, London: Sage.

Storey, J. and Sisson, K. (1993) *Managing Human Resources and Industrial Relations*, Buckingham: Open University Press.

Stringfellow, M. (1994) 'Assessing for competence at Safeway Stores plc', in A. Mumford (ed.) *Gower Handbook of Management Development*, Aldershot: Gower, 293–300.

Tate, W. (1995a) *Developing Corporate Competence: A High-Performance Agenda for Managing Organizations*, London: Gower.

—— (1995b) *Developing Managerial Competence: A Critical Guide to Methods and Materials*, London: Gower.

Taylor, F.J.W. (1994) *Working Party Report: The Way Ahead 1994–2001: Management Development to the Millennium Research*, Corby: Institute of Management [see Institute of Management (1994)].

Taylor, F.W. (1911) *The Principles of Scientific Management*, New York: Harper.

Taylor, P. and Thackwray, B. (1995) *Investors in People Explained*, London: Kogan Page.

Temporal, P. (1990) 'Linking management development to the corporate future – the role of the professional', *Journal of Management Development*, 9, 5: 7–15.

Thomas, A. (1992) 'Developing managers and their teams', *Management Education and Development*, 23, 1: 30–2.

Thomas, A., Wells, M. and Willard, J. (1992) 'A novel approach to developing managers and their teams: BPX uses upward feedback', *Management Education and Development*, 23, 1: 30–2.

Thomson, A., Storey, J., Mabey, C., Henderson, E. and Thomson, R. (1997) *A Portrait of Management Development*, London: Institute of Management.

Thorpe, R. and Holman, D. (1997) 'A critical analysis of the Management Charter Initiative', Department of Management, Manchester Metropolitan University (mimeo).

Thurbin, P. (1995) *Leveraging Knowledge: The 17 Day Program for a Learning Organization*, London: Pitman.

Tobin, D.R. (1993) *Re-Educating the Corporation: Foundations for the Learning Organization*, Essex Junction, VT: Omneo.

Torrington, D. (1988) 'How Does Human Resources Management Change the Personnel Function?', *Personnel Review*, 17, June, 6: 3–9.

Tovey, L. (1991) *Management Training and Development in Large UK Business Organisations*, London: Harbridge Consulting Group.

—— (1992) *Competency Assessment: A Strategic Approach*, London: Harbridge Consulting Group.

Toye, J. and Vigor, P. (1994) *Implementing NVQs: The Experience of Employers, Employees and Trainees*, Report 265, Brighton: Institute for Manpower Studies.

Trades Union Congress (1989) *Skills 2000*, London: TUC.

—— (1990) *Joint Action over Training*, London: TUC.

—— (1992) *Opportunities for All*, London: TUC.

—— (1993) *Learning for Life*, London: TUC.

—— (1994a) *A New Partnership for Company Training*, London: TUC.

—— (1994b) *Human Resource Management: A Trade Union Response*, London: TUC.

—— (1995a) *Funding Lifelong Learning*, London: TUC.

—— (1995b) *Bargaining for Skills*, London: TUC.

—— (1995c) *Working for a World Class Work Force: TUC Submission to the Review of the Top 100 NVQs/SVQs*, London: TUC.

—— (1996a) *Partners for Lifelong Learning*, London: TUC.

—— (1996b) *Bargaining for Skills: Training in the Workplace: a Negotiators' Guide*, London: TUC.

Training Agency (1988) *The Definition of Competences and Performance Criteria*, Guidance Note 3 in Development of Assessable Standards for National Certification Series, Sheffield: Employment Department.

—— (1989) *Development of Assessable Standards for National Certification*, Sheffield: Employment Department.

Training Commission (1988) *Classifying the Components of Management Competences*, Sheffield: Training Commission.

Training Services Agency (1977) *A Discussion Document on Management Development*, London: TSA.

Tsui, A.S., Pearce, J.L., Porter, L.W. and Tripoli, A.M. (1997) 'Alternative approaches to the employee–organization relationship: does investment in employees pay off?', *Academy of Management Journal*, 40, 5: 1089–121.

Tyson, S. (1995) *Human Resource Strategy: Towards a General Theory of Human Resource Management*, London: Pitman.

Varney, G.H. (1976) *An Organization Development Approach to Management Development*, Reading, MA: Addison-Wesley.

Vicere, A.A., Taylor, M.A. and Freeman, V.A. (1994) 'Executive development in major corporations: a ten year study', *Journal of Management Development*, 13, 1: 4–22.

Wallace, J.B. (1991) *Developing Better Managers*, London: Kogan Page.

Walton, R.E. and Lawrence, P.R. (1985) *Human Resource Management Trends and Challenges*, Boston, MA: Harvard Business School.

Waterman, R.H. (1994) *The Frontiers of Excellence: Learning from Companies that Put People First*, London: Nicholas Brealey.

Watkins, K. (1989) 'Business and industry', in S. Merriam and P. Cunningham (eds) *Handbook of Adult and Continuing Education*, San Francisco: Jossey-Bass.

Watkins, K.E. and Marsick, V.J. (1992) 'Building the learning organization: a new role for human resource developers', *Studies in Continuing Education*, 14, 2: 115–29.

Whitely, R. (1989) 'On the nature of managerial tasks and skills: their distinguishing characteristics and organisation', *Journal of Management Studies*, 26, 3: 209–24.

Whittington, R. (1993) *What is Strategy and Does it Matter?*, London: Thomson.

Wickens, P.D. (1995) *The Ascendant Organisation*, London: Macmillan.

Wild, R. (1993) 'Management development in a changing world', *Management Decision*, 31, 5: 10–17.

Wille, E. (1989) 'Managerial competencies and management development', *Training Officer*, 25, 11: 326–8.

—— (1990) 'Should management development just be for managers?', *Personnel Management*, August, 34–7.

Williamson, O.E. (1991) 'Strategizing, economizing and economic organization', *Strategic Management Journal*, 12, Winter: 75–94.

Wilson, B. (1989) 'Towards competitive company operation', *International Journal of Manpower*, 10, 6: 17–25.

—— (1993) 'Demythologizing management development', *Management Development Review*, 6, 3: 7–10.

Winterton, J. (1994) *Assessment and Recognition of Skills and Competences: New Trends and Policy Implications*, Report to OECD, December.

Winterton, J. and Taplin, I. (1997) 'Restructuring clothing', in I. Taplin and J. Winterton (eds) *Rethinking Global Production: A Comparative Analysis of Restructuring in the Clothing Industry*, Aldershot: Ashgate, 1997, 1–17.

Winterton, J. and Winterton, R. (1992) *Strategic Implications of Proposed Colliery Closures*, Bradford: Work Organisation Research Unit, University of Bradford Management Centre.

—— (1993a) 'Coal', in A. Pendleton and J. Winterton (eds) *Public Enterprise in Transition: Industrial Relations in State and Privatized Corporations*, London: Routledge, 69–99.

—— (1993b) 'Contractual policy and training supply at sector level in the UK', *La Politica Contrattuale nel Campo della Formazione Professionale Continua: Esperienze Europee*, Atti della Conferenza Force in Italia, Rome, 14–15 October, CE/ISFOL/Ministero del Lavoro, 85–109.

—— (1994) *Collective Bargaining and Consultation over Continuing Vocational Training*, RM.7, Sheffield: Employment Department.

—— (1995) *Implementing NVQs: Barriers to Individuals*, Sheffield: Employment Department.

—— (1996) *The Business Benefits of Competence-Based Management Development*, Department for Education and Employment, Research Studies RS16, London: HMSO.

—— (1997) 'Workplace training and enskilling', in S. Walters (ed.) *Globalization, Adult Education and Training: Impacts and Issues*, London: Zed Books, 154–64.

—— (1998) *Validation and Recognition of Competences and Qualifications in the UK*, Final UK Report for Leonardo da Vinci Project VALID, Edinburgh: Employment Research Institute, Napier University.

Womack, J.P., Jones, D.T. and Roos, D. (1990) *The Machine that Changed the World*, New York: Harper.

Woodruffe, C. (1990) *Assessment Centres: Identifying and Developing Competences*, London: Institute of Personnel Management

—— (1991) 'Competent by any other name', *Personnel Management*, September, 30–3.

Yin, R.K. (1981) 'The case study crisis: some answers', *Administrative Science Quarterly*, 26, 58–65.

—— (1984) *Case Study Research: Design and Methods*, London: Sage.

—— (1993) *Applications of Case Study Research*, London: Sage.

Youndt, M.A., Snell, S.A., Dean, J.W. and Lepak, D.P. (1996) 'Human resource management, manufacturing strategy, and firm performance' *Academy of Management Journal*, 33, 4: 836–66.

Zairi, M. (1996) *Benchmarking for Best Practice*, Oxford: Butterworth-Heinemann.

Index